Datsun Owners Workshop Manual

by J H Haynes
Member of the Guild of Motoring Writers

and M B Gilmour

Models covered:

UK: Datsun Cherry (100A) F-II Saloon & Estate. 988 cc
        Datsun Cherry (120A) F-II Coupe. 1171 cc
USA: Datsun F10 Sedan, Hatchback & Wagon. 85·24 cu in (1397 cc)

Does not cover automatic transmission models

ISBN 0 85696 368 2

Printed in England   *(368-6K1)*

HAYNES PUBLISHING GROUP
SPARKFORD YEOVIL SOMERSET BA22 7JJ ENGLAND
distributed in the USA by
HAYNES PUBLICATIONS INC
861 LAWRENCE DRIVE
NEWBURY PARK
CALIFORNIA 91320
USA

Acknowledgements

Thanks are due to Nissan Motor Company Limited of Japan for the supply of technical information and certain illustrations. Castrol Limited provided lubrication details, and the Champion Sparking Plug Company provided the illustrations showing the various spark plug conditions. The bodywork repair photographs used in this manual were provided by Lloyds Industries Limited who supply 'Turtle Wax', 'Dupli-color Holts', and other Holts range products.

Lastly special thanks are due to all of those people at Sparkford who helped in the production of this manual; particularly, Martin Penny and Les Brazier who carried out the mechanical work and took the photographs respectively, John Austin who edited the text and Stanley Randolph for planning the layout of each page.

About this manual

Its aim

The aim of this manual is to help you get the best value from your car. It can do so in several ways. It can help you decide what work must be done (even should you choose to get it done by a garage), provide information on routine maintenance and servicing, and give a logical course of action and diagnosis when random faults occur. However, it is hoped that you will use the manual by tackling the work yourself. On simpler jobs it may even be quicker than booking the car into a garage, and going there twice, to leave and collect it. Perhaps most important, a lot of money can be saved by avoiding the costs a garage must charge to cover its labour and overheads.

The book has drawings and descriptions to show the function of the various components so that their layout can be understood. Then the tasks are described and photographed in a step-by-step sequence so that even a novice can cope with complicated work. Such a person is the very one to buy a car needing repair yet be unable to afford garage costs.

The jobs are described assuming only normal spanners are available, and not special tools. However, a reasonable outfit of tools will be a worthwhile investment. Many special workshop tools produced by the makers merely speed the work, and in these cases guidance is given as to how to do the job wihout them, the oft quoted example being the use of a large hose clip to compress the piston rings for insertion in the cylinder. On the very few occasions the special tool is essential to prevent damage to components, then its use is described. Though it might be possible to borrow the tool such work may have to be entrusted to the official agent.

To reduce labour costs a garage will often give cheaper repair by fitting a reconditioned assembly. The home mechanic can be helped by this book to diagnose the fault and make a repair using only a minor spare part.

The manufacturer's official workshop manuals are written for their trained staff, and so assume special knowledge; therefore detail is left out. This book is written for the owner, and so goes into detail.

Using the manual

The manual is divided into twelve Chapters. Each Chapter is divided into numbered Sections which are headed in **bold type** between horizontal lines. Each Section consists of serially numbered paragraphs.

There are two types of illustration: (1) Figures which are numbered according to Chapter and sequence of occurrence in that Chapter, (2) Photographs which have a reference number on their caption. All photographs apply to the Chapter in which they occur so that the reference number pinpoints the pertinent Section and paragraph number.

Procedures, once described in the text, are not normally repeated. If it is necessary to refer to another Chapter the reference will be given in Chapter number, Section number and where necessary, paragraph number. Cross references given without use of the word 'Chapter' apply to Section and/or paragraphs in the same Chapter (eg; 'see Section 8' also means 'in this Chapter').

When the left or right side of the car is mentioned it is as if one is seated in the driver's seat looking forward.

Whilst every care is taken to ensure that the information in this manual is correct, no liability can be accepted by the authors or publishers for loss, damage or injury caused by any errors in, or omissions from, the information given.

Contents

Use of English

As this book has been written in England, it uses the appropriate English component names, phrases, and spelling. Some of these differ from those used in America. Normally, these cause no difficulty, but to make sure, a glossary is printed below. In ordering spare parts remember the parts list will probably use these words:

Glossary

English	American	English	American
Accelerator	Gas pedal	Leading shoe (of brake)	Primary shoe
Alternator	Generator (AC)	Locks	Latches
Anti-roll bar	Stabiliser or sway bar	Motorway	Freeway, turnpike etc.
Battery	Energizer	Number plate	Licence plate
Bonnet (engine cover)	Hood	Paraffin	Kerosene
Boot lid	Trunk lid	Petrol	Gasoline
Boot (luggage compartment)	Trunk	Petrol tank	Gas tank
Bottom gear	1st gear	'Pinking'	'Pinging'
Bulkhead	Firewall	Propellor shaft	Driveshaft
Camfollower or tappet	Valve lifter or tappet	Quarter light	Quarter window
Carburettor	Carburetor	Retread	Recap
Catch	Latch	Reverse	Back-up
Choke/venturi	Barrel	Rocker cover	Valve cover
Circlip	Snap ring	Roof rack	Car-top carrier
Clearance	Lash	Saloon	Sedan
Crownwheel	Ring gear (of differential)	Seized	Frozen
Disc (brake)	Rotor/disk	Side indicator lights	Side marker lights
Drop arm	Pitman arm	Side light	Parking light
Drop head coupe	Convertible	Silencer	Muffler
Dynamo	Generator (DC)	Spanner	Wrench
Earth (electrical)	Ground	Sill panel (beneath doors)	Rocker panel
Engineer's blue	Prussion blue	Split cotter (for valve spring cap)	Lock (for valve spring retainer)
Estate car	Station wagon	Split pin	Cotter pin
Exhaust manifold	Header	Steering arm	Spindle arm
Fast back (Coupe)	Hard top	Sump	Oil pan
Fault finding/diagnosis	Trouble shooting	Tab washer	Tang; lock
Float chamber	Float bowl	Tailgate	Liftgate
Free-play	Lash	Tappet	Valve lifter
Freewheel	Coast	Thrust bearing	Throw-out bearing
Gudgeon pin	Piston pin or wrist pin	Top gear	High
Gearchange	Shift	Trackrod (of steering)	Tie-rod (or connecting rod)
Gearbox	Transmission	Trailing shoe (of brake)	Secondary shoe
Halfshaft	Axle-shaft	Transmission	Whole drive line
Handbrake	Parking brake	Tyre	Tire
Hood	Soft top	Van	Panel wagon/van
Hot spot	Heat riser	Vice	Vise
Indicator	Turn signal	Wheel nut	Lug nut
Interior light	Dome lamp	Windscreen	Windshield
Layshaft (of gearbox)	Counter shaft	Wing/mudguard	Fender

Miscellaneous points

An "Oil seal" is fitted to components lubricated by grease!

A "Damper" is a "Shock absorber" it damps out bouncing, and absorbs shocks of bump impact. Both names are correct, and both are used haphazardly.

Note that British drum brakes are different from the Bendix type that is common in America, so different descriptive names result. The shoe end furthest from the hydraulic wheel cylinder is on a pivot; interconnection between the shoes as on Bendix brakes is most uncommon. Therefore the phrase "Primary" or "Secondary" shoe does not apply. A shoe is said to be Leading or Trailing. A "Leading" shoe is one on which a point on the drum, as it rotates forward, reaches the shoe at the end worked by the hydraulic cylinder before the anchor end. The opposite is a trailing shoe, and this one has no self servo from the wrapping effect of the rotating drum.

Introduction to the Datsun F10 series

The Datsuns covered by this workshop manual are known as the F10 series. Introduced in 1976, the UK range, consisting of saloon, coupe and station wagon, is designated: 100A F-II with a 988 cc engine and 120A F-II with a 1171 cc engine. In North America the range, consisting of sedan, hatchback, station wagon and sports wagon models, is designated F10 and has a 85.24 cu in (1397 cc) engine.

The F10 series is based on the Cherry 100A and 120A, having the same well proven mechanical layout but with a new, slightly larger body. The construction is very strong with vibration and sound-proofing materials used in the floor, bulkheads and body panels, making the car unusually quiet for its size and type.

Quick reference general data

Engine model	A10	A12	A14
Capacity cc (cu/in)	988 (60.3)	1171 (71.5)	1397 (85.2)
Firing order	1–3–4–2	1–3–4–2	1–3–4–2
Idling speed (rpm)	700	700	700
Ignition timing (BTDC) degree rpm	8°/700	7°/700	10°/700
Spark plug gap in (mm)	0.028 – 0.031 (0.7 – 0.8)	0.031 – 0.035 (0.8 – 0.9)	0.039 – 0.043 (1.0 – 1.1)
Contact breaker gap in (mm)	0.018 – 0.022 (0.45 – 0.55)	0.018 – 0.022 (0.45 – 0.55)	0.018 – 0.022 (0.45 – 0.55)
Distributor air gap (Californian models) in (mm)	N/A	N/A	0.008 – 0.016 (0.2 – 0.4)
Inlet and exhaust valve clearance (Hot) in (mm)	0.014 (0.35)	0.014 (0.35)	0.014 (0.35)

Capacities:	Imperial	Metric	US
Fuel tank			
Saloon, Coupe and sports wagon	8¾ gals	40 litres	10⅝ gals
Station wagon	7¾ gals	35 litres	9¼ gals
Cooling system (with heater):			
A10 and A12 engines	4¾ qts	5.4 litres	5¾ qts
A14 engines	5⅞ qts	6.6 litres	7 qts
Engine oil:			
Without oil filter change	2½ qts	2.8 litres	3 qts
With oil filter change	2⅞ qts	3.3 litres	3½ qts
Transmission	4 pts	2.3 litres	4⅞ pts

Overall dimensions in (mm)

100A F-II and 120A F-II models	Saloon, coupe and station wagon
Length	150.59 (3825)
Width	59.06 (1500)
Height	52.76 (1340)
Wheelbase	94.29 (2395)

F10 models	Sedan	Hatchback	Station wagon
Length	156.9 (3985)	156.9 (3985)	157.3 (3995)
Width	59.8 (1520)	59.8 (1520)	59.8 (1520)
Height	53.0 (1345)	51.8 (1315)	53.7 (1365)
Wheelbase	94.3 (2395)	94.3 (2395)	94.3 (2395)

F-II Coupe

F-II four-door Saloon

Buying spare parts and vehicle identification numbers

Buying spare parts

Spare parts are available from many sources, for example: Datsun garages, other garages and accessory shops, and motor factors. Our advice regarding spare parts is as follows:

Officially appointed Datsun garages – This is the best source of parts which are peculiar to your car and otherwise not generally available (eg complete cylinder heads, internal gearbox components, badges, interior trim etc). It is also the only place at which you should buy parts if your car is still under warranty; non-Datsun components may invalidate the warranty. To be sure of obtaining the correct parts it will always be necessary to give the storeman your car's engine and chassis number, and if possible, to take the old part along for positive identification. Remember that many parts are available on a factory exchange scheme – any parts returned should always be clean! It obviously makes good sense to go straight to the specialists on your car for this type of part for they are best equipped to supply you.

Other garages and accessory shops – These are often very good places to buy material and components needed for the maintenance of your car (eg oil filter, spark plugs, bulbs, fan belts, oils and grease, touch-up paint, filler paste etc). They also sell general accessories, usually have convenient opening hours, charge lower prices and can often be found not far from home.

Motor factors – Good factors will stock all the more important components which wear out relatively quickly (eg clutch components, pistons, valves, exhaust systems, brake cylinders/pipes/hoses /seals/shoes and pads etc). Motor factors will often provide new or reconditioned components on a part exchange basis – this can save a considerable amount of money.

Vehicle identification numbers

Modifications are a continuing and unpublished process in vehicle manufacture quite apart from major model changes. Spare parts manuals and lists are compiled upon a numerical basis, the individual vehicle numbers being essential to correct identification of the component required.

The car identification plate is located on the left-hand wheel apron in the engine compartment. The car serial number is stamped on the centre of the bulkhead in the engine compartment. The car serial number is preceded by the engine model designation, A10, A12 or A14.

The engine number is stamped on the right rear side of the cylinder block.

Car identification plate

Car serial number stamped on the bulkhead

The engine number is stamped on the cylinder block

Routine maintenance

Maintenance is essential for ensuring safety and desirable for the purpose of getting the best in terms of performance and economy from the car. Over the years the need for periodic lubrication — oiling, greasing and so on — has been drastically reduced if not totally eliminated. This has unfortunately tended to lead some owners to think that because no such action is required the items either no longer exist or will last for ever. This is a serious delusion. It follows therefore that the largest initial element of maintenance is visual examination. This may lead to repairs or renewals.

In the summary given here the 'essential for safety' items are shown in **bold type**. These **must** be attended to at the regular frequencies shown in order to avoid the possibility of accidents and loss of life. Neglect results in unreliability, increased running costs, more rapid wear and more rapid depreciation of the vehicle in general.

Every 250 miles (400 km) or weekly — whichever comes first

Steering
Check the tyre pressures.
Examine tyres for wear or damage.
Is steering smooth and accurate?

Brakes
Check reservoir fluid level.
Is there any fall off in braking efficiency?
Try an emergency stop. Is adjustment necessary?

Lights, wipers and horns
Do all bulbs work at the front and rear?
Are the headlamp beams aligned properly?
Do the wipers and horns work?
Check windscreen washer fluid level

Engine
Check the sump oil level and top-up if required.
Check the radiator coolant level and top-up if required.
Check the battery electrolyte level and top-up the level with distilled water as needed.

Every 6000 miles (10 000 km)

Engine
Change oil. (If short distance driving, extensive idling or driving in dusty conditions, change oil every 3000 miles)
Renew engine oil filter.
Clean and check spark plugs.
Check distributor cap, rotor and contact points.
Lubricate distributor shaft and cam.
Check drive belts for cracks, fraying, wear and correct tension.
Check battery terminals.
Check for coolant, oil and fuel leaks.

Steering
Examine all steering linkages, joints and bushes for signs of wear or damage.
Check front wheel hub bearings and adjust if necessary.
Check security of steering gear mounting.
Rotate road wheels and rebalance if necessary.

Brakes
Examine disc pads and drum shoes for wear. Renew if necessary.
Examine all hydraulic pipes, hoses and unions for chafing, corrosion or dents. Check for any signs of leaks.
Adjust drum type brakes.

Topping-up with engine oil

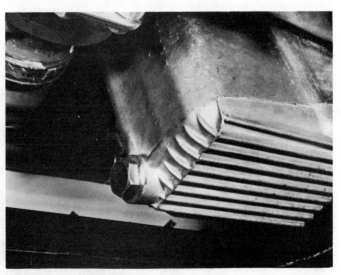
Engine oil sump drain plug

Suspension

Examine all nuts, bolts and shackles securing the suspension units, front and rear. Tighten if necessary.
Examine the rubber bushes for signs of wear and play.

Transmission

Check oil level and top-up if necessary.
Examine driveshaft boots for splits or deterioration.

Clutch

Check fluid reservoir and top-up if necessary.
Check pedal free-movement and adjust if necessary.

Body

Check seat belts, buckles and anchors.
Lubricate all locks and hinges.
Check that water drain holes at bottom of doors are clear.

Every 12 000 miles (20 000 km)

Engine

Check cylinder head bolt torque setting.
Check valve clearances and adjust if necessary.
Check positive crankcase ventilation system
Check fuel storage evaporative emission control system
Check exhaust emission control system.
Fit new spark plugs.
Fit new distributor points.
Clean carburettor float chamber and jets.
Check HT leads for deterioration

Steering

Check shock absorber operation

Transmission

Check security of driveshaft bolts.

Every 24 000 miles (40 000 km)

Engine

Flush the cooling system and refill with the correct anti-freeze coolant mixture (Ethylene glycol base).
Renew fuel filter.
Renew air cleaner element, and air pump air cleaner filter (if fitted).
Renew carbon canister filter (if fitted).

Topping-up with transmission oil

Brakes

Lubricate handbrake linkage.

Every 30 000 miles (50 000 km)

Brakes

Drain hydraulic system, renew all cylinder seals and refill with fresh fluid. Bleed system.

Clutch

Drain hydraulic system, renew master and slave cylinder seals, refill with fresh fluid. Bleed system. If it is a mechanical system it is sound practice to renew the cable.

Additionally the following items should be attended to as time can be spared:

Cleaning

Examination of components requires that they be cleaned. The same applies to the body of the car, inside and out, in order that deterioration due to rust or unknown damage may be detected. Certain parts of the body frame, if rusted badly, can result in the vehicle being declared unsafe and it will not pass the annual test for roadworthiness.

Exhaust system

An exhaust system must be leakproof, and the noise level must be kept to a minimum. Excessive leaks may cause carbon monoxide fumes to enter the passenger compartment. Excessive noise constitutes a public nuisance. Both these faults may cause the vehicle to be kept off the road. Repair or renew defective sections when symptoms are apparent.

Other aspects of Routine Maintenance

Jacking-up

Always chock a wheel on the opposite side, in front and behind. Always support the car on stands as well as on the jack. Use only the support strong points shown in the associated illustrations.

Wheel nuts

These should be cleaned and lightly smeared with grease as necessary during work, to keep them moving easily. If the nuts are stubborn to undo due to dirt and overtightening, it may be necessary to hold them by lowering the jack till the wheel rests on the ground. Normally if the wheel brace is used across the hub centre a foot or knee held against the tyre will prevent the wheel from turning, and so save

Transmission drain plug

the wheels and nuts from wear if the nuts are slackened with weight on the wheel. After refitting a wheel make a point later of rechecking the nuts again for tightness.

Safety

Whenever working, even partially, under the car, put an extra strong box or piece of timber underneath onto which the car will fall rather than on you.

Cleanliness

Whenever you do any work allow time for cleaning. When something is in pieces or components removed to improve access to other areas, give an opportunity for a thorough clean. This cleanliness will allow you to cope with a crisis on the road without getting yourself dirty. During bigger jobs when you expect a bit of dirt it is less extreme and can be tolerated at least whilst removing a component. When an item is being taken to pieces there is less risk of ruinous grit finding its way inside. The act of cleaning focuses your attention onto parts and you are more likely to spot trouble. Dirt on the ignition components is a common cause of poor starting. Large areas such as the engine compartment, inner wings or bulkhead should be brushed thoroughly with grease solvent, allowed to soak and then very carefully hosed down. Water in the wrong places, particularly the carburettor or electrical components will do more harm than dirt. Use petrol or paraffin and a small paintbrush to clean the more inaccessible places.

Waste disposal

Old oil and cleaning paraffin must be destroyed. Although it makes a good base for a bonfire the practice is dangerous. It is also illegal to dispose of oil and paraffin down domestic drains. By buying your new engine oil in one gallon cans you can refill them with old oil and take them to the local garage who have facilities for disposal.

Long journeys

Before taking the car on long journeys, particularly such trips as continental holidays, make sure that the car is given a thorough check in the form of the next service due, plus a full visual inspection well in advance so that any faults found can be rectified in time.

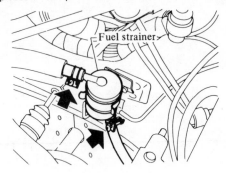

Renewing the fuel filter

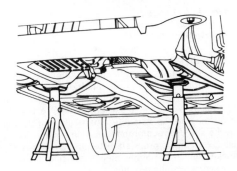

Front support positions

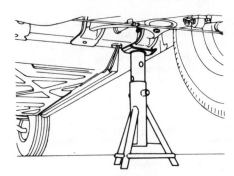

Rear support positions (saloon and coupe)

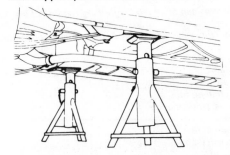

Rear support positions (station wagon)

Front towing point

Rear towing point (saloon and coupe)

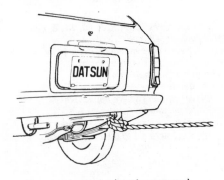

Rear towing point (station wagon)

Tools and working facilities

Introduction

A selection of good tools is a fundamental requirement for anyone contemplating the maintenance and repair of a motor vehicle. For the owner who does not possess any, their purchase will prove a considerable expense, offsetting some of the savings made by doing-it-yourself. However, provided that the tools purchased are of good quality, they will last for many years and prove an extremely worthwhile investment.

To help the average owner to decide which tools are needed to carry out the various tasks detailed in this manual, we have compiled three lists of tools under the following headings: *Maintenance and minor repair, Repair and overhaul,* and *Special.* The newcomer to practical mechanics should start off with the *Maintenance and minor repair* tool kit and confine himself to the simpler jobs around the vehicle. Then, as his confidence and experience grows, he can undertake more difficult tasks, buying extra tools as, and when, they are needed. In this way, a *Maintenance and minor repair* tool kit can be built-up into a *Repair and overhaul* tool kit over a considerable period of time without any major cash outlays. The experienced do-it-yourselfer will have a tool kit good enough for most repair and overhaul procedures and will add tools from the *Special* category when he feels the expense is justified by the amount of use these tools will be put to.

It is obviously not possible to cover the subject of tools fully here. For those who wish to learn more about tools and their use there is a book entitled *How to Choose and Use Car Tools* available from the publishers of this manual.

Maintenance and minor repair tool kit

The tools given in this list should be considered as a minimum requirement if routine maintenance, servicing and minor repair operations are to be undertaken. We recommend the purchase of combination spanners (ring one end, open-ended the other); although more expensive than open-ended ones, they do give the advantages of both types of spanner.

> Combination spanners - 6, 7, 8, 9, 10, 11, & 12 mm
> Adjustable spanner - 9 inch
> Engine sump/gearbox/rear axle drain plug key (where applicable)
> Spark plug spanner (with rubber insert)
> Spark plug gap adjustment tool
> Set of feeler gauges
> Brake adjuster spanner (where applicable)
> Brake bleed nipple spanner
> Screwdriver - 4 in long x $\frac{1}{4}$ in dia (flat blade)
> Screwdriver - 4 in long x $\frac{1}{4}$ in dia (cross blade)
> Combination pliers - 6 inch
> Hacksaw, junior
> Tyre pump
> Tyre pressure gauge

Grease gun (where applicable)
Oil can
Fine emery cloth (1 sheet)
Wire brush (small)
Funnel (medium size)

Repair and overhaul tool kit

These tools are virtually essential for anyone undertaking any major repairs to a motor vehicle, and are additional to those given in the *Maintenance and minor repair* list. Included in this list is a comprehensive set of sockets. Although these are expensive they will be found invaluable as they are so versatile - particularly if various drives are included in the set. We recommend the $\frac{1}{2}$ in square-drive type, as this can be used with most proprietary torque wrenches. If you cannot afford a socket set, even bought piecemeal, then inexpensive tubular box spanners are a useful alternative.

The tools in this list will occasionally need to be supplemented by tools from the *Special* list.

> Sockets (or box spanners) to cover range in previous list
> Reversible ratchet drive (for use with sockets)
> Extension piece, 10 inch (for use with sockets)
> Universal joint (for use with sockets)
> Torque wrench (for use with sockets)
> 'Mole' wrench - 8 inch
> Ball pein hammer
> Soft-faced hammer, plastic or rubber
> Screwdriver - 6 in long x $\frac{5}{16}$ in dia (flat blade)
> Screwdriver - 2 in long x $\frac{5}{16}$ in square (flat blade)
> Screwdriver - $1\frac{1}{2}$ in long x $\frac{1}{4}$ in dia (cross blade)
> Screwdriver - 3 in long x $\frac{1}{8}$ in dia (electricians)
> Pliers - electricians side cutters
> Pliers - needle nosed
> Pliers - circlip (internal and external)
> Cold chisel - $\frac{1}{2}$ inch
> Scriber (this can be made by grinding the end of a broken hacksaw blade)
> Scraper (this can be made by flattening and sharpening one end of a piece of copper pipe)
> Centre punch
> Pin punch
> Hacksaw
> Valve grinding tool
> Steel rule/straight edge
> Allen keys
> Selection of files
> Wire brush (large)
> Axle stands
> Jack (strong scissor or hydraulic type)

Special tools

The tools in this list are those which are not used regularly, are expensive to buy, or which need to be used in accordance with their manufacturers' instructions. Unless relatively difficult mechanical jobs are undertaken frequently, it will not be economic to buy many of these tools. Where this is the case, you could consider clubbing together with friends (or a motorist's club) to make a joint purchase, or borrowing the tools against a deposit from a local garage or tool hire specialist.

The following list contains only those tools and instruments freely available to the public, and not those special tools produced by the vehicle manufacturer specifically for its dealer network. You will find occasional references to these manufacturer's special tools in the text of this manual. Generally, an alternative method of doing the job without the vehicle manufacturer's special tool is given. However, sometimes, there is no alternative to using them. Where this is the case and the relevant tool cannot be bought or borrowed you will have to entrust the work to a franchised garage

Valve spring compressor
Piston ring compressor
Balljoint separator
Universal hub/bearing puller
Impact screwdriver
Micrometer and/or vernier gauge
Carburettor flow balancing device (where applicable)
Dial gauge
Stroboscopic timing light
Dwell angle meter/tachometer
Universal electrical multi-meter
Cylinder compression gauge
Lifting tackle
Trolley jack
Light with extension lead

Buying tools

For practically all tools, a tool factor is the best source since he will have a very comprehensive range compared with the average garage or accessory shop. Having said that, accessory shops often offer excellent quality tools at discount prices, so it pays to shop around.

Remember, you don't have to buy the most expensive items on the shelf, but it is always advisable to steer clear of the very cheap tools. There are plenty of good tools around at reasonable prices, so ask the proprietor or manager of the shop for advice before making a purchase.

Care and maintenance of tools

Having purchased a reasonable tool kit, it is necessary to keep the tools in a clean serviceable condition. After use, always wipe off any dirt, grease and metal particles using a clean, dry cloth, before putting the tools away. Never leave them lying around after they have been used. A simple tool rack on the garage or workshop wall, for items such as screwdrivers and pliers is a good idea. Store all normal spanners and sockets in a metal box. Any measuring instruments, gauges, meters, etc., must be carefully stored where they cannot be damaged or become rusty.

Take a little care when tools are used. Hammer heads inevitably become marked and screwdrivers lose the keen edge on their blades from time-to-time. A little timely attention with emery cloth or a file will soon restore items like this to a good serviceable finish.

Working facilities

Not to be forgotten when discussing tools, is the workshop itself. If anything more than routine maintenance is to be carried out, some form of suitable working area becomes essential.

It is appreciated that many an owner mechanic is forced by circumstances to remove an engine or similar item, without the benefit of a garage or workshop. Having done this, any repairs should always be done under the cover of a roof.

Wherever possible, any dismantling should be done on a clean flat workbench or table at a suitable working height.

Any workbench needs a vice: one with a jaw opening of 4 in (100 mm) is suitable for most jobs. As mentioned previously, some clean dry storage space is also required for tools, as well as the lubricants, cleaning fluids, touch-up paints and so on which become necessary.

Another item which may be required, and which has a much more general usage, is an electric drill with a chuck capacity of at least $\frac{5}{16}$ in (8 mm). This, together with a good range of twist drills, is virtually essential for fitting accessories such as wing mirrors and reversing lights.

Last, but not least, always keep a supply of old newspapers and clean, lint-free rags available, and try to keep any working area as clean as possible.

Spanner jaw gap comparison table

Jaw gap (in)	Spanner size
0·250	$\frac{1}{4}$ in AF
0·275	7 mm AF
0·312	$\frac{5}{16}$ in AF
0·315	8 mm AF
0·340	11/32 in AF; $\frac{1}{8}$ in Whitworth
0·354	9 mm AF
0·375	$\frac{3}{8}$ in AF
0·393	10 mm AF
0·433	11 mm AF
0·437	$\frac{7}{16}$ in AF
0·445	$\frac{3}{16}$ in Whitworth; $\frac{1}{4}$ in BSF
0·472	12 mm AF
0·500	$\frac{1}{2}$ in AF
0·512	13 mm AF
0·525	$\frac{1}{4}$ in Whitworth; $\frac{5}{16}$ in BSF
0·551	14 mm AF
0·562	$\frac{9}{16}$ in AF
0·590	15 mm AF
0·600	$\frac{5}{16}$ in Whitworth; $\frac{3}{8}$ in BSF
0·625	$\frac{5}{8}$ in AF
0·629	16 mm AF
0·669	17 mm AF
0·687	$\frac{11}{16}$ in AF
0·708	18 mm AF
0·710	$\frac{3}{8}$ in Whitworth; $\frac{7}{16}$ in BSF
0·748	19 mm AF
0·750	$\frac{3}{4}$ in AF
0·812	$\frac{13}{16}$ in AF
0·820	$\frac{7}{16}$ in Whitworth; $\frac{1}{2}$ in BSF
0·866	22 mm AF
0·875	$\frac{7}{8}$ in AF
0·920	$\frac{1}{2}$ in Whitworth; $\frac{9}{16}$ in BSF
0·937	$\frac{15}{16}$ in AF
0·944	24 mm AF
1·000	1 in AF
1·010	$\frac{9}{16}$ in Whitworth; $\frac{5}{8}$ in BSF
1·023	26 mm AF
1·062	$1\frac{1}{16}$ in AF; 27 mm AF
1·100	$\frac{5}{8}$ in Whitworth; $\frac{11}{16}$ in BSF
1·125	$1\frac{1}{8}$ in AF
1·181	30 mm AF
1·200	$\frac{11}{16}$ in Whitworth; $\frac{3}{4}$ in BSF
1·250	$1\frac{1}{4}$ in AF
1·259	32 mm AF
1·300	$\frac{3}{4}$ in Whitworth; $\frac{7}{8}$ in BSF
1·312	$1\frac{5}{16}$ in AF
1·390	$\frac{13}{16}$ in Whitworth; $\frac{15}{16}$ in BSF
1·417	36 mm AF
1·437	$1\frac{7}{16}$ in AF
1·480	$\frac{7}{8}$ in Whitworth; 1 in BSF
1·500	$1\frac{1}{2}$ in AF
1·574	40 mm AF; $\frac{15}{16}$ in Whitworth
1·614	41 mm AF
1·625	$1\frac{5}{8}$ in AF
1·670	1 in Whitworth; $1\frac{1}{8}$ in BSF
1·687	$1\frac{11}{16}$ in AF
1·811	46 mm AF
1·812	$1\frac{13}{16}$ in AF
1·860	$1\frac{1}{8}$ in Whitworth; $1\frac{1}{4}$ in BSF
1·875	$1\frac{7}{8}$ in AF
1·968	50 mm AF
2·000	2 in AF
2·050	$1\frac{1}{4}$ in Whitworth; $1\frac{3}{8}$ in BSF
2·165	55 mm AF
2·362	60 mm AF

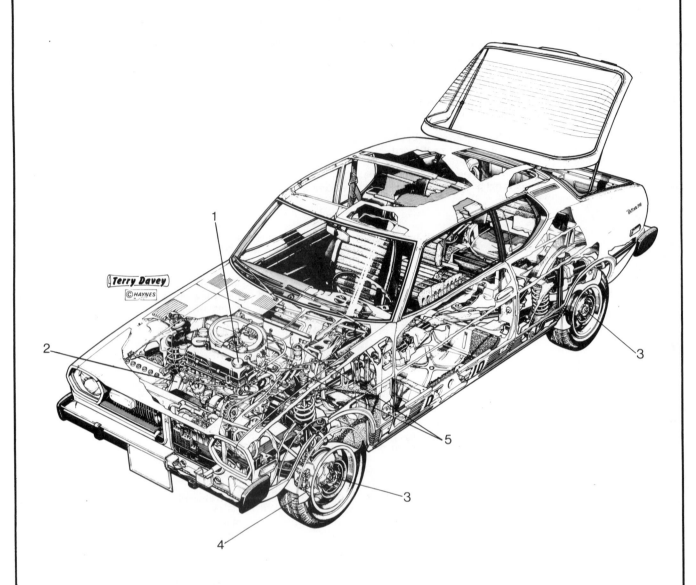

Recommended lubricants

Component	Specification	Castrol grade
Engine (1)	SAE 20W-50	**Castrol GTX**
Gearbox (2)	Gear oil (Sae 80EP or 90EP; API GL-4)	**Castrol Hypoy Light or Castrol Hypoy**
Wheel bearings (3)	Grease (NLGI No. 1 or 2)	**Castrol LM Grease**
Suspension balljoints (4)	Grease (NLGI No. 1 or 2)	**Castrol LM Grease**
Brake and clutch systems (5)	Hydraulic fluid (SAE 70R-3; DOT 3)	**Castrol Girling Universal Brake and Clutch Fluid**

Note: *The above are general recommendations only. Lubrication requirements vary from territory-to-territory. If in doubt, consult the driver's handbook or the nearest official agent.*

Chapter 1 Engine

Contents

Specifications

All dimensions are shown as in (mm) unless otherwise stated. The word 'ditto' denotes that it has the same dimension as given on its left; eg the compression ratio for the A12 engine is the same as that given for the A10. Where a dimension is applicable to all three engine types, it is centred under the three headings, eg the firing order for all engines is 1, 3, 4, 2.

Engine model	A10	A12	A14
Cylinder arrangement		four in line	
Capacity cc (cu/in)	988 (60.3)	1171 (71.5)	1397 (85.24)
Bore	2.87 (73)	ditto	2.99 (76)
Stroke	2.32 (59)	2.76 (70)	3.03 (77)
Compression ratio	9 : 1	ditto	8.5 : 1
Firing order		1 – 3 – 4– 2	
Ignition timing		Refer to Chapter 4	
Cylinder block			
Material		cast iron	
Bore inner diameter	2.874 – 2.876 (73.000 – 73.050)	ditto	2.9921 – 2.9941 (76.000 – 76.050)
Wear limit		0.0079 (0.20)	
Surface flatness (maximum limit)		0.0039 (0.10)	
Pistons			
Material		Aluminium	
Diameter:			
Standard	2.8735 – 2.8755 (72.987 – 73.037)	ditto	2.9908 – 2.9927 (75.967– 76.017)
Oversize (0.50)	2.8924 – 2.8944 (73.467 – 73.517)	ditto	3.0105 – 3.0124 (76.467 – 76.517)
Oversize (1.00)	2.9121 – 2.9140 (73.967 – 74.017)	ditto	3.0301 – 3.0321 (76.967 – 77.017)
Oversize (1.50)	2.9318 – 2.9337 (74.467 – 74.517)	ditto	–

Piston rings

Number		Two compression and one oil control	
Side clearance:			
Top ring		0.0016 – 0.0028 (0.04 – 0.07)	
2nd ring	0.0016 – 0.0028 (0.04 – 0.07)	ditto	0.0012 – 0.0024 (0.03 – 0.06)
Oil ring	0.0118 – 0.0354 (0.30 – 0.90)	ditto	Combined ring
Ring gap:			
Top ring		0.0079 – 0.0138 (0.20 – 0.35)	
2nd ring	0.0079 – 0.0138 (0.20 – 0.35)	ditto	0.0059 – 0.0118 (0.15 – 0.30)
Oil ring		0.0118 – 0.0354 (0.30 – 0.90)	

Gudgeon pin

Diameter	0.6869 – 0.6871 (17.447 – 17.452)	ditto	0.7478 – 0.7480 (18.995 – 19.000)
Clearance in piston at 20°C (68°F)	0.00004 – 0.00051 (0.001 – 0.013)	ditto	0.0003 – 0.0005 (0.008 – 0.012)
Interference fit in connecting rod	0.0008 (0.020)	ditto	0.0007 – 0.014) (0.017 – 0.035)

Crankshaft

Number of main bearings	3	5	ditto
Journal diameter		1.9666 – 1.9671 (49.951 – 49.964)	
Main journal ovality		0.0004 (0.01)	
Crankpin diameter		1.7701 – 1.7706 (44.961 – 44.974)	
Maximum crankpin ovality	0.0004 (0.01)	ditto	0.0012 (0.03)
Main bearing thickness		0.0719 – 0.0722 (1.827 – 1.835)	
Main bearing clearance		0.0008 – 0.0024 (0.020 – 0.062)	
Main bearing clearance (wear limit)		0.0059 (0.15)	
Crankshaft end play		0.0020 – 0.0059 (0.05 – 0.15)	
Wear limit		0.0118 (0.30)	

Connecting rods

Bearing thickness	0.0591 – 0.0594 (1.500 – 1.508)
Big-end end play	0.008 – 0.012 (0.2 – 0.3)
Endplay wear limit	0.016 (0.40)
Big-end bearing clearance	0.0008 – 0.0020 (0.020 – 0.050)
Weight difference between rods	0.18 oz (5 g) maximum

Camshaft

Number of bearings		five, bored in line	
Endplay		0.0004 – 0.0020 (0.01 – 0.05)	
Maximum endplay (wear limit)		0.0039 (0.10)	
Lobe lift:			
Intake	0.211 (5.35)	0.222 (5.65)	0.2224 (5.65)
Exhaust	0.211 (5.35)	0.222 (5.65)	0.2331 (5.92)
Journal diameter:			
1st		1.7237 – 1.7242 (43.783 – 43.796)	
2nd		1.7041 – 1.7046 (43.283 – 43.296)	
3rd		1.6844 – 1.6849 (42.783 – 42.796)	
4th		1.6647 – 1.6652 (42.283 – 42.296)	
5th		1.6224 – 1.6299 (41.208 – 41.221)	
Bearing inner diameter:			
1st		1.7257 – 1.7261 (43.833 – 43.843)	
2nd		1.7056 – 1.7060 (43.323 – 43.333)	
3rd		1.6865 – 1.6868 (42.836 – 42.846)	
4th		1.6663 – 1.6667 (42.323 – 42.333)	
5th		1.6243 – 1.6247 (41.258 – 41.268)	

Cylinder head

Material	Aluminium alloy
Surface flatness (maximum limit)	0.0039 (0.10)

Valves

Valve clearance:	
Intake (hot)	0,014 (0.35)
(cold)	0.010 (0.25)
Exhaust (hot)	0.014 (0.35)
(cold)	0.010 (0.25)
Valve head diameter:	
Inlet	1.46 (37)
Exhaust	1.18 (30)
Valve stem diameter:	
Inlet	0.3138 – 0.3144 (7.970 – 7.985)
Exhaust	0.3128 – 0.3134 (7.945 – 7.960)

Valve length, inlet and exhaust:
    A10 and A12 . . . .   4.030 – 4.041 (102.35 – 102.65)
    A14 . . . .   4.0807 – 4.0925 (103.65 – 103.95)
Valve spring free length:
    A10 . . . .   1.799 (45.7)
    A12 and A14 . . . .   1.831 (46.5)
Valve guide length 1.929 (49)
Valve guide height from head surface:
    A10 and A12 . . . .   0.709 (18)
    A14 . . . .   0.728 (18.5)
Valve stem to guide clearance:
    Inlet . . . .   0.0006 – 0.0018 (0.015 – 0.045)
    Exhaust . . . .   0.0016 – 0.0028 (0.040 – 0.070)
Valve seat width:
    Inlet 0.051 (1.3)
    Exhaust 0.071 (1.8)
Valve seat angle:
    Inlet and exhaust . . . .   45°
Valve guide interference fit . . . .   0.0009 – 0.0017 (0.022 – 0.044)
Valve seat interference fit . . . .   0.0025 – 0.0038 (0.064 – 0.096)

Timing chain
Type . . . .   Double roller

Lubrication system
Type . . . .   Pressure feed
Filter . . . .   Canister, disposable type

Oil pump
Type . . . .   Rotor, camshaft gear driven
Rotor side clearance . . . .   0.0020 – 0.0047 (0.05 – 0.12)
    Wear limit 0.0078 (0.20)
Rotor tip clearance . . . .   less than 0.0047 (0.12)
    Wear limit 0.0078 (0.20)
Outer rotor to body clearance . . . .   0.0059 – 0.0083 (0.15 – 0.21)
    Wear limit 0.0196 (0.50)
Gap between body and rotor 0.0020 (0.05)
    Wear limit 0.0078 (0.20)

Oil pressure regulator valve
Oil pressure at idling . . . .   more than 11 lb/in^2 (0.8 kg/cm^2)
Oil pressure at 3000 rpm . . . .   54 – 74 lb/in^2 (3.8 – 5.2 kg/cm^2)
Regulator valve spring:
    Free length 1.7122 (43.49)

Sump and filter capacity (approx) . . . .   6 pints (3.3 litre)

Torque wrench settings

	lbf ft	kgf m
Cylinder head bolts:		
A10	43 – 47	6 – 6.5
A12 and A14	51 – 54	7 – 7.5
Rocker shaft pillar bolts	14 – 18	2 – 2.5
Connecting rod big-end nuts:		
A10	22 – 26	3 – 3.6
A12 and A14	23 – 27	3.2 – 3.8
Flywheel bolts:		
A10	41 – 43	5.6 – 6
A12	47 – 54	6.5 – 7.5
A14	54 – 61	7.5 – 8.5
Main bearing cap bolts	36 – 43	5 – 6
Camshaft sprocket bolt	29 – 35	4 – 4.8
Oil sump bolts	11 – 14	1.5 – 2
Oil pump bolts	7 – 10	0.9 – 1.4
Sump drain plug	14 – 22	2 – 3
Camshaft plate bolts	3 – 4	0.4 – 0.5
Water pump bolts	7 – 10	0.9 – 1.4
Timing chain cover bolts	4 – 5	0.5 – 0.7
Crankshaft pulley bolt	108 – 145	15 – 20
Engine mounting bolts	14 – 18	1.9 – 2.5

1   General description

The engine fitted to the 100A F-II is the A10. It is a three-bearing 988 cc (60.3 cu in) engine transversely mounted and inclined at 5° from the vertical on a subframe.

The A12 engine fitted to the 120A F-II and the A14 engine fitted to the F10 (USA) series are basically the same except that they have a five-bearing crankshaft and capacities of 1171 cc (71.5 cu in) and 1397 cc (85.24 cu in) respectively.

Apart from the difference in the number of crankshaft bearings, and the capacity, the following description encompasses both engines. All the photographs in the ensuing Sections are of the A10 engine, but are nearly all applicable to the A12 and A14 engines.

All the engines are of the four-cylinder, in-line overhead valve, water-cooled design. The crankshaft is of forged steel construction and incorporates oil drillings for lubrication of the main bearings.

The pistons are made of aluminium with flat crowns on the A10 engine, and with concave crowns on the A12 and A14 engines. The connecting rods are of forged steel with gudgeon pins which are an interference fit in the connecting rod small ends but fully floating in the pistons.

A cast iron crankshaft is fitted, which is supported by renewable bearings, the number depending on engine type, and drives the camshaft by a double roller chain. The cylinder head is of aluminium with pressed in valve seats. The overhead valve mechanism comprises conventional camshaft operated tappets, pushrods and rocker shaft and arms. The valves are fitted with single coil springs and split cotters are employed to retain the valve spring caps.

The inlet manifold is aluminium and the exhaust manifold is cast iron and incorporates a quick warm-up valve.

The power unit is mounted at three points, one at the sump, one at the clutch housing and one on the transmission housing. The mountings are of bonded rubber/metal acting under compression of steel brackets.

2   Major operations with engine in the car

The following major operations can be carried out on the engine with it in place in the bodyframe:

a)   *Removal and refitting of the cylinder head assembly.*
b)   *Removal and refitting the oil pump*
c)   *Removal and refitting the clutch assembly.*

3   Major operations with engine removed

The following major operations require the removal of the engine/transmission assembly from the bodyframe:
a)   *Removal and refitting of the main bearings*
b)   *Removal and refitting the crankshaft*
c)   *Removal and refitting the flywheel*
d)   *Removal and refitting of the crankshaft rear bearing oil seal*
e)   *Removal and refitting of the timing chain*
f)   *Removal and refitting of the camshaft*
g)   *Removal and refitting of big-end bearings, pistons and connecting rods*

4   Engine removal – general

The engine and transmission are removed as an assembly. The engine cannot be removed as a separate unit because of the method of utilizing the clutch housing as part of the transmission casing and the limited access to split them when fitted in the vehicle.

Before beginning work it would be worthwhile getting all the dirt and oil cleaned off the engine, either by a service station, using steam cleaning equipment, or doing it yourself using a grease solvent and a garden hose. This will make dismantling the engine that much more pleasant, and cleaner.

A good hoist, and two strong axle stands will be required if a inspection pit is not available. Removal will be much easier if there is someone to assist, especially during the later stages.

In most cases, it is better to lift out the engine with all the

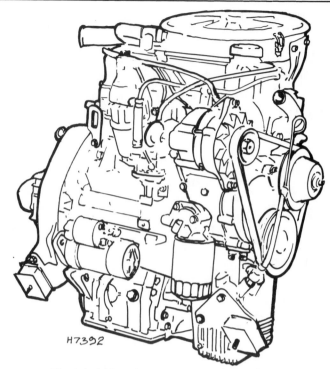

H7392

Fig. 1.1. A12 engine and transmission assembly

ancillaries (alternator, distributor, carburettor, starter motor, exhaust manifold and air pump, if fitted) still attached as they are easier to remove with the engine out of the car.

5   Engine – removal

1   Using a pencil, mark the outline of the bonnet hinge on either side to act as a datum point for refitting. With the help of an assistant, undo and remove the two bolts and washers securing the bonnet to the hinge (photo) and carefully lift the bonnet up and then over the front of the car. Store it in a safe place where it will not get damaged. Push the hinges down out of the way.
2   Protect the top surface of the front wings with covers to prevent damage to the paintwork during the removal operations.
3   Disconnect the earth lead from the negative (–) terminal of the battery.
4   Drain the cooling system and remove the radiator as described in

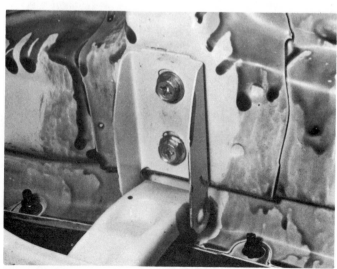

5.1   Remove the bonnet hinge securing bolts

Chapter 2, Section 2.
5   Remove the air cleaner as described in Chapter 3 Section 2 or 4. Cover the carburettor air inlet to prevent the entry of dirt or foreign objects.
6   Disconnect the accelerator and choke control cables from the carburettor (photos)
7   Disconnect the following electrical wiring and hoses:

   a)   *Coil to distributor HT lead.*
   b)   *Coil earth lead at the clutch housing.*
   c)   *Starter motor connections.*
   d)   *Lead from the reverse lamp switch (photo).*
   e)   *LT lead to the distributor*
   f)   *Lead to the oil pressure switch*
   g)   *Alternator leads*
   h)   *Lead to the thermal transmitter*
   j)   *Lead to the anti-dieseling solenoid*
   k)   *Heater inlet and outlet hoses*
   l)   *Fuel hose at the fuel pump, plug the hose after removal*
   m)   *Brake servo vacuum hose at the inlet manifold*

   On A14 engines most of the electrical connections are disconnected at the connectors on the wiring harness, also the following additional hoses have to be disconnected:

   n)   *Fuel return hose from the carburettor*
   p)   *Carbon canister hose.*
   q)   *Air pump cleaner hose.*

8   Remove the air pump cleaner, carbon canister and auxiliary fan (A14 engines only)
9   Remove the washer tank, and the radiator as described in Chapter 2.
10 Disconnect the clutch operating cable at its forked clevis (right-hand drive vehicles) or on left-hand drive vehicles, remove the slave cylinder securing bolt after disconnecting the operating rod from the clutch release arm. The slave cylinder may then be swung up out of the way without disturbing the hydraulic circuit which would necessitate subsequent bleeding of the clutch hydraulic system.

11 Disconnect the exhaust down pipe from the exhaust manifold by removing the two flange securing nuts.
12 Disconnect the speedometer cable from the transmission (photo).
13 Since one has to work under the vehicle jack it up and support it on axle stands or some other equally secure support.
14 Disconnect the bracket, not just the clamp, from the exhaust pipe to differential casing (photo)
15 Unhook the return spring on the gearchange linkage, then disconnect the radius link assembly from the differential casing by removing the two securing bolts. Disconnect the spring clip at the end of the control rod; this enables you to ease the radius link rod away from the control rod, but be ready to collect the spring and nylon inserts from inside the joint. The main rod will now drop away (photo).
16 Unclip the remaining single linkage from the selector mechanism on the differential.
17 Remove the three bolts securing each driveshaft to the differential side flanges (photo). Lower the driveshafts to rest on the subframe.
18 Remove the single mounting nut on the rear mounting assembly (photo).
19 Disconnect the right and left buffer rods from the brackets on the engine and swing them out of the way (photo).
20 Remove the nuts on the engine from mountings (photo). Before connecting a hoist and sling to the engine, make a final check that there are no more items to disconnect and that there is nothing likely to get caught up when the engine and transmission assembly is removed.
21 The engine can be lifted either by a sling placed round each end of the assembly, or by attaching lifting hooks at the appropriate points, see Fig. 1.3.
22 With suitable lifting tackle connected securely to the engine, hoist the assembly out of the car. The engine mountings are lifted out with the engine/transmission assembly (photo).

6   Engine/transmission assembly – separation

1   With the engine/transmission assembly removed from the car, the

5.6a   Disconnect the accelerator control cable ...

5.6b   ... and the choke control cable

5.7   Disconnect the lead from the reverse lamp switch

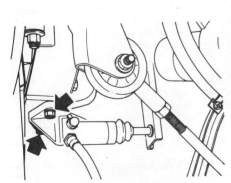
Fig. 1.2. Removing the clutch slave cylinder – LH drive models (Sec. 5)

5.12   Disconnect the speedometer cable from the transmission

5.14   Remove the bolts securing the exhaust pipe bracket to the differential casing

5.15   Disconnecting the gearchange linkage

5.17   Removing the driveshaft to differential side flange securing bolts ...

5.18   ... and then the single nut on the rear mounting

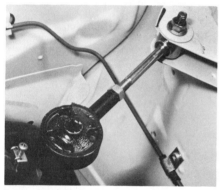

5.19   Disconnect the buffer rods from the brackets on the engine

5.20   Remove the nuts from the front engine mountings

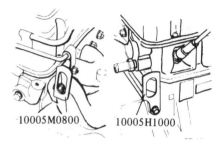

10005M0800   10005H1000

Fig. 1.3. Engine lifting points
The past numbers are for the Datsun lifting eyes, but any suitable attachment can be used (Sec. 5)

5.22   Lifting the engine out of the engine compartment

6.2a   Removing the transmission to engine bracket securing bolt

6.2b   Separating the transmission from the engine

next task is to separate the two units, this is necessary whether one is working on the engine or tranmission
2   Remove the bolts and bracket bolt securing the transmission to the engine (photo) and separate the transmission from the engine (photo). The clutch assembly remains attached to the engine.

7   Engine dismantling – general

1   It is best to mount the engine on a dismantling stand but if one is not available, then stand the engine on a strong bench so as to be at a comfortable working height. Failing this, the engine can be stripped down on the floor.
2   During the dismantling process the greatest care should be taken to keep the exposed parts free from dirt. As an aid to achieving this, it is a sound scheme to thoroughly clean down the outside of the engine, removing all traces of oil and congealed dirt, if it has not been done already.
3   Use paraffin or a good grease solvent. The latter compound will

make the job much easier, as, after the solvent has been applied and allowed to stand for a time, a vigorous jet of water will wash off the solvent and all the grease and filth. If the dirt is thick and deeply embedded, work the solvent into it with a wire brush.
4   Finally wipe down the exterior of the engine with a rag and only then, when it is quite clean should the dismantling process begin. As the engine is stripped, clean each part in a bath of paraffin or petrol.
5   Never immerse parts with oilways in paraffin, eg the crankshaft, but to clean, wipe down carefully with a petrol dampened rag. Oilways can be cleaned out with wire. If an air line is present all parts can be blown dry and the oilways blown through as an added precaution.
6   Re-use of old engine gaskets is false economy and can give rise to oil and water leaks, if nothing worse. To avoid the possibility of trouble after the engine has been reassembled **always** use new gaskets throughout.
7   Do not throw the old gaskets away as it sometimes happens that an immediate replacement cannot be found and the old gasket is then very useful as a template. Hang up the old gaskets as they are removed on a suitable hook or nail.

8 To strip the engine it is best to work from the top down. The sump provides a firm base on which the engine can be supported in an upright position. When this stage where the sump must be removed is reached, the engine can be turned on its side and all other work carried out with it in this position.

9 Wherever possible, refit nuts, bolts and washers fingertight from wherever they were removed. This helps avoid later loss and muddle. If they cannot be refitted then lay them out in such a fashion that it is clear from where they came.

8 Ancillary components – removal

1 With the engine removed from the vehicle and separated from the gearbox, the ancillary components should now be removed before dismantling of the engine unit commences.

2 Loosen the alternator mounting bolts and the adjustment strap bolt. Push the alternator in towards the engine and remove the drivebelt. Remove the alternator mounting bolts and adjustment strap bolt and lift the unit away (photo).

3 Remove the idler pulley, air pump drivebelt and idler pulley bracket. Remove the air pump and air pump bracket (A14 engines only).

4 Remove the oil level dipstick.

5 Unscrew and remove the cartridge type oil filter (photo). It may be necessary to employ a small chain or strap wrench where the filter is stuck tight.

6 Unscrew and remove the bolts which secure the oil pump body to the exterior of the crankcase. Withdraw the oil pump complete with drive gear.

7 Unscrew and remove the spark plugs.

8 Disconnect and remove the vacuum tube which runs between the distributor vacuum capsule and the carburettor.

9 Unscrew and remove the setscrew which retains the distributor plate to the engine crankcase. Withdraw the distributor from its crankcase location.

10 Disconnect the fuel pump to carburettor fuel pipe at the carburettor end. Unscrew and remove the carburettor to manifold flange nuts and washers. Lift the carburettor away.

11 Unscrew and remove the rocker cover screws and lift off the rocker cover.

12 Unscrew and remove the thermostat cover retaining bolts and lift the cover away. If it is stuck do not insert a blade and attempt to prise it off as this will damage the mating faces. Tap it sideways with a plastic faced hammer until it is free.

13 Withdraw the thermostat. If it is stuck in its seating, do not try and pull it out with a pair of pliers but cut round its periphery with a sharp pointed knife to free it.

14 Remove the EGR control valve (A14 engine).

15 Unscrew and remove the inlet and exhaust manifold securing nuts and remove the manifold assemblies and gasket.

16 Remove the PCV hose (pipe connector to control valve).

17 Unscrew the water pump pulley securing bolts, use a strap wrench to hold the pulley, and remove it (photo).

18 Unscrew and remove the nuts which secure the water pump to the upper front face of the timing cover.

19 Unscrew and remove the securing nuts from the fuel pump and lift it from its crankcase location. Carefully note the exact number and sequence of gaskets and spacers between the pump and crankcase.

20 Remove the clutch assembly as described in Chapter 5.

9 Cylinder head – removal

1 Unscrew the rocker shaft pillar securing bolts. Lift the rocker shaft assembly from the cylinder head (photo).

2 Unscrew each of the cylinder head bolts a turn or two each at a time in the sequence shown in Fig. 1.4. finally removing them.

3 Withdraw each of the pushrods and keep them in sequence so that they can be returned to their original positions. A piece of wood with two rows of holes drilled in it and numbered will provide a very useful rack for both pushrods and valves.

4 Lift off the cylinder head. Should it be stuck, do not attempt to prise it from the engine block but tap it all round using a hardwood block or plastic faced mallet. Remove the cylinder head gasket.

8.2 Remove the alternator

8.5 Unscrew the oil filter

8.17 Using a chain wrench to hold the water pump pulley while removing the bolts

9.1 Lifting off the rocker shaft assembly

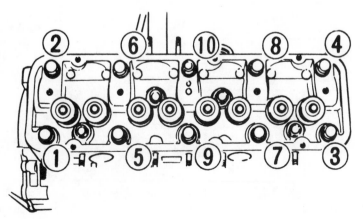

Fig. 1.4. Loosening sequence of cylinder head bolts (Sec. 9)

10 Inlet and exhaust valves – removal

1   The valves can be removed from the cylinder head by the following method. Compress each spring in turn with a valve spring compressor until the two halves of the collet can be removed (photo). Release the compressor and remove the spring and spring retainer.

2   If, when the valve spring compressor is screwed down, the valve spring retaining cap refuses to free to expose the split collet, do not continue to screw down on the compressor as there is a likelihood of damaging it.

3   Gently tap the top of the tool directly over the cap with a light hammer. This will free the cap. To avoid the compressor jumping off the valve spring retaining cap when it is tapped, hold the compressor firmly in position with one hand.

4   Slide the rubber oil control seal off the top of each valve stem and then drop out each valve through the combustion chamber.

5   It is essential that the valves are kept in their correct sequence unless they are so badly worn that they are to be renewed.

11 Rocker assembly – dismantling

1   Remove the bolts from the rocker pillars and slide the rocker pillars, rocker arms and springs off the rocker shaft.

2   If the original components are to be refitted, identify their fitting sequence with a piece of masking tape.

12 Engine oil sump – removal

1   Unscrew and remove the sump drain plug, catching the oil in a container of adequate capacity. Refit the plug.

2   Unscrew and remove the sump retaining bolts and lift the sump away (photo).

3   The gauge strainer and oil suction pipe is now exposed and can be detached by removing the two suction pipe flange securing bolts

(photo).

13 Timing cover, gear and chain – removal

1   Unscrew the crankshaft pulley securing bolt. To do this it will be necessary to restrain the crankshaft from turning by wedging the flywheel (see photo). One or two heavy blows with a club hammer on the end of the spanner should loosen the nut.

2   Lever off the crankshaft pulley, using two screwdrivers or similar levers.

3   Unscrew the timing cover securing bolts and remove the timing cover.

4   Withdraw the oil thrower disc from the crankshaft. Unscrew the securing bolts and remove the timing chain tensioner from the front of the engine block (photo).

5   Unscrew and remove the camshaft sprocket securing bolt.

6   Remove the camshaft and crankshaft sprockets simultaneously, complete with double roller chain (photo). Use tyre levers behind each gear and lever them equally and a little at a time. If they are stuck on their shafts, the use of a puller may be required.

7   When the sprockets and chain are removed, extract the two Woodruff keys from the crankshaft and retain safely.

14 Pistons and connecting rods – removal

1   With the cylinder head and sump removed undo the big-end retaining bolts.

2   The connecting rods and pistons are lifted out from the top of the cylinder block, after the carbon or 'wear' ring at the top of the bore has been scraped away.

3   Remove the big-end caps one at a time, taking care to keep them in the right order and the correct way round. Also ensure that the shell bearings are kept with their correct connecting rods and caps unless they are to be renewed. Normally, the numbers 1 to 4 are stamped on adjacent sides of the big-end caps and connecting rods, indicating

Fig. 1.5. Valve assembly components (Sec. 10)

10.1   Removing the valve collets

12.2   Remove the oil sump and ...

12.3   ... then the oil strainer

13.1   Restrain the flywheel from turning

13.4   Removing the timing chain tensioner securing bolt

13.6 Pull off the camshaft and crankshaft sprockets with the timing chain

14.3 The connecting rods and caps are numbered

15.1 Remove the flywheel retaining bolts

16.1 Removing the main bearing caps

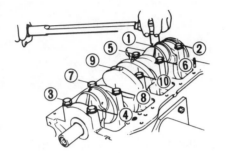

Fig. 1.6. Main bearing cap bolts – loosening sequence (Sec. 16)

16.4 Take the shell bearing out of the crankcase

which oap fits on which rod and which way round the cap fits (photo). If no numbers or lines can be found, then, with a sharp screwdriver or file, scratch mating marks across the joint from the rod to the cap. One line for connecting rod No. 1, two for connecting rod No. 2 and so on. This will ensure there is no confusion later as it is most important that the caps go back in the correct position on the connecting rods from which they were removed.

4   If the big-end caps are difficult to remove they may be gently tapped with a soft hammer.

5   To remove the shell bearings, press the bearings opposite the groove in both the connecting rod, and the connecting rod caps and the bearings will slide out easily.

6   Withdraw the pistons and connecting rods upwards and ensure they are kept in the correct order for refitting in the same bore. Refit the connecting rod caps and bearings to the rods to prevent the caps and rods getting mixed up.

15 Flywheel – removal

1   Unscrew and remove the flywheel retaining bolts (photo). It will be necessary to restrain the crankshaft from turning while undoing the bolts. To do this wedge the flywheel (refer to Section 13, paragraph 1) or place a block of wood between a crankshaft web and the side of the crankcase.

2   Lift the flywheel off the crankshaft flange.

3   The endplate behind the flywheel can now be removed.

16 Main bearings and crankshaft – removal

1   Unscrew and remove the securing bolts from the main bearing caps (photo). Gradually loosen the bolts in two or three stages in the sequence shown in Fig. 1.6. On the three-bearing crankshaft fitted to the A10 engine, the main bearing cap at the timing case end has a raised circular flange in the centre. The other two bearing caps can easily be confused so it is as well to identify them before dismantling. On the five-bearing crankshaft fitted to the A12 and A14 engines the

caps are numbered 1 to 5, starting from the timing cover end of the engine, and arrows, marked on the caps, point towards the timing cover to ensure correct orientation of the caps when refitting.

2   Withdraw the bearing caps complete with the shell bearing.

3   Remove the rear oil seal.

4   Lift the crankshaft out of the crankcase and then remove the shell bearings.

5   Remove the baffle plate and the steel mesh screen from the crankcase (A12 and A14 engines only).

17 Camshaft and tappets – removal

1   Remove the two bolts which secure the camshaft end plate and take off the plate.

2   Carefully withdraw the camshaft (photo). Rotate the camshaft during the removal operation and take particular care not to damage the camshaft bearings as the lobes of the camshaft pass through them.

3   The tappets can now be removed from the crankcase. Identify the tappets so that they can be refitted in their original positions.

18 Piston rings – removal

1   If the same piston rings are to be refitted, care must be taken that the rings are not broken when being removed. Starting with the top ring (all rings must be removed from the top of the piston) ease one end out of its groove and place a thin piece of metal behind it.

2   Then move the metal strip carefully behind the ring, at the same time easing the ring upward so that it rests on the surface of the piston above the groove, until the whole ring is clear and can be slid off. With the second and third rings which must come off from the top, arrange the strip of metal to carry them over the other grooves.

3   Identify the rings so that they can be refitted to the same pistons, by piercing a piece of paper with each ring, showing its location, top 1, middle 1, etc.

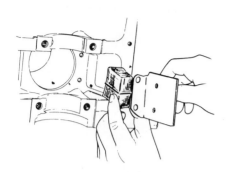

Fig. 1.7. Removing the baffle plate and steel mesh screen – A 12 and A14 engines (Sec. 16)

17.2　Withdrawing the camshaft

21.3　Removing the oil pressure regulator plug, spring and valve

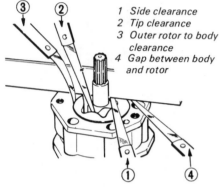

1　Side clearance
2　Tip clearance
3　Outer rotor to body clearance
4　Gap between body and rotor

Fig. 1.8. Checking the oil pump rotor clearance (Sec. 21)

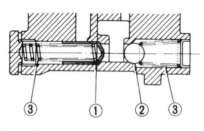

Fig. 1.9. Oil system regulator valve and relief valve (Sec. 21)

1　Regulator valve　　　　3　Valve spring
2　Relief valve

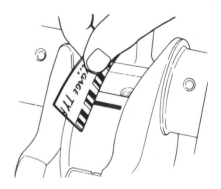

Fig. 1.10. Using Plastigage to measure the main bearing clearance (Sec. 23)

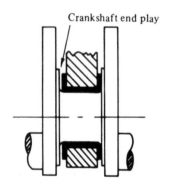

Crankshaft end play

Fig. 1.11. Checking crankshaft endplay (Sec. 23)

23.5　Measuring the crankshaft endplay

23.6 Check the bush in the rear end of the crankshaft (A12 and A14 engines only)

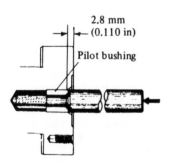

2.8 mm (0.110 in)

Pilot bushing

Fig. 1.12. Pressing in a new crankshaft pilot bush ((Sec. 23)

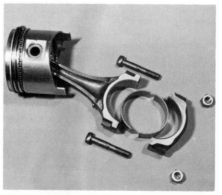

24.2　Piston and connecting rod assembly

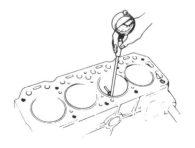

Fig. 1.13. Measuring the cylinder bore (Sec. 25)

19 Gudgeon pins – removal

1   The gudgeon pins are an interference fit in the connecting rod small ends.
2   To separate the pistons from the connecting rods considerable pressure is required to press out the gudgeon pins and this requires a proper press. Attempts with other methods will probably result in bent connecting rods or broken pistons. Therefore this is a job best left to your local Datsun dealer, as in the event of new pistons being needed it is necessary to heat the connecting rod when refitting the gudgeon pins and this requires experience to prevent distortion of the connecting rod.

20 Lubrication system – description

The engine lubrication system is of the pressure feed type. An oil pump mounted on the right-hand side of the cylinder block is driven by a meshing gear on the camshaft which also drives the distributor drive shaft. Oil is drawn from the sump through a filter screen and tube, by the rotor type pump, through the full flow oil filter to the main crankcase oil gallery.

The main oil gallery supplies oil to the crankshaft main bearings and big-end bearings through drillings and a regulated quantity of oil ejected from small holes in the connecting rods lubricates the gudgeon pins and cylinder walls.

The timing chain is fed with oil from the main gallery and the chain tensioner is held against the timing chain partly by oil pressure and partly by a coil spring.

The camshaft bearings are lubricated with oil from the main gallery, and the rocker shaft and valve gear obtain their lubrication through a drilling from the camshaft centre bearing.

21 Oil pump – inspection and servicing

1   Having removed the oil pump as described in Section 8, unscrew and remove the bolt securing the pump cover to the pump body.
2   Slide out the outer rotor from the pump body.
3   Remove the oil pressure regulator, plug, washer, shim, spring and valve (photo).
4   Thoroughly clean all parts in cleaning solvent. Use a brush to clean the inside of the pump housing and pressure regulator valve chamber.
5   Examine all the parts for damage and excessive wear.
6   Check the inner rotor shaft for looseness in the pump body, the regulator valve for wear or scoring and the spring for chafing or a permanent set.
7   Check the following clearances using a feeler gauge and straight edge, see Fig. 1.8.

    a)   Side clearance between inner and outer rotors
    b)   Clearance between outer rotor and the pump body
    c)   Rotor tip clearance
    d)   Gap between body and rotor

If the clearances exceed the limits given in the Specifications at the beginning of this Chapter, the pump must be renewed as a complete assembly, as individual parts are not available.
8   The oil pressure relief valve, located in the oil pump cover, bypasses the oil into the main oil gallery when the oil filter element is excessively clogged. With the regulator valve removed check the valve operation.
9   Reassembly of the oil pump is the reverse of the dismantling procedure. Always use a new gasket between the pump cover and pump body.

22 Inspection and renovation – general

Having dismantled the engine and thoroughly cleaned all the parts, everything should now be examined and checked for damage and wear. The following Sections describe the inspection procedure and the renovation or renewal operations as necessary.

23 Crankshaft and main bearings – inspection and renovation

1   Examine the crankpin and main journal surfaces for signs of scoring or scratches. Check the ovality of the crankpins at different positions with a micrometer. If more than 0.001 in (0.025 mm) out of round the crankpin will have to be reground. It will also have to be reground if there are any scores or scratches present. Also check the journals in the same fashion.
2   If it is necessary to regrind the crankshaft and fit new bearings your local Datsun garage or engineering works will be able to decide how much metal to grind off and the size of new bearing shells.
3   Full details of crankshaft regrinding tolerances and bearing undersizes are given in Specifications.
4   The main bearing clearances may be established by using a strip of Plastigage between the crankshaft journals and the main bearing/shell caps. Tighten the bearing cap bolts to a torque of between 36 and 43 lbf ft (5 and 6 kgf m). Do not turn the crankshaft while the Plastigage is in place. Remove the cap and compare the flattened Plastigage strip with the scale printed on the Plastigage envelope. Check that the clearance is within the limit specified in the Specifications at the beginning of this Chapter.
5   Temporarily fit the crankshaft in the crankcase, with main bearing shells, and tighten the bearing caps to a torque of 36 – 43 lbf ft (5 – 6 kgf m). Push the crankshaft as far as possible to one end and, inserting a feeler gauge as shown in Fig. 1.11, measure the crankshaft endplay between the crankshaft thrust face and the flange of the centre main bearing (photo). Check that the end play is within the specified limit.
6   On A12 and A14 engines check the crankshaft pilot bush at the rear end of the crankshaft for wear or damage (photo). Renew the bush if defective. When fitting a new bush, press the bush in so that its height above the flange end is 0.11 in (2.8 mm). Do **not** oil the bush.

24 Connecting rods and bearings – inspection and renovation

1   Big-end bearing failure is indicated by a knocking from within the crankcase and a slight drop in oil pressure.
2   Examine the big-end bearing surfaces for pitting and scoring (photo). Renew the shells in accordance with the size specified in the Specifications. Where the crankshaft has been reground, the correct undersize big-end shell bearings will be supplied with the crank.
3   Should there be any suspicion that a connecting rod is bent, or twisted, or the small-end bush no longer provides an interference fit for the gudgeon pin, then the complete connecting rod assembly should be exchanged for a reconditioned one but ensure that the comparative weight of the two rods is within the specified tolerance (see Specifications).
4   Measurement of the big-end bearing clearances may be carried out in a similar manner to that described for the main bearings in the previous Section but tighten the securing nuts on the cap bolts to 23 – 26 lbf ft (3.2 – 3.6 kgf m).

25 Cylinder bores and crankcase – inspection and renovation

1   The cylinder bores must be examined for taper, ovality, scoring and scratches. Start by carefully examining the top of the cylinder bores. If they are at all worn a very slight ridge will be found on the thrust side. This marks the top of the piston ring travel. The owner will have a good indication of the bore wear prior to dismantling the engine, or removing the cylinder head. Excessive oil consumption accompanied by blue smoke from the exhaust is a sure sign of worn cylinder bores and piston rings.
2   Measure the bore diameter just under the ridge with an internal micrometer and compare it with the diameter at the bottom of the bore, which is not subject to wear. If the difference between the two measurements is more than 0.008 in (0.20 mm) then it will be necessary to fit special pistons and rings or to have the cylinders rebored and fit oversize pistons. Oversize pistons are available as listed in Specifications.
3   These are accurately machined to just below the indicated measurements so as to provide correct running clearances in bores machined out to the exact oversize dimensions.
4   If the bores are slightly worn but not so badly worn as to justify reboring them, then special oil control rings and pistons can be fitted

which will restore compression and stop the engine burning oil. Several different types are available and the manufacturers' instructions concerning their fitting must be followed closely.

5   If new pistons are being fitted and the bores have not been rebored, it is essential to slightly roughen the hard glaze on the sides of the bores with fine glass paper so that the new piston rings will have a chance to bed in properly.

26 Pistons and piston rings – inspection and renovation

1   If the original pistons are to be refitted, carefully remove the piston rings as described in Section 18.

2   Clean all carbon off the rings and grooves, taking care not to scratch the aluminium surface of the pistons. Ensure that the oil slots in the bottom land of oil ring groove are cleaned out.

3   Before fitting the rings to the pistons, check the ring gap. Place the ring in the cylinder bore and press it down to the bottom of the cylinder with a piston, and using a feeler gauge, check that the gap is as given in the Specifications at the beginning of this Chapter. If the ring gap is too large the ring will have to be renewed, if too small the gap can be increased by filing one end of the ring with a fine file. Be careful not to break the rings as they are very brittle. Ensure that the gap is not less than that specified; if it closes under normal operating temperatures the ring will break.

4   Check that each ring gives a side clearance in the piston groove according to the Specifications. If the gap is too large, new pistons and rings will be required if Datsun spares are used. However, independent specialist manufacturers of pistons and rings can normally provide the rings required separately. If new Datsun pistons and rings are being obtained it will be necessary to have the ridge ground away from the top of the cylinder bores. If specialist oil control rings are being obtained from an independent supplier the ridge removal will not be necessary as the top rings will be stepped to provide the necessary clearance. If the top ring, of a new set, is not stepped it will hit the ridge made by the previous ring and break.

5   If new pistons are obtained the rings will be included, so it must be emphasised that the top ring be stepped if fitted to a cylinder which has not been rebored, or had the ridge at the top removed.

6   The groove clearance of new rings on old pistons should be within the specified tolerance. If it is not enough the rings could stick in the grooves, causing loss of compression and oiling-up. If it is too loose, this accelerates wear on the sides of the ring grooves.

7   If the piston appears slack on the gudgeon pin, then both the piston and the gudgeon pin should be renewed. This is a job for the local Datsun dealer as mentioned in Section 19.

27 Camshaft and camshaft bearings – inspection and renovation

1   Carefully examine the camshaft bearings for wear. If the bearings are obviously worn or pitted then they must be renewed. This is an operation for your local Datsun dealer or local engineering works as it demands the use of specialized equipment. The bearings are removed with a special drift after which new bearings are pressed in, and in-line bored, care being taken to ensure the oil holes in the bearings line up with those in the block.

2   The camshaft itself should show no signs of wear, but, if very slight scoring on the cams is noticed, the score marks can be removed by very gently rubbing down with a very fine emery cloth. The greatest care should be taken to keep the cam profiles smooth.

3   Examine the skew gear for wear, chipped teeth or other damage.

4   Check the camshaft endplay by fitting the camshaft thrust plate and camshaft sprocket in their respective positions. Measure the endplay with a feeler gauge. If the endplay exceeds 0.0039 in (0.10 mm), renew the thrust plate.

28 Valves and valve seats – inspection and renovation

1   Examine the heads of the valves for pitting and burning, especially the heads of the exhaust valves. The valve seats should be examined at the same time. If the pitting on valve and seat is very slight the marks can be removed by grinding the seats and valves together with coarse, and then fine, valve grinding paste.

2   Where bad pitting has occurred to the valve seats it will be necessary to recut them and fit new valves. If the valve seats are so worn that they cannot be recut, then it will be necessary to fit new valve seat inserts. These latter two jobs should be entrusted to the local Datsun agent or engineering works. In practice it is very seldom that the seats are so badly worn that they require renewal. Normally, it is the valve that is too badly worn for refitting, and the owner can easily purchase a new set of valves and match them to the seats by valve grinding.

3   Valve grinding is carried out as follows: Smear a trace of coarse carborundum paste on the seat face and apply a suction grinder tool to the valve head. With semi-rotary motion, grind the valve head to its seat, lifting the valve occasionally to redistribute the grinding paste. When a dull matt even surface finish is produced on both the valve seat and the valve, wipe off the paste and repeat the process with fine carborundum paste, lifting and turning the valve to redistribute the paste as before. A light spring placed under the valve head will greatly ease this operation. When a smooth unbroken ring of light grey matt finish is produced, on both valve and valve seat faces, the grinding operation is completed.

4   Scrape away all carbon from the valve head and the valve stem. Carefully clean away every trace of grinding compound, taking great care to leave none in the ports or in the valve guides. Clean the valves and valve seats with a paraffin soaked rag then with a clean rag, and finally, if an air line is is available, blow the valves, valve guides and valve ports clean.

29 Valve guides – inspection and renewal

1   Check each valve in its guide for wear. After a considerable mileage, the valve guide bore may wear oval. This can best be checked by inserting a new valve in the guide and moving it from side to side. If the top of the valve stem deflects by about 0.0080 in (0.20 mm) then it must be assumed that the tolerance between the stem and guide is greater than the permitted maximum (0.0039 in /0.10 mm).

2   New valve guides (oversize available – see Specifications) may be pressed or drifted into the cylinder head after the worn ones have been removed in a similar manner. The cylinder head must be heated to 200°C (392°F) before carrying out these operations and although this can be done in a domestic oven, it must be remembered that the new guide will have to be reamed after installation and it may therefore be preferable to leave this work to your Datsun dealer.

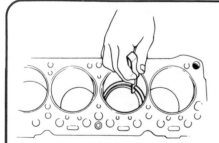

Fig. 1.14. Checking the piston ring gap (Sec. 26)

Fig. 1.15. Measuring the piston ring side clearance in the piston groove (Sec. 26)

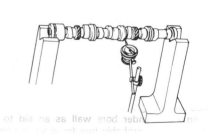

Fig. 1.16. Checking the camshaft for bend (Sec. 27)

30 Rockers and rocker shaft – inspection and renewal

1   Thoroughly clean the rocker shaft and then check the shaft for straightness by rolling it on plate glass. It is most unlikely that it will deviate from normal, but if it does, purchase a new shaft. The surface of the shaft should be free from any worn ridges, caused by the rocker arms. If any wear is present, renew the shaft.

2   Check the rocker arms for wear of the rocker bushes, for wear at the rocker arm face which bears on the valve stem, and for wear of the adjusting ball ended screws. Wear in the rocker arm bush can be checked by gripping the rocker arm tip and holding the rocker arm in place on the shaft, noting if there is any lateral rocker arm shake. If shake is present, and the arm is very loose on the shaft, a new bush or rocker arm must be fitted.

3   Check the top of the rocker arm where it bears on the valve head for cracking or serious wear on the case hardening. If none is present re-use the rocker arm. Check the lower half of the ball on the end of the rocker arm adjusting screw.

4   Reassemble the rocker arms, springs and pillars on the rocker shaft and retain with the rocker pillar bolts.

31 Tappets and pushrods – inspection and renewal

1   Examine the bearing surface of the mushroom tappets which lie on the camshaft. Any indentation in this surface or any cracks indicate serious wear and the tappets should be renewed. Thoroughly clean them out, removing all traces of sludge. It is most unlikely that the sides of the tappets will prove worn, but, if they are a very loose fit in their bores and can readily be rocked, they should be exchanged for new units. It is very unusual to find any wear in the tappets, and any wear is likely to occur only at very high mileages.

2   Check the pushrods for straightness by rolling them on a piece of glass. Check the ends for roughness or excessive wear. Renew any that are bent or worn.

32 Cylinder head – decarbonising, inspection and renovation

1   With the cylinder head removed, use a blunt scraper to remove all traces of carbon deposits from the combustion spaces and ports. Remember that the cylinder head is aluminium alloy and can be damaged easily during the decarbonising operations. Scrape the cylinder head free from scale or old pieces of gasket or jointing compound. Clean the cylinder head by washing it in paraffin and take particular care to pull a piece of rag through the ports and cylinder head bolt holes. Any grit remaining in these recesses may well drop onto the gasket or cylinder block mating surface as the cylinder head is lowered into position and could lead to a gasket leak after reassembly is complete.

2   With the cylinder head clean test for distortion if a history of coolant leakage has been apparent. Carry out this test using a straight-edge and feeler gauge or a piece of plate glass. If the surface shows any warping in excess of 0.0039 in (0.10 mm) then the cylinder head will have to be resurfaced which is a job for a specialist engineering company.

3   Clean the pistons and top of the cylinder bores. If the pistons are still in the block then it is essential that great care is taken to ensure that no carbon gets into the cylinder bores as this could scratch the cylinder walls or cause damage to the piston and rings. To ensure this does not happen, first turn the crankshaft so that two of the pistons are at the top of their bores. Stuff rag into the other two bores or seal them off with paper and masking tape. The waterways should also be covered with small pieces of masking tape to prevent particles of carbon entering the cooling system and damaging the water pump.

4   There are two schools of thought as to how much carbon should be removed from the piston crown. One school recommends that all carbon should be removed from the piston head. The other recommends that a ring of carbon should be left round the edge of the piston and on the cylinder bore wall as an aid to low oil consumption. Although this is probably true for older engines with worn bores, on newer engines the thought of the first school can be applied; which is that for effective decarbonisation all traces of carbon should be removed.

5   If all traces of carbon are to be removed, press a little grease into

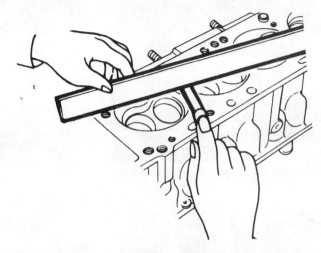

Fig. 1.17. Checking the cylinder head for distortion (Sec. 32)

the gap between the cylinder walls and the two pistons which are to be worked on. With a blunt scraper carefully scrape away the carbon from the piston crown, taking great care not to scratch the aluminium. Also scrape away the carbon from the surrounding lip of the cylinder wall. When all carbon has been removed, scrape away the grease which will now be contaminated with carbon particles, taking care not to press any into the bores. To assist prevention of carbon build-up, the piston crown can be polished with a metal polish. Remove the rags or masking tape from the other two cylinders and turn the crankshaft so that the two pistons which were at the bottom are now at the top. Place rag or masking tape in the cylinders which have been decarbonised and proceed as just described.

6   If a ring of carbon is going to be left round the piston then this can be helped by inserting an old piston ring into the top of the bore to rest on the piston and ensure that the carbon is not accidentally removed. Check that there are no particles of carbon in the cylinder bores. Decarbonising is now complete.

33 Timing chain, tensioner and sprockets – inspection and renewal

1   Examine the teeth on both the crankshaft sprocket and the camshaft sprocket for wear or damage. If any sign of wear is present the sprockets must be renewed.

2   Check the timing chain for stepped wear on the rollers or any other damage. Check the links of the chain for side slackness. Renew the chain if any defect is apparent.

3   Check the chain tensioner slipper head for wear or grooving. Check that the spring loaded plunger is free in its bore and that the spring is not distorted or damaged.

34 Flywheel starter ring gear – inspection and renewal

1   If the teeth on the flywheel starter ring are badly worn, or if some are missing then it will be necessary to remove the ring and fit a new one, or preferably exchange the flywheel for a reconditioned unit.

2   Either split the ring with a cold chisel after making a cut with a hacksaw blade between two teeth, or use a soft headed hammer (not steel) to knock the ring off, striking it evenly and alternately at equally spaced points. Take great care not to damage the flywheel during this process.

3   Heat the new ring in either an electric oven to about 200°C (392°F) or immerse in a pan of boiling oil.

4   Hold the ring at this temperature for five minutes and then quickly fit it to the flywheel so the chamfered portion of the teeth faces the gearbox side of the flywheel.

5   The ring should be tapped gently down onto its register and left to cool naturally when the contraction of the metal on cooling will ensure that it is a secure and permanent fit. Great care must be taken not to overheat the ring, indicated by it turning light metallic blue, as if this

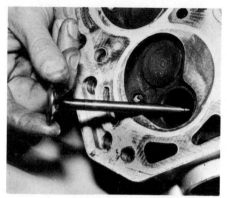

36.1   Insert the valve in its original position

36.2a   ... and fit a new oil seal

36.2b   Fitting the valve spring and retainer

36.3   Compress the spring and fit the collets

37.3   Insert the tappets in their original locations

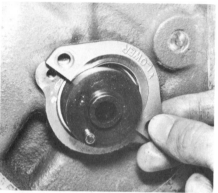

37.5   Fit the camshaft locking plate with the word 'lower' to the bottom with the engine right way up

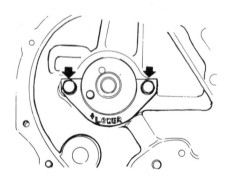

Fig. 1.18. The camshaft locking plate fitted (Sec. 37)

37.6a   Fitting the main bearing shells in the crankcase

37.6b   Oil the bearing surfaces ...

37.6c   ... and lower the crankshaft into position

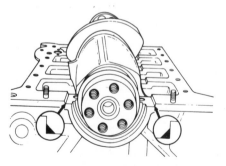

Fig. 1.19. Apply sealant when fitting rear main bearing cap (Sec. 37)

37.7a   Fitting the rear main bearing cap

happens the temper of the ring will be lost.

35 Engine reassembly – general

1   To ensure maximum life with minimum trouble from a rebuilt engine, not only must everything be correctly assembled, but everything must be spotlessly clean: all the oilways must be clear, locking washers and spring washers must always be fitted where indicated and all bearing and other working surfaces must be thoroughly lubricated during assembly.

2   Before assembly begins renew any bolts or studs the threads of which are in any way damaged, and whenever possible use new spring washers.

3   Apart from your normal tools, a supply of clean rags, an oil can filled with engine oil (an empty plastic detergent bottle thoroughly cleaned and washed out will invariably do just as well); a new supply of assorted spring washers; a set of new gaskets; and a torque wrench, should be collected together.

36 Cylinder head – reassembly

1   Oil the valve guides and fit the valves to the seats into which they have been previously ground (Section 28) (photo).

2   Fit a valve spring seat and a new oil seal (photo), then the valve spring and valve spring retainer on each valve (photo).

3   Fit the base of the spring compressor tool on the valve head and compress the valve spring until the collets can be fitted in the grooves on the valve stem (photo). Release the compressor tool and repeat for the remaining valves. When all the collets have been fitted, tap the valve stems with a hammer to ensure all the parts are seated correctly.

37 Engine – reassembly

1   Check the cylinder block for cracks, probe the oil passages and holes with a piece of wire and clean the external surfaces.

2   Renew all gaskets and seals and use plenty of clean engine oil to lubricate the components as they are fitted. Observe absolute cleanliness.

3   Lubricate and refit the tappet blocks to their original locations with the engine block in the inverted position (photo).

4   Oil the camshaft bearings and gently slide the camshaft into position taking care not to scratch or damage the bearing surfaces as the cam lobes pass through.

5   Fit the camshaft locking plate so that the word 'lower' is to the bottom when the engine is the right way up (photo). Tighten the securing bolts to 3.6 lbf ft (0.5 kgf m).

6   Install the main bearing shells into their crankcase locations and into the bearing caps (photo). Oil the bearing surfaces and carefully lower the crankshaft into position in the crankcase (photos). Apply some lithium based grease to the inner face of the rear oil seal. It can now be positioned approximately on the crankshaft boss.

7   Fit the main bearing caps, complete with shells. Refer to Section 16 for the difference between the main bearing caps of the A10 engine and the A12 and A14 engines. Ensure that the caps are refitted in their original locations. Tighten the main bearing caps bolts, in four stages in the reverse order to Fig. 1.6; to a torque of 36 - 43 lbf ft (5 - 6 kgf m). **Note**: when fitting the rear main bearing cap apply gasket sealant to each contact corner of the crankcase as shown in Fig. 1.19 (photos).

8   Check that the crankshaft rotates smoothly and re-check the crankshaft endfloat (Section 23).

9   Position the new rear oil seal and then fit the endplate in position. Fit the flywheel on the crankshaft and tighten the retaining bolts to the torque wrench setting given in the Specifications at the beginning of this Chapter (photo).

10   The pistons, piston rings, and connecting rods, having been assembled with new big-end bearings and gudgeon pins as required, can now be fitted in the cylinders. Arrange the piston ring gaps as shown in Fig. 1.20. Liberally lubricate the rings and pistons. Fit a piston ring compressor on the piston to compress the rings and insert the connecting rod and piston into the cylinder bore. Ensure that it is the correct piston/connecting rod assembly for that particular bore and that the number stamped on the piston head faces to the front of the engine (photos).

11   The piston will slide into the cylinder only as far as the piston ring clamp. Gently tap the piston into the bore with a hammer shaft (photo). This should drive the piston and rod assembly into the bore. If this action does not have the desired effect then either the piston rings have not been sufficiently compressed with the 'piston ring compressor, or the connecting rod has jammed on the crankshaft.

12   Connect each big-end to its appropriate crankshaft journal and fit the big-end cap complete with shells (photo). The caps and rods are numbered 1 to 4 commencing at the timing gear end of the engine and when correctly fitted will have the cap and rod numbers adjacent. Tighten the big-end bolt nuts to the torque given in Specifications (photo). Use plenty of oil when fitting the connecting rods to the crankshaft and turn the crankshaft so that each big-end bearing is engaged when the respective crankshaft journal is at its lowest point.

13   Check the endfloat of each connecting rod big-end after refitting; this should be between 0.008 and 0.012 in (0.20 and 0.30 mm) (Fig. 1.21).

14   Refit the crankcase baffle and gauze filter screen.

15   Temporarily refit the camshaft and crankshaft sprockets.

16   Place the crankshaft and camshaft sprockets within the timing chain and fit both sprockets complete with timing chain to the crankshaft and camshaft simultaneously. When correctly installed, a line drawn through the sprocket centres should also pass through the crankshaft dowel hole and the crankshaft sprocket keyway. A double check is the alignment of the sprocket dot punch marks and the matching marks on the chain side plates (Fig. 1.22) (photo). Installation of the timing gear will call for rotation of the camshaft and the crankshaft and repositioning of the camshaft sprocket within the loop of the chain on a trial and error basis until the alignment is correct.

17   When the timing is correct, tighten the camshaft sprocket securing bolt to a torque wrench setting of between 29 to 35 lbf ft (4 and 4.8 kgf m) (photo).

18   Fit the timing chain tensioner and tighten the securing bolts (photo).

19   Check that the gap between the body of the tensioner and the rear face of the slipper does not exceed 0.59 in (15 mm), dimension L in Fig. 1.23. If the gap is greater than specified, either the chain has

37.7b   Tighten the main bearing caps with a torque wrench

37.9   Fit the endplate and then the flywheel

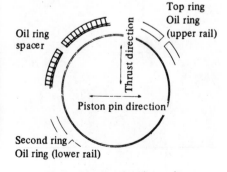

Fig. 1.20. Positioning the piston ring gap (Sec. 37)

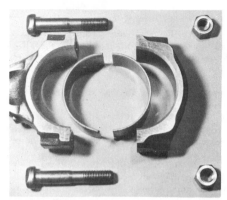

37.10a   Connecting rod big-end

37.10b   Insert the piston and connecting rod assembly in the cylinder bore

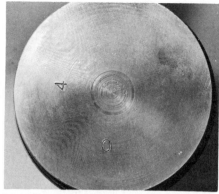

37.10c   Check that the number on the piston crown faces to the front of the engine

37.11   Tapping the piston into the cylinder with a hammer shaft

37.12a   Fit the big-end bearing caps ...

37.12b   ... and tighten them with a torque wrench

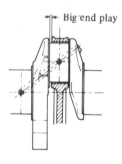

Fig. 1.21. Check the endfloat of the connecting rod big-end (Sec. 37)

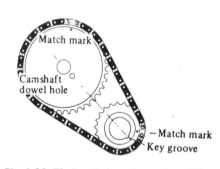

Fig. 1.22. Timing chain and sprocket aligning marks (Sec. 37)

37.16   The punch mark on the sprocket lines up with the marks on the chain side plates

37.17   Tighten the camshaft sprocket retaining bolt

37.18   Fitting the timing chain tensioner

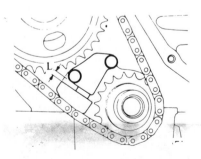

Fig. 1.23. Checking the gap between the chain tensioner body and the rear face of the slipper (Sec. 37)

stretched badly or the tensioner slipper has worn away and in either event the component must be renewed.

20 Fit the oil thrower disc to the crankshaft ensuring that the projecting rim is towards the timing chain cover (photo).

21 Drift out the timing cover oil seal using a piece of tubing for this purpose. Fit a new seal, ensuring that the lips face inwards. Renew the chain slipper if it is worn.

22 Apply a thin film of gasket cement to the mating surfaces of the timing cover and the cylinder block. Use a new gasket and fit the cover. Secure the cover with the retaining bolts and tighten them to a torque of 4 – 5 lbf ft (0·5 – 0·7 kgf m) (photo).

23 Refit the oil pump intake pipe and gauze filter (photo).

24 Apply a thin film of gasket cement to the lower face of the crankcase and stick a new sump gasket into position, so that the holes in the gasket are in alignment with the bolt holes of the crankcase. Apply more gasket cement to the mating surfaces of the sump, being particularly liberal with it at the front and rear and in the corners adjacent to the main bearing caps and timing cover. Offer up the sump and insert the securing bolts. Tighten them progressively in a diametrically opposite sequence (photo).

25 Fit the water pump (photo). Always use a new gasket. Tighten the attaching bolts to 7 – 10 lbf ft (0.9 – 1.4 kgf m).

26 Fit the Woodruff key on the crankshaft and then fit the crankshaft pulley (photo). Tighten the pulley securing bolt to 108 – 145 lbf ft (15 – 20 kgf m). Restrain the crankshaft from turning by wedging the flywheel, during the tightening operation.

27 After checking that both the cylinder block and cylinder head mating faces are perfectly clean, lubricate each cylinder bore with engine oil.

28 Always use a new cylinder head gasket as the old gasket will be compressed and not capable of giving a good seal (photo).

29 The cylinder head gasket is of the laminated type, having a steel sheet surface on one side and this surface should make contact with the face of the cylinder block. Due to the possiblity of oil leakage from the cylinder head gasket on the pushrod side, the gasket has been partially treated with sealant in this area only. It is recommended however, that both the mating faces of head and block are smeared with a thin coat of non-setting gasket cement as this will help to protect the surface of the alloy head against corrosion as well as providing a reliable seal.

30 Place the gasket in position on the block (steel side down, jointing material visible). Lightly smear the threads of the cylinder head bolts with heavy grade grease and push two of the bolts through the head so that as the head is gently lowered into position they will serve as locating dowels to locate the gasket and head (photo).

31 Note that one of the cylinder head bolts is smaller in diameter than the others and has a hollow head. It must be fitted on the right side centre of the cylinder head, position '1' in Fig. 1.4 (photo)

32 Fit the remaining bolts then tighten them in two or three steps, in the reverse sequence shown in Fig. 1.4. to a torque of 43 – 47 lbf ft (6 – 6.5 kgf m) for A10 engines and 51 – 54 lbf ft (7 – 7.5 kgf m) for A12 and A14 engines (photo).

33 Refit the pushrods in their original positions (photo).

34 Refit the rocker shaft assembly, tightening the pillar bolts to 14 – 18 lbf ft (2 – 2.5 kgf m). Tighten the centre bolt first and work outwards.

35 Fit a new manifold gasket and then fit the inlet and exhaust manifold assembly (photos). Tighten the securing nuts to 6.5 – 10 lbf ft (0.9 – 1.4 kgf m) on A10 and A12 engine and to 11 – 14 lbf ft (1.5 – 2 kgf m) on A14 engines.

36 Fit the EGR control valve (A14 engines with exhaust gas recirculation emission control system).

37 The valve clearances should now be adjusted. Rotate the engine during the adjustment procedure by using a spanner or socket on the crankshaft pulley bolt.

38 The valve clearances obviously will have to be set with the engine cold to start with but when the unit is refitted to the vehicle and run up to normal operating temperature, then they will have to be checked and readjusted when the engine is hot.

39 The valve adjustments may be made with the engine cold but are more accurate when the engine is hot. The importance of correct rocker arm/valve stem clearances cannot be overstressed as they vitally affect the performance of the engine. If the clearances are set too open, the efficiency of the engine is reduced as the valves open

37.20 Fit the oil thrower disc with projecting rim towards the timing chain cover

37.22 Fitting the timing chain cover

37.23 Fit the oil pump intake pipe and filter ...

37.24 ... and then the oil sump

37.25 Fitting the water pump

37.26 Fitting the crankshaft pulley

37.28   Always fit a new cylinder head gasket

37.30   Lowering the cylinder head into position

37.31   Fit the bolt with the small diameter on the right side centre of the cylinder head

37.32   Tighten the cylinder head bolts to the specified torque with a torque wrench

37.33   Fit the pushrods in their original positions

37.35a   Fit a new manifold gasket ...

37.35b   ...and then the manifold assembly

37.42   Adjusting the valve clearances

37.43   Fitting the oil pump with the filter already screwed on

37.45   Fit the drivebelt pulley on the water pump

37.48   Fitting the fuel pump

37.50   Crankshaft pulley and timing chain cover marks

late and close earlier than was intended. If, on the other hand, the clearances are set too close there is a danger that the stems will expand upon heating and not allow the valves to close properly which will cause burning of the valve head and seat and possible warping.

40 It is important that the valve clearance is set when the tappet of the valve being adjusted is on the heel of the cam (the lowest point) so that the valve is fully seated. One of two methods may be employed; first place a finger over No 1 spark plug hole, turn the engine and as soon as compression is felt, either observe the piston crown until it reaches its highest point (TDC) and descends about $\frac{1}{8}$ inch (3.175 mm) or using a length of wire as a measure, stop rotating the engine when the wire has passed its highest point and descended about $\frac{1}{8}$ inch (3.175 mm). Both the valves for No 1 cylinder may be set to the specified clearances.

41 The firing order is 1–3–4–2 and the alternative method of valve clearance adjustment which avoids the necessity of turning the engine excessively is to apply the adjustment sequence shown in the following table.

Valve fully open	Check & Adjust
Valve No. 8	Valve No. 1
Valve No. 6	Valve No. 3
Valve No. 4	Valve No. 5
Valve No. 7	Valve No. 2
Valve No. 1	Valve No. 8
Valve No. 3	Valve No. 6
Valve No. 5	Valve No. 4
Valve No. 2	Valve No. 7

Counting from the timing cover end of the engine, inlet valves are nos. 2–3–6–7, exhaust valves are nos. 1–4–5–8.

42 Adjustment of the clearance is made by conventional screw and locknut. Insert the feeler blade between the rocker arm face and the valve stem end face. Loosen the locknut, turn the screw until the blade cannot be withdrawn and then loosen the screw until the blade can be just withdrawn (stiffly), by a hard pull. Holding the slotted adjustment screw quite still, tighten the locknut with a ring spanner (photo). When all the valve clearances have been adjusted, recheck them again before fitting the rocker box cover complete with a new sealing gasket.

43 Using a new gasket, fit the oil pump to the crankcase, checking that the drive gear meshes correctly (photo).

44 Screw a new oil filter cartridge into position. Lightly grease the rubber sealing ring before fitting it and tighten it by hand pressure only.

45 Using new gaskets, fit the thermostat and thermostat cover. Fit the drive belt pulley on the water pump (photo). Hold the pulley with a strap or chain wrench when tightening the bolts.

46 Fit the alternator to its mountings and reconnect the slotted adjustment strap.

47 Locate the drive belt over the crankshaft, water pump and alternator pulleys and then prise the alternator away from the engine until the belt has a total deflection of $\frac{1}{2}$ in at the centre of its longest run. Tighten the adjustment strap bolt and mounting bolts of the alternator.

48 Fit the carburettor to the manifold (if not previously combined with the exhaust manifold) and the fuel pump to the crankcase, ensuring that new gaskets similar to those originally fitted are used (photo).

49 Reconnect the fuel pipe between the pump and the carburettor.

50 The distributor should now be refitted. To do this, turn the engine until No 1 cylinder is at TDC. This position can be observed from the alignment of the crankshaft pulley and timing cover marks (photo). A secondary check can be made by seeing that both the inlet and exhaust valves of No 1 cylinder are fully closed.

51 When installed the distributor rotor should take up the position shown in Fig. 1.24. To achieve this, hold the distributor over the engine and position the rotor as shown. Now turn the rotor approximately 30° in a clockwise direction, this is to compensate for movement of the rotor as the distributor is pushed into mesh with the camshaft gear. The action of meshing will return the rotor to the position illustrated (photo) which shows the rotor point to No 1 spark plug HT lead segment in the distributor cap. Tighten the distributor clamp plate bolt. It will be necessary to check the ignition timing in accordance with Chapter 4, when the engine is fitted.

52 Fit the spark plugs, cleaned and correctly gapped (refer to Chapter 4).

53 Fit the distributor cap and HT leads. Connect the HT leads to the spark plugs.

54 Fit the pipe connector to control valve hose and right-hand engine mounting bracket.

55 Fit the distributor vacuum hose.

56 Fit the oil level dipstick.

57 Fit the clutch assembly to the flywheel as described in Chapter 5. Then refit the transmission to the engine using the reverse of the procedure described in Section 6 of this Chapter.

58 On A14 engines with the air injection emission control system fit the air pump bracket, air pump and air pump pulley. Fit the idler pulley bracket, air pump drive belt and idler pulley. Adjust the air pump belt tension so that a deflection of 0.39 – 0.55 in (10 – 14 mm) is obtained when a pressure of 22 lb (10 kg) is applied midway between the crank pulley and the air pump pulley.

38 Positive crankcase ventilation (PCV) system

1 The closed type of crankcase ventilation system fitted to models covered by this manual draws air from the air cleaner and passes it through a mesh type flame trap to a hose connected to the rocker cover. The air is then passed through the inside of the engine and back to the inlet manifold via a hose and control valve. This means that fumes in the crankcase are drawn into the combustion chambers, burnt and passed to the exhaust system.

2 When the car is being driven at full throttle conditions, the inlet manifold depression is not sufficient to draw all the fumes through the control valve and into the inlet manifold. Under these operating conditions the crankcase ventilation flow is reversed with the fumes passing into the air cleaner instead of the inlet manifold.

3 To prevent engine oil being drawn into the inlet manifold a baffle plate and steel nut is positioned in the crankcase.

4 Maintenance of the system simply involves inspection and renewal of any suspect parts. Check the condition of the rocker cover to air cleaner hose and crankcase to inlet manifold hose. Check for blockage, deterioration or collapse of the hoses and renew as necessary.

5 Inspect the seats on the engine oil filler and dipstick. If defective renew the seals.

6 Operation of the control valve may be checked by running the

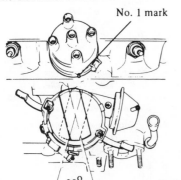

Fig. 1.24. Fitting the ignition distributor (Sec. 37)

37.51 Position of rotor after fitting the distributor on the crankcase

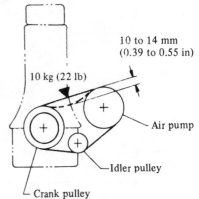

Fig. 1.25. Tensioning the air pump drivebelt – A14 engine with air injection system (Sec. 37)

engine at a steady idle speed and disconnecting the hose from the control valve. Listen for a hissing noise from the valve when the hose has been detached. Now place a finger over the valve inlet and a strong depression should be felt immediately as the finger closes the inlet.

7   If the valve is faulty it must be renewed as it is not practical to dismantle it.

39 Engine/transmission refitting – general

1   Although the engine can be replaced by one man using a suitable winch, it is easier if two are present: one to lower the assembly into the engine compartment and the other to guide the assembly into position and to ensure it does not foul anything.

2   At this stage one or two tips may come in useful. Ensure all the loose leads, cables, etc are tucked out of the way. If not it is easy to

40.2   Lowering the engine/transmission assembly into the engine compartment

trap one and so cause much additional work after the engine is replaced.

3   Two pairs of hands are better than one when refitting the bonnet. Do not tighten the bonnet securing bolts fully until it is ascertained that the bonnet is on straight.

40 Engine/transmission – refitting

1   Raise the engine/transmission unit and either roll the vehicle forward under it or if the hoist is mobile roll it forward so that the unit is suspended above the engine compartment.

2   Lower the assembly into the engine compartment. Ensure that nothing is fouled during the operation (photo).

3   The engine is installed by following, in the reverse order, the procedures given for removal. The following points must be noted:

a) *Do not let the weight of the engine be fully taken on the mounting insulators until the bolts have been tightened.*

b) *The rear insulator has a locking pawl attached to the rubber mount. Take care that this part is not damaged whilst lowering the engine into position.*

c) *Ensure that the mounting insulator stud bolts are seated in the groove of the mounting bracket and check the clearance between the subframe and clutch housing, H in Fig. 1.27. Standard clearance is 0.394 – 0.472 in (10 – 12 mm). If the clearance is less than 0.276 in (7 mm), adjust by fitting adjusting shims between the mounting insulator and mounting bracket of the subframe. Do not use more than two shims at each insulator. Standard thickness of shims – 0.0787 in (2 mm).*

d) *Tighten the exhaust pipe by starting at the manifold connection.*

e) *Fit the buffer rods only after the engine mounting insulators have been tightened (photo). The buffer rods must not be fitted under stress. The standard length of the rods, I in Fig. 1.28, is as follows*

> *A10 and A12 engines, right side – 8.15 in (207 mm)*
> *left side – 5.51 in (140 mm)*
> *A14 engine, right side – 8.27 in (210 mm)*
> *left side – 5.43 in (138 mm)*

Start with the rods at this length, and adjust if necessary, to remove any stress on the engine mountings.

4   Reconnect the driveshafts (Chapter 7).

5   Reconnect the gearchange linkage.

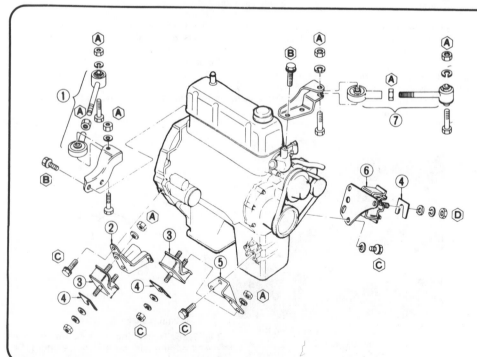

Fig. 1.26. Exploded view of engine mountings (Sec. 40)

1   *Buffer rod assembly (RH)*
2   *Engine support bracket (RH)*
3   *Front engine mounting insulator*
4   *Engine mounting shim*
5   *Engine support bracket (LH)*
6   *Rear engine mounting insulator*
7   *Buffer rod assembly (LH)*

Tightening torque of bolts or nuts kgf m (lbf ft)

A   0.8 to 1.2 (5.8 to 8.7)
B   1.5 to 2.1 (11 to 15)
C   1.9 to 2.6 (14 to 19)
D   2.8 to 3.8 (20 to 27)

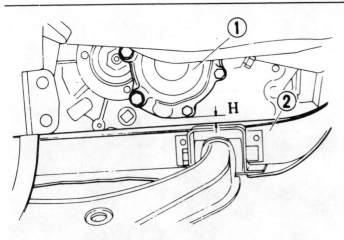

Fig. 1.27. Clearance between subframe and clutch housing (Sec. 40)

1 *Clutch housing* 2 *Subframe*

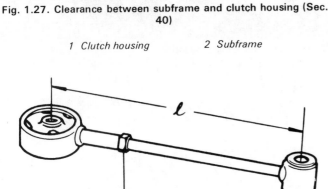

Tightening torque
0.8 to 1.2 kgf m (5.8 to 8.7 lbf ft)

Fig. 1.28. Adjusting the buffer rod length (Sec. 40)

6 Reconnect the speedometer drive.
7 Remove the plug and reconnect the fuel line to the fuel pump.
8 Reconnect the reversing lamp leads.
9 Reconnect the alternator leads.
10 Reconnect the clutch cable or hydraulic slave cylinder according to vehicle type.
11 Reconnect the choke and accelerator controls and refit the air cleaner.
12 Reconnect the LT lead to the distributor, the HT lead between the distributor and the coil.
13 Connect the oil pressure and water temperature lead.
14 Refit the radiator and heater hoses. Reconnect the leads to the electrically-operated fan.
15 Connect the negative battery lead.
16 Refit the bonnet.
17 Refill the cooling system (Chapter 2).
18 Refill the engine sump with the correct grade and quantity of oil (photo).
19 Check the level of oil in the transmission.

41 Engine – adjustment after major overhaul

1 With the engine refitted to the vehicle, give a final visual check to see that everything has been reconnected and that no loose rags or tools have been left within the engine compartment.
2 Turn the engine slow running screw in about $\frac{1}{2}$ turn (to increase slow running once the engine is started). (Chapter 3).
3 Pull the choke fully out and start the engine. This may take a little longer than usual as the fuel pump and carburettor will be empty and need initial filling.
4 As soon as the engine starts, push the choke in until the engine runs at a fast tickover and examine the engine for leaks. Check

40.3 Attach the buffer rods to the brackets on the engine

40.18 Refilling the engine oil sump

particularly the water hoses and oil filter and fuel hose unions.
5 Run the vehicle on the road until normal operating temperature is reached. Check the valve clearances while the engine is hot, as described in Section 37 of this Chapter. Re-adjust engine idling speed (Chapter 3).
6 After 500 miles (800 km) running, the engine oil should be changed particularly where the majority of the internal components have been renewed or reconditioned.)
7 After 500 miles (800 km) check the torque setting of the cylinder head bolts with the cylinder head **cold** . Follow the reverse of the sequence given in Fig. 1.4.

42 Engine mountings – renewal

1 With time the bonded rubber insulators will perish causing undue vibration and noise from the engine. Severe juddering when reversing or when moving off from rest is also likely and is a further sign of worn mounting rubbers (photos).
2 The mounting rubber insulators can be changed with the engine in the car.
3 Apply the handbrake firmly, jack-up the front of the car, and place stands under the front of the car.
4 Lower the jack, and place the jack under the sump to take the weight of the engine.

42.1a   A front engine mounting and ...

42.1b   ... the rear engine mounting

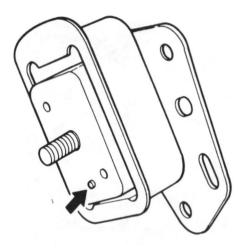

Fig. 1.29. Rear insulator locking pawl (Sec. 42)

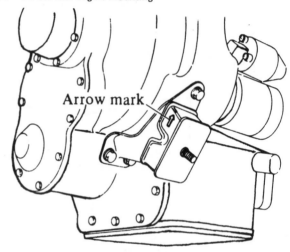

Fig. 1.30. Fit front insulator with arrow mark pointing upwards
(Sec. 42)

5   Undo the large bolt which holds each of the engine mountings to the subframe.
6   Raise the engine sufficiently high to enable the mounting insulator brackets to be disconnected from the sump, clutch housing and transmission. If the engine is raised too high the buffer rods and exhaust pipe could be damaged. If you are uncertain it is better to disconnect them.
7   Fitting new flexible insulators is a reversal of removal but note the following points:

a)   When installing rear insulator to subframe, check to be sure that locking pawl is properly positioned. Do not damage locking pawl while fitting.
b)   The front insulator should be installed so that arrow on side is pointing upwards.
c)   Check the clearance between the subframe and clutch housing as described in Section 40 paragraph 3 (c).
d)   Adjust the length of the buffer rods; refer to Section 40 paragraph 3 (e).

43 Fault diagnosis – Engine

Note: When investigating starting and uneven running faults do not be tempted into snap diagnosis. Start from the beginning of the check procedure and follow it through. It will take less time in the long run. Poor performance from an engine in terms of power and economy is not normally diagnosed quickly. In any event the ignition and fuel systems must be checked first before assuming any further investigation needs to be made.

Symptom	Reason/s	Remedy
Engine will not turn over when starter switch is operated	Flat battery Bad battery connections Bad connections at solenoid switch and/or starter motor	Check that battery is fully charged and that all connections are clean and tight.
	Starter motor jammed	Rock the car back and forth with a gear engaged. If this does not free pinion remove starter.
	Defective solenoid	Bridge the main terminals of the solenoid switch with a piece of heavy duty cable in order to operate the starter.
	Starter motor defective	Remove and overhaul starter motor.
Engine turns over normally but fails to start	No spark at plugs	Check ignition system according to procedures given in Chapter 4.
	No fuel reaching engine	Check fuel system according to procedures given in Chapter 3.
	Too much fuel reaching the engine (flooding)	Check the fuel system as above.
Engine starts but runs unevenly and misfires	Ignition and/or fuel system faults	Check the ignition and fuel systems as though the engine had failed to start.
	Incorrect valve clearances	Check and reset clearances.
	Burnt out valves	Remove cylinder head and examine and overhaul as necessary.
	Worn out piston rings	Remove cylinder head and examine pistons and cylinder bores. Overhaul as necessary.
Lack of power	Ignition and/or fuel system faults	Check the ignition and fuel systems for correct ignition timing and carburettor settings.
	Incorrect valve clearances	Check and reset the clearances.
	Burnt out valves	Remove cylinder head and examine and overhaul as necessary.
	Worn out piston rings	Remove cylinder head and examine pistons and cylinder bores. Overhaul as necessary.
Excessive oil consumption	Oil leaks from crankshaft rear oil seal, timing cover gasket and oil seal, rocker cover gasket, oil filter gasket, sump gasket, sump plug washer.	Identify source of leak and renew seal as appropriate.
	Worn piston rings or cylinder bores resulting in oil being burnt by engine	Fit new rings or rebore cylinders and fit new pistons, depending on degree of wear.
	Worn valve guides and/or defective valve stem seals	Remove cylinder heads and recondition valve stem bores and valves and seals as necessary.
Excessive mechanical noise from engine	Wrong valve to rocker clearances	Adjust valve clearances.
	Worn crankshaft bearings Worn cylinders (piston slap)	Inspect and overhaul where necessary.
	Slack or worn timing chain and sprockets	Adjust chain and/or inspect timing mechanism

Chapter 2 Cooling system

Contents

Specifications

System type	Thermo-syphon with pump assistance
Radiator type	Corrugated fin
Filler cap opening pressure	13 lb/in² (0.9 kg/cm²)

Thermostat

Type	Wax pellet
Opening temperature:	
Standard	177– 182°F (80.5 – 83.5°C)
Cold climates	188 – 193°F (86.5 – 89.5°C)

Fan motor

Voltage	12
Wattage	95
Speed	2350 – 2650 rpm

Temperature sensing switch

Radiator cooling fan:	
On	181 – 189°F (83 – 87°C)
Off	172 – 178°F (78 – 81°C)
Auxiliary cooling fan (A14 engine):	
On	163 – 171°F (73 – 77°C)
Off	154 – 160°F (68 – 71°C)

Coolant capacity

	Imp	Litre	US
100A F-II and 120A F-II:			
With heater	4.75 qt	5.4	5.75 qt
Without heater	4.25 qt	4.8	5.12 qt
F10 (A14 engine)	5.8 qt	6.6	7 qt

Torque wrench settings

	lbf ft	kgf m
Pump securing nuts	7 – 10	0.96 – 1.38
Temperature sensing switch	14 – 18	2 – 2.5

1 General description

The cooling system comprises the radiator, top and bottom water hoses, water pump, cylinder head and block water jackets, radiator cap with pressure relief valve and flow and return heater hoses. An electrically operated and controlled fan is mounted directly on the radiator with a coolant temperature sensing switch fitted at the radiator outlet. A thermostat is located in a recess at the front of the cylinder head. On A14 engine an auxiliary fan is fitted behind the engine, near the carburettor to eliminate problems encountered when restarting a hot engine in extremely hot weather. The operation of the auxiliary cooling fan is controlled by a water temperature sensing switch located at the radiator outlet.

The pressure type radiator filler cap operates the cooling system at higher than atmospheric pressure. The higher pressure raises the boiling point of the coolant and increases the cooling efficiency of the system.

The principle of the system is that cold coolant in the bottom of the radiator circulates through the bottom radiator hose to the water pump, where the pump impeller pushes the coolant round the cylinder block and head, through the various passages to cool the cylinder

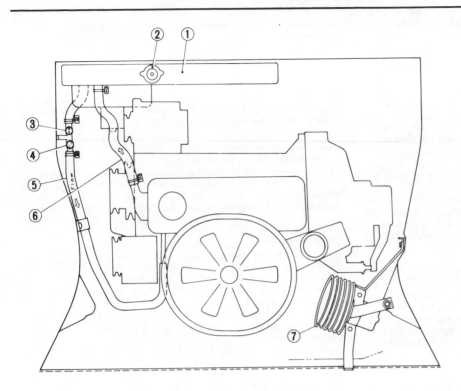

Fig. 2.1. Cooling system

1 *Radiator*
2 *Filler cap*
3 *Temperature sensing switch (cooling fan)*
4 *Temperature sensing switch (auxiliary fan)*
5 *Inlet hose*
6 *Outlet hose*
7 *Auxiliary electric cooling fan (if fitted)*

bores, combustion areas and valve seats. When sufficient heat has been absorbed by the coolant, and the engine has reached an efficient working temperature, the coolant passes from the cylinder head, past the now open thermostat into the top radiator hose and then into the radiator header tank. The coolant then travels down the radiator tubes where it is rapidly cooled by the in-rush of air, when the vehicle is in motion, and by the cooling fan. The coolant, now cooled, reaches the bottom of the radiator and the cycle is repeated.

When the engine is cold the thermostat remains closed until the coolant reaches a pre-determined temperature (see Specifications). This assists the rapid warm-up of the engine.

Water temperature is measured by an electro-sensitive capsule located immediately below the thermostat housing. Connection between the transmitter capsule and the temperature gauge is made by a single lead and Lucar type connector. The cooling system also provides heat for the heating system. The heater matrix is fed directly with coolant from the hottest part of the cooling system, the cylinder head, returning through a connection on the bottom radiator hose.

2 Cooling system – draining

1 Should the system have to be left empty for any reason, both the cylinder block and radiator must be drained, otherwise with a partly drained system corrosion of the water pump impeller seal face may occur with subsequent early failure of the pump seal and bearing.

2 Place the car on a level surface and have ready a container having a capacity of two gallons which will slide beneath the radiator and sump

3 Move the heater control on the facia to 'warm' and unscrew and remove the radiator cap. If hot, unscrew the cap very slowly, first covering it with a cloth to remove the danger of scalding when the pressure in the system is released.

4 Unscrew the radiator drain tap (photo) at the base of the radiator and then when coolant ceases to flow into the receptacle, repeat the operation by unscrewing the cylinder block plug located on the engine (photo). If the coolant has recently been renewed, retain it for further

2.4a Radiator drain tap

2.4b Coolant drain plug on cylinder block

use. The coolant should be renewed every 24 000 miles (40 000 km) or 2 years.

3 Cooling system – flushing

1   The radiator and waterways in the engine after some time may become restricted or even blocked with scale or sediment which reduce the efficiency of the cooling system. When this condition occurs or the coolant appears rusty or dark in colour the system should be flushed. In severe cases reverse flushing may be required as described later.

2   Place the heater controls to the 'warm' position and unscrew fully the radiator and cylinder block drain taps.

3   Remove the radiator filler cap and place a hose in the filler neck. Allow water to run through the system until it emerges from both drain taps quite clear in colour. Do not flush a hot engine with cold water.

4   In severe cases of contamination of the coolant and the system, reverse flush by first removing the radiator cap and disconnecting the lower radiator hose at the radiator outlet pipe.

5   Remove the top hose at the radiator connection end and remove the radiator, as described in Section 6.

6   Invert the radiator and place a hose in the bottom outlet pipe. Continue flushing until clear water comes from the radiator top tank.

7   To flush the engine water jackets, remove the thermostat as described later in this Chapter and place a hose in the thermostat location until clear water runs from the water pump inlet. Cleaning by the use of chemical compounds is not recommended.

4 Cooling system – filling

1   Place the heater control to the 'warm' position.

2   Screw in the radiator drain tap and the cylinder block drain plug.

3   Pour coolant slowly into the radiator so that air can pass through the thermostat bleed hole without being trapped in a coolant passage.

4   Fill to the correct level, which is 1 inch (25.4 mm) below the radiator filler neck, and refit the filler cap.

5   Run the engine to normal operating temperature, check for leaks and recheck the coolant level.

5 Antifreeze mixture

1   The cooling system should be filled with antifreeze coolant (ethylene glycol base) or fresh soft water. The antifreeze solution should be renewed every 2 years. Systems using soft water should be drained and refilled with fresh water every 6000 miles (10 000 km). Antifreeze solutions of good quality will prevent corrosion and rusting.

2   Before adding antifreeze to the system, check all hose connections and check the tightness of the cylinder head bolts as such solutions are searching. The cooling system should be drained and refilled with clean water as previously explained, before adding antifreeze.

3   The quantity of antifreeze which should be used for various levels of protection is given in the table below, expressed as a percentage of the system capacity.

Antifreeze volume	Protection to	Safe pump circulation
25%	$-26°C (-15°F)$	$-12°C (10°F)$
30%	$-33°C (-28°F)$	$-16°C (3°F)$
35%	$-38°C (-38°F)$	$-20°C (-4°F)$

4   Where the cooling system contains an antifreeze solution any topping-up should be done with a solution made up in similar proportions to the original in order to avoid dilution.

6 Radiator – removal, inspection and refitting

The radiator is a conventional down flow type having top and bottom tanks to distribute the coolant flow uniformly through the vertical tubes of the radiator core. The radiator filler cap is designed to maintain a pre-set pressure of 13 lb/in² (0·9 kg/cm²) above atmospheric pressure.

1   Drain the cooling system as described in Section 2.

2   Disconnect the radiator upper and lower hoses (photo).

3   Disconnect the wiring to the fan motor, remove the fan motor retaining bolts and lift the fan motor assembly out. The fan motor assembly can be left fitted to the radiator and removed with the radiator as an assembly.

4   Remove the radiator grille securing screws and take off the grille (this is not essential but the radiator bolts are more accessible with the grille removed).

5   Remove the radiator retaining bolts and lift out the radiator (photo).

6   Clean the exterior of the radiator matrix by using a compressed air jet or a strong jet of water to clean away road dirt, flies or other foreign matter.

7   With the radiator out of the car any leaks can be repaired by soldering. Clean the inside of the radiator by flushing, particularly reverse flushing, as described in Section 3.

8   Inspect the radiator hoses for cracks, internal and external deterioration and damage by overtightening of the securing clips. Check that the overflow pipe is clear. Renew any suspect hoses and hose clips.

9   Refitting of the radiator is the reverse of the removal procedure. Take care not to damage the radiator fins and core tubes when refitting the radiator in the car.

10   Fill the cooling system and check for leaks as described in Section 4.

7 Thermostat – removal, testing and refitting

1   The wax pellet type thermostat is located in the thermostat housing at the cylinder head coolant outlet. The thermostat controls the flow of coolant, facilitating fast engine warm-up and regulating coolant temperature. The thermostat is designed to open and close at predetermined temperatures, and if suspect, should be removed and tested as described below.

2   Drain off enough coolant through the radiator drain tap so that the coolant level is below the thermostat housing joint face. A good indication that the correct level has been reached is when the cooling tubes are exposed when viewed through the radiator filler cap.

6.2   Disconnect the lower hose

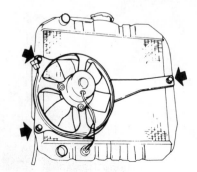

Fig. 2.2. Removing the fan motor assembly (Sec. 6)

6.5   Lifting out the radiator with fan assembly

3 Disconnect the upper radiator hose at the coolant outlet and on engines with an air injection system, disconnect the air hose at the check valve. Unscrew the retaining bolts and remove the thermostat cover, gasket and thermostat (photo).

4 To test whether the unit is serviceable, suspend the thermostat by a piece of string in a pan of water being heated. Using a thermometer, with reference to the opening and closing temperature in Specifications, its operation may be checked. The thermostat should be renewed if it is stuck open or closed or it fails to operate at the specified temperature. The operation of a thermostat is not instantaneous and sufficient time must be allowed for movement during testing. Never refit a faulty unit – leave it out if no new unit is available immediately.

5 Refitting of the thermostat is a reversal of the removal procedure. Ensure the mating faces of the housing are clean. Use a new gasket with jointing compound. The word 'TOP' which appears on the thermostat face must be visible from above.

6 Top up the cooling system and check for leaks.

8 Water pump – description

The water pump is of the conventional impeller type, driven by a pulley belt from the crankshaft. The impeller chamber is built into, and forms part of, the timing cover. The water pump detachable body is of die-cast aluminium in which runs the shaft. The shaft is fitted with bearings which are a shrink fit in the body, therefore the water pump should not be dismantled. In the event of leakage or failure of the water pump, it must be renewed as an assembly on an exchange basis.

9 Water pump – removal and refitting

1 Drain the cooling system as described in Section 2.

2 Slacken the alternator mountings and adjustment strap bolt, push the alternator in towards the engine and slip the belt from the driving pulleys.

3 Unscrew and remove the four bolts which secure the pulley to the hub. Hold the pulley from turning with a strap wrench.

4 Unscrew and remove the securing nuts and bolts from the water pump housing flange and withdraw the water pump. Should the pump be stuck to the face of the timing cover, do not attempt to prise the mating flange apart as this will damage the soft aluminium and cause leaks after refitting. Grip the shaft extension housing firmly and lever from side to side to break the seal.

5 Refitting is a reversal of removal but ensure that the mating faces are clean and free from old pieces of gasket. Use a new gasket coated both sides with jointing compound and tighten the securing nuts to a torque of between 7 and 10 lbf ft (0.967 and 1.382 kgf m).

6 Adjust the tension of the drivebelt, as described in Section 9 of Chapter 10.

7 Refill the cooling system (Section 4).

10 Drivebelt – adjustment

1 The correct tension of the drivebelt must be maintained. If it is overtightened the bearings in the water pump and the alternator may wear prematurely. If it is slack, it will slip and cause overloading and a discharged battery through low alternator output.

2 The drivebelt is correctly tensioned when a total movement of $\frac{1}{2}$ in (12 mm) can be obtained at the centre of the longest run of the belt.

3 Always adjust the drivebelt with the engine cold. Slacken the alternator mounting bolts and the slotted adjustment strap bolt. Prise the alternator away from the engine until the correct tension is obtained. It will be easier to achieve the correct tension if the alternator bolts are only slackened sufficiently to permit it to move stiffly. Always apply leverage to the drive end housing when tilting the alternator and never to the diode end housing, or the alternator will be damaged at the casing. Always recheck the drivebelt tensions after the alternator mounting and adjustment strap bolts have been tightened.

11 Radiator cooling fan – testing, removal and refitting

1 If the water temperature gauge is showing a high reading then one obviously suspects the thermostat or cooling fan, if nothing more obvious like coolant leaks are the case.

2 In the case of an electrical cooling fan it is not easy to determine when, or if, it is working, especially since it is thermostatically controlled and is not always running.

3 Obviously, if the engine has been working hard (eg after climbing a longish hill), then one simply looks at the fan and sees whether it is working or not. If it is, then you have some other reason for the high temperature, and should check the fault diagnosis chart in this Chapter.

4 Having decided the fan is not working; proceed as follows. First, turn on the ignition and then short-circuit the thermostat switch: this is in the insert pipe in the bottom hose on the left-hand side, and stands up like a tee-piece. If the fan now runs the thermostat is faulty and should be renewed. If not check that the white feed cable to the thermostat is live, using a test lamp or voltmeter.

5 If all is satisfactory so far, check the black/white cable at the fan relay: this should be live when the thermostat is short-circuited. If it is, next check the yellow cable at the fan relay: this should always be live. If not check the fused end of the cable at the fuse box.

6 If all tests have been satisfactory so far, next check the blue wire at the fan relay: this should only be live when the thermostat is short-circuited. If it is all right it indicates that the fan motor is probably defective: this must be removed and renewed.

7 Disconnect the Lucar connectors to the fan and then remove the bolts that secure it to the radiator. The fan can now be lifted out. Refitting is the reverse of removal.

12 Water temperature sensing switch – removal, testing and refitting

1 The water temperature sensing switch for controlling the radiator cooling fan (photo) is located in the insert pipe in the bottom radiator hose. On A14 engines there are two sensing switches, one for the radiator fan and the other for the auxiliary cooling fan.

2 Drain the cooling system as described in Section 2.

3 Remove the windscreen washer tank by pulling it up.

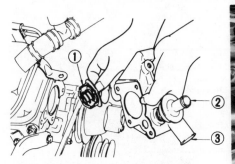

Fig. 2.3. Removing the thermostat (Sec. 7)

1 Thermostat
2 Air check valve
3 Water outlet

7.3 Removing the thermostat cover and thermostat

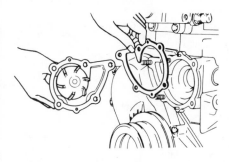

Fig. 2.4. Removing the water pump (Sec. 9)

12.1   Temperature sensor switch for radiator
cooling fan

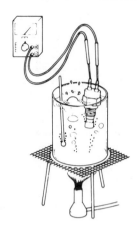

Fig. 2.5. Checking the water temperature
sensing switch (Sec. 12)

13.2   Water temperature gauge transmitter
unit fitted in cylinder head

4   Disconnect the leads and unscrew the water temperature sensing
switch.
5   Check the operation of the switch by submerging the temperature
sensing unit in water as shown in Fig. 2.5. Gradually heat the water to
194° F (90°C). Never boil the water.
6   Check that the switch comes on in the range given in the
Specifications at the beginning of this Chapter and goes off when the
temperature is outside the specified range. Renew a defective switch.
7   Refitting is the reverse of removal procedure. Tighten the switch to
14 to 18 lbf ft (2 to 2.5 kgf m).
8   Refill the cooling system and check for leaks as described in
Section 4.

13 Water temperature gauge – fault finding

1   Correct operation of the water temperature gauge is very

important as the engine can otherwise overheat without it being
observed.
2   The gauge is an electrically operated instrument comprising a
transmitter unit screwed into the front of the cylinder head (photo) and
transmitting through a Lucar type connector and cable to the dial
mounted on the facia instrument panel. The instrument only operates
when the ignition is switched on.
3   Where the water temperature gauge reads high-low intermittently,
or not at all, then first check the security of the connecting cable
between the transmitter unit and the gauge.
4   Disconnect the Lucar connector from the transmitter unit, switch
on the ignition when the gauge should read COLD. Now earth the
cable to the engine block when the gauge needle should indicate HOT.
This test proves the gauge to be functional and the fault must
therefore lie in the cable or transmitter unit. Renew as appropriate.
5   If the fuel gauge shows signs of malfunction at the same time as
the water temperature gauge then a fault in the voltage stabilizer may
be the cause.

14 Fault diagnosis – Cooling system

Symptom	Reason/s	Remedy
Overheating	Electrical fan faulty	Trace fault.
	Low coolant level	Top up.
	Pump drivebelt slack	Adjust tension.
	Thermostat not operating	Renew.
	Radiator pressure cap faulty or of wrong type	Renew.
	Defective water pump	Renew.
	Cylinder head gasket blowing	Fit new gasket.
	Radiator core clogged	Clean.
	Radiator blocked	Reverse flush.
	Binding brakes	Rectify
Engine running too cool	Defective thermostat	Renew.
	Faulty water temperature gauge	Renew.
	Faulty temperature sensing switch	Renew.
Loss of coolant	Leaking radiator or hoses	Renew or tighten.
	Cylinder head gasket leaking	Renew gasket.
	Leaking cylinder block core plugs	Renew.
	Faulty radiator filler cap or wrong type fitted	Replace with correct type.

Chapter 3 Carburation; fuel, exhaust and emission control systems

Contents

Specifications

Fuel pump

Type	Mechanical, driven by camshaft eccentric
Output at 3,000 rpm	$1\frac{1}{8}$ Imp. pt (600 cc, $1\frac{1}{4}$ US pt) per minute
Static fuel pressure:	
A10 and A14 engine	3.4 lb/in² (0.24 kg/cm²)
A12	2.6 lb/in² (0.18 kg/cm²)

Fuel tank

Location	Rear mounted
Capacity:	
Saloon and Coupe	8.75 Imp. gall (40 litre, 10.5 US gall)
Estate	7.75 Imp. gall (35 litre, 9.25 US gall)

Air cleaner

A10 and A12 engine	Standard, paper element
A14 engine	Automatic temperature control type with paper element

Carburettors

Type:	
A10 engine	Hitachi DCG 286–6D manual choke
A12 engine	Hitachi DCG 306–6D manual choke
A14 engine:	
Non-California model	Hitachi DCH 306–16A automatic choke
California model	Hitachi DCH 306–17A automatic choke

	DCG 286–6D		DCH 306–6D	
	Primary	*Secondary*	*Primary*	*Secondary*
Outer diameter in (mm)	1.024 (26)	1.102 (28)	1.024 (26)	1.181 (30)
Venturi diameter in (mm)	0.748 (19)	0.945 (24)	0.787 (20)	1.024 (26)
Main jet	92	140	96	150
Main air bleed	80	80	80	80
Slow air bleed	220	100	220	100
Power jet		45		60
Main nozzle in (mm)	0.083 (2.1)	0.091 (2.3)	0.083 (2.1)	0.110 (2.8)
Engine idling speed		700 rpm		700 rpm

	DCH 306–16A		DCH 306–17A	
	Primary	*Secondary*	*Primary*	*Secondary*
Outer diameter in (mm)	1.02 (26)	1.181 (30)	1.02 (26)	1.181 (30)
Venturi diameter in (mm)	0.906 (23)	1.063 (27)	0.906 (23)	1.063 (27)
Main jet	105	145	106	145
Main air bleed	95	80	95	80
Slow jet	45	50	45	50
Power jet		40		40
Engine idling/CO% (air off)	700 rpm/CO 2 $\pm$ 1%			

1 General description

The fuel system comprises a fuel tank at the rear of the vehicle, a mechanical fuel pump located on the front of the engine and a Hitachi carburettor. A disposable type fuel filter is fitted in the fuel line between the tank and the fuel pump.

The fuel pump drains petrol from the fuel tank and delivers it to the carburettor. The level of the petrol in the carburettor float chamber is controlled by a flat operated needle valve. Petrol flows past the needle valve until the float rises sufficiently to close the valve. The pump will then freewheel under slight back pressure until the petrol level drops. The needle valve will open and petrol will again flow past the needle valve until the level in the float chamber rises again to close the needle valve.

Three types of emission control system may be fitted to the Datsun model F10 series of vehicles. The crankcase emission control system is used on all vehicles. The exhaust emission control and evaporative emssion control systems are used on models exported to Canada and USA.

Vehicles being operated in areas controlled by the US Federal Regulations on air pollution must have their engines and ancillary equipment modified and accurately tuned so that carbon monoxide, hydro-carbons and nitrogen produced by the engine are within finely controlled limits.

To achieve this there are several systems used. Depending on the anti-pollution standard required, the systems may be fitted singly or as a combination of them all. This is achieved by modifying various parts of the engine and fuel system.

2 Standard air cleaner – servicing

1   The standard air cleaner comprises a body in which is housed a paper element type filter, a lid and the necessary connecting hoses and brackets.

2   Every 24 000 miles (40 000 km) the element should be renewed (photo). Other than renewal, no servicing is required.

3   Unscrew and remove the wing nut which secures the air cleaner lid in position, remove the lid and extract the paper element.

4   Wipe the interior of the air cleaner body free from oil and dirt and install the new element.

5   On some models a WINTER/SUMMER selector lever is used on the air inlet (photo). The lever should be set accordingly and in winter will admit air heated from proximity to the exhaust manifold.

3 Automatic temperature control (ATC) air cleaner – description

The ATC air cleaner fitted to A14 engines is designed to reduce hydrocarbon emission when the engine compartment temperature is below 38°C (100°F). The automatic temperature control system maintains the temperature of air being drawn into the carburettor at 40°C (110°F), thus allowing a weaker mixture setting for the carburettor. In addition the automatic temperature control system

2.2   Renewing the air cleaner

2.5   The Winter/Summer selector lever

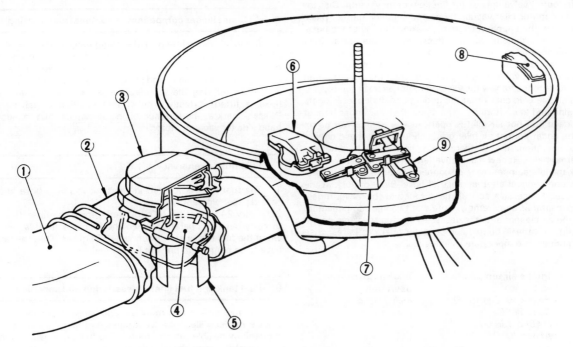

Fig. 3.1 Automatic temperature control air cleaner (A14 engine) (Sec.3)

1 Fresh air duct
2 Air inlet pipe
3 Vacuum motor assembly

4 Air control valve
5 Hot air pipe
6 Temperature sensor

7 Idle compensator
8 Blow-by gas filter
9 Altitude compensator

effectively improves the warm-up characteristics of the engine and prevents the carburettor icing-up.
   The ATC air cleaner consists of the following devices:

a) *A viscous paper type filter which should be renewed every 24 000 miles (40 000 km). It should not be cleaned.*
b) *The air control valve which is actuated by inlet manifold vacuum to control the intake air flow circuit. The temperature sensor detects the intake air temperature and opens or closes the vacuum passage.*
c) *A hot air duct mounted on the exhaust manifold. The air warmed up between the exhaust manifold and the hot air duct passes to the air cleaner.*
d) *A blow-by gas filter which removes dirt and oil from the blow-by gas sucked into the air cleaner from the engine rocker cover.*
e) *An idle compensator which introduces the air directly from the air cleaner to the inlet manifold to compensate for abnormal enrichment of the mixture in high idling temperature.*
f) *An altitude compensator (California models only).*

4 ATC air cleaner – removal and refitting

1 Remove the bolts securing the air cleaner to the air cleaner bracket.
2 Disconnect the following hoses when removing the air cleaner from the carburettor:

a) *Under bonnet air inlet hose.*
b) *Hot air inlet hose.*
c) *Vacuum hose – sensor to inlet manifold.*
d) *Vacuum hose – sensor to vacuum motor.*
e) *Vacuum hose – idle compensator to inlet manifold.*
f) *Air pump to air cleaner hose.*
g) *AB valve to air cleaner hose.*
h) *Carburettor to air cleaner hose.*
j) *Blow-by hose – air cleaner to rocker cover.*

3 Refitting is the reverse of the removal procedure.

5 Hot air control system – checking

1 In warm weather, it is difficult to detect malfunction of the hot air control system. In cold weather, however, malfunction of the air control valve, due to a defective or disconnected vacuum hose between the inlet manifold and the vacuum motor, or a faulty control valve will result in poor engine performance, such as engine stalling, lack of power and an increase in fuel consumption. If these faults become apparent, check the hot air control system before checking the carburettor.
2 Check that vacuum hoses are securely connected in the correct position and that they are in good condition.
3 Place a mirror at the end of the air cleaner inlet, as shown in Fig. 3.2, and check that the air inlet is open and the hot air inlet closed.

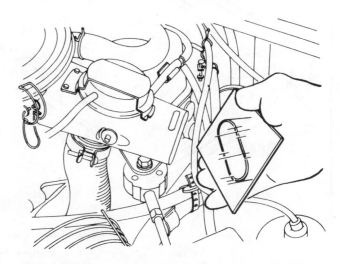

Fig. 3.2 Checking the valve position (Sec. 5)

Check the air control valve linkage for freedom of movement. Disconnect the vacuum motor inlet vacuum hose and connect another piece of hose to the inlet, then apply vacuum by sucking the end of the hose. Using a mirror check that the air inlet is closed and the hot air inlet open. Pinch the hose to cut off the vacuum and check that the hot air inlet remains open for more than 30 seconds. If the diaphragm spring actuates the air control valve by spring force to open the under bonnet air inlet with 30 seconds, renew the vacuum motor as an assembly.

4   With the engine cold check that the under bonnet air inlet is open. Start the engine and keep it idling, then check that the under bonnet air inlet is closed and hot air inlet is open. As the engine warms up check that the under bonnet air inlet gradually opens. If these checks reveal faulty operation, the temperature sensor must be checked against a thermometer. Renew a defective temperature sensor.

5   To check the idle compensator, disconnect the hose leading to the compensator and connect another piece of hose. Blow or suck at the end of the hose. If excessive air leakage is found at the valve, renew the idle compensator as an assembly. Note that two idle compensators are fitted to the air cleaner and it is necessary to plug the valve of one while checking the other. The idle compensator operates in response to the under bonnet air temperature as follows:

Bi-metal	Intake air temperature	Idle compensator operation
No. 1	Below 60°C (140°F)	Fully closed
	60 to 70°C (140 to 158°F)	Close to open
	Above 70°C (158°F)	Fully open
No. 2	Below 70°C (158°F)	Fully closed
	70 to 80°C (158 to 176°F)	Close to open
	Above 80°C (176°F)	Fully open

6   ATC air cleaner components – removal and refitting

1   Removal and refitting of the component parts is straightforward after removing the top cover and filter element from the air cleaner. **Note:** The gasket between the temperature sensor and air cleaner is bonded to the air cleaner and should not be removed.

2   When refitting the temperature sensor ensure that the vacuum hose is fitted correctly. The correct position is: left-hand side to 'Nissan' mark at the top face of the sensor for inlet manifold – right-hand side for vacuum motor.

7   Fuel filter – renewal

1   The fuel filter is located in the tank to pump hose and is of the sealed paper element type.

2   Every 24 000 miles (40 000 km), renew the filter. It is preferable to carry out this operation when the fuel tank level is low otherwise when the fuel hoses are disconnected from the filter, the tank line will have to be plugged to prevent loss of fuel.

8   Fuel tank and fuel lines – description and servicing

1   The fuel tank is rear mounted and varies in capacity according to vehicle model. Filler tube, vent pipes and fuel lines are connected to the tank by flexible tubing (photo). The fuel level gauge is mounted in the top of the tank and a drain plug is conveniently located. The tank on the station wagon is of a different shape and is mounted in a slightly different manner.

2   To remove the fuel tank, drain the tank and disconnect the fuel gauge sending unit harness and the fuel lines.

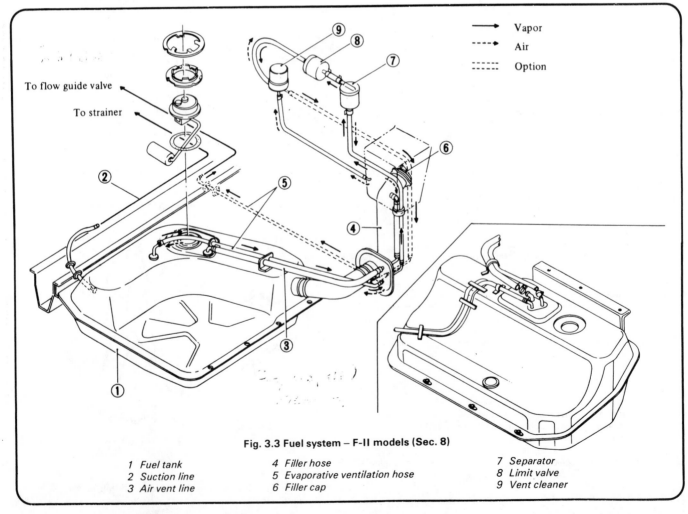

Fig. 3.3 Fuel system – F-II models (Sec. 8)

1 Fuel tank	4 Filler hose	7 Separator
2 Suction line	5 Evaporative ventilation hose	8 Limit valve
3 Air vent line	6 Filler cap	9 Vent cleaner

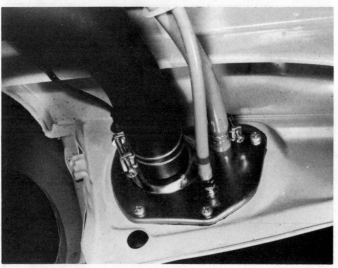

8.1   Fuel tank filler tube and vent pipes

3   Loosen the clamps at the fuel filler hose, ventilation hose and air vent hose.
4   Unscrew and remove the securing bolts and anchor plates from the fuel tank flanges. When working on the saloon or station wagon work should commence at the bolts at the front of the tank. The station wagon tank should be lowered just far enough to rest against

the rear axle before removing the remaining bolts.
5   Withdraw the tank from its location.
6   If the tank contains a lot of sediment or sludge, shake it vigorously using two or three changes of paraffin and then allow it to drain thoroughly.
7   Should a leak develop in the fuel tank do not be tempted to solder over the hole. Fuel tank repair is a specialist job and unless lengthy safety precautions are observed, can be a very dangerous procedure.
8   Occasionally drain the tank when there is very little fuel left in it so that any accumulated water or sediment will be flushed out and discarded. This action will safeguard the tank against corrosion and help to prevent clogging of the fuel line filter.
9   Refitting the fuel tank is a reversal of removal, but check that the vent tubes which are connected to the filler neck are not trapped and are securely clipped in position. Do not forget to install spring and plain washers on tank mounting bolts since the mounting holes in the tank flange are elongated to provide for adjustment.

9   Fuel pump – description

The fuel pump is a diaphragm type, consisting of a body, rocker arm and link assembly, diaphragm, diaphragm spring, seal, inlet and outlet valves.
The diaphragm is made of specially treated rubber, which is not affected by petrol, held together by two metal discs and a pull rod.
The fuel pump is actuated by the movement of the rocker arm on a camshaft eccentric. This movement is transferred to the flexible diaphragm which draws the fuel from the tank and delivers it under pressure to the carburettor float chamber. The inlet and outlet valves control the flow of fuel.

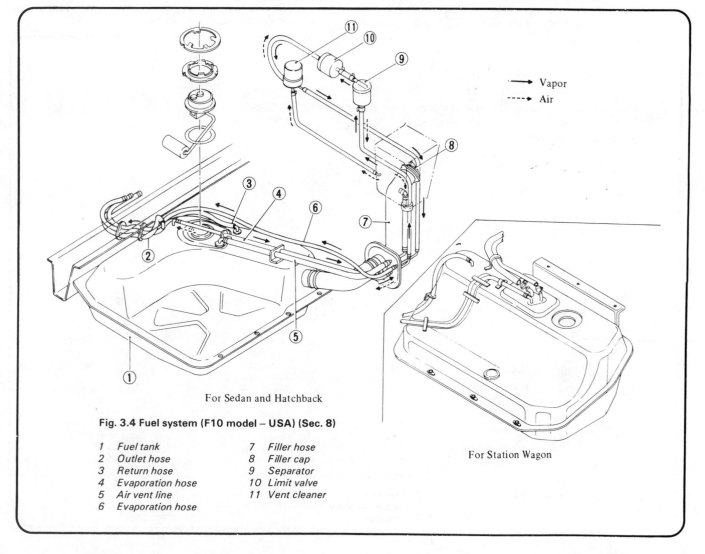

For Sedan and Hatchback

Fig. 3.4 Fuel system (F10 model – USA) (Sec. 8)

1	Fuel tank	7	Filler hose
2	Outlet hose	8	Filler cap
3	Return hose	9	Separator
4	Evaporation hose	10	Limit valve
5	Air vent line	11	Vent cleaner
6	Evaporation hose		

For Station Wagon

10 Fuel pump – checking operation

Assuming that the fuel lines and unions are in good condition and that there are no leaks anywhere, check the performance of the fuel pump in the following manner: Disconnect the fuel pipe at the carburettor inlet union, and the high tension lead to the coil, and with a suitable container or a large rag in position to catch the ejected fuel, turn the engine over on the starter motor solenoid. A good spurt of petrol should emerge from the end of the pipe every second revolution.

11 Fuel pump – removal and refitting

1   Disconnect the fuel pipes by unscrewing their two unions on the fuel pump which is located on the front of the engine. Where the fuel tank contains more than a small amount of fuel it will probably be necessary to plug the inlet fuel line from the tank.
2   Remove the two nuts which secure the fuel pump to the crankcase. Lift away the pump noting carefully the number of gaskets used between the pump and crankcase mating faces.

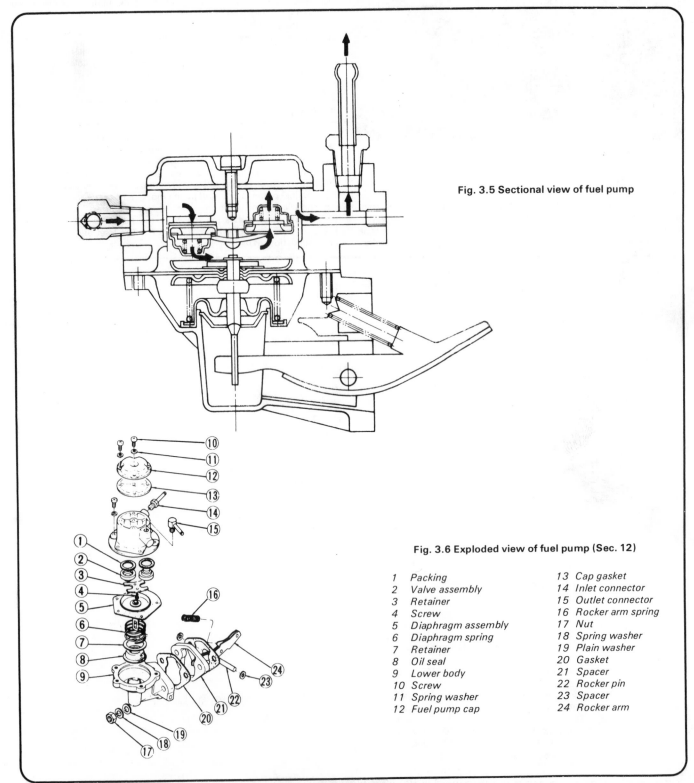

Fig. 3.5 Sectional view of fuel pump

Fig. 3.6 Exploded view of fuel pump (Sec. 12)

1 Packing	13 Cap gasket
2 Valve assembly	14 Inlet connector
3 Retainer	15 Outlet connector
4 Screw	16 Rocker arm spring
5 Diaphragm assembly	17 Nut
6 Diaphragm spring	18 Spring washer
7 Retainer	19 Plain washer
8 Oil seal	20 Gasket
9 Lower body	21 Spacer
10 Screw	22 Rocker pin
11 Spring washer	23 Spacer
12 Fuel pump cap	24 Rocker arm

3   Refitting is the reverse of removal. Always use new gaskets

12 Fuel pump – dismantling, inspection and reassembly

1   Before dismantling, clean the exterior of the pump and then make a mark across the centre and base mating flanges so that they can be refitted in their original position.
2   Remove the screws securing the cap to the upper body and take off the cap and cap gasket.
3   Separate the upper body and lower body by removing the securing screws and lifting off the upper body. It is possible for the diaphragm to stick to the mating flanges; if this happens use a sharp knife to free it.
4   To remove the diaphragm, diaphragm spring, lower body seal washer and lower body seal from the lower body, press down on the diaphragm to counter the action of the diaphragm spring and while doing this, tilt the diaphragm so that the rectangular part in the lower end of the pull rod is unhooked from the rocker arm link.
5   Check the upper and lower bodies for cracks or damage.
6   Check the valve assembly for wear of valve and valve spring.
7   Hold the diaphragm up to the light and examine for splits or pin holes.
8   Check the rocker arm pin for wear as a worn pin may cause oil leakage. Check the rocker arm for wear on the mating face with the camshaft.
9   Renew defective parts as necessary. Always use a new gasket.
10 Reassembly is the reverse of the dismantling procedure. Before refitting the pump to the engine lubricate the rocker arm link and rocker arm pin.
11 After the pump has been reassembled, functionally test it by either placing a finger over the inlet and actuating the rocker arm when a good suction noise should be heard or by connecting it to the tank fuel line and after actuating the rocker arm a few times, each successive

stroke should be accompanied by a spurt of fuel from the pump outlet. Collect the fuel in a container.

13 Fuel gauge sender unit – removal and refitting

1   Remove the fuel tank as described in Section 8.
Note: An access hole is not provided for removal of the fuel gauge sender unit.
2   Turn the lockplate with a screwdriver then remove the gauge unit (bayonet type).
3   To refit the fuel gauge sender unit, align the notches and then turn the lockplate, see Fig. 3.3. Always use a new gasket.
4   Refit the fuel tank as described in Section 8

14 Accelerator control linkage (manual choke) – removal and refitting

1   Remove the outer casing clamp and accelerator cable on the carburettor end. Before removing the cable, hold the throttle valve fully open so as to slacken the cable.
2   Remove the cable from the clevis at the accelerator pedal arm and pull into the drivers compartment. On right-hand drive models, remove the clip and pin from the arm end.
3   Refitting is the reverse of the removal procedure. Before securing the accelerator cable, ensure that the inner cable slides smoothly without binding.

15 Choke control (manual) – removal and refitting

1   Remove the choke knob by holding the inner wire with a pair of pliers and push the knob in, then rotate the knob through 90° and pull it off.

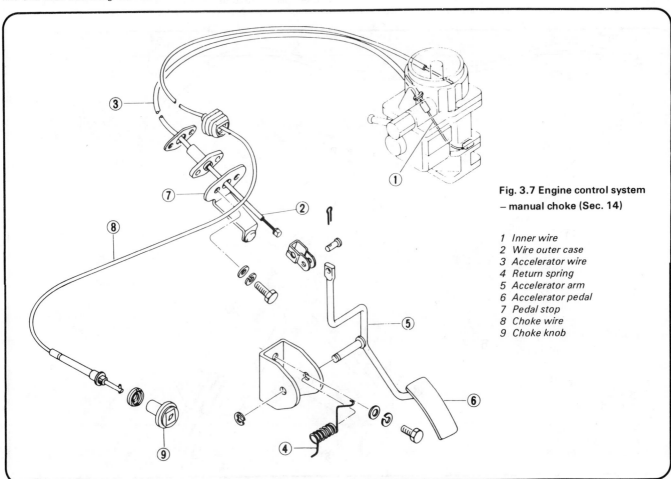

Fig. 3.7 Engine control system
– manual choke (Sec. 14)

1 Inner wire
2 Wire outer case
3 Accelerator wire
4 Return spring
5 Accelerator arm
6 Accelerator pedal
7 Pedal stop
8 Choke wire
9 Choke knob

2   Disconnect the choke control wire from the choke control lever at the carburettor.

3   Remove the escutcheon from the dash panel and pull the choke cable assembly into the engine compartment.

4   Refitting the choke cable assembly is the reverse of the removal sequence.

5   Adjust the choke valve so that it opens fully when the choke knob is pushed in all the way and closes when the knob is pulled out.

16 Accelerator control linkage (automatic choke) – removal, refitting and adjustment

1   Removal and refitting procedure is the same as described in Section 14.

2   To adjust the control linkage, loosen the locknut, 'A' in Fig. 3.8, in direction 'X' as far as possible. Unscrew nut 'C' in direction 'X' until it comes off the thread. Pull the accelerator outer cable until the clearance between the end of the inner wire and clevis is zero, and tighten adjusting nut 'B' until clearance to part 'D' is 0 – 0.118 in (0 – 3mm). Tighten nut 'C' fully to part 'D'. When tightening nut 'C' take care to avoid turning the adjusting nut 'B' at the same time. Finally tighten locknut 'A' to secure the adjusting nut 'B'.

17 Carburettor (DCG 286 and DCG 306) – general description

The carburettor fitted to all models is of the downdraught twin choke type. The DCG type carburettors fitted to the A10 and A12 engine have a manual choke and the DCH type on the A14 engine has an automatic choke.

Full specifications of the carburettors used are given in the Specifications at the beginning of this Chapter.

The carburettor is conventional in operation and incorporates a primary and main jet system and a mechanically operated accelerator pump.

Manually operated choke: This comprises a butterfly valve which closes one of the venturi choke tubes and is so synchronized with the throttle valve plate that the latter opens sufficiently to provide a rich mixture and an increased slow running speed for easy starting.

For idling and slow running, the fuel passes through the slow running jet, the primary slow air bleed and the secondary slow air bleed. The fuel is finally ejected from the bypass and idle holes (Fig. 3.9).

The accelerator pump is synchronized with the throttle valve. During periods of heavy acceleration, the pump which is of simple piston and valve construction, provides an additional metered quantity of fuel to enrich the normal mixture. The quantity of fuel metered can be varied according to operating climatic conditions by adjusting the stroke of the pump linkage.

The secondary system provides a mixture for normal motoring conditions by means of a main jet and air bleed. The float chamber is fed with fuel pumped by the mechanically operated pump on the crankcase. The level in the chamber is critical and must at all times be maintained as specified. The power valve system utilizes the vacuum in the intake manifold to open or close the valve. During light load running the valve is closed, but is opened during full load running or acceleration, thus furnishing more fuel.

18 Idling speed – adjustment

1   Run the engine to normal operating temperature and then set the throttle adjusting screw (Fig. 3.10) to provide an engine speed of 700 rpm.

2   If the vehicle is fitted with a tachometer then the setting of engine speed will be no problem. Where an instrument is not available then a useful guide may be obtained from the state of the ignition warning lamp. This should be just going out at the correct idling speed.

3   Setting of the mixture screw may be carried out using 'Colortune' or a vacuum gauge attached to the inlet manifold. In either case follow the equipment manufacturers' instructions.

4   In certain territories, the use of a CO meter is essential and if this is used then the throttle adjusting screw and the mixture screw must be turned to provide a reading on the meter of 2 ± 1% at the specified

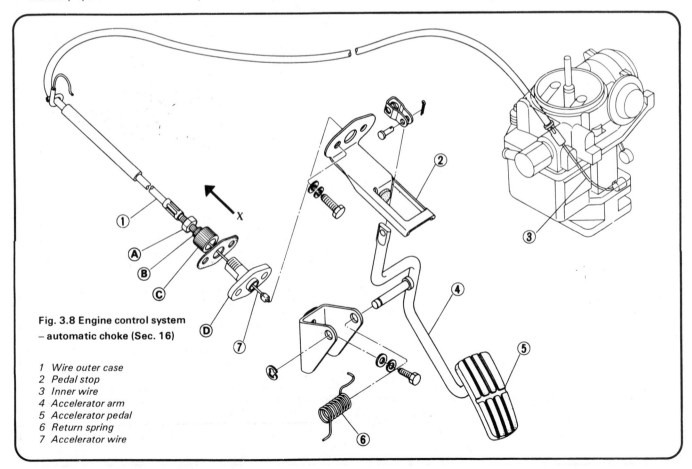

Fig. 3.8 Engine control system
– automatic choke (Sec. 16)

1   *Wire outer case*
2   *Pedal stop*
3   *Inner wire*
4   *Accelerator arm*
5   *Accelerator pedal*
6   *Return spring*
7   *Accelerator wire*

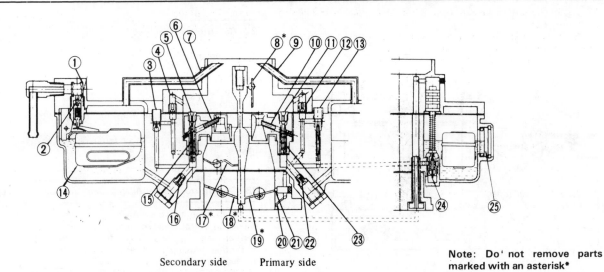

Note: Do' not remove parts marked with an asterisk*

Secondary side   Primary side

Fig. 3.9 Sectional view of DCG type carburettor (Sec. 17)

1 Filter	10 Primary main nozzle	18 *Secondary throttle valve
2 Needle valve	11 Primary main air bleed	19 *Primary throttle valve
3 Secondary slow jet	12 Primary slow air bleed	20 Idle hole
4 Secondary slow air bleed	13 Primary slow jet	21 Bypass hole
5 Secondary main air bleed	14 Float	22 Primary main jet
6 Secondary main nozzle	15 Secondary emulsion tube	23 Primary emulsion tube
7 Secondary air vent	16 Secondary main jet	24 Power valve
8 *Choke valve	17 *Auxiliary valve	25 Level gauge
9 Primary air vent		

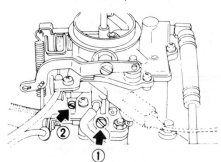

Fig. 3.10 Adjusting screws (Sec. 18)

1 Throttle adjusting screw
2 Idle adjusting screw

"h" Hold up

Fig. 3.11 Float adjustment (Sec. 19)

1 Float   3 Float seat
2 Float stop   4 Needle valve

20.1   Carburettor float level sight glass

engine idling speed.

5   As a temporary measure, the adjustment screws may be rotated progressively, first one and then the other until the engine idles at the correct speed without any 'hunting' or stalling. Turning the mixture screw clockwise weakens the mixture and anti-clockwise richens it.

19 Float level – adjustment

1   Where the appropriate adjustments have been carried out and there is evidence of fuel starvation or conversely, flooding or excessively rich mixture, the float level should be checked.
2   Remove the carburettor, as described in Section 22.
3   Disconnect choke connecting rod, accelerator pump lever and return spring.
4   Unscrew and remove the five securing screws which secure the upper choke chamber to the main body.
5   Turn the float chamber upside down and check the dimension 'H' with the float hanging down under its own weight. This should be 0.472 in (12.0 mm) (Fig. 3.11).
6   Now gently push the float upwards to the full extent of its travel

and check the clearance between the endface of the inlet needle valve and the float tongue. This should be 0.051 to 0.067 in (1.3 to 1.7 mm) when the float is fully raised, dimension 'h' in Fig. 3.11. Adjustment to correct either of these dimensions is carried out by bending the float seat or the stopper tag.

20 Float chamber fuel level – checking

1   The fuel level can be checked in the float chamber sight glass (photo).
2   The level should be maintained within the range of 0.71 - 0.79 in (18 - 20 mm) as shown in Fig. 3.12.

21 Interlock opening of primary and secondary throttle valves – checking and adjustment

1   Open the primary side throttle valve 48° from the fully closed position and measure the clearance, 'G' in Fig. 3.13, between the throttle valve and throttle chamber inner wall.

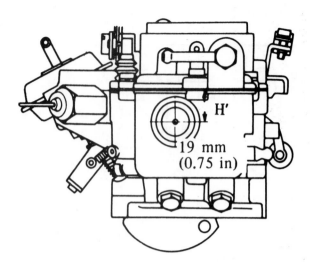

Fig. 3.12 Checking the fuel level (Sec. 20)

"G1"   5.83 mm (0.230 in)

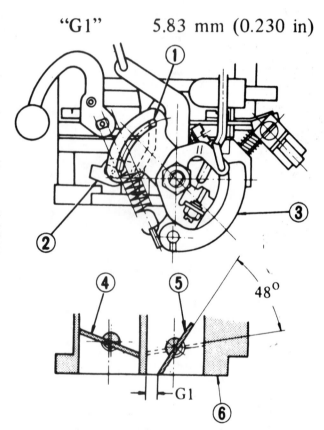

Fig. 3.13 Adjusting interlock opening of primary and secondary throttle valves (Sec. 21)

1 Connecting rod	4 Secondary throttle valve
2 Secondary connecting lever	5 Primary throttle valve
3 Throttle lever	6 Throttle chamber

2   Without disturbing the above setting, bend the rod which connects the two throttle valves, as necessary, so that the secondary valve is about to open.

3   After adjustment check that the link system operates smoothly.

22 Carburettor – removal and refitting

1   Remove the air cleaner assembly.
2   Disconnect the fuel and vacuum hoses from the carburettor, also the choke and accelerator controls.
3   Remove the four nuts and washers which secure the carburettor to the inlet manifold.
4   Lift the carburettor from the manifold and discard the flange gasket.
5   Refitting is a reverse of removal, but always use a new flange gasket.

23 Carburettor dismantling and reassembly – general

1   With time the component parts of the Hitachi carburettor will wear and petrol consumption will increase. The diameter of drillings and jet may alter, and air and fuel leaks may develop round spindles and other moving parts. Because of the high degree of precision involved it is recommended that an exchange rebuilt carburettor is purchased. This is one of the few instances where it is better to buy a new component rather than to rebuild the old one.
2   The accelerator pump itself may need attention and gaskets may need renewal. Providing care is taken there is no reason why the carburettor may not be completely reconditioned at home, but ensure a full repair kit can be obtained before you strip the carburettor down. **Never** poke out jets with wire or similar to clean them but blow them out with compressed air or air from a car tyre pump.

24 Carburettor – dismantling and reassembly

1   The main jets and needle valves are accessible from the exterior of the carburettor.
2   These should be unscrewed, removed and cleaned by blowing them through with air from a tyre pump; **never** probe a jet or needle valve seat with wire.
3   Detach the choke chamber by removing the connecting rod, accelerator pump lever, return spring and the five securing screws.
4   The primary and secondary emulsion tubes are accessible after removing the main air bleeds.
5   Remove the accelerator pump cover, retaining the spring, piston and ball valve carefully.
6   Separate the float chamber from the throttle housing by unscrewing and removing three securing screws. Slide out the float pivot pin and remove the float
7   Unless imperative, do not dismantle the throttle butterfly valves from their spindles.
8   Take great care when disconnecting the interlock rods that they are not bent or twisted or the settings and adjustments will be upset.
9   With the carburettor dismantled, clean all components in clean fuel and blow through the internal body passages with air from a tyre pump.
10 Inspect all components for wear and the body and chamber castings for cracks.
11 Clean the small gauze filter and if corroded or clogged, renew it.
12 If wear is evident in the throttle spindle, the carburettor should be renewed on an exchange basis.
13 Check all jet and air bleed sizes with those specified in Specifications in case a previous owner has changed them for ones of an incorrect size.
14 Check the ejection of fuel when the accelerator pump is actuated.
15 Reassembly is a reversal of dismantling using all the items supplied in the repair kit.
16 When the carburettor is being reassembled, check the float movement (Section 19) and when it is refitted to the engine, carry out all the checks and adjustments described in this Chapter

25 Carburettor (DCH 306) – general description

The DCH 306 carburettor fitted on A14 engines is basically similar to the DCG 306 except for the choke, which is automatically operated, and the addition of a throttle opener control system to reduce

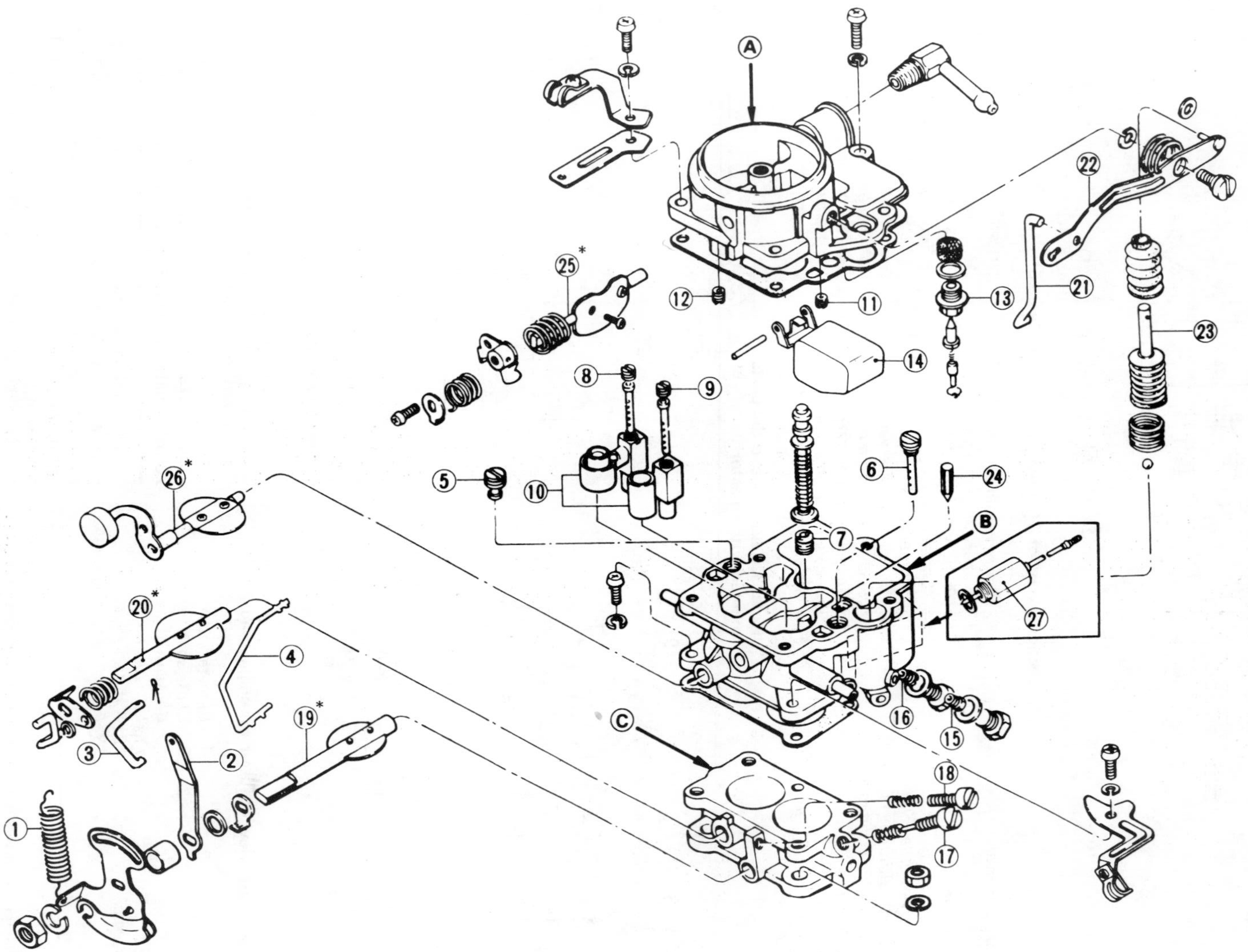

Fig. 3.14 Exploded view of DCG type carburettor (Sec. 24)

A   Choke chamber
B   Centre body
C   Throttle chamber

1   Return spring
2   Starting lever
3   Connecting rod
4   Choke connecting rod
5   Secondary slow jet
6   Primary slow jet
7   Power jet
8   Secondary main air bleed
9   Primary main air bleed
10 Small venturi
11 Primary slow air bleed
12 Secondary slow air bleed
13 Needle valve
14 Float
15 Primary main jet
16 Secondary main jet
17 Idle adjust screw
18 Throttle adjust screw
19 *Primary throttle valve
20 *Secondary throttle valve
21 Accelerating pump-rod
22 Accelerating pump lever
23 Accelerating pump
24 Injector weight
25 *Choke valve
26 *Auxiliary valve
27 Anti-dieseling solenoid valve (A12 Engine only)

Note: Do not remove the parts marked with an asterisk*

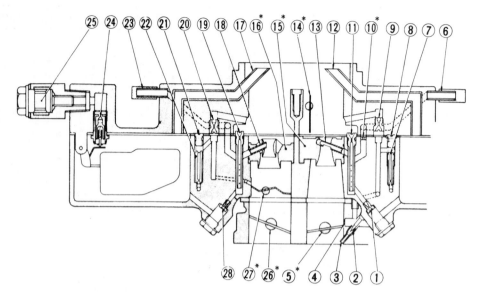

3.15 Sectional view of DCH type carburettor (Sec. 25)

1   Primary main jet
2   Idle adjust screw
3   Idle nozzle
4   Bypass hole
5   *Primary throttle valve
6   Primary altitude compensator pipe (for California)
7   Primary slow jet
8   Plug
9   Primary slow air bleed
10 *Safe orifice

11 Primary main air bleed
12 Primary air vent pipe
13 Primary main nozzle
14 *Choke valve
15 *Primary small venturi
16 *Secondary small venturi
17 Secondary air vent pipe
18 Secondary main nozzle
19 Secondary main air bleed
20 Secondary slow air bleed

21 Plug
22 Secondary slow jet
23 Secondary altitude compensator pipe (for California)
24 Needle
25 Fuel filter
26 *Secondary throttle valve
27 *Auxiliary valve
28 Secondary main jet

Note: Do not remove the parts marked with an asterisk *

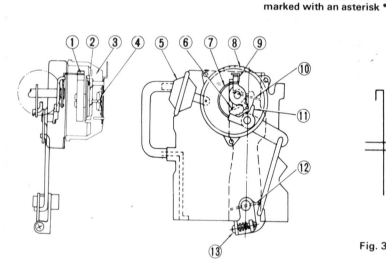

Fig. 3.16 Sectional view of automatic choke (Sec. 26)

1   Bi-metal
2   Heater
3   Bi-metal cover
4   Bi-metal switch
5   Vacuum diaphragm
6   Fast idle cam
7   Bi-metal

8   Bi-metal index mark
9   Choke shaft lever
10 Choke valve
11 Unloader tang
12 Throttle valve
13 Fast idle adjusting screw

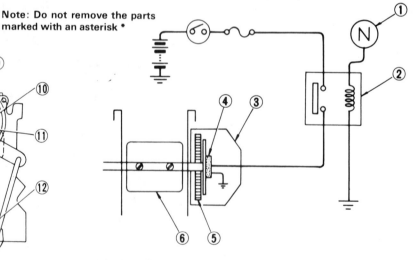

Fig. 3.17 Circuit diagram of automatic choke heater (Sec. 26)

1   Alternator
2   Automatic choke relay
3   Automatic choke cover

4   PTC heater
5   Bi-metal spring
6   Choke valve

---

26   Automatic choke (DCH 306 carburettor) – description

An electric heater warms a bi-metal, interconnected to the choke valve, and controls the position of the choke valve and throttle valve in accordance with the time elapsed, the warm-up condition of the engine and the ambient temperature. The function of each part is as follows:

1   *Bi-metal and heater in thermostat cover:* electric current flows through the heater as the engine starts, and warms the bi-metal. The deflection of the bi-metal is transmitted to the choke valve through the

hydrocarbon emissions and a dashpot to ensure smooth deceleration. A manually operated altitude compensator is fitted on California models.

choke valve lever.

2 *Fast idle cam:* the fast idle cam determines the opening of the throttle valve so that the proper amount of mixture, corresponding to the opening of the choke valve, will be obtained. The opening of the choke is dependent upon the warm-up condition of the engine.

3 *Fast idle adjusting screw:* this screw adjusts the opening of the throttle valve by the fast idle cam.

4 *Unloader:* when accelerating the engine during the warm-up period, that is, before the choke valve opens sufficiently, the unloader forces the choke valve open a little so as to obtain an adequate air-fuel mixture.

5 *Vacuum diaphragm:* after the engine has been started, this diaphragm forces the choke valve open to the predetermined extent so as to provide the correct air-fuel ratio.

6 *Bi-metal case index mark:* this mark is used for setting the movement of the bi-metal which controls the air-fuel mixture ratio required for starting the engine.

27 Fast idle adjustment – automatic choke (DCH 306 carburettor)

1 Remove the carburettor from the engine.
2 Remove the bi-metal cover.
3 Place the fast idle arm on the second step of the fast idle cam and then adjust the fast idle adjusting screw as shown in Fig. 3.18. The clearance at 'A' should be 0.0287 - 0.0343 in (0.73 - 0.87 mm) at 1900 to 2700 rpm.
4 To check the fast idle cam setting by engine speed, warm up the engine, set the fast idle cam at the second step and check the engine speed. The rpm should be within the above specifications.

28 Vacuum break (DCH 306 carburettor) – adjustment

1 Close the choke valve completely.

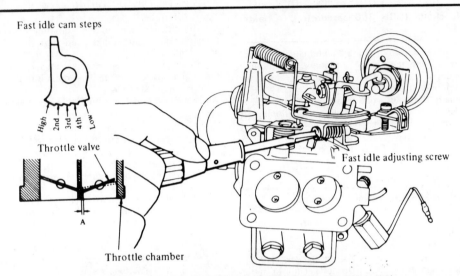

Fig. 3.18 Adjusting the fast idle – DCH 306 carburettor (Sec. 27)

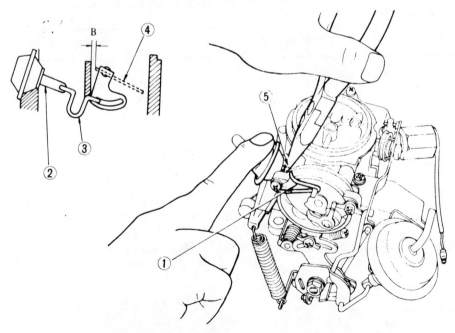

Fig. 3.19 Adjusting the vacuum break – DCH 306 carburettor (Sec. 28)

1 Rubber band
2 Vacuum break stem
3 Vacuum break rod
4 Choke valve
5 Vacuum break stem

2   Hold the choke valve by stretching a rubber band between the choke shaft lever and fixed part of the carburettor, refer to Fig. 3.19.
3   Grip the vacuum break stem with pliers, pull it fully straight and then adjust the gap, 'B' in Fig. 3.19 between the choke valve and carburettor body to 0.0567 - 0.0614 in (1.44 - 1.56 mm).

29 Choke unloader (DCH 306 carburettor) – adjustment

1   Repeat the operations in paragraphs 1 and 2 of Section 28.
2   Pull the throttle lever to fully open the throttle and then adjust the clearance, 'C' in Fig. 3.20, between the choke valve and the carburettor body to 0.079 in (2.01 mm) by bending the unloader tongue.
3   Ensure that the throttle valve opens fully when the carburettor is fitted on the engine. If the throttle valve fails to open fully, the unloader becomes inoperative and results in poor acceleration.

30 Electric automatic choke (DCH 306 carburettor) – heater circuit check

1   Connect a circuit tester as shown in Fig. 3.21 and check for continuity between 'A' and 'B' with the engine stationary. If continuity exists the heater is functioning. If there is no continuity, check for disconnected connector or open heater circuit.
2   With the engine idling check for voltage across 'A' and 'B'. If voltmeter reading is 12 volts the heater circuit is functioning. If voltmeter reading is zero, check for disconnected connector, open circuit or faulty automatic choke relay.
3   If the above checks indicate a faulty part or unit, renew as necessary.

31 Automatic choke (DCH 306 carburettor) – checking

1   Before starting the engine, fully depress the accelerator pedal to ensure that the choke valve closes.
2   Push the choke valve with a finger to check for binding.
3   Check that the bi-metal cover index mark is set at the centre of the choke housing index as shown in Fig. 3.22. Do not set the bi-metal cover index mark at any position other than the centre of the choke housing index marks.
4   Check the automatic choke heater wiring connections then start the engine.
5   After warming up the engine, check that the choke valve is fully

open.
6   If the automatic choke heater wiring is in order and the choke valve does not operate after warm-up, renew the bi-metal cover.

32 Idling speed and mixture ratio (DCH 306 carburettor) – adjustment

Idle mixture adjustment requires the use of a CO meter. When measuring CO percentage, insert the probe more than 16 in (40 cm) into the tail pipe.
1   Disconnect the air hose from the air check valve and fit a cap on the air check valve. Ensure that the carburettor pipes are correctly fitted.
2   Warm-up the engine to normal operating temperature.
3   Adjust the throttle adjusting screw until the engine speed is 700 rpm.
4   Adjust the idle adjusting screw so that the CO percentage is 2 ± 1% at 700 rpm.
5   Run the engine up to approximately 1700 rpm two or three times, under no load, and make sure that the CO percentage is within specification.
6   Remove the cap and connect the air hose to the air check valve. If the engine speed increases, re-adjust it to the specified speed with the throttle adjusting screw.
7   If a CO meter is not available, the following procedures may be used:

a) *Proceed as above but adjust the throttle screw until the engine speed is 740 rpm, then adjust the idle mixture screw until maximum rpm is obtained.*
b) *Repeat the procedures at (a) above until the engine speed, at best idle mixture, is 740 rpm.*
c) *Turn the idle adjustment clockwise until the engine speed drops off below the specified rpm. If the idle limiter cap prevents correct adjustment, remove it. To refit the idle limiter cap refer to Section 33.*
d) *If the engine speed rises when the air hose is reconnected to the air check valve, re-adjust to the specified speed with the throttle adjusting screw.*

33 Idle limiter cap (DCH 306 carburettor) – adjustment

Do not remove the idle limiter cap unless necessary. If it is

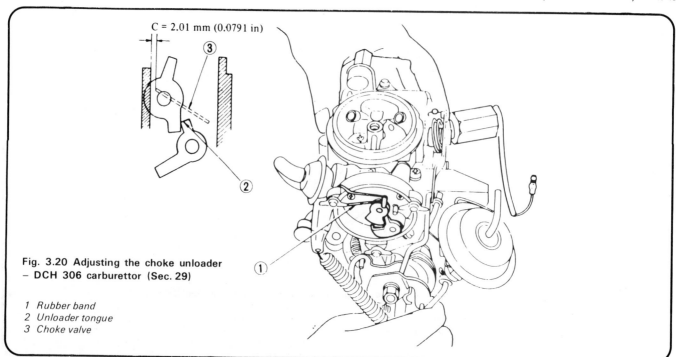

Fig. 3.20 Adjusting the choke unloader
– DCH 306 carburettor (Sec. 29)

1 *Rubber band*
2 *Unloader tongue*
3 *Choke valve*

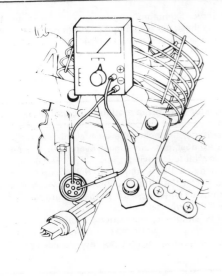

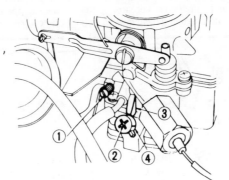

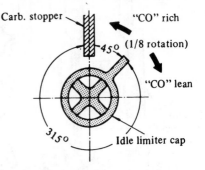

Fig. 3.21 Checking the choke heater circuit – DCH 306 carburettor (Sec. 30)

1 Ignition key
2 Fuse
3 Automatic choke relay
   Engine stop: OFF
   Engine start: ON
4 Automatic choke heater
5 Function test connector
6 'N' terminal of alternator

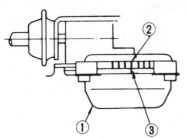

Fig. 3.22. Position of bi-metal cover (Sec. 31)

1 Bi-metal cover
2 Choke housing index marks
3 Bi-metal cover index marks

Fig. 3.23 Carburettor adjusting screws (Sec. 32)

1 Throttle adjusting screw
2 Idle adjusting screw
3 Stop
4 Idle limiter cap

Fig. 3.24. Setting the idle limiter cap (Sec. 33)

removed it must be adjusted when being refitted.
1   After adjusting the throttle or idle speed adjusting screws, check that the CO percentage in the exhaust gases is within the specified limit.
2   Fit the idle limiter cap in position, making sure that the adjusting screw can rotate a further $\frac{1}{8}$ turn in the CO-Rich direction, see Fig. 3.24.

34   Dashpot (DCH 306 carburettor) – adjustment

1   The dashpot assembly is fitted to the carburettor on the A14 engines and is interlocked with the primary throttle valve through a link mechanism. Its function is to prevent the engine from stalling from sudden release of the accelerator pedal after it has been depressed. The throttle lever strikes the dashpot stem at the specified rpm. This condition creates a dampening effect on the primary throttle valve and thus prevents the engine from stalling on sudden deceleration.
2   For this adjustment an electric tachometer will be required. If one is not available have the local Datsun dealer carry out the adjustment.
3   Start the engine and run it until it reaches its normal operating temperature.
4   Gradually increase the engine speed until the tachometer reads 2300 – 2400 rpm (for California models 1900 – 2000 rpm). At this speed the dashpot stem should be in contact with the primary throttle lever.
5   Should the dashpot not be in contact with the throttle lever, then release the dashpot locknuts and adjust the dashpot until the stem just touches the primary throttle lever. Retighten the locknuts.
6   With the engine running and the tachometer registering the specified rpm, (paragraph 4 above) release the throttle suddenly and check that the engine speed drops smoothly from 2000 to 1000 rpm in approximately 3 seconds.

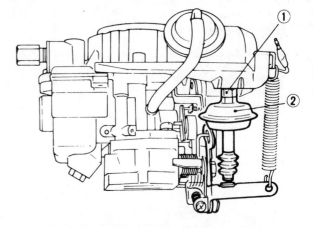

Fig. 3.25 Adjusting the dashpot (Sec. 34)

1 Locknut   2 Dashpot

7   If necessary, slacken the locknuts once more and readjust the dashpot until the required action is obtained.

35   Throttle opening control system (TOCS) – description and operation (DCH 306 carburettor)

1   The throttle opener is designed to open the throttle valve of the carburettor slightly during deceleration. During deceleration manifold vacuum rises and the quantity of mixture in the engine is not sufficient

for normal combustion, resulting in increased emission of hydrocarbon gases in the exhaust.

2 Carburettors equipped with the throttle opener supply the engine with an adequate charge of mixture to maintain correct combustion during deceleration and thereby reducing the HC emission.

3 The system for the manual transmission models consists of servo diaphragm, vacuum control valve, throttle opener solenoid valve, speed detecting switch and amplifier. An altitude connector fitted to the vacuum control valve serves to regulate automatically the operating pressure in the system with variation of atmospheric pressure.

4 When the manifold vacuum increases on deceleration, the vacuum control valve opens to transfer the manifold vacuum to the servo diaphragm chamber and the throttle valve opens slightly. Under this condition the correct amount of fresh air is sucked into the combustion chamber. This additional air assists in the complete combustion of the fuel and the amount of HC in the exhaust gases is reduced.

5 The throttle opener solenoid valve is controlled by a speed detecting switch which is actuated by the speedometer needle. As the car speed falls below 10 mph (16 km/h), this switch is actuated and produces a signal which is led to the amplifier and amplified to actuate the throttle opener solenoid valve. The throttle opener solenoid valve is

actuated and the servo-diaphragm chamber is opened to the atmosphere. In this case the servo-diaphragm does not operate.

6 Generally, the throttle opener control system does not require adjusting, but should it become suspect, the vehicle should be taken to a Datsun dealer for checking and adjusting.

36 Altitude compensator (California models) – description

1 The higher the altitude, the richer the air-fuel mixture ratio and therefore the higher exhaust gas emissions, even with the engine correctly adjusted for low altitude driving.

2 At high altitudes, additional air is supplied to the carburettor by the altitude compensator. When the altitude compensator lever is set at 'H' air is conducted through an air passage to the carburettor. The air passage is closed when the lever is set at 'L'.

3 Make sure that the altitude compensator to carburettor hose is securely connected and that it is not cracked or blocked. Check that the altitude compensator lever is set at 'L' for low altitudes or 'H' for high altitudes.

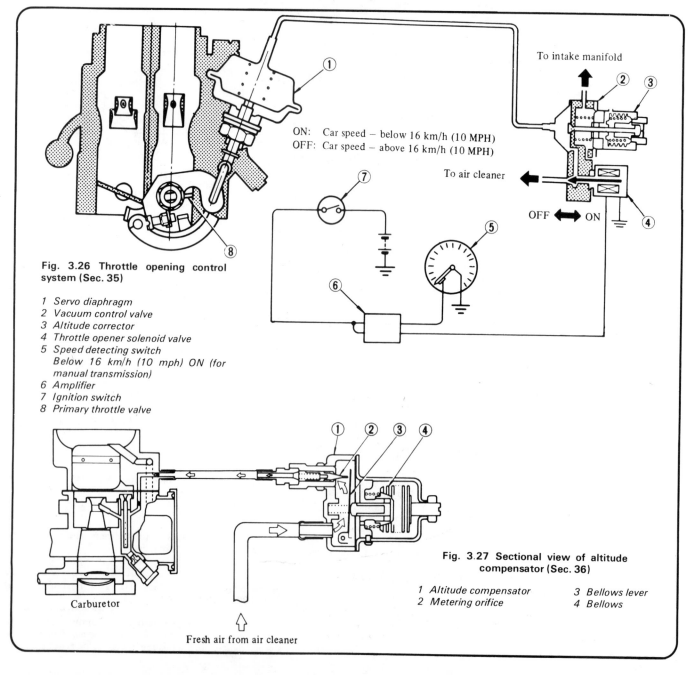

Fig. 3.26 Throttle opening control system (Sec. 35)

1 Servo diaphragm
2 Vacuum control valve
3 Altitude corrector
4 Throttle opener solenoid valve
5 Speed detecting switch
   Below 16 km/h (10 mph) ON (for manual transmission)
6 Amplifier
7 Ignition switch
8 Primary throttle valve

ON: Car speed – below 16 km/h (10 MPH)
OFF: Car speed – above 16 km/h (10 MPH)

To intake manifold

To air cleaner

OFF ⬌ ON

Carburetor

Fresh air from air cleaner

Fig. 3.27 Sectional view of altitude compensator (Sec. 36)

1 Altitude compensator
2 Metering orifice
3 Bellows lever
4 Bellows

37 DCH 306 carburettor – dismantling and reassembly

Dismantling and reassembly of the DCH 306 carburettor can be carried out by following the procedure described in Section 24 in conjunction with the exploded view in Fig. 3.28.

38 Emission control systems – general

Three types of emission control systems may be used: a closed type crankcase emission control system, exhaust emission control system and an evaporative emission control system.

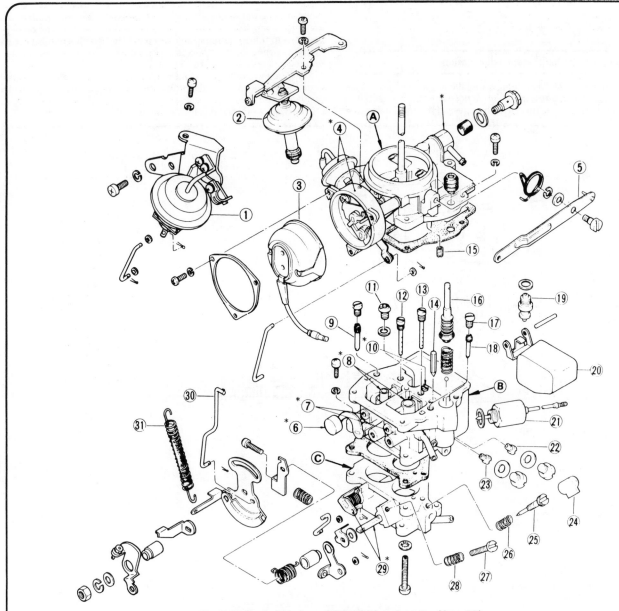

Fig. 3.28 Exploded view of DCH 306 carburettor (Sec. 37)

A	Choke chamber	9	Secondary slow jet	23	Secondary main jet
B	Centre body	10	*Safe orifice	24	Idle limiter cap
C	Throttle chamber	11	Power valve	25	Idle adjust screw
		12	Secondary main air bleed	26	Spring
1	Servo diaphragm of throttle opener	13	Primary main air bleed	27	Throttle adjust screw
2	Dashpot	14	Injector weight	28	Spring
3	Automatic choke cover	15	Primary slow air bleed	29	Primary and secondary throttle valve
4	*Automatic choke body and diaphragm chamber	16	Accelerating pump	30	Accelerating pump rod
5	Accelerating pump lever	17	Plug	31	Throttle return spring
6	*Auxiliary valve	18	Primary slow jet		
7	*Venturi stopper screw	19	Needle valve		**Note: Do not remove the parts marked with an asterisk ***
8	*Primary and secondary small venturi	20	Float		
		21	Anti-dieseling solenoid valve		
		22	Primary main jet		

Periodic inspection and servicing of these systems should be carried out to reduce air pollution by carbon monoxide, hydrocarbons and nitrogen gases. The following should also be checked regularly as they play an important part in reducing harmful emissions:

a) *Valve clearance.*
b) *Ignition timing.*
c) *Contact breaker points.*
d) *Spark plugs.*
e) *Carburettor adjustments.*

39 Crankcase ventilation system – description

This system draws clean air from within the air cleaner and passes it through a mesh flame arrester and into a hose which is connected to the top of the rocker cover. This air is then passed through the engine and into the inlet manifold via an oil separator, hose and regulating valve. This means any crankcase vapours are passed back into the combustion chambers and burnt.

The oil dipstick and filler cap are sealed to prevent the passing of vapours to the atmosphere.

The operation of this system is most efficient under part throttle conditions when there is a relatively high induction vacuum in the inlet manifold so as to allow the regulation valve to open and allow all crankcase vapours to be drawn from the crankcase. Under full throttle conditions the inlet manifold vacuum is not sufficient to draw all vapours from the crankcase and into the inlet manifold. In this case the crankcase ventilation air flow is reversed, with the fumes being drawn into the air cleaner instead of the inlet manifold.

Positioned within the crankcase is a baffle plate and filter mesh which will prevent engine oil from being drawn upwards into the inlet manifold.

Servicing information on this Section will be found in Chapter 1.

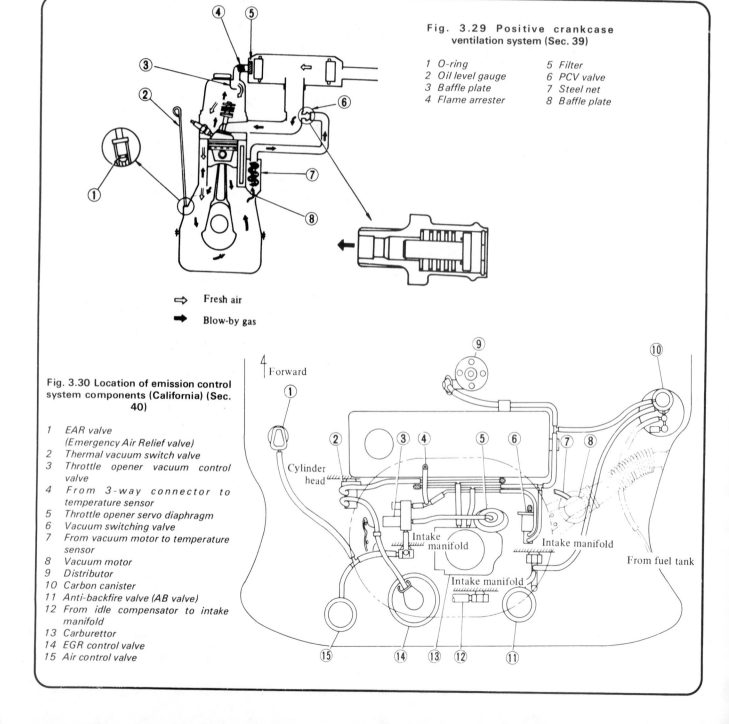

Fig. 3.29 Positive crankcase ventilation system (Sec. 39)

1 *O-ring*	5 *Filter*
2 *Oil level gauge*	6 *PCV valve*
3 *Baffle plate*	7 *Steel net*
4 *Flame arrester*	8 *Baffle plate*

⇨ Fresh air

➡ Blow-by gas

Fig. 3.30 Location of emission control system components (California) (Sec. 40)

1 *EAR valve (Emergency Air Relief valve)*
2 *Thermal vacuum switch valve*
3 *Throttle opener vacuum control valve*
4 *From 3-way connector to temperature sensor*
5 *Throttle opener servo diaphragm*
6 *Vacuum switching valve*
7 *From vacuum motor to temperature sensor*
8 *Vacuum motor*
9 *Distributor*
10 *Carbon canister*
11 *Anti-backfire valve (AB valve)*
12 *From idle compensator to intake manifold*
13 *Carburettor*
14 *EGR control valve*
15 *Air control valve*

40 Exhaust emission control system – general

The exhaust emission control system consists of the following:

a) *Early fuel evaporative system (EFE).*
b) *Air injection system.*
c) *Exhaust gas recirculation (EGR) control system.*
d) *Catalytic converter (California models).*
e) *Throttle opener control device; refer to Section 35.*
f) *Altitude compensator (California models); refer to Section 36.*

41 Early fuel evaporative system (EFE) – description and operation

Refer to Fig. 3.31. A heat control valve, welded to the valve shaft, is fitted in the exhaust manifold. The heat control valve is actuated by the coil spring, thermostat spring and counterweight which are assembled on the valve shaft projecting to the rear of the exhaust manifold. The counterweight is secured to the valve shaft with a key bolt and circlip.

The EFE system is provided with a chamber above a manifold stove mounted between the inlet and exhaust manifolds. During engine warm-up, air-fuel mixture in the carburettor is heated in the chamber by the exhaust gas. This results in improved evaporation of fuel droplets in the mixture and therefore reduces the hydrocarbons (HC) in the exhaust gas especially in cold weather. The exhaust gas flow from the engine is obstructed by the heat control valve in the exhaust manifold and changes direction as shown by the solid lines in Fig. 3.31. The exhaust gas heats the manifold stove.

Open-close operation of the heat control valve is controlled by the counterweight and thermostat spring which is sensitive to the ambient temperature around the exhaust manifold.

The counterweight rotates counterclockwise and stops at the stopper pin mounted on the exhaust manifold while the engine temperature is low. With this condition, the heat control valve is in the fully closed position, obstructing the flow of exhaust gas. As the engine temperature goes up and the ambient temperature becomes high enough to actuate the thermostat spring, the counterweight begins to rotate clockwise, and again comes into contact with the stopper pin. With this condition, the heat control valve is in the fully open position, and exhaust gas passes through the exhaust manifold as shown by the dotted lines in Fig. 3.31, without heating the manifold stove.

42 EFE system – removal, refitting and checking

1   Refer to Fig. 3.32.
2   Remove the circlip and lock bolt, then detach the key, counterweight, thermostat spring and coil spring from the heat control valve shaft.
Note: The heat control valve is welded to the valve shaft and cannot be dismantled.
3   Refitting is the reverse of the removal procedure.
4   For some time after starting the engine in cold weather the counterweight turns counterclockwise until it comes into contact with the stopper pin, then as the engine warms up the counterweight should gradually move down clockwise as the temperature around the exhaust manifold rises. When the heat control valve is in the fully open position, the counterweight moves further clockwise until again coming into contact with the stopper pin.
5   With the engine stopped, visually examine the EFE system for damage or wear. Check the axial clearance between the heat control valve and the exhaust manifold. The clearance should be 0.028 - 0.059 in (0.7 – 1.5 mm). Renew parts as necessary.

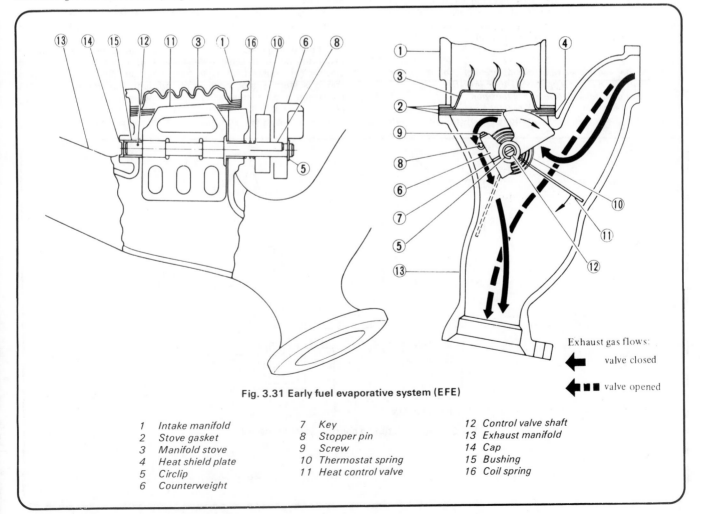

Exhaust gas flows:
⬅ valve closed
⬅▪▪▪ valve opened

Fig. 3.31 Early fuel evaporative system (EFE)

1	Intake manifold	7 Key	12 Control valve shaft
2	Stove gasket	8 Stopper pin	13 Exhaust manifold
3	Manifold stove	9 Screw	14 Cap
4	Heat shield plate	10 Thermostat spring	15 Bushing
5	Circlip	11 Heat control valve	16 Coil spring
6	Counterweight		

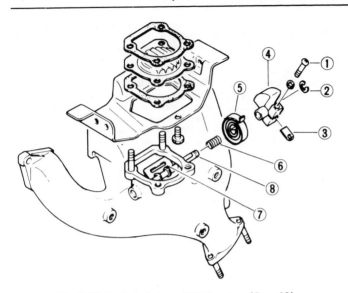

Fig. 3.32 Exploded view of EFE system (Sec. 42)

1 Lock bolt	5 Thermostat spring
2 Circlip	6 Coil spring
3 Key	7 Heat control valve
4 Counterweight	8 Valve shaft

43 Ignition timing control system – description

The ignition timing control system controls the distributor vacuum advance under varying driving conditions to reduce HC and NOx emissions. The system consists of a thermal vacuum valve – TCS, a vacuum switching valve, a top detecting switch and vacuum hoses.

The ignition timing fully advances under all the following four conditions:

    a) Thermal vacuum valve in 'closed' state or coolant temperature below 53° F (12° C) or above 140°F (60° C)
    b) Vacuum switching valve in 'ON' position.
    c) Top detecting switch in 'ON' or transmission in top gear.
    d) Carburettor vacuum port positioned below the throttle valve.

Except under the above conditions ignition timing advances very slightly because of inlet manifold vacuum discharged into the atmosphere.

A schematic diagram of the ignition timing control system is shown in Fig. 3.33.

Thermal vacuum valve – TCS (transmission controlled system)

The thermal vacuum valve – TCS monitors the coolant temperature in order to control the inlet manifold vacuum applied to the distributor vacuum pressure chamber.

44 Ignition timing control system – removal and refitting

1   To remove the thermal vacuum valve – TCS, disconnect the air intake duct at the air cleaner. Remove the vacuum hose, heat shield plate and then the thermal vacuum valve.
2   Disconnect the electrical leads and two vacuum hoses from the vacuum switching valve and then remove the valve.
3   Disconnect the electrical leads from the top detecting switch and remove the switch.
4   Refitting is the reverse of the removal procedure. Fit the thermal vacuum valve – TCS tilted at an angle of 30° and tighten it to 16 lbf ft (2.2 kgf m). Check that there is no coolant leak.

45 Ignition timing control system – checking

1   Ensure that all wiring and hose connections are secure.
2   Connect a timing light. Have an assistant start the engine and run it at approximately 1600 rpm. After the engine is warmed up, disengage the clutch and shift the gear lever through the different gear positions.
3   Check the ignition timing; the system is functioning correctly if the timing, when top gear is selected, is about 10° to 15° further advanced than in the other gear positions.
4   If the timing does not vary at all it is recommended that the car be taken to the local Datsun dealer and have the system checked electronically rather than try to trace the fault; the exhaust emission control system is dependent on the efficient operation of all parts of the system and if a fault occurs it can, in fact, give symptoms of a completely different fault. Without experience of emission control systems and the necessary test equipment, fault tracing is virtually impossible.

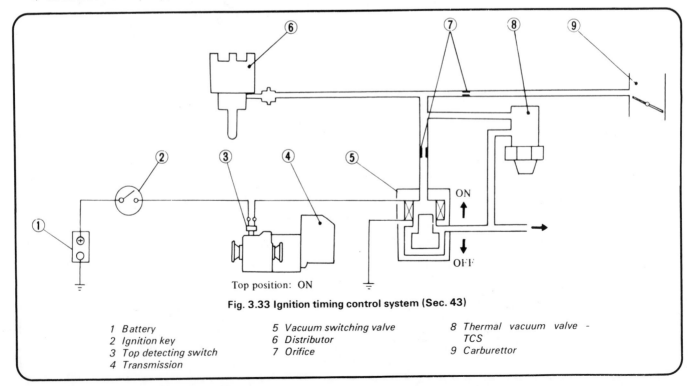

Fig. 3.33 Ignition timing control system (Sec. 43)

1 Battery	5 Vacuum switching valve	8 Thermal vacuum valve – TCS
2 Ignition key	6 Distributor	
3 Top detecting switch	7 Orifice	9 Carburettor
4 Transmission		

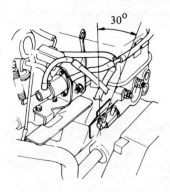

Fig. 3.34 Fitting with thermal vacuum valve (Sec. 44)

46 Air injection system – description

An air injection system is used with other systems to reduce the amount of polluting gases being emitted from the exhaust system to the atmosphere.

The principle of operation is that clean filtered air is injected into the exhaust port of each cylinder where unburnt carbon monoxide and hydrocarbons are present; a chemical reaction is able to take place which will bring the exhaust gases to an acceptable level.

The system comprises an air pump, air injection gallery and nozzle, check valve and anti-backfire valve. Models for California are fitted with a combined air control valve (CAC valve). The California model includes a system which controls injection of secondary air so as to ensure proper function of the catalytic converter, and a system to prevent abnormal temperature rise in the catalytic converter.

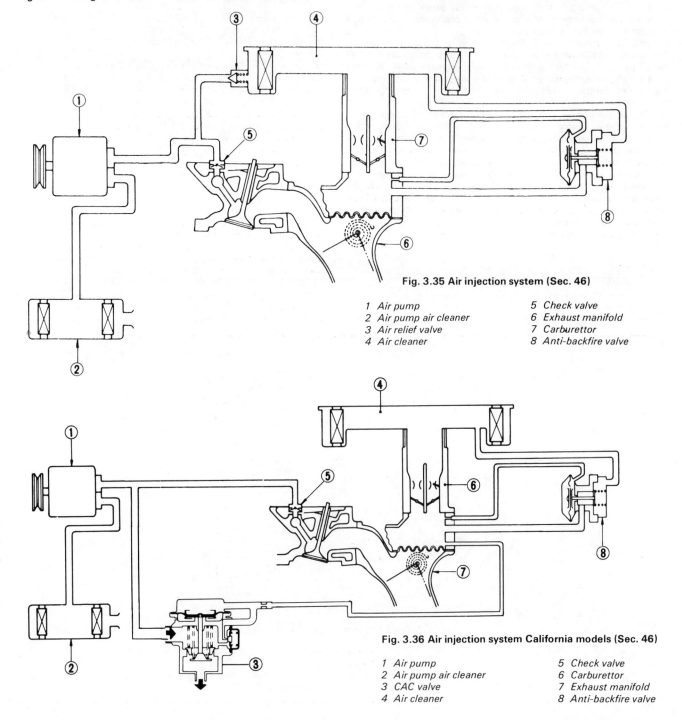

Fig. 3.35 Air injection system (Sec. 46)

1 Air pump	5 Check valve
2 Air pump air cleaner	6 Exhaust manifold
3 Air relief valve	7 Carburettor
4 Air cleaner	8 Anti-backfire valve

Fig. 3.36 Air injection system California models (Sec. 46)

1 Air pump	5 Check valve
2 Air pump air cleaner	6 Carburettor
3 CAC valve	7 Exhaust manifold
4 Air cleaner	8 Anti-backfire valve

Clean air is drawn by the air pump and compressed by the two vanes of the pump and passed to the air injection gallery and nozzle assembly on the exhaust manifold. The air injector nozzle protrudes down at an angle into the exhaust manifold ports, in the area of the exhaust valves. The fresh air is injected into the manifold at these points. The air injection gallery and nozzle assembly is designed to ensure that an even distribution of air, which is drawn through a check valve, is passed to each exhaust manifold port.

To prevent backfiring in the exhaust system when the throttle is closed at high speed, and a coasting condition exists, a special 'anti-backfire' valve is fitted between the inlet manifold and air delivery line. The valve supplies the inlet manifold with a certain amount of air which will burn completely in the combustion chamber and not in the exhaust manifold during these coasting conditions. It is controlled by a small sensor hose which is able to relay high manifold depression to the 'anti-backfire' valve sensing chamber. The valve diaphragm is spring loaded and reacts on this vacuum and is drawn downwards to open the air valve so as to supply air pump pressure to the inlet manifold. The valve will only remain open in proportion to the degree of depression felt by the diaphragm.

The check valve is fitted in the delivery line at the injection gallery. The function of this valve is to prevent any exhaust gases passing into the air pump should the manifold pressure be greater than the pump injection pressure. It is designed to close against the exhaust manifold pressure should the air pump fail as a result, for example, of a broken drive belt.

The air pump relief valve controls the injection of secondary air into the exhaust system when the engine is running at high speed under heavy load conditions. It minimizes exhaust gas temperature rise and power loss resulting from air injection into the exhaust system. It also protects the air pump from excessive back pressure.

The CAC valve controls the amount of secondary air fed from the air pump, according to load conditions, and it discharges the secondary air into the atmosphere to prevent overheating of the catalytic converter. It is operated by inlet manifold vacuum and air pump discharge pressure.

47 Air injection system components – removal and refitting

Air pump air cleaner
1   Remove the windscreen washer tank.
2   Remove the air pump to air pump air cleaner, air hose and the air cleaner bracket.
3   Remove the air pump air cleaner.

Air pump
4   Disconnect the air hoses from the air pump.
5   Loosen the air pump adjusting bar securing bolts and the air pump mounting bolts, then remove the air pump drivebelt.
6   Remove the air pump from the mounting bracket

Anti-backfire valve
7   Disconnect the air hose and vacuum hose from the anti-backfire valve and then remove the valve.

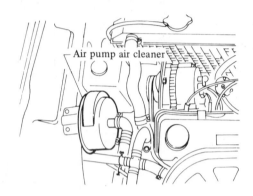

Fig. 3.37 Air pump air cleaner (Sec. 47)

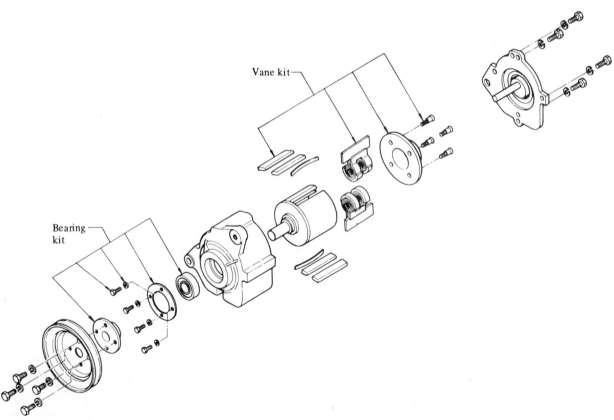

Fig. 3.38 Exploded view of air pump (Sec. 47)

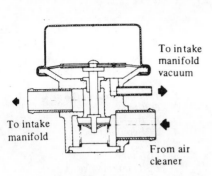

Fig. 3.39 Sectional view of anti-backfire valve (Sec. 47)

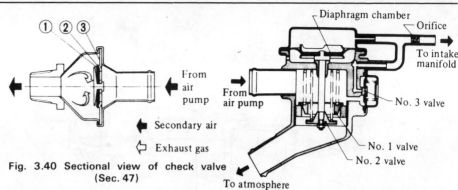

Fig. 3.40 Sectional view of check valve (Sec. 47)

1 Spring   3 Seat
2 Rubber valve

Fig. 3.41 Sectional view of CAC valve (Sec. 47)

Check valve

8 Detach the air supply hose from the check valve and then remove the check valve.

Air pump relief valve (non–California models)

9 Loosen the carburettor air cleaner securing screws and remove the air pump relief valve.

CAC valve (California models)

10 Remove the windscreen washer tank.
11 Disconnect the CAC valve to 3-way connector air hose.
12 Remove the air pump air cleaner bracket and the CAC valve.
13 Refitting of the components is the reverse of the removal procedure. Adjust the air pump belt tension so that when thumb pressure is applied midway between crankshaft pulley and pump there is a deflection of 0.40 – 0.55 in (10 – 14 mm).

---

48 Air injection system – checking

Air injection system hoses

1 Check the air system hoses for loose connections, cracks or deterioration. Tighten or renew as necessary.

Air pump

2 Run the engine until it reaches normal operating temperature and inspect all hoses and hose connections for leaks.
3 Check air pump drivebelt tension; refer to Section 47.
4 Disconnect the air supply hose at the check valve.
5 Disconnect the vacuum hose from the air control valve (California models).
6 Fit a test gauge to the open end of the air supply hose.
7 Fit a tachometer to the engine and with engine speed of 2600 rpm note the pressure on the test gauge; it should be 3.94 in (100 mm) Hg or more.
8 Should the air pressure reading be less than specified disconnect the air supply hose from the anti-backfire valve. Plug the hose and repeat the check at paragraph 7.
9 With the engine speed at 1500 rpm, close the hole of the test gauge with a finger. If leaking air is heard or felt at the relief valve the relief valve is defective and should be renewed.
10 If, after carrying out the above checks, the pump pressure is still below the specified pressure, the air pump assembly should be renewed.

Check valve

11 Start the engine and warm it up to the normal operating temperature.
12 Disconnect the air supply hose from the check valve.
13 Run the engine at approximately 2000 rpm and then let it return to idling.
14 Check for any signs of leaks. If leaks are detected renew the check valve.

Air pump relief valve

15 Disconnect the check valve and air control valve hoses from the air hose connector. Blank off the connector.
16 With the engine running at approximately 3000 rpm place your hand on the air outlet of the air pump relief valve and check for a discharge of air. If no air is felt, renew the air pump relief valve.

Anti-backfire valve

17 With the engine at the normal operating temperature, disconnect the hose from the air cleaner and place a finger near the outlet.
18 Run the engine at approximately 3000 rpm then quickly return it to idling. A suction force should be felt on your finger if the valve is operating normally. If no suction is felt, the anti-backfire valve is defective and must be renewed.

CAC valve (California models)

19 A vacuum pump and test gauge is required for checking the CAC valve and it is recommended that the car is taken to the local Datsun dealer for this check to be carried out.

---

49 Exhaust gas recirculation (EGR) system – description and operation

In the EGR control system, some of the exhaust gas is returned to the combustion chamber to lower the temperature during combustion. This results in a reduction of the nitrogen oxide content in the exhaust emissions.

The system consists of an EGR control valve, a thermal vacuum valve and a back pressure transducer (BPT) valve.

The thermal vacuum valve and BPT valve are located in the vacuum line between the carburettor and the EGR control valve. They operate according to changes in the coolant temperature and exhaust gas pressure respectively.

Exhaust gases are recirculated in the inlet manifold when manifold

Fig. 3.42 Checking the air pump relief valve (Sec. 48)

Fig. 3.43 Checking the anti-backfire valve (Sec. 48)

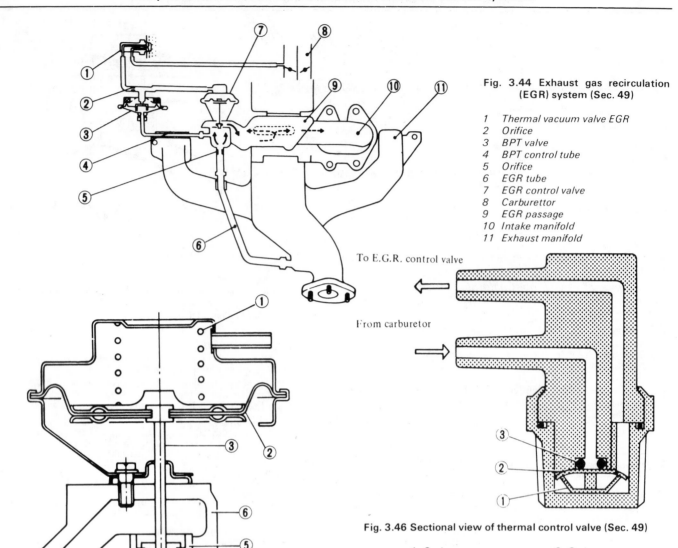

Fig. 3.44 Exhaust gas recirculation
(EGR) system (Sec. 49)

1   Thermal vacuum valve EGR
2   Orifice
3   BPT valve
4   BPT control tube
5   Orifice
6   EGR tube
7   EGR control valve
8   Carburettor
9   EGR passage
10 Intake manifold
11 Exhaust manifold

To E.G.R. control valve

From carburetor

Fig. 3.46 Sectional view of thermal control valve (Sec. 49)

1 Spring   3 O-ring
2 Bi-metal

Fig. 3.45 Sectional view of EGR control valve (Sec. 49)

1 Diaphragm spring   4 Valve
2 Diaphragm   5 Valve seat
3 Valve shaft   6 Valve chamber

pressure is high enough to open the thermal vacuum valve and to close the BPT valve.

The EGR system does not operate under any of the following conditions:

a) Idle or full throttle under heavy load, as the inlet manifold vacuum is insufficient to lift the EGR control   valve.
b) Thermal valve closed: when coolant temperature is below 135°F (57°C), no inlet manifold vacuum being admitted to the EGR control valve vacuum chamber.
c) Exhaust pressure applied to the BPT valve below 0.65 in (17 mm) H_2O. Inlet manifold vacuum not high enough to lift the EGR control valve since the BPT valve vacuum chamber is open to the atmosphere.

The EGR system operates under the following conditions:

a) Engine at other than idling or full throttle.
b) Thermal vacuum valve open or coolant temperature above 135 – 145°F (57 – 63°C).

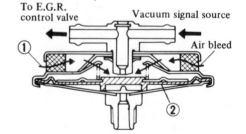

To E.G.R.
control valve   Vacuum signal source

                                              Air bleed

Exhaust pressure

Fig. 3.47 Sectional view of BPT valve (Sec. 49)

1 Air filter   2 Diaphragm

c) Exhaust pressure applied to BPT valve is above 0.65 – 1.47 in (17 – 37 mm) H_2O.

The BPT valve monitors exhaust pressure to actuate the diaphragm controlling inlet manifold vacuum applied to the EGR control valve.

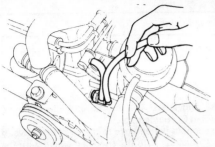

Fig. 3.48 Checking the thermal vacuum valve (Sec. 50)

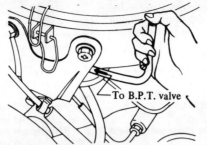

Fig. 3.49 Checking the BPT valve (Sec. 50)

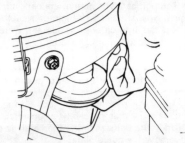

Fig. 3.50 Checking the EGR valve (Sec. 50)

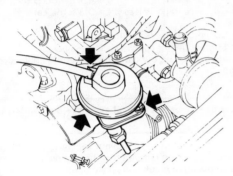

Fig. 3.51 Removing the EGR control valve (Sec. 50)

Fig. 3.52 Cleaning the EGR control valve (Sec. 50)

50 EGR system – checking

1   Inspect the EGR control valve for binding or sticking by moving the diaphragm of the control valve upwards with your finger.

2   With the engine running and the coolant temperature below 104°F (40°C), disconnect the BPT valve side of the vacuum hose connecting the thermal vacuum valve to the BPT valve. Increase the engine speed from idling to 3000 – 3500 rpm and check that the thermal vacuum valve is closed and that carburettor vacuum does not exist at the end of the vacuum hose. If a vacuum is present, renew the thermal vacuum valve.

3   With the engine running and engine coolant temperature above 145°F (63°C) check the thermal vacuum valve, BPT valve and EGR control valve as follows:

a) *Disconnect one end of the hose connecting the thermal vacuum valve to the BPT valve and then increase the engine speed from idling to 3000 – 3500 rpm. Check that the thermal vacuum valve is open and that the carburettor vacuum is present at the end of the vacuum hose. If vacuum is weak or not present at all, renew the thermal vacuum valve.*

b) *Disconnect the EGR control valve to BPT valve vacuum hose at the EGR valve and increase the engine speed from idling to*

3000 – 3500 rpm. Check that the BPT valve operates and that the carburettor vacuum increases at the open end of the hose. Iffif the vacuum does not vary, renew the BPT valve.

c) *Check that the EGR control valve operates when the engine speed i increased from idling to 3000 – 3500 rpm, by placing a finger on the diaphragm of the EGR valve, to check for valve movement. If the diaphragm does not move, remove the EGR control valve and clean it with a brush and compressed air. Recheck and if necessary renew the valve.*

51 Catalytic converter (California models) – description and operation

The catalytic converter, fitted on cars for California, accelerates the chemical reaction of hydrocarbons and carbon monoxide in the exhaust gas and changes them into carbon dioxide (CO_2) and water (H_2O). The air pump supplies the correct amount of air (secondary air) required for this chemical reaction process.

In this system, the secondary air is drawn from the check valve and injected into the exhaust manifold. With this injection of secondary air the hydrocarbons (HC) and carbon monoxide (CO) in the exhaust gas are gradually oxidised with oxygen and converted into carbon dioxide and water.

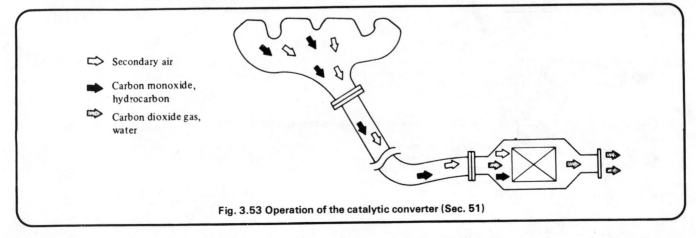

⇨ Secondary air

➡ Carbon monoxide, hydrocarbon

⇨ Carbon dioxide gas, water

Fig. 3.53 Operation of the catalytic converter (Sec. 51)

Through catalytic action, the catalytic converter further cleans the engine exhaust gas by changing residual HC and CO contained in the exhaust gas into carbon dioxide and water before the exhaust gas is discharged into the atmosphere.

52 Catalytic converter – removal and refitting

1   Apply the parking brake, jack up the car and support it on axle stands. Ensure that the catalytic converter is cold.
2   Undo the bolts securing the catalytic converter lower guard plate and remove the guard plate.
3   Undo the attaching bolts and remremove the catalytic converter from the exhaust system.
4   Refitting is the reverse of removal procedure. Tighten the catalytic converter attaching bolts to 19 - 25 lbf ft (2·6 – 3·4 kgf m).

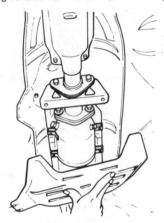

Fig. 3.54 Removing the catalytic converter (Sec. 52)

53 Catalytic converter – checking

The catalytic converter condition can be checked by noting the variation in CO percentage.
1   Visually inspect the catalytic converter for cracks or damage.
2   Remove the air hose from the air check valve and fit a cap on the air check valve.
3   Return to Section 32 and adjust the throttle and idle adjusting screws to obtain the specified CO percentage.
4   Remove the cap and connect the air hose to the air check valve. If the idling speed increases, readjust it to the specified speed with the throttle adjusting screw.
5   Run the engine for about four minutes and 2000 rpm, then at idling speed for one minute and then check the CO percentage.
6   If the CO percentage is less than 0·3% the catalytic converter is serviceable.
7   If the CO percentage is more than 0·3%, check the air injection system and renew the air check valve. Re-check the CO percentage; if it is still more than 0·3% the catalytic converter is defective and must be renewed.

54 Evaporative emission control system – description and checking

1   This system is designed to prevent vapour from the tank escaping into the atmosphere and is fitted to vehicles operating in areas where stringent anti-pollution regulations are enforced.
2   The system comprises a sealed filler cap, a liquid separator, a vent cleaner, a flow guide valve and a limit valve. On models for North America a fuel check valve and carbon canister is also fitted. The canister is filled with activated charcoal to absorb the fuel vapours when the engine is stationary or at idling.
3   The principle of operation is such that with the engine switched off, the vent line, the separator and fuel tank are filled with fuel vapour. When the pressure of this vapour reaches a pre-determined level it

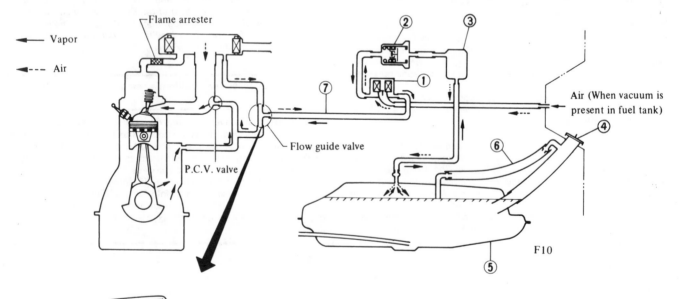

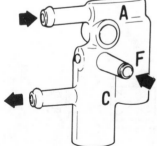

Fig. 3.55 Evaporative emission control system (Sec. 54)

1 Vent cleaner	*5 Fuel tank*
2 Limit valve	*6 Air vent hose*
3 Liquid separator	*7 Vapour line*
4 Positive sealing cap	

actuates a flow guide valve and passes to the crankcase. When the engine is started, the vapour which has accumulated in the crankcase, manifold and air cleaner is drawn into the inlet manifold for combustion within the engine cylinders. When the vapour pressure in the system becomes negative, then the flow guide valve will permit entry of fresh air to the fuel tank from the air cleaner.

4   Periodic preventative maintenance of the system should be carried out. Inspect all hoses and the fuel filler cap for damage or deterioration. Leakage at the fuel cap can only be determined by fitting a three-way connector, cock and manometer (U-shaped glass tube will do) into the vent line as shown (Fig. 3.56).

5   Blow through the cock until the level in the U-tube is approximately at the higher level illustrated. Close the cock and after a period of $2\frac{1}{2}$ minutes check that the level in the U-tube has not dropped more than 0·98 in (25 mm)H_2O. If the levels in the U-tube quickly become equalised, then the filler cap is not sealing correctly.

6   Assuming the previous test has proved satisfactory, again blow into the U-tube and shut the cock. Remove the filler cap quickly when the height of the liquid in the U-tube should immediately drop to zero, failure to do this will indicate a clogged or obstructed vent line.

7   The fuel filler cap incorporates a vacuum release valve and this may be checked by gently sucking with the mouth. A slight resistance accompanied by a click shows the valve is in good condition. Further suction will cause the resistance to cease as soon as the valve clicks.

8   To check the operation of the flow guide valve, apply air pressure from a tyre pump in the following sequence:

a) *Air applied to fuel tank nozzle should emerge freely from crankcase nozzle.*
b) *Air applied to crankcase nozzle should not enter or emerge from any other nozzles.*
c) *Air applied to air cleaner nozzle should emerge from one or both of the other two nozzles.*

Any deviations from the foregoing tests will necessitate renewal of the components as assemblies.

55 Carbon canister – servicing

1   To check the carbon canister purge control valve for leakage, disconnect the hose, in the line between the T-connector and carbon canister.

2   Suck air into the rubber hose running to the vacuum hole in the carbon canister and check that there is no leak.

3   If there is a leak, remove the top cover from the purge control valve and check for a damaged diaphragm. If necessary repair it with a diaphragm kit, consisting of a retainer, diaphragm and spring.

4   The carbon canister filter element should be renewed every 25 000 miles (40 000 km). The element can be removed from the bottom of the canister.

56 Exhaust system – description and servicing

1   All models in the range are fitted with a two section exhaust system. The front downpipe is connected to a socket at the forward end of the silencer and the silencer body and tailpipe are a combined unit. The station wagon is slightly different in that the pipe run is changed and an additional pipe joint is introduced in front of the silencer. On California models a catalytic converter is fitted in the front downpipe and protected by a guard.

2   The system is suspended at the front pipe by brackets bolted to the transmission and at the tailpipe by a flexible support (photo).

3   Examination of the exhaust pipe and silencers at regular intervals is worthwhile as small defects may be repairable when, if left they will almost certainly require renewal of one of the sections of the system. Also, any leaks, apart from the noise factor, may cause poisonous exhaust gases to get inside the car which can be unpleasant, to say the least, even in mild concentrations. Prolonged inhalation could cause sickness and giddiness.

4   As the sleeve connections and clamps are usually very difficult to

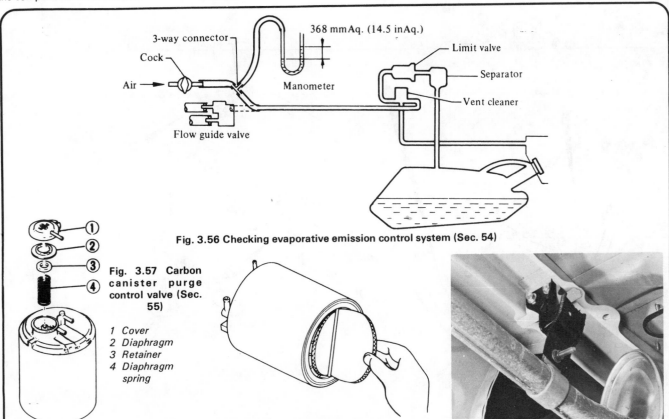

Fig. 3.56 Checking evaporative emission control system (Sec. 54)

Fig. 3.57 Carbon canister purge control valve (Sec. 55)

1 Cover
2 Diaphragm
3 Retainer
4 Diaphragm spring

Fig. 3.58 Renewing the carbon canister filter (Sec. 55)

56.2   Exhaust pipe flexible support

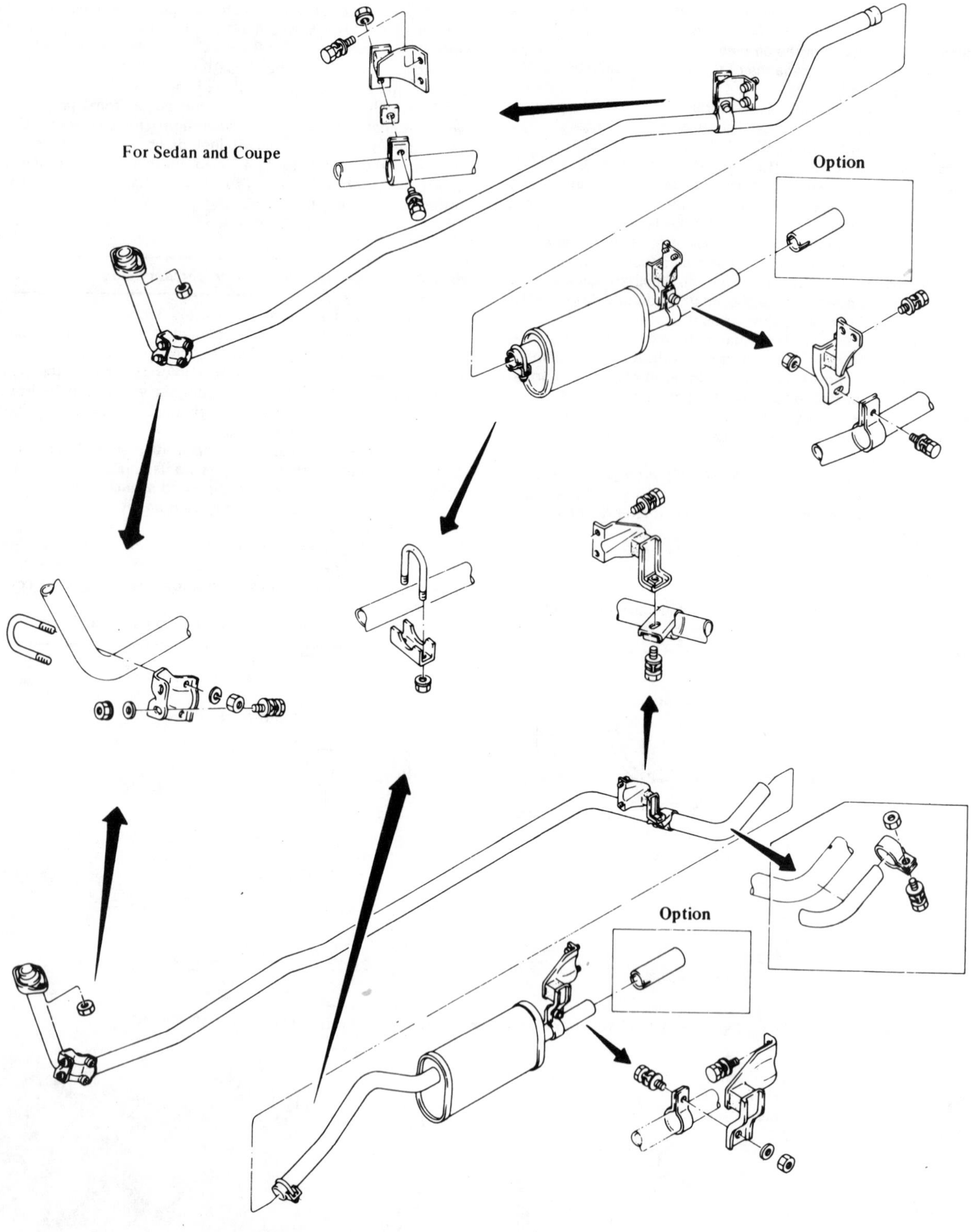

For Sedan and Coupe

Option

Option

For Station Wagon

Fig. 3.59 Exploded view of exhaust system (Sec. 56)

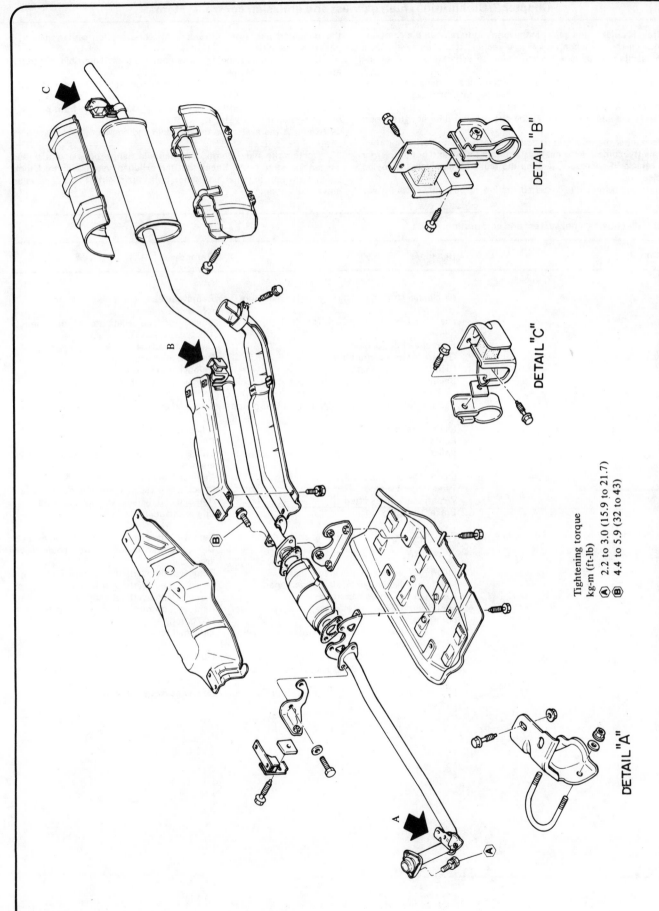

DETAIL "B"

DETAIL "C"

DETAIL "A"

Tightening torque
kg-m (ft-lb)
Ⓐ 2.2 to 3.0 (15.9 to 21.7)
Ⓑ 4.4 to 5.9 (32 to 43)

Fig. 3.60 Exhaust system – California model – Sedan and Hatchback (Sec. 56)

separate it is quicker and easier in the long run to remove the complete system from the car when renewing a section. It can be expensive if another section is damaged when trying to separate a bad section from it.

5   To remove the system first remove the bolts holding the tail pipe bracket to the body. Support the rear silencer on something to prevent cracking or kinking the pipes elsewhere.

6   Disconnect the front pipe at the chassis and differential support brackets.

7   Disconnect the manifold to downpipe connecting flange and then withdraw the complete exhaust system from below and out to the rear of the vehicle. If necessary, jack-up the rear of the vehicle to provide more clearance.

8   When separating the damaged section to be renewed cut away the damaged part from the adjoining good section rather than risk damaging the latter.

9   If small repairs are being carried out it is best, if possible, not to try and pull the sections apart.

10   Refitting should be carried out after connecting the two sections together. De-burr and grease the connecting socket and make sure that the clamp is in good condition and slipped over the front pipe but do not tighten it at this stage.

11   Connect the system to the manifold and connect the rear support strap.

12   Tighten the pipe clamp, the manifold flange nuts and the rear suspension strap bolts. Check that the exhaust system will not knock against any part of the vehicle when deflected slightly in a sideways or upward direction.

57 Fault diagnosis – Fuel system and carburation

Symptom	Reason/s	Remedy
Fuel consumption excessive	Air cleaner choked and dirty giving rich mixture	Remove, clean, renew element and refit air cleaner.
	Fuel leaking from carburettor, fuel pump or fuel lines	Check for and eliminate all fuel leaks. Tighten fuel line union nuts.
	Float chamber flooding	Check and adjust float level.
	Generally worn carburettor	Remove, overhaul or renew.
	Distributor condenser faulty	Remove and fit new unit.
	Balance weights or vacuum advance mechanism in distributor faulty	Remove and overhaul distributor.
	Carburettor incorrectly adjusted, mixture too rich	Tune and adjust carburettor.
	Idling speed too high	Adjust idling speed.
	Contact breaker gap incorrect	Check and reset gap.
	Valve clearances incorrect	Check rocker arm to valve stem clearances and adjust as necessary.
	Incorrectly set spark plugs	Remove, clean and re-gap.
	Tyres under-inflated	Check tyre pressures and inflate if necessary.
	Wrong spark plugs fitted	Remove and replace with correct units.
	Brakes dragging	Check and adjust brakes.
Insufficient fuel delivery or weak mixture due to air leaks	Partially clogged filters in pump and carburettors	Remove and clean filters. Remove and clean out float chamber and needle valve assembly.
	Incorrectly seating valves in fuel pump	Remove, and overhaul or fit new fuel pump.
	Fuel pump diaphragm leaking or damaged	Remove, and overhaul or fit new fuel pump.
	Gasket in fuel pump damaged	Remove, and overhaul or fit new fuel pump.
	Fuel pump valves sticking due to petrol gumming	Remove and overhaul or thoroughly clean fuel pump.
	Too little fuel in fuel tank (prevalent when climbing steep hills)	Refill fuel tank.
	Union joints on pipe connections loose	Tighten joints and check for air leaks.
	Split in fuel pipe on suction side of fuel pump	Examine, locate and repair. Test by pouring oil along joints – bubbles indicate leak.
	Inlet manifold to head or inlet manifold to carburettor gasket leaking	Renew gasket as appropriate.

58 Fault diagnosis – Emission control systems

Symptom	Reason/s	Remedy
High idling speed	Sticking anti-stall dashpot	Adjust or renew dashpot.
	Binding accelerator linkage	Check and rectify as necessary.
	Faulty throttle opener system	Check for loose hose connections. Renew components as necessary.
	Automatic choke faulty	Adjust or renew components as necessary.
Rough or unstable idling speed	Incorrect idle adjustment	Re-adjust idling speed.
	Incorrect automatic choke setting	Adjust.
	Faulty vacuum motor, sensor or hoses of air cleaner	Check for loose hoses. Renew system components as necessary.
	Idle compensator in air cleaner faulty	Renew.
	Defective EGR control valve	Clean or renew.
	Carbon canister purge line hose damaged or disconnected	Re-connect or renew.
Backfire or after-burning	Faulty ATC air cleaner	Check for loose vacuum hoses. Rectify as necessary.
	Defective anti-backfire valve	Renew.
	Defective EGR control valve	Renew.
Air pump noisy	Damaged air pump	Renew air pump.
Lack of power	Altitude compensator setting incorrect (California models)	Correct H–L lever setting.

Chapter 4 Ignition system

Contents

Specifications

Spark plugs
Type:
A10 engine . . . . Hitachi L46W, NGK B5ES or BR5ES
A12 engine . . . . Hitachi L46PW, NGK BP5ES or BPR5ES
A14 engine . . . . Hitachi L46PW–11, NGK BP5ES–11
Spark plug gap:
A10 engine . . . . 0.028 – 0.031 in (0.7 – 0.8 mm)
A12 engine . . . . 0.031 – 0.035 in (0.8 – 0.9 mm)
A14 engine . . . . 0.039 – 0.043 in (1.0 – 1.1 mm)
Firing order . . . . 1 – 3 – 4 – 2

Coil
Make . . . . Hitachi or Hanskin
Type:
A10 and A12 engine . . . . 6CR – 205 or HP5 – 13E11
A14 engine:
Non-California model . . . . C6R – 618 or H5 – 15 – 18
California model . . . . C1T – 16 or STC – 9

Condenser
Capacity . . . . 0.20 to 0.24 mfd

Ignition timing
A10 engine . . . . 8° BTDC at 700 rpm
A12 engine . . . . 7° BTDC at 700 rpm
A14 engine . . . . 10° BTDC and 700 rpm

Distributor, A10 and A12 engines

	A10 engine	A12 engine
Make	Hitachi	Hitachi
Type	D413 – 67	D411 – 89
Direction of rotation	Counterclockwise	Counterclockwise
Dwell angle	49 – 55°	49 – 55°
Contact breaker points gap	0.018 – 0.022 in (0.45 – 0.55 mm)	0.018 – 0.022 in (0.45 – 0.55 mm)

Distributor, A14 engine

	With breaker	Breakerless
Make	Hitachi	Hitachi
Type	D4A5 – 13	D4F5 – 04
Direction of rotation	Counterclockwise	Counterclockwise
Dwell angle	49 – 55°	N/A
Contact breaker points gap	0.018 – 0.022 in (0.45 – 0·55 mm)	N/A
Air gap	N/A	0.008 – 0.16 in (0.2 – 0.4 mm)

Torque wrench settings

	lbf ft	kgf m
Spark plugs	11 – 14	1.5 – 2.0

1 General description

In order that the engine can run correctly it is necessary for an electrical spark to ignite the fuel/air mixture in the combustion chamber at exactly the right moment in relation to engine speed and load. The ignition system is based on feeding low tension (LT) voltage from the battery to the coil where it is converted to high tension (HT) voltage. The high tension voltage is powerful enough to jump the spark plug gap in the cylinders many times a second under high compression pressures, providing that the system is in good condition and that all adjustments are correct.

The ignition system is divided into two circuits. The low tension circuit and the high tension circuit.

The low tension (sometimes known as the primary) circuit consists of the battery lead to the control box, lead to the ignition switch, lead from the ignition switch to the low tension or primary coil windings (terminal SW), and the lead from the low tension coil windings (coil terminal CB) to the contact breaker points and condenser in the distributor.

The high tension circuit consists of the high tension or secondary coil windings, the heavy ignition lead from the centre of the coil to the centre of the distributor cap, the rotor arm, and the spark plug leads and spark plugs.

The system functions in the following manner. Low tension voltage is changed in the coil into high tension voltage by the opening and closing of the contact breaker points in the low tension circuit. High tension voltage is then fed via the carbon brush in the centre of the distributor cap to the rotor arm of the distributor cap, and each time it comes in line with one of the four metal segments in the cap, which are connected to the spark plug leads, the opening and closing of the contact breaker points causes the high tension voltage to build up, jump the gap from the rotor arm to the appropriate metal segment and so via the spark plug lead to the spark plug, where it finally jumps the spark plug gap before going to earth.

The ignition is advanced and retarded automatically, to ensure the spark occurs at just the right instant for the particular load at the prevailing engine speed.

The ignition advance is controlled both mechanically and by a vacuum operated system. The mechanical governor mechanism comprises two lead weights, which move out from the distributor shaft as the engine speed rises due to centrifugal force. As they move outwards they rotate the cam relative to the distributor shaft, and so advance the

spark. The weights are held in position by two light springs and it is the tension of the springs which is largely responsible for correct spark advancement.

The vacuum control consists of a diaphragm, one side of which is connected via a small bore tube to the carburettor, and the other side to the contact breaker plate. Depression in the inlet manifold and carburettor, which varies with engine speed and throttle opening, causes the diaphragm to move, so moving the contact breaker plate, and advancing or retarding the spark. A fine degree of control is achieved by a spring in the vacuum assembly.

On California models a breakerless distributor is fitted and a transistor ignition unit is added to the circuit. In the conventional

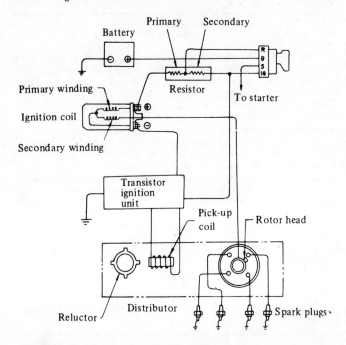

Fig. 4.1. Circuit diagram of breakerless type ignition system

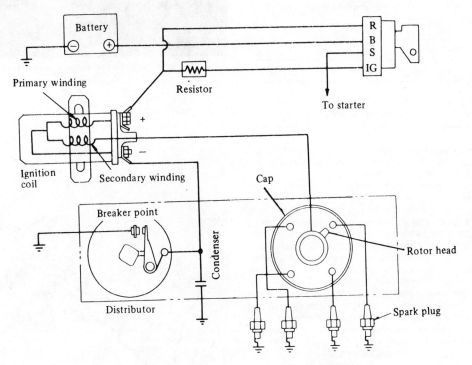

Fig. 4.2. Circuit diagram of ignition system

distributor the ignition timing is detected by the cam and breaker arm; with the breakerless system it is detected by the reluctor on the distributor shaft and the pick-up coil which are fitted in place of the contact breaker.

An electrical signal is generated in the pick-up coil and passed to the transistor ignition unit which breaks the primary circuit and induces a high voltage in the secondary winding of the coil. The transistor unit re-makes the primary circuit again after a fixed time.

The centrifugal and vacuum advance mechanism is of the conventional type.

2   Contact breaker – adjustment

1   To adjust the contact breaker points to the correct gap, first pull off the two clips securing the distributor cap to the distributor body, and lift away the cap (photo). Clean the cap inside and out with a dry cloth. It is unlikely that the four segments will be badly burned or scored, but if they are the cap will have to be renewed.

2   Inspect the carbon brush contact located in the top of the cap – see that it is unbroken and stands proud of the plastic surface.

3   Check the contact spring on the top of the rotor arm. It must be clean and have adequate tension to ensure good contact.

4   Gently prise the contact breaker points open to examine the condition of their faces. If they are rough, pitted, or dirty, it will be necessary to remove them for resurfacing, or for new points to be fitted.

5   Assuming the points are satisfactory, or that they have been cleaned and refitted, measure the gap between the points by turning the engine over until the heel of the breaker arm is on the highest point of the cam.

6   A 0.020 in (0.50 mm) feeler gauge should now just fit between the points (photo). The specifications allow a tolerance of 0.018 in (0.45 mm) to 0.022 in (0.55 mm) but the optimum gap of 0.020 in (0.50 mm) should be set if possible. This will allow the normal changes in the gap due to wear, to still fall in the permitted tolerance.

7   If the gap varies from this amount slacken the contact plate securing screw.

8   Adjust the contact gap by inserting a screwdriver in the notched hole, in the breaker plate. Turn clockwise to increase and anticlockwise to decrease the gap. When the gap is correct tighten the securing screw and check the gap again.

9   Making sure the rotor is in position refit the distributor cap and clip the spring blade retainers into position.

3   Contact breaker points – removal and refitting

1   Slip back the spring clips which secure the distributor cap in position. Remove the distributor cap and lay it to one side, only removing one or two of the HT leads from the plugs, if necessary, to provide greater movement of the cap.

2   Pull the rotor from the distributor shaft.

3   Unscrew the contact breaker securing screws a turn or two and disconnect the LT lead from the contact breaker arm.

4   If necessary, unscrew the securing screws a turn or two more and slide the contact breaker arms sideways to remove them.

5   Inspect the faces of the contact points. If they are only lightly burned or pitted then they may be ground square on an oilstone or by rubbing a carborundum strip between them. Where the points are found to be severely burned or pitted, then they must be renewed and at the same time the cause of the erosion of the points established. This is most likely to be due to poor earth connections from the battery negative lead to body earth or the engine to earth strap. Remove the connecting bolts at these points, scrape the surfaces free from rust and corrosion and tighten the bolts using a star type lock washer. Other screws to check for security are: the baseplate to distributor body securing screws, the condenser securing screw and the distributor body to lockplate bolt. Looseness in any of these could contribute to a poor earth connection. Check the condenser (Section 4).

6   Refitting the contact breaker assembly is a reversal of removal and when fitted, adjust the points gap as described in the preceding Section.

2.1   Distributor with cap removed

2.6   Checking the contact breaker gap with feeler gauge

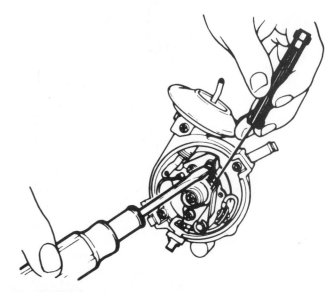
Fig. 4.3. Adjusting the contact breaker gap (Sec. 3)

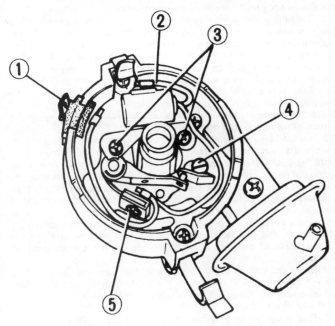

Fig. 4.4. Removing the contact breaker points (Sec. 3)

1 *Primary lead terminal*　　4 *Adjuster*
2 *Earth lead*　　　　　　　 5 *Screw*
3 *Set screw*

4 Condenser (capacitor) – removal, testing and refitting

1 The condenser ensures that with the contact breaker points open, the sparking between them is not excessive as this would cause severe pitting.
2 Testing for an unserviceable condenser may be effected by switching on the ignition and separating the contact points by hand. If this action is accompanied by a blue flash then condenser failure is indicated. Difficult starting, missing of the engine after several miles running and badly pitted points are other indications of a faulty condenser.
3 The surest test is by substitution of a new unit.
4 Removal of the condenser is by means of withdrawing the screw which retains it to the distributor. Refitting is a reversal of this procedure.

5 Distributor – removal and refitting

1 To remove the distributor complete with cap from the engine, begin by pulling the plug lead terminals off the four spark plugs, but first mark the leads so that you know where to refit them. Free the HT lead from the centre of the coil to the centre of the distributor by undoing the lead retaining cap from the coil.
2 Pull off the rubber pipe holding the vacuum tube to the distributor vacuum advance and retard take off pipe.
3 Disconnect the low tension wire from the coil.
4 Undo and remove the bolt which holds the distributor clamp plate to the distributor and lift out the distributor. Mark the relative positions of the distributor and the block to aid replacement if the engine is not going to be turned.
5 To refit the distributor, if the engine has been rotated, turn the engine by hand using a spanner on the crankshaft pulley securing bolt until number one piston is at TDC on compression stroke. This position is indicated when the mark on the crankshaft pulley is in alignment with the 0° mark on the timing indicator on the front cover (compression stroke, both number one cylinder valves closed).
6 When correctly fitted, the distributor rotor should align with the mark on the distributor cap, see Fig. 1.24 of Chapter 1. Due to the meshing action of the distributor and camshaft drive gears however, the distributor driveshaft must be turned back (clockwise) by approximately 30 degrees from the position it will finally take up. Insert the distributor into its crankcase location and check the rotor alignment as shown in Fig. 1.24 (Chapter 1) (photos).
7 Reconnect the HT and LT leads and then time the ignition as described in Section 6.

6 Ignition – timing

1 This operation should be required only if the distributor has been removed for overhaul or the ignition timing otherwise disturbed.
2 Connect a timing light (stroboscope) between number one spark plug and number one HT lead terminal.
3 Mark the indicator on the timing cover at the specified BTDC mark (see the Specifications at the beginning of this Chapter) and the mark on the crankshaft pulley with white paint or chalk. Loosen the distributor clamp plate bolt (Fig. 4.5).
4 Warm up the engine to the normal operating temperature and run it at the specified idling speed (700 rpm).
5 By directing the timing light onto the chalked marks, the mark on the crankshaft pulley will appear to be stationary. Having previously loosened the distributor body clamp plate bolt, the distributor may be rotated slightly until the timing marks are in alignment. Where the limited adjustment provided by the oval clamp plate bolt hole is found to be sufficient to attain the correct alignment, then the distributor

5.6a　Fitting the distributor

5.6b　The rotor should be in this position after fitting the distributor must be removed and re-meshed with the camshaft as described in the preceding Section.

6   When the timing is correct, tighten the distributor body to clamp plate bolt.

7   An alternative method is to turn the engine in the normal direction of rotation until on the compression stroke (felt by placing finger over No 1 plug hole) the timing cover mark and the timing mark on the pulley are aligned (see Specifications for correct timing).

8   Rotate the engine in an anticlockwise direction just past the mark then clockwise so that the timing marks are aligned. The foregoing procedure ensures that all backlash is removed from the timing assembly.

9   Remove the distributor cap and check that the rotor arm points towards No 1 cylinder firing position. Reference to the No 1 HT lead connection in the cap will determine this position.

10 Slacken the distributor clamp plate pinch bolt and rotate the

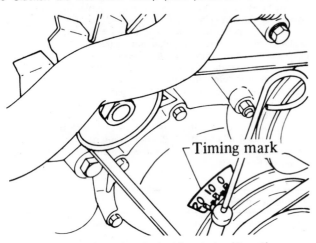

Fig. 4.5. Checking the ignition timing (Sec. 6)

distributor body until the points are just opening.

11 Difficulty is sometimes experienced in determining exactly when the contact breaker points open. This can be ascertained most accurately by connection of a 12 volt bulb in parallel with the contact breaker points (one lead to earth and the other from the distributor low tension terminal). Switch on the ignition and with the distributor adjusting plate securing screw slack turn the distributor until the bulb lights up, indicating that the points have just opened. Retighten the securing screw.

Note: When timing the ignition on the breakerless type system, a stroboscopic timing light **must** be used.

12 It should be noted that to get the very best setting the final adjustment must be made on the road. The distributor can be moved slightly until the best setting is obtained. The amount of wear in the engine, quality of petrol used, and amount of carbon in the combustion chambers, all contribute to make the recommended settings no more than nominal ones. To obtain the best setting under running conditions start the engine and allow to warm up to normal temperature, and then accelerate in top gear from 30-50 mph, listening for heavy pinking. If this occurs, the ignition needs to be retarded slightly until just the faintest trace of pinking can be heard under these operating conditions.

13 Since the ignition advance adjustment enables the firing point to be related correctly in relation to the grade of fuel used, the fullest advantage of any change of fuel will be obtained only by re-adjustment of the ignition settings.

14 Finally, tighten the distributor body to clamp plate bolt.

---

7   Distributor (contact breaker type) – dismantling, inspection and reassembly

---

1   Remove the distributor cap, rotor and contact breaker points as described in Section 3.

2   Remove the vacuum control assembly.

3   Remove the two securing screws and remove the breaker plate.

4   Remove the packing from the top of the cam assembly and unscrew the rotor shaft setscrew. Mark the cam and shaft so that they can be refitted in their original position.

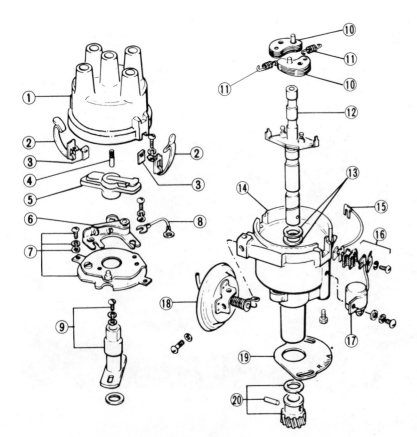

Fig. 4.6. Exploded view of distributor – contact breaker type (Sec. 7)

1	Cap assembly
2	Cap clamp set
3	Dust seal
4	Carbon point assembly
5	Rotor head
6	Contact set
7	Breaker plate
8	Earth wire
9	Cam set assembly
10	Governor weight
11	Governor spring
12	Shaft assembly
13	Thrust washer
14	Housing
15	Lead wire
16	Terminal assembly
17	Condenser assembly
18	Vacuum control assembly
19	Fixing plate
20	Pinion set

5 Using a suitable drift, drive out the pin retaining the drive pinion on the end of the shaft.

6 Withdraw the distributor driveshaft complete with the mechanical advance assembly.

7 If it is necessary to dismantle this assembly, take care not to stretch the springs during removal and mark their respective positions: also mark the governor weights in relation to their pivots so that they can be refitted in their original locations.

8 With the distributor dismantled, clean all the parts and check for wear or damage. Check the distributor cap for signs of tracking, indicated by a thin black line between the segments. If wear in the shaft, bushes, governor weight pivots or holes is excessive, then the distributor should be renewed on an exchange basis.

9 Reassembly is the reverse of dismantling. Align the marks made so that parts are assembled to their original positions. Apply grease to the cam and wick. Adjust the points gap as described in Section 2.

8 Distributor (breakerless type) – dismantling, inspection and reassembly

1 Remove the distributor cap and rotor.

2 Remove the two securing screws and detach the vacuum controller.

3 Unscrew the two retaining screws and remove the pick-up coil assembly.

4 Using two screwdrivers, prise the reluctor from the shaft. Be careful not to distort or damage the teeth of the reluctor. Remove the roll pin.

5 Remove the baseplate setscrews and remove the baseplate assembly.

6 Drive out the roll pin and remove the drive pinion.

7 Remove the rotor shaft and driveshaft assembly.

8 Match mark the rotor shaft and driveshaft. Remove the packing from the top of the rotor shaft and unscrew the rotor shaft retaining screw then separate the rotor shaft from the driveshaft.

9 Mark one governor spring and its bracket. Also mark one of the governor weights and its pivot pin.

10 Carefully unhook and remove the governor springs, then remove the governor weights.

11 Clean all the parts and inspect for wear or damage. If wear in the

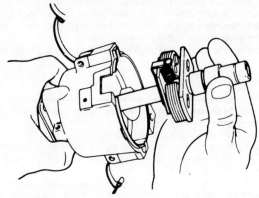

Fig. 4.7. Removing the rotor shaft and driveshaft assembly (Sec. 8)

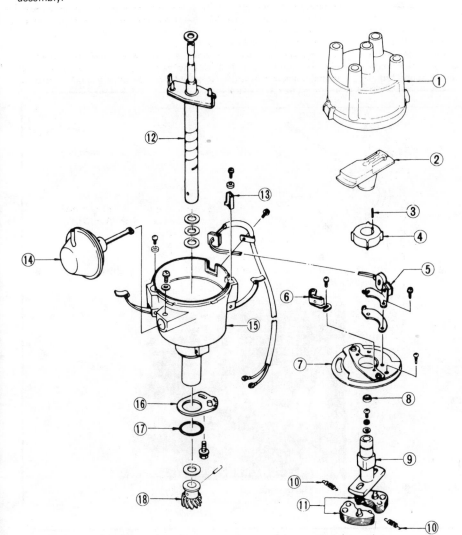

Fig. 4.8. Exploded view of distributor – breakerless type (Sec. 8)

1 Cap assembly
2 Rotor head assembly
3 Roll pin
4 Reluctor
5 Pick-up coil
6 Contactor
7 Breaker plate assembly
8 Packing
9 Rotor shaft
10 Governor spring
11 Governor weight
12 Shaft assembly
13 Cap setter
14 Vacuum controller
15 Housing
16 Fixing plate
17 O-ring
18 Pinion

shaft, bushes, governor weight pivots or holes is excessive, then the distributor should be renewed on an exchange basis. Check the distributor cap for tracking, indicated by a thin black line between the segments. Renew the cap if any sign of tracking is apparent.

12 Reassembly is the reverse of dismantling. Align the match marks so that parts are reassembled in their original positions. If for any reason the contactor was removed from the baseplate, adjust the cam-to-contactor clearance to 0.012 in (0.3 mm), as shown in Fig. 4.9, after refitting the distributor to the engine.

13 Ensure that the reluctor is correctly fitted on the shaft. Always drive in the roll pin with its slit towards the outer end of the shaft (see Fig. 4.10). Be sure to use a new roll pin on reassembly.

14 When fitting the pinion on the shaft, align the punch mark on the pinion with the mark on the distributor housing so that the rotor points to No 1 segment of the distributor cap.

15 Apply grease to the top of the rotor shaft sparingly; do not over grease.

16 Adjust the air gap as described in Section 10.

9 Air gap (breakerless distributor) – adjustment

1 Remove the distributor cap and rotor.

2 Using a feeler gauge measure the gap between the reluctor and pick-up coil, as shown in Fig. 4.11. The standard air gap is 0.008 to 0.016 in (0.2 to 0.4 mm).

3 Adjust, if necessary, by loosening the pick-up coil securing screws and repositioning the pick-up coil to obtain the specified gap. Tighten the pick-up coil securing screws.

4 Refit the rotor and distributor cap.

10 Transistor ignition unit (California models)

1 The transistor ignition unit is located on the right-hand dash side panel in the passenger compartment. It makes and breaks the electric current in the primary circuit of the ignition coil. The component parts of the unit are very reliable; however, should any part be found faulty,

the complete assembly must be renewed.

2 To remove the unit disconnect the battery leads then remove the parcel tray. Disconnect the wiring from the unit, remove the two securing setscrews and lift out the unit.

3 Refitting is the reverse of the removal procedure. Be sure to connect the wiring to the correct terminals, see Fig. 4.12, as failure to do so will damage the unit.

11 Coil – description and polarity

1 High tension current should be negative at the spark plug terminals. To ensure this, check the LT connections to the coil are correctly made (photo).

2 The LT wire from the distributor must connect with the (–) negative terminal on the coil.

3 The coil (+) positive terminal is connected to the ignition/starter switch.

4 An incorrect connection can cause as much as a 60% loss of spark efficiency and can cause rough idling and misfiring at speed.

12 Spark plugs and HT leads

1 The correct functioning of the spark plugs is vital for the correct running and efficiency of the engine. The plugs fitted as standard are listed on the Specification page.

2 At intervals of 6000 miles (10 000 km) the plugs should be removed, examined, cleaned and, if worn excessively, renewed. The condition of the spark plug will also tell much about the overall condition of the engine.

3 If the insulator nose of the spark plug is clean and white, with no deposits, this is indicative of a weak mixture, or too hot a plug (a hot plug transfers heat away from the electrode slowly – a cold plug transfers it away quickly).

4 If the top and insulator nose is covered with hard black looking deposits, then this is indicative that the mixture is too rich. Should the plug be black and oily, then it is likely that the engine is fairly worn, as

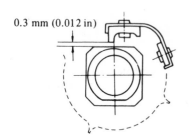

Fig. 4.9. Adjusting the cam-to-contactor clearance (Sec. 3)

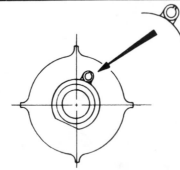

Fig. 4.10. Fitting the pinion retaining roll pin (Sec. 8)

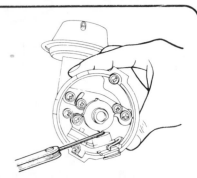

Fig. 4.11. Checking the air gap (Sec. 9)

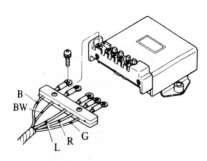

Fig. 4.12. Transistor ignition unit (Sec. 10)

11.1 The ignition coil is located beside the battery

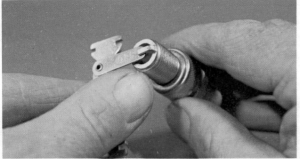

Measuring plug gap. A feeler gauge of the correct size (see ignition system specifications) should have a slight 'drag' when slid between the electrodes. Adjust gap if necessary

Adjusting plug gap. The plug gap is adjusted by bending the earth electrode inwards, or outwards, as necessary until the correct clearance is obtained. Note the use of the correct tool

Normal. Grey-brown deposits, lightly coated core nose. Gap increasing by around 0.001 in (0.025 mm) per 1000 miles (1600 km). Plugs ideally suited to engine, and engine in good condition

Carbon fouling. Dry, black, sooty deposits. Will cause weak spark and eventually misfire. Fault: over-rich fuel mixture. Check: carburettor mixture settings, float level and jet sizes; choke operation and cleanliness of air filter. Plugs can be re-used after cleaning

Oil fouling. Wet, oily deposits. Will cause weak spark and eventually misfire. Fault: worn bores/piston rings or valve guides; sometimes occurs (temporarily) during running-in period. Plugs can be re-used after thorough cleaning

Overheating. Electrodes have glazed appearance, core nose very white – few deposits. Fault: plug overheating. Check: plug value, ignition timing, fuel octane rating (too low) and fuel mixture (too weak). Discard plugs and cure fault immediately

Electrode damage. Electrodes burned away; core nose has burned, glazed appearance. Fault: pre-ignition. Check: as for 'Overheating' but may be more severe. Discard plugs and remedy fault before piston or valve damage occurs

Split core nose (may appear initially as a crack). Damage is self-evident, but cracks will only show after cleaning. Fault: pre-ignition or wrong gap-setting technique. Check: ignition timing, cooling system, fuel octane rating (too low) and fuel mixture (too weak). Discard plugs, rectify fault immediately

well as the mixture being too rich.

5   If the insulator nose is covered with light tan to greyish brown deposits, then the mixture is correct and it is likely that the engine is in good condition.

6   If there are any traces of long brown tapering strains on the outside of the white portion of the plug, then the plug will have to be renewed, as this shows that there is a faulty joint between the plug body and the insulator, and compression is being allowed to leak away.

7   Plugs should be cleaned by a sand blasting machine, which will free them from carbon more thoroughly than cleaning by hand. The machine will also test the condition of the plugs under compression. Any plug that fails to spark at the recommended pressure should be renewed.

8   The spark plug gap is of considerable importance, as, if it is too large or too small the size of the spark and its efficiency will be seriously impaired. The spark plug gap should be set to the specified dimension (refer to the Specifications at the beginning of this Chapter) for the best results.

9   To set it, measure the gap with a feeler gauge, and then bend open, or close, the outer plug electrode until the correct gap is achieved. The centre electrode should never be bent as this may crack the insulation and cause plug failure, if nothing worse.

10 When refitting the plugs, remember to use new plug washers and replace the leads from the distributor in the correct firing order 1, 3, 4, 2; No 1 cylinder being the one nearest the left side of the vehicle, looking forward.

11 The plug leads require no routine attention other than being kept clean and wiped over regularly.

13 Ignition system – fault diagnosis (general)

Failure of the ignition system will either be due to faults in the HT or LT circuits. Initial checks should be made by observing the security of spark plug terminals, Lucar type terminals, coil and battery connection. More detailed investigation and the explanation and remedial action in respect of symptoms of ignition malfunction are described in the next Section.

14 Ignition system – fault diagnosis

Engine fails to start

1   If the engine fails to start and the car was running normally when it was last used, first check there is fuel in the fuel tank. If the engine turns over normally on the starter motor and the battery is evidently well charged, then the fault may be in either the high or low tension circuits. First check the HT circuit. **Note:** If the battery is known to be fully charged, the ignition light comes on, and the starter motor fails to turn the engine **check the tightness of the leads on the battery terminals** and also the secureness of the earth lead to its **connection to the body.** It is quite common for the leads to have worked loose, even if they look and feel secure. If one of the battery terminal posts gets very hot when trying to work the starter motor this is a sure indication of a faulty connection to that terminal.

2   One of the commonest reasons for bad starting is wet or damp spark plug leads and distributor. Remove the distributor cap. If condensation is visible internally, dry the cap with a rag and also wipe over the leads. Replace the cap.

3   If the engine still fails to start, check that current is reaching the plugs, by disconnecting each plug lead in turn at the spark plug end, and hold the end of the cable about $\frac{3}{16}$ in (5 mm) away from the cylinder block. Spin the engine on the starter motor.

4   Sparking between the end of the cable and the block should be fairly strong with a regular blue spark. (Hold the lead with rubber to avoid electric shocks.) If current is reaching the plugs, then remove them and clean and regap them. The engine should now start.

5   If there is no spark at the plug leads take off the HT lead from the centre of the distributor cap and hold it to the block as before. Spin the engine on the starter once more. A rapid succession of blue sparks between the end of the lead and the block indicate that the coil is in order and that the distributor cap is cracked, the rotor arm faulty, or

the carbon brush in the top of the distributor cap is not making good contact with the spring on the rotor arm. Possibly the points are in bad condition. Clean and reset them as described in this Chapter.

6   If there are no sparks from the end of the lead from the coil, check the connections at the coil end of the lead. If it is in order start checking the low tension circuit.

7   Use a 12v voltmeter or a 12v bulb and two lengths of wire. With the ignition switch on and the points open test between the low tension wire to the coil (it is marked SW or +) and earth. No reading indicates a break in the supply from the ignition switch. Check the connections at the switch to see if any are loose. Refit them and the engine should run. A reading shows a faulty coil or condenser, or broken lead between the coil and the distributor.

8   Take the condenser wire off the points and earth. If there now is a reading, then the fault is in the condenser. Fit a new one and the fault is cleared.

9   With no reading from the moving point to earth, take a reading between earth and the CB or – terminal of the coil. A reading here shows a broken wire which will need to be replaced between the coil and distributor. No reading confirms that the coil has failed and must be replaced, after which the engine will run once more. Remember to refit the condenser wire to the points assembly. For these tests it is sufficient to separate the points with a piece of dry paper while testing with the points open.

Engine misfires

10 If the engine misfires regularly run it at a fast idling speed. Pull off each of the plug caps in turn and listen to the note of the engine. Hold the plug cap in a dry cloth or with a rubber glove as additional protection against a shock from the HT supply.

11 No difference in engine running will be noticed when the lead from the defective circuit is removed. Removing the lead from one of the good cylinders will accentuate the misfire.

12 Remove the plug lead from the end of the defective plug and hold it about $\frac{3}{16}$ in (4.7 mm) away from the block. Restart the engine. If the sparking is fairly strong and regular the fault must lie in the spark plug.

13 The plug may be loose, the insulation may be cracked, or the points may have burnt away giving too wide a gap for the spark to jump. Worse still, one of the points may have broken off. Either renew the plug, or clean it, reset the gap, and then test it.

14 If there is no spark at the end of the plug lead, or if it is weak and intermittent, check the ignition lead from the distributor to the plug. If the insulation is cracked or perished, renew the lead. Check the connections at the distributor cap.

15 If there is still no spark, examine the distributor cap carefully running between two or more electrodes, or between an electrode and some other part of the distributor. These lines are paths which now conduct electricity across the cap thus letting it run to earth. The only answer is a new distributor cap.

16 Apart from the ignition timing being incorrect, other causes of misfiring have already been dealt with under the section dealing with the failure of engine to start. To recap – these are that:

a) *The coil may be faulty giving an intermittent misfire.*
b) *There may be a damaged wire or loose connection in the low tension circuit.*
c) *The condenser may be short circuiting.*
d) *There may be a mechanical fault in the distributor (broken driving spindle or contact breaker spring).*

17 If the ignition timing is too far retarded, it should be noted that the engine will tend to overheat, and there will be a quite noticeable drop in power. If the engine is overheating and the power is down, and the ignition timing is correct, then the carburettor should be checked, as it is likely that this is where the fault lies.

15 Breakerless ignition system (California models) – fault diagnosis

Diagnosing faults in the HT circuit of the breakerless ignition system is the same as described in Section 14. For checking the LT circuit special test equipment is required and this job should be done by your local Datsun dealer.

Chapter 5 Clutch

Contents

Specifications

Clutch type	Single, dry disc, diaphragm spring	

Clutch disc

	A10	**A12 and A14**
Facing size		
Outer dia. x inner dia. x thickness	6.30 x 4.33 x 0.138 in	7.48 x 5,19 x 0.138 in
	(160 x 110 x 3.5 mm)	(190 x 132 x 3.5 mm)
Thickness of disc assembly (compressed)	0.287 – 0.303 in (7.3 – 7.7 mm)	
Number of damper springs	6	
Min allowable depth of rivet below facing surface	0.012 in (0.(0.3 mm)	
Runout limit of facing	0.020 in (0.5 mm)	

Clutch pedal

Pedal height:		
Left-hand drive model	6.65 – 6.89 in (169 – 175 mm)	
Right-hand drive model	6.50 – 6.73 in (165 – 171 mm)	
Free play:		
Left-hand drive model	0.236 – 0.551 in (6 – 14 mm)	
Right-hand drive model	1.220 (31 mm)	

Torque wrench setting

	lbf ft	kgf m
Clutch assembly to flywheel bolt	7.2	1.0

1 General description

All vehicles are fitted with a diaphragm spring, single plate clutch. The unit comprises a pressed steel cover, pressure plate and diaphragm spring.

The clutch disc is free to slide along the splined primary drive gear assembly, and is held in position between the cover and the pressure plate by the pressure of the pressure plate spring. Friction lining material is riveted to the clutch disc and it has a spring cushioned hub to absorb transmission shocks and to help ensure a smooth take-off.

The clutch disc and cover can be removed or replaced without the need to dismantle any other components, and has one or two features that distinguish it from more conventional clutches. These are: the relative assembled location of clutch cover and disc, the selection of a pushrod that operates the clutch through the primary drive gear, and, finally, the unusual type of release bearing mechanism.

The clutch is either actuated hydraulically (LHD vehicles) or mechanically by a cable (RHD vehicles). Where the clutch is actuated hydraulically, the pendant clutch pedal is connected to the clutch master cylinder and hydraulic fluid reservoir by a short pushrod. The master cylinder and hydraulic reservoir are mounted on the engine side of the bulkhead in front of the driver.

Depressing the clutch pedal moves the piston in the master cylinder forwards, so forcing hydraulic fluid through the clutch hydraulic pipe to the slave cylinder.

The piston in the slave cylinder moves forward on the entry of the fluid and actuates the clutch release arm by means of a short pushrod.

The release arm pushes the release bearing forwards to bear against the pressure plate through a pushrod that runs through the centre of the primary drive gear assembly, so moving the centre of the diaphragm spring inwards, and disengaging the pressure plate from the clutch disc.

When the clutch pedal is released the diaphragm spring forces the pressure plate into contact with the high friction linings on the clutch disc. The clutch disc is now firmly sandwiched between the pressure plate and the covers so the drive is taken up.

As the friction linings on the clutch disc wear, the pressure plate automatically moves closer to the disc to compensate. There is then no need to periodically adjust the clutch.

Where a cable type clutch actuating mechanism is fitted, the principle of operation is similar to that already described for the hydraulic type but correct adjustment must at all times be maintained, as described in Section 3 of this Chapter.

2 Hydraulically operated clutch – adjustment

1   Locate the clutch pedal stop on the pedal bracket and adjust it to give a floor to clutch pedal top surface dimension of 6.6 to 6.9 in (169 to 175 mm). Secure the pedal stop locknut. Now check the adjustment of the slave cylinder rod.

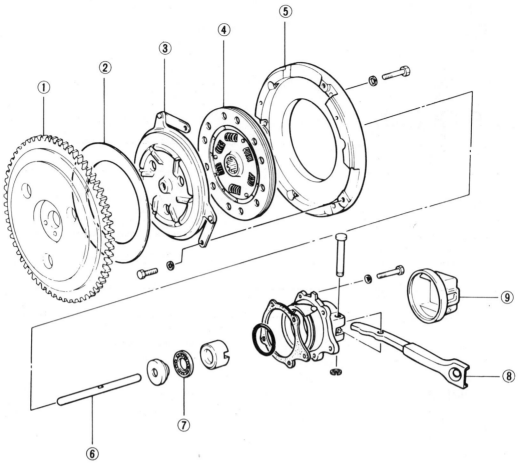

Fig. 5.1. Exploded view of clutch assembly

1 Flywheel
2 Diaphragm spring
3 Pressure plate

4 Clutch disc
5 Clutch cover
6 Pushrod

7 Release bearing
8 Withdrawal lever
9 Rubber cover

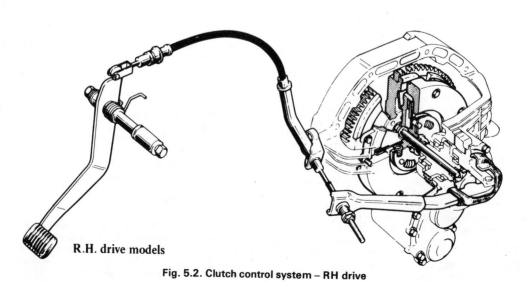

R.H. drive models

Fig. 5.2. Clutch control system – RH drive

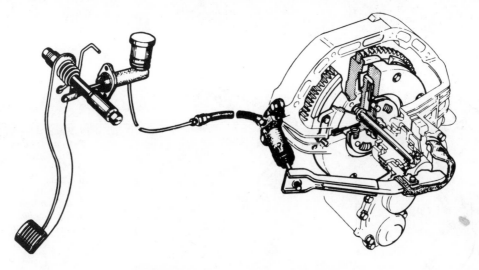

Fig. 5.3. Clutch control system – LH drive

2   Loosen the locknut on the slave cylinder rod, then turn the adjusting nut so that it moves further from the slave cylinder. Continue rotating the nut until the release lever is pressed against the release bearing and any free-movement has been eliminated.

3   Now turn the adjusting nut back 1¼ turns and secure it in position with the locknut. This adjustment will give the correct clearance between the release lever and the release bearing.

4   Finally, check the stroke and free-play of the pedal in accordance with the Specifications. Adjust the free play by slackening the pushrod yoke locknut and rotate the pushrod until the correct clearance exists at the clevis pin. Tighten the locknut.

3   Cable operated clutch – adjustment

1   Adjust the clutch pedal arm stop to provide a floor to the surface of the pedal pad dimension of between 6.5 and 6.7 in (165 and 171 mm). Tighten the stop locknut.

2   Tighten the adjusting nut at the end of the withdrawal lever until pedal free play is eliminated, then depress the clutch pedal fully several times.

3   Refer to Fig. 5.5 and loosen adjusting nut. Adjust clearance between adjusting nut and ball seat to 0.472 in (12 mm). Tighten the locknut when the correct clearance has been obtained.

4   The free play at the pedal pad should be 1.122 in (31 mm).

4   Clutch pedal (hydraulic) – removal and refitting

1   Detach the return spring from the pedal arm (Figs. 5.6 and 5.7).

2   Loosen the locknut on the master cylinder pushrod and screw the rod out of the clevis fork on the pedal arm.

3   Unscrew and remove the nut and lockwasher from the pedal cross-shaft and then slide the pedal arm from the shaft.

4   Refitting is a reversal of removal but always check the adjustment, as described in Section 2.

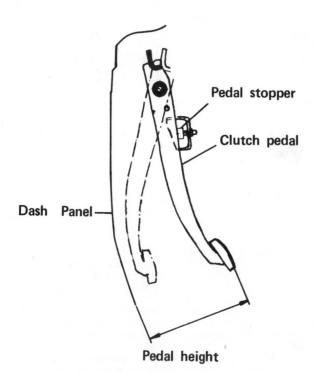

Fig. 5.4. Adjusting the clutch pedal height (Sec. 2)

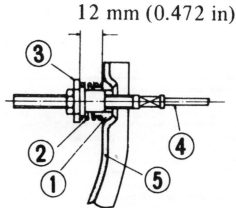

Fig. 5.5. Clutch free play adjustment (cable actuation) (Sec. 3 and 5)

1 Ball seat	4 Clutch cable
2 Preload spring	5 Withdrawal lever
3 Adjusting nut	

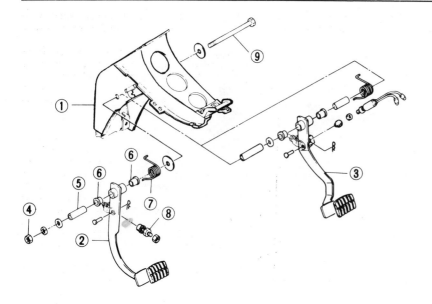

Fig. 5.6. Clutch pedal assembly – LH
          drive (Sec. 4 and 5)

1 Pedal bracket
2 Clutch pedal
3 Brake pedal
4 Nut
5 Spacer
6 Bushing
7 Return spring
8 Stopper bolt
9 Fulcrum shaft

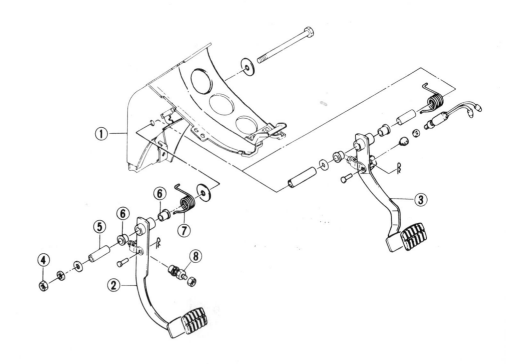

Fig. 5.7. Clutch pedal assembly – RH
          drive (Secs. 4 and 5)

1 Pedal bracket
2 Clutch pedal
3 Brake pedal
4 Nut
5 Spacer
6 Bushing
7 Return spring
8 Stopper bolt

5 Clutch pedal and cable – removal and refitting

1 Remove the locknut and the adjusting nut and then detach the
clutch cable from the withdrawal lever (see Fig. 5.5). Collect the dome,
spring and spring bearer from the end of the cable.
2 Remove the clutch pedal return spring. Take out the bolt which
secures the clutch and brake pedals. Pull the clutch control cable out
from the upper portion of the pedal rod and detach the clutch pedal.
3 Check the pedal and associated parts for wear and damage.
Ensure that the cable has not become stretched. Renew defective
parts.
4 Refitting is the reverse of the removal procedure. Apply grease to
the clutch pedal shaft. Check the clutch adjustment as described in
Section 3.
5 When reconnecting the clutch cable to the release lever, remember that the dome abuts the face of the lever and is tensioned by the
spring on the bearer.

6 Hydraulic system – bleeding

1 The need for bleeding the cylinders and fluid line arises when air
gets into the system, because of a joint or seal leaking or when any
part of the system is being dismantled. Air also gets into the system if
the level in the fluid reservoir becomes too low. Bleeding is the process
of excluding air from the system.
2 Make sure the reservoir is filled and obtain a piece of $\frac{3}{16}$ in (4.76
mm) bore diameter rubber tube about 2 to 3 feet long and a clean
glass jar. A small quantity of fresh, clean hydraulic fluid is also
necessary.
3 Detach the cap (if fitted) on the bleed nipple at the clutch slave
cylinder and clean up the nipple and surrounding area. Unscrew the
nipple $\frac{3}{4}$ turn and fit the tube over it. Put about $\frac{1}{2}$ in (13 mm) of fluid in
the jar and put the other end of the pipe in it. The jar can be placed on
the ground under the car.
4 The clutch pedal should then be depressed quickly and released

slowly until no more air bubbles come from the pipe. Quick pedal action carries the air along rather than leaving it behind. Keep the reservoir topped-up.

5   When the air bubbles stop, tighten the nipple at the end of a down stroke.

6   Check that the operation of the clutch is satisfactory. Even though there may be no exterior leaks it is possible that the movement of the pushrod from the clutch cylinder is inadequate because fluid is leaking internally past the seals in the master cylinder. If this is the case, it is best to renew all seals in both cylinders.

7   Always use clean hydraulic fluid which has been stored in an airtight container and has remained unshaken for the preceding 24 hours.

7   Master cylinder – removal, servicing and reassembly

1   The master cylinder and fluid reservoir are a single unit and indication of something wrong with it is if the pedal travels down without operating the clutch efficiently (assuming, of course, that the system has been bled and there are no leaks).

2   To remove the unit from the car first seal the cap with a piece of film to reduce fluid wastage whilst dismantling the pipes. Alternatively, the fluid may be pumped out from the clutch cylinder bleed nipple by opening the nipple and depressing the pedal several times.

3   From inside the car remove the locknut which attaches the pushrod assembly to the clevis, and disconnect the pushrod.

4   Disconnect the fluid line which runs between the master cylinder and the slave (operating) cylinder.

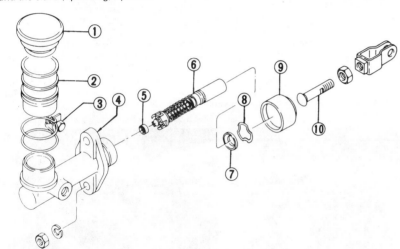

5   Unscrew and remove the two bolts which secure the master cylinder to the engine rear bulkhead.

6   Withdraw the master cylinder from the bulkhead.

7   Peel back the rubber dust cover from the end of the master cylinder, remove the circlip and inlet valve stop pin.

8   The internal components may then be ejected, either by tapping the end of the cylinder on a piece of wood or by applying air pressure from a tyre pump at the fluid outlet pipe.

9   Clean all components in clean hydraulic fluid or methylated spirit. Examine the internal surfaces of the master cylinder for scoring or bright areas; also the surface of the piston. Where these are apparent, renew the complete master cylinder assembly.

10 Discard all rubber seals, making sketches if necessary before removing them from the piston so that the new seals will be fitted with their lips and chamfers the correct way round.

11 Obtain a repair kit and examine all the items supplied for damage, particularly the seals for cuts or deterioration in storage.

12 Commence reassembling by dipping the new seals in clean hydraulic fluid and fitting them to the piston, using only the fingers to manipulate them into their grooves. Ensure that they are correctly located with regard to the contour as originally fitted.

13 Use all the new items supplied in the repair kit and reassemble in the reverse order to dismantling, lubricating each component in clean hydraulic fluid before it is fitted into the master cylinder.

14 When all the internal components have been installed, fit a new circlip and screw in the inlet valve stop pin.

15 Bolt the master cylinder to the engine rear bulkhead. Once the

master cylinder has been installed and the pushrod connected to the clutch pedal arm then the adjustment described in Section 2 must be carried out.

16 Reconnect the fluid pipe between the master and slave cylinders, fill the reservoir with clean hydraulic fluid and bleed the system. Probe the reservoir vent hole in the cap to ensure that it is not clogged.

Note: Two makes of master cylinder are available, Nabco and Tokico. The repair kits or component parts are not interchangeable, so be sure to use the correct replacement parts.

8   Slave (operating) cylinder – removal, servicing and reassembly

1   Disconnect the fluid pipe from the slave cylinder. To do this, uncouple the union at the master cylinder and plug the union outlet to prevent loss of fluid. Now unscrew the flexible pipe from the slave cylinder, taking care not to twist the pipe, and retaining the sealing washer.

2   Remove the adjusting nut and locknut from the slave cylinder operating rod and then disconnect the operating rod from the clutch release lever.

3   Unscrew and remove the slave cylinder to clutch housing securing bolts and lift the cylinder away.

4   Peel back the dust cover and remove the circlip.

5   Eject the internal components of the slave cylinder either by tapping the end of the unit on a piece of wood or by applying air pressure from a tyre pump at the fluid hose connection.

6   Wash all components in clean hydraulic fluid or methylated spirit.

Fig: 5.8. Exploded view of clutch master cylinder (Sec. 7)

1   Reservoir cap
2   Reservoir
3   Reservoir band
4   Cylinder body
5   Supply valve
6   Piston assembly
7   Piston stopper plate
8   Piston stopper ring
9   Boot
10 Push rod

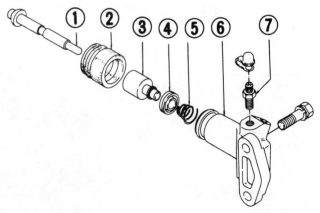

Fig. 5.9. Exploded view of clutch slave (operating) cylinder

1 Push rod	5 Piston spring
2 Dust cover	6 Cylinder body
3 Piston	7 Bleeder screw
4 Piston cup	

Discard the seals and examine the piston and cylinder bore surfaces for scoring or bright areas. Where these are evident, renew the complete assembly.

7 Obtain a repair kit and examine all the items supplied for damage, particularly the seals for cuts or deterioration in storage.

8 Commence reassembling by dipping the new seals in clean hydraulic fluid and fitting them to the piston, using the fingers only to manipulate them.

9 Use all the new items supplied in the repair kit and reassemble in reverse order to dismantling, lubricating each component in clean hydraulic fluid before it is fitted into the cylinder bore.

10 When all the internal components have been installed, fit a new circlip and the new rubber dust cover supplied with the repair kit.

11 Refit the slave cylinder to the clutch housing, reconnect the fluid supply pipe and the operating pushrod to the clutch release lever.

12 Bleed the hydraulic system, as described in Section 6.

13 Adjust the operating rod nut, as described in Section 2.

Note: Two makes of operating cylinder are available, Nabco and Tokico. The repair kits or component parts are not interchangeable, so be sure to use the correct replacement parts.

9 Clutch assembly – removal

1 Disconnect the battery leads.

2 Detach the clutch control cable, or slave cylinder operating rod, from the clutch withdrawal lever. This will depend on whether it is a LHD or RHD model.

3 Remove the inspection cover from the clutch housing (photo). Remove the six bolts which secure the clutch cover. These bolts should be slackened off gradually and evenly, after first marking the relative positions of the clutch and flywheel (photo).

4 Disconnect the clutch operating lever by first pulling off the rubber shroud, and then removing the spring clip that secures the lever pivot pin. The operation lever can be lifted away when the pin is pulled out (photo).

5 Remove the six bolts on the bearing housing, and withdraw the primary drive gear assembly through the opening on the right-hand side wheel housing. The opening can be revealed by removing the three screws that secure the cover on the opening, from inside the wheel housing.

6 Lift the clutch cover and disc out through the inspection opening in the upper part of the clutch housing.

7 Remove the strap bolts which secure the pressure plate to the cover (photo), and take off the clutch disc (see Fig. 5.11). Note that the relative position of pressure plate and cover are indicated on the edge of the assembly either by white paint spots or by an arrow and raised pointer.

10 Clutch assembly – inspection and renovation

1 Since the clutch on this vehicle is so easily removed, there is no reason to delay when renewal becomes necessary. The only positive indication that something needs doing is when the clutch starts to slip or when squealing noises on engagement indicate that the friction lining has worn down to the rivets. In such instances it can only be hoped that the friction surfaces on the cover and pressure plate have not been badly worn or scored. A clutch will wear according to the way in which it is used. Much intentional slipping of the clutch while driving – rather than the correct selection of gears – will accelerate wear.

2 Examine the surfaces of the pressure plate and cover for signs of scoring. If this is only light it may be left, but if very deep the pressure plate and cover assembly will have to be renewed as a unit because they are a balanced assembly.

3 The friction plate lining surfaces should be at least 0.012 in (0.3 mm) above the rivets, otherwise the disc is not worth putting back. If the lining material shows signs of breaking up or black areas where oil contamination has occurred it should also be renewed. If facilities are readily available for obtaining and fitting new friction pads to the existing disc, this may be done, but the saving is relatively small compared with obtaining a complete new disc assembly, which ensures that the shock absorbing springs and the splined hub are renewed also. An allowance is usually given for exchange units.

9.3a Removing the inspection cover from the clutch housing

9.3b Slacken off the securing bolts evenly

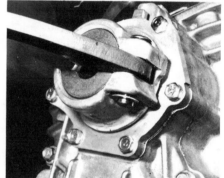
9.4 Clutch withdrawal lever pivot pin

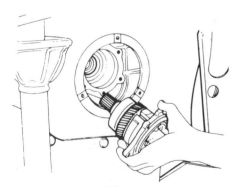
Fig. 5.10. Removing the primary drive gear assembly (Sec. 9)

9.7 Remove the stop bolts securing the pressure plate to the cover

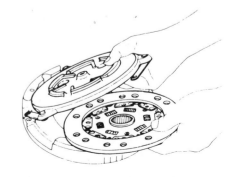
Fig. 5.11. Removing the clutch disc (Sec. 9)

11 Pushrod and release bearing assembly – removal and refitting

1   In order to remove the pushrod and release bearing it is first necessary to remove the primary drive gear as described in Section 9.
2   Place the primary drive gear on end, splines uppermost, with the two outer flanges supported. Using a hammer and a piece of wood on the pushrod, lightly tap the assembly out of the end of the drivegear. A drift will be required to completely remove the pushrod.
3   Prise out the O-ring in the bearing housing.
4   Reassembly is the reverse of the removal procedure. Apply a light coating of multi-purpose grease to the sliding part of the withdrawal lever and the primary gear splines.

12 Pushrod – selection

1   If any parts of the clutch or release mechanism are replaced, it will be necessary to check the pushrod clearance and renew the pushrod if necessary.
2   With the primary drive gear, and the release mechanism, in position and bolted up, gently press the release bearing, and thus the pushrod, until movement is arrested by the pressure plate. Then measure the depth 'A' as shown in Fig. 5.12. Select a pushrod from the table below to keep the clearance at 'A' to the specified value of 0.020 to 0.098 in (0.5 to 2.5 mm) on A14 engines and 0.055 to 0.063 in (1.4 to 1.6 mm) on A10 and A12 engines.

Length of notch on rod	Length of pushrod A14 engine	Length of pushrod A10 and A12 engine
6.0 mm (0.236 in)	115 mm (4.53 in)	130 mm (5.118 in)
None	114 mm (4.49 in)	129 mm (5.078 in)
3.5 mm (0.138 in)	113 mm (4.45 in)	128 mm (5.039 in)

3   As shown in Fig. 5.13 each pushrod is marked with a notch of a specified length which indicates the pushrod overall length.

13 Clutch assembly – refitting

1   Insert the clutch disc between the clutch cover and pressure plate and, before securing the assembly, ensure that the two marks on the cover and pressure plate are aligned. Note that the raised centre of the clutch disc faces towards the clutch cover (ie. away from the flywheel).
2   Offer up the clutch assembly to the flywheel aligning the marks made prior to dismantling and insert the retaining bolts finger tight. Where a new clutch assembly is being fitted, locate it to the flywheel in a similar relative position to the original by reference to the index marking and dowel positions.
3   Insert a guide tool through the splined hub of the driven plate so that the end of the tool locates in the pressure plate. This action of the guide tool will centralise the driven plate by causing it to move in a sideways direction.
4   Insert and remove the guide tool two or three times to ensure that the driven plate is fully centralised and then tighten the securing bolts a turn at a time and in a diametrically opposite sequence, to a torque of 7.2 lbf ft (1.0 kgf m) to prevent distortion of the pressure plate cover. If a guide tool is not available it is acceptable to insert the clutch assembly and then replace the primary drive gear assembly, before bolting the clutch assembly to the flywheel. This will have the effect of centralising the clutch disc.
5   The remainder of clutch refitting is the reverse of dismantling.
6   Adjust the clutch free-movement, according to type, as described in Section 2 or 3.

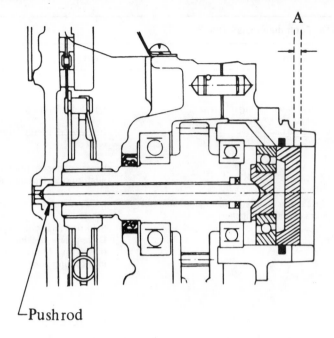

Pushrod

Fig. 5.12. Selecting correct length of pushrod (Sec. 12)

Identification mark

Fig. 5.13. Identification mark (or length) of pushrod (Sec. 12)

Fig. 5.14. Align the marks on the clutch cover and pressure plate at assembly (Sec. 13)

See overleaf for 'Fault diagnosis – Clutch'

14 Fault diagnosis – Clutch

Symptom	Reason/s	Remedy
Judder when taking up drive	Loose engine or gearbox mountings	Tighten and inspect rubber insulators for deterioration
	Badly worn friction surfaces or contaminated with oil	Renew driven plate and rectify oil leakage, probably crankshaft rear oil seal or input shaft oil seal.
	Worn splines on primary drive gear input shaft or driven plate hub	Renew component.
Clutch spin (failure to disengage) so that gears cannot be meshed	Incorrect release bearing clearance	Adjust according to type, see Sections 2 or 3.
	Incorrect pushrod	Select another pushrod.
	Driven plate sticking on input shaft splines due to rust. May occur after vehicle standing idle for long period	As temporary remedy, engage top gear, apply handbrake, depress clutch and start engine. If driven plate badly stuck, engine will not turn. When engine running, rev up and slip clutch until normal clutch disengagement is possible. Renew driven plate at earliest opportunity.
	Damage or misaligned pressure plate assembly	Renew pressure plate assembly.
Clutch slip (increase in engine speed does not result in increase in vehicle road speed – particularly on gradients)	Incorrect release bearing clearance	Adjust clearance according to type, see Sections 2 or 3.
	Friction surfaces worn out or oil contaminated	Renew driven plate and rectify oil leakage.
	Incorrect pushrod	Select another pushrod.
Noise evident on depressing clutch pedal	Dry, worn or damaged release bearing	Renew bearing.
	Insufficient pedal free travel	Adjust according to type see Sections 2 or 3.
	Weak or broken pedal return spring	Renew.
	Weak or broken clutch release lever return	Renew.
Noise evident as clutch pedal released	Distorted driven plate	Renew.
	Broken or weak driven plate cushion coil springs	Renew driven plate as an assembly.
	Insufficient pedal free travel	Adjust according to type, see Section 2 or 3.
	Weak or broken clutch pedal return spring	Renew.
	Weak or broken release lever return spring	Renew.
	Distorted or worn input primary gear shaft splines	Renew primary gear and driven plate if necessary.
	Release bearing loose on retainer hub	Renew hub and bearing.

Chapter 6 Transmission

Contents

Specifications

	F4WF60A	F5WF60A
Type		
Number of speeds	4 forward, 1 reverse	5 forward, 1 reverse
Gearchange	Floor mounted, remote control	

Gear ratios

	F4WF60A	F5WF60A
1st	3.673 : 1	4.018 : 1
2nd	2.217 : 1	2.475 : 1
3rd	1.448 : 1	1.720 : 1
4th	1.000 : 1	1.254 : 1
5th	–	1.000 : 1
Reverse	4.093 : 1	4.093 : 1

Synchromesh type . . . . Warner

Final drive gear ratio . . . . 3.471 : 1

Oil capacity . . . . 4 Imp pints (2.3 litre, $4\frac{1}{8}$ US pints)

General clearances in (mm)
Gear backlash

	F4WF60A	F5WF60A
Primary drive gear } Primary idler gear }	0.0024 – 0.0063 (0.06 – 0.16)	
Main drive gear	0.0012 – 0.0051 (0.03 – 0.13)	
1st gear 2nd gear 3rd gear } . . . . 4th gear Reverse idler gear }	0.0020 – 0.0059 (0.05 – 0.15)	
Counter reverse gear		0.0032 – 0.0063 (0.08 – 0.16)
Final gear	0.0024 – 0.063 (0.06 – 0.16)	0.0024 – 0.0059 (0.06 – 0.15)

End play

	F4WF60A	F5WF60A
1st gear } 2nd gear } . . . . 3rd gear }	0.0079 – 0.0138 (0.20 – 0.35)	
4th gear	–	0.0079 – 0.0138 (0.20 – 0.35)
Reverse idler input gear	–	0 – 0.0146 (0 – 0.37)

Clearance between baulk ring and gear
Standard	0.047 (1.2)	
Allowable limit	0.020 (0.5)	

Main shaft bearing adjusting shim	–	0.0012 (0.03) 0.0020 (0.05) 0.0028 (0.07) 0.0039 (0.10) 0.0118 (0.30) 0.0197 (0.50) 0.0276 (0.70) 0.0354 (0.90)
1st/reverse counter gear adjusting shim	–	0.0079 (0.20)
Primary idler gear adjusting spacer		0.268 (6.80) 0.269 (6.85) 0.272 (6.90) 0.274 (6.95) 0.276 (7.00)
Differential side bearing adjusting shim		0.0079 (0.20) 0.0118 (0.30)
Differential side gear thrust washer		0.0276 (0.70) 0.0315 (0.80) 0.0354 (0.90) 0.0394 (1.0) 0.0433 (1.1)

Torque wrench settings

	lbf ft	kgf m
Main drive gear nut	43 – 58	6 – 8
Reverse idler shaft locknut	72 – 87	10 – 12
Mainshaft locknut	36 – 43	5 – 6
Final gear bolts	43 – 51	6 – 7
Side flange securing nuts	87 – 101	12 – 14
Reverse lamp switch	14 – 22	2 – 3
Interlock plugs	8 – 12	1.1 – 1.5

1 General description

The power from the engine is transmitted through the clutch, primary gear train to the main drive input gear, and subsequently to the mainshaft in the gearbox.

The gearbox is fairly standard having a 4-speed mainshaft and layshaft (countershaft). A 5-speed transmission is fitted to the model F10 Hatchback. The mainshaft transmits the drive to the final drive and differential unit which shares the same housing with the gearbox. A common lubrication system is shared by the two assemblies.

The final gear used in the final drive is a helical gear which is of the same design as that used in the transmission, requiring no adjustment for gear contact pattern.

The transmission gearchange is of a remote control floor shift type. It consists essentially of a hand lever, a linkage which connects the hand lever to the transmission, and a radius link assembly which supports the linkage at the location between the control rod and the transmission.

The reverse stop mechanism is incorporated in the socket located at the lower end of the hand lever.

2 Transmission removal – general

The gearbox and differential assembly are removed from the vehicle together with the engine as described in Chapter 1, Section 5. In this Chapter it is assumed that the complete assembly has been removed from the vehicle and then the transmission separated from the engine as described in Chapter 1, Section 6.

3 Transmission dismantling – general

1 Ensure that an exceptionally clean area is available for the dismantling, and that a good supply of clean fluff-free rags is available, together with various jars and containers in which to store items.
2 It is sound policy to replace bolts, after a component has been dismantled, to aid replacement. Failing this identify them in some other way.
3 As a general aid it is a good policy to have the following tools at hand:

a) *Good quality circlip pliers; 2 pairs, 1 expanding and 1 contracting.*
b) *Copper head mallet, at least 2 lbs.*
c) *Drifts, steel $\frac{3}{8}$ in and brass $\frac{3}{8}$ in.*
d) *Small containers for needle rollers.*
e) *Engineer's vice mounted on firm bench.*

4 Any attempt to dismantle the gearbox without the foregoing is not necessarily impossible, but will certainly be very difficult and inconvenient resulting in possible injury or damage.
5 Take care not to let the synchromesh hub assemblies come apart before you want them to. It accelerates wear if the splines of hub and sleeve are changed in relation to each other. As a precaution it is advisable to make a line up mark with a dab of paint.
6 Before finally going ahead with dismantling first ascertain the availability of spare parts. If several major components need replacing, work out the total cost. It could well be that a reconditioned unit is cheaper in the long run.

4 Transmission (4-speed) – dismantling

1 Support the assembly on a stand or on a bench. The housing is made of aluminium alloy, so great care must be taken, as it is easily damaged. Prior to dismantling the unit clean all dirt and grease from it with a good grease solvent. Remove the drain plug, drain the oil into a container and refit the drain plug.
2 Remove the bolts that secure the clutch thrust bearing housing and the primary drive gear. Withdraw the assembly (photo).
3 Remove the bolts that secure the primary gear cover and remove the cover by tapping it with a soft hammer (photo). This might be a little difficult owing to the bearings in the cover. **Do not** prise it off with a screwdriver. It will be noted that some bolts either have a white or green protective resin on the threads, in order to prevent oil leakage. When replacing any bolts of this type a protective coating of non-setting gasket sealer should be applied to the threads.

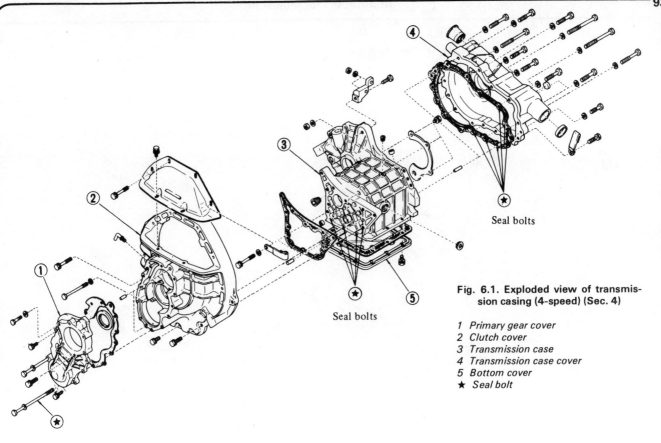

Seal bolts

Seal bolts

**Fig. 6.1. Exploded view of transmis-
sion casing (4-speed) (Sec. 4)**

1 Primary gear cover
2 Clutch cover
3 Transmission case
4 Transmission case cover
5 Bottom cover
★ Seal bolt

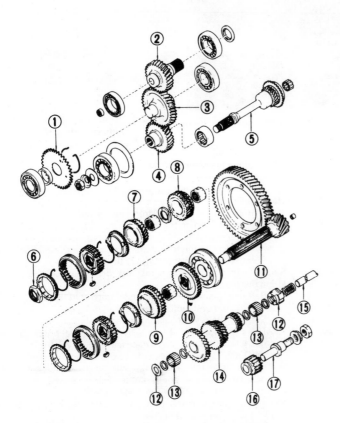

**Fig. 6.2. Exploded view of transmis-
sion gear assembly (4-speed) (Sec. 4)**

1 Sub-gear
2 Primary drive gear
3 Primary idler gear
4 Main drive input gear
5 Main drive shaft
6 Lock nut
7 3rd gear
8 2nd gear
9 1st gear
10 Reverse gear
11 Main shaft
12 Thrust washer
13 Needle bearing
14 Idler gear
15 Idler gear shaft
16 Reverse idler gear
17 Reverse idler shaft

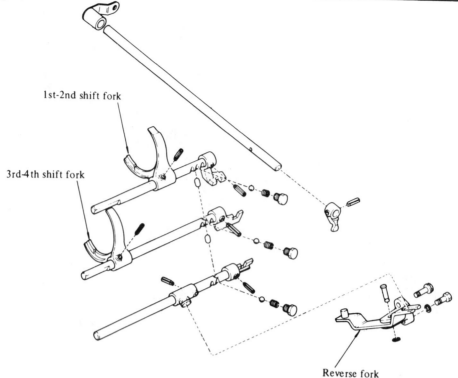

1st-2nd shift fork

3rd-4th shift fork

Reverse fork

Fig. 6.3. Gearchange shafts and forks (Sec. 4)

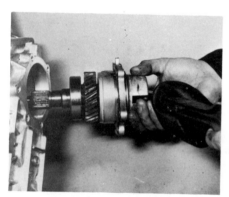

4.2   Removing the primary drive gear

4.3   Remove the primary gear cover securing bolts

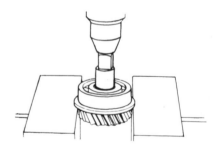

Fig. 6.4. Removing the main drive input gear bearing (Sec. 4)

4   Detach the bottom cover from the transmission case by removing the retaining bolts. Using a screwdriver, mesh the reverse gear and 1st gear (or 2nd) at the same time. Unscrew the main drive gear nut and remove the main drive input gear. Collect the lockwasher and thrust washer under the nut.

5   Remove the primary idler gear, preferably by using a slide hammer type of puller: if this is not available, an ordinary three-legged type of puller will do.

6   Remove the clutch housing bolts and lift away the clutch housing.

7   Drive out the primary drive and primary idler gear bearings with a press. Press out the ball bearing of the main drive input gear, using the bearing retainer as a support.

8   Remove the nuts securing the driving flanges (one each side) to the differential and top off the flanges using a block of wood and a hammer. If they do not come off easily it may be necessary to use a puller. When undoing the flange securing nuts it is necessary to restrain the flange from turning (photos); Fig. 6.5 shows the special Datsun tool for this, but two bolts and a suitable bar can be used as shown in the associated photograph.

9   Remove the bolts securing the transmission case cover and remove the cover (photo). It will probably be necessary to separate the cover from the case by using a hammer and a block of wood. Note the bolts with resin on the threads.

10   Remove the speedometer pinion gear (photo).

11   Lift out the differential unit.

12   Remove the detent plugs and take out the locking springs and steel balls.

13   Remove the taper plug from the casing; this provides access to drive out the roll pin on the 1st/2nd gearchange fork (photos).

14   Using a suitable drift, drive out the roll pin that secures the gearchange fork to the fork shaft, then remove the shaft and fork.

15   Remove the bolts that retain the reverse gear fork and bracket. Separate the bracket from the fork by unclipping the pivot pin and lifting out the fork.

16   Remove the bolts and double nuts that secure the mainshaft bearing retainer and remove the retainer (photo).

17   Remove the reverse idler gear and its shaft.

18   The next step can be a a little tricky. In order to remove the counter shaft (layshaft) it is necessary to drive it out using either a special Datsun tool or a piece of rod of the same diameter as the shaft and the same length as the distance between the two faces of the gearbox casing. One could argue that the tool, or rod, is more important when replacing the layshaft (in order to retain the needle bearings in position) but it is just as well to use it at this stage to ensure that it fits and no needle bearings are lost.

19   Drive out the countershaft, using the tool described above, then

4.8a   Restraining the flange from turning with a suitable bar and two bolts

4.8b   Removing the flange securing nut

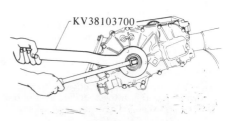

Fig. 6.5. Undoing the drive flange securing nuts (Sec. 4)

4.9   Separate the cover from the transmission case

4.10   Removing the speedometer pinion gear

Fig. 6.6. Lifting out the differential unit (Sec. 4)

4.13a   Remove the taper plug from the casings ...

4.13b   ... and drive out the roll pin on the 1st/2nd gearchange fork

4.16   The mainshaft bearing retainer is secured by through-bolts and double nuts

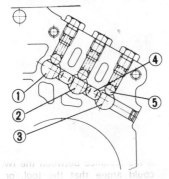

Fig. 6.7. Position of detent balls and interlock plungers (Sec. 4)

1 1st/2nd fork   4 Interlock plungers
2 3rd/4th fork shaft   5 Detent balls
3 Reverse fork shaft

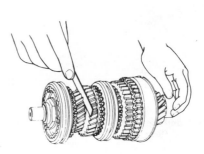

Fig. 6.8. Measuring the endplay of mainshaft gears (Sec. 4)

remove the countershaft and gear cluster, and collect the counter gear spring and thrust washer.

20 Using a suitable drift, remove the roll pins from each of the remaining selector forks and pull each selector shaft out through the casing, complete with the attached dogs. Collect the selector forks and store in a safe place. The interlock plungers can now be removed from their housing in the casing between the selector shafts (Fig. 6.7).

21 Lift the gear mainshaft assembly and the main drive input gear out of the casing through the final drive side. Collect the needle bearing from the mainshaft nose.

22 Measure the endplay present in each gear of the mainshaft, as shown in Fig. 6.8. If the specified limit of 0.0079 to 0.0118 in (0.2 to 0.3 mm) is exceeded new parts will have to be fitted.

5   Mainshaft – dismantling

1 Place the mainshaft in a vice, but ensure that some form of padding is used so as not to damage the gears.

2 Remove the locknut from the end of the mainshaft. **The lock nut is staked, so when it is removed be sure to clean the threaded portion of the mainshaft until all the metal chips are removed. The lock nut should be discarded and should not be re-used.**

3 Remove the 3rd and 4th synchronizer, 3rd gear, main gear bushing, main gear spacer, 2nd gear, main gear bushing, 1st and 2nd synchronizer, 1st and main gear bushing from mainshaft in the order enumerated.

4 Press out the bearing from the mainshaft. This can be done by resting the outer face of the bearing on the vice, and with a piece of wood interposed, lightly tapping the shaft down through the bearing. Leave the circlip on the bearing outer face.

6   Final drive and differential – dismantling

1 Place the final drive assembly in a vice, using padded jaws, and pull off the differential side bearings using a puller.

2 Remove the bolts that secure the final drive gear to the differential.

3 Detach the differential case. Withdraw the differential pinion, by using a drift and hammer, from the mainshaft, and then remove the differential side gears and pinion.

7   Countershaft – dismantling and reassembly

1 Place the countershaft in a vice with padded jaws. Although the countershaft is out of the gear assembly at this stage, it is now necessary to remove the dummy shaft and then the needle roller bearings and spacers.

2 Reassembly is the reverse of dismantling. Insert the spacers and needle rollers into both sides of the countergear. Apply grease liberally

to the bearing needles (this will keep them in position), and fit the dummy shaft, thrust washer and spring (photo).

3 The assembly is now ready for fitting in the gearbox during final assembly of the transmission.

8   Primary drive gear and idler gear – dismantling and reassembly

1 The primary drive gear can be dismantled by first using a piece of bar and lightly tapping the pushrod through the assembly so that the thrust bearing and its two-piece carrier block emerges. Then tap the pushrod right through.

2 The front section of the drive gear can now be removed by using a suitable drift and driving it out.

3 The bearings on the drive gear and idler gear can be pressed out in a vice, always ensuring that soft jaws are used and that suitably spaced blocks of wood carry the pressure.

4 Replacement is the reverse of dismantling, but if any clutch components have been renewed it is most important that the length of the pushrod is selected as covered in Chapter 5.

9   Transmission components – inspection and checking

1 Thoroughly clean all parts in cleaning solvent, and blow dry with compressed air. Check each part for wear, damage, or other defective conditions.

2 Inspect the primary gear cover, clutch housing, transmission case and transmission case cover. Repair or renew parts if burrs, pitting or damage is apparent on their mating surfaces.

3 Repair or renew a dowel pin if it is distorted or other damage is apparent.

4 Make sure that each bearing is thoroughly cleaned and free from dirt.

5 Check ball bearings to ensure that they roll freely and are free from cracked, pitted, or worn balls. Also check outer and inner races and balls for indications of bearing creepage. Renew if any of the above conditions are apparent.

6 Renew needle roller bearing, if worn or damaged.

7 Check all the gears for wear, damaged or chipped teeth. Where such damage is evident, the driven and driving gears should be renewed as a set. Where the gearbox has covered a substantial period of service it will be appropriate to test for backlash and endfloat with the gear train assembled on the mainshaft and countershaft and installed in the gearbox. Use a dial gauge to check for backlash, turning each gearwheel as far as it will go whilst holding the mainshaft perfectly still. The permitted backlash tolerance is given below. Use a feeler gauge to check for endplay. The correct tolerance is 0.0079 to 0.0118 in (0.2 to 0.3 mm).

8 Where the backlash or endplay is greater than that specified, consideration should be given to purchasing a reconditioned gearbox as

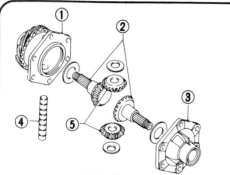

Fig. 6.9. Exploded view of differential unit (Sec. 6)

1 Differential case A
2 Side gear
3 Differential case B
4 Pinion shaft
5 Pinion

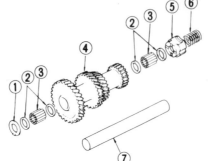

Fig. 6.10. Countershaft and gear assembly (Sec. 7)

1 Thrust washer
2 Spacer
3 Needle bearing
4 Counter gear
5 Thrust washer
6 Spring
7 Counter shaft

7.2   Apply grease when fitting the needle rollers in the countershaft

the cost of a complete set of gears and other internal components will probably prove uneconomical by comparison.

Standard backlash

Primary drive gear Primary idler gear	0.0020 to 0.0055 in (0.05 to 0.14 mm)
Main drive input gear Main drive gears, 1st, 2nd, 3rd gears, reverse idler gear Final gear	0.0020 to 0.0059 in (0.05 to 0.15 mm)

9   Check baulk rings for evidence of wear, pitting, cracking, or damage. If any of the above conditions are apparent, renew the baulk rings.

10 Measure the clearance between the baulk ring end and cone (Fig. 6.11). The standard clearance is 0.0472 in (1.2 mm). If it is less than 0.0197 in (0.5 mm) replace the baulk ring with a new one.

10   Transmission reassembly – general

1   Ensure that all parts are thoroughly cleaned and lubricated with oil before reassembly. Do not use any liquid sealants between the casing mating surfaces.

2   Apply a non-setting gasket sealant to the threads of the bolts specified as seal bolts (see Fig. 6.1) prior to assembly.

3   Always use new gaskets and oil seals.

11   Mainshaft – reassembly

1   Ensure that the sliding surfaces of the mainshaft bushes are lubricated with oil before assembly.

2   Press the ball bearing onto the mainshaft (photo) and fit the reverse gear (photo). Slide the bush into position on the mainshaft, so that the oil holes are aligned (photo). Fit the first gear, baulk ring and synchronizer hub (photos). Make sure that the insert is correctly seated in the groove of the baulk ring.

3   Fit the second gear bush with its oil hole aligned with the hole in the mainshaft and then fit the second gear (photos).

4   Fit the main gear spacer, followed by the bush and third gear. Fit the baulk ring and synchronizer hub (photos).

5   Mount the mainshaft in a vice equipped with soft faced jaws, to avoid damage to the gears.

6   Fit the mainshaft locknut (photo) and tighten to a torque of 36 - 43 lbf ft (5 – 6 kgf m).

7   Recheck the endplay, and if within the specified limit, stake the locknut to the shaft (photo).

12   Final drive and differential – reassembly

1   Press the differential side bearings into the differential case. If a proper press is not available use a hammer and block of wood to spread the load over the face of the bearing. Tap the bearing home gently.

2   The next stage is slightly more complex and involves the use of a dial gauge. Fit the final drive assembly on a testing tool like that shown in Fig. 6.13. If you cannot obtain the official Datsun tool there should be no problem in making one up locally. Using the dial gauge adjust each side gear endplay to less than 0.008 in (0.2 mm) by selective thrust washers. Sizes of thrust washers available are given in the Specifications.

3   Fit the final drive gear on the differential assembly. Apply thread locking compound to the bolts and tighten them to a torque of 43 to 51 lbf ft (60 to 7.0 kgf m).

13   Transmission – reassembly

1   Lubricate the lip of the differential side flange oil seal with multi-purpose grease, and press it into position using a block of wood between the faces of a vice. Note that the lip should be innermost.

2   Ensure the main drive gear bearing is in position in the casing,

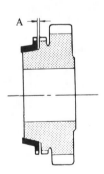

Fig. 6.11. Baulk ring-to-cone clearance (Sec. 9)

11.2a   Press the ball bearing onto the mainshaft

11.2b   Fit the reverse gear ...

11.2c   ... then slide the bush into position, with the oil holes aligned with the mainshaft oil holes

11.2d   ... followed by the 1st gear, baulk ring ...

11.2e   ... and synchronizer hub

11.3a   Fit the 2nd gear bush …

11.3b   … and then the 2nd gear

11.4a   Fit the main gear spacer …

11.4b   … followed by the bush …

11.4c   … then the 3rd gear, baulk ring …

11.4d   … and synchronizer hub

11.6   Fitting the mainshaft locknut

11.7   Recheck the gear endplay with a feeler gauge

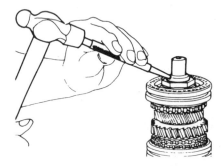

Fig. 6.12. Staking the mainshaft locknut (Sec. 11)

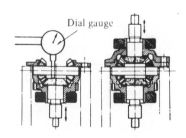

Fig. 6.13. Measuring the side gear endplay (Sec. 12)

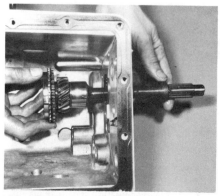

13.2a   Position the main drive gear in the casing …

13.2b   … fit the needle bearing …

then ease the main drive gear through the bearing and into position. Fit the needle bearing in the main drive gear and then fit the mainshaft in the casing (photos).

3   Insert the bottom selector shaft, slide the fork over it and engage the fork with the nearest coupling sleeve on the mainshaft. Secure in position with a roll pin. Insert the interlock plunger through the bore in centre selector shaft housing (photo).

4   Insert the centre selector shaft, slide the fork over it and engage the fork with the end coupling sleeve on the mainshaft. Secure in position with a roll pin. Insert the interlock plunger (photos).

5   Hold the countergear in position in the transmission case, with the thrust washers and spring correctly located, and then insert the countershaft into the counter gear and drive out the dummy shaft. Make sure that the cut out part of the countershaft is lined up with the bearing retainer (photos).

6   Fit the reverse idler shaft, reverse idler gear and the bearing retainer. Make sure that the cut out part of the reverse idler shaft is lined up with the bearing retainer. Tighten the idler shaft retaining nuts (double nuts) to a torque of 72 – 87 lbf ft (10 – 12 kgf m) and the

bearing retainer bolts to 12 – 16 lbf ft (1.6 – 2.2 kgf m) (photos).

7   Insert the reverse fork shaft, slide the reverse fork pivot over the shaft and secure with a roll pin (photo).

8   Fit the reverse fork bracket and secure with two bolts. Fit the reverse fork on the pivot and secure to the bracket with a clevis pin and clip (photos).

9   Fit the steel balls. locking springs and retaining plugs (photos). Manipulate the selector shafts to ensure that all gears can be selected.

10   Before fitting the differential unit, measure the side bearing height, 'H' in Fig. 6.15. After selecting a suitable shim from the following table, fit the differential assembly (photos):

Available shim thickness in (mm)

Height 'H'	Thickness
4.720 to 4.730 (119.91 to 120.10)	Unnecessary
4.715 to 4.719 (119.76 to 119.90)	0.0078 (0.2)
4.710 to 4.714 (119.66 to 119.75)	0.0118 (0.3)

11   Fit the transmission case cover, applying non-setting gasket

13.2c   … and then fit the mainshaft to engage with the main drive gear

13.3   Fitting the bottom selector shaft and interlock plunger

13.4a   Fit the centre selector shaft and fork …

13.4b   … and secure with a roll pin …

13.4c   … then fit the interlock plunger

13.5a   Fit the countershaft in the countergear

13.5b   Countergear thrust washer and spring

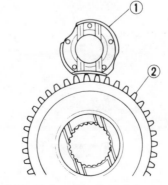

Fig. 6.14. Fitting direction of thrust washer (Sec. 13)

1 Thrust washer   2 Reverse gear

13.5c   Ensure that the cut-out on the countershaft is positioned to line up with the bearing retainer

13.6a   Fit the reverse idler shaft and gear ...

13.6b   ... and then the bearing retainer and idler shaft nuts

13.7   Insert the reverse fork shaft and pivot

13.8a   The reverse fork bracket is retained by two bolts

13.8b   Fit the reverse fork on the pivot and secure to the bracket with a clevis pin

13.9a   Insert the detent balls and springs ...

13.9b   ... and fit the retaining plugs

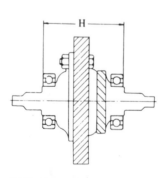

Fig. 6.15. Side bearing height (Sec. 13)

13.10a   Position the selected shim on the casing ...

13.10b   ... and fit the differential assembly

13.11   The transmission case cover ready for fitting

13.12   Fit the differential side flanges

13.13   Fitting the reversing lamp switch

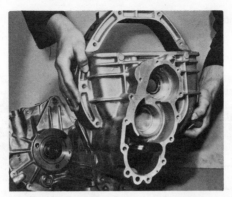

13.14   When refitting the clutch housing don't forget to apply sealant to the seal bolts

13.16a   Position the primary idler sub-gear with a bar and fit the main drive input gear and

13.16b   ... then the thrust washer, lockwasher and main drive gear nut

13.18   Fitting the primary gear cover

sealant to the seal bolts and tightening them to 13 – 18 lbf ft (1.8 – 2.5 kgf m) and the other bolts to 12 – 16 lbf ft (1.6 – 2.2 kgf m) (photo).

12   Apply thread-locking compound to the threads of the differential side flanges, then fit them and tighten the retaining nuts to a torque of 87 – 101 lbf ft (12 – 14 kgf m). Restrain the flanges from turning; refer to Section 4, paragraph 8 (photo).

13   Fit the reversing lamp switch in its housing in the casing (photo).

14   Fit the clutch housing. Apply non-setting gasket sealant to the threads of the seal bolts (photo).

15   Drive the primary idler gear a short way into the clutch housing with a wooden mallet, making sure that its sub-gear side is towards the primary gear cover.

16   Fit the main drive input gear. Fit the primary idler sub-gear to the correct position by inserting a bar through the hole in the sub-gear and into the hole in the primary idler gear, then fit the main drive input gear and bearing. Next fit the thrust washer, lockwasher and main drive gear nut. The nut for the main drive gear must be fitted with the chamfered side facing the lockwasher (photos).

17   Engage two gears at the same time, to prevent the main drive from turning, then tighten the nut to a torque of 43 – 58 lbf ft (6 – 8 kgf m) and bend over the lockwasher to lock the nut.

18   Fit the primary gear cover on the clutch housing (photo).

19   Fit the speedometer pinion gear and the bottom cover.

20   Do not fit the bearing housing assembly and primary drive gear at this stage because of the difficulty of lining up with the flywheel and clutch assembly.

21   Refit the clutch operating lever and secure in position with a pivot pin through the primary drive gear flange. Fit a locking clip over the pin. Fit the protective rubber boot.

22   Reconnect the transmission to the engine, first by the single bolt through the transmission flange and engine stay rod, then by the bolts through the clutch housing to the engine endplate. The clutch should still be in position on the flywheel.

23   Now replace the primary drive gear and bearing assembly. If the clutch has been removed it is most likely that you will have to use some form of centring tool to line-up the clutch with the primary drive gear splines. Another way of tackling it is to loosen the clutch bolts, insert the primary drive gear, and adjust the clutch position until the

two are correctly mated. Then tighten the bolts.

24   Replace the clutch inspection cover. The assembly is now ready for replacing in the car. Refer to Chapter 1 for these details.

14   Transmission (5-speed) – general

Dismantling and reassembly procedures are almost the same as those for the 4-speed transmission. Unless otherwise described, refer to the relevant Section for 4-speed transmission. The inspection procedure is the same as for the 4-speed transmission.

15   Transmission (5-speed) – dismantling

1   Remove the differential side flanges and primary gear.

2   Remove the speedometer pinion gear.

3   Remove the bolts securing the transmission case cover and lift off the cover. Take care not to lose the lock ball when removing the cover.

4   Detach the counter thrust bush from first and reverse counter gear.

5   Remove the detent ball plugs and take out the steel balls.

6   Drive the roll pin out of the reverse shift fork, using a parallel pin punch. Drive out the first and reverse fork shaft from the clutch housing side with a suitable drift.

7   To remove the cover side taper roller bearing, apply a suitable puller to the first gear and remove the bearing together with the retainer washer, first synchronizer assembly, first gear needle bearing, first and reverse counter gear and reverse idler input gear. Then remove the reverse idler gear and reverse shift fork.

8   Lift out the differential unit.

9   Remove the plug from the service hole and drive the roll pins out of the shift forks and then withdraw the fork shafts. When removing the 4th/5th shift fork roll pin, shift to 5th gear and then drive the pin out.

10   Remove the bearing retainer.

11   Remove the mainshaft gear assembly and main drive gear from the transmission case towards the final drive gear side by tapping the

main drive gear lightly.

12 Remove the countershaft and gear assembly, the 2nd/3rd shift fork and the 4th/5th shift fork.

13 Remove the mainshaft locknut.

14 From the mainshaft remove the 4th/5th synchronizer, 4th gear, main gear bush, main gear spacer, 3rd gear, main gear needle bearing, main gear bush, 2nd/3rd synchronizer, 2nd gear, main gear needle bearing, main gear bush, reverse gear and bearing housing in that order; see Fig. 6.17.

15 If necessary remove the mainshaft bearing with a puller. If the bearing is removed it should be discarded and a new bearing fitted at reassembly.

16 Transmission (5-speed) – reassembly

1   Press the mainshaft bearing onto the shaft.

2   Insert the bearing outer race into the bearing housing, then fit the bearing housing and reverse gear on the mainshaft. Ensure that the cut out part of the reverse gear is aligned with the 2nd main gear bush.

3   Fit the 2nd gear bush, needle bearing, 2nd main gear, baulk ring, 2nd/3rd synchro-hub assembly and the 3rd main gear bush. When fitting the 3rd main gear bush ensure that the claw is lined up with the main gear spacer. When fitting the 2nd/3rd synchro-hub, the thinner spline tooth side must be towards the 3rd gear; see Figs. 6.18 and 6.19.

4   Fit the needle bearing, baulk ring, 3rd gear and main gear spacer. When fitting the main gear spacer ensure that the uneven surface side is towards the 4th gear.

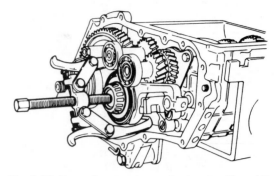

Fig. 6.16. Removing the taper roller bearing (Sec. 15)

5   Fit the 4th gear bush, 4th gear, baulk ring, 4th/5th synchro-hub and mainshaft locknut. Tighten and then stake the locknut.

6   Fit the differential side flange oil seals.

7   Fit the main drive gear and mainshaft assembly into the transmission case and at the same time insert the 2nd/3rd shift fork, 4th/5th shift fork and counter gear with thrust washer into the case.

8   Slide the 2nd/3rd fork shaft through the casing and the 2nd/3rd shift fork, then secure it to the shift fork with a new roll pin.

9   Fit the 2nd/3rd detent ball, spring and plug. Align the notch in the 2nd/3rd shaft with the ball and place in neutral position.

10   Insert the interlock plunger between 2nd/3rd and 4th/5th fork

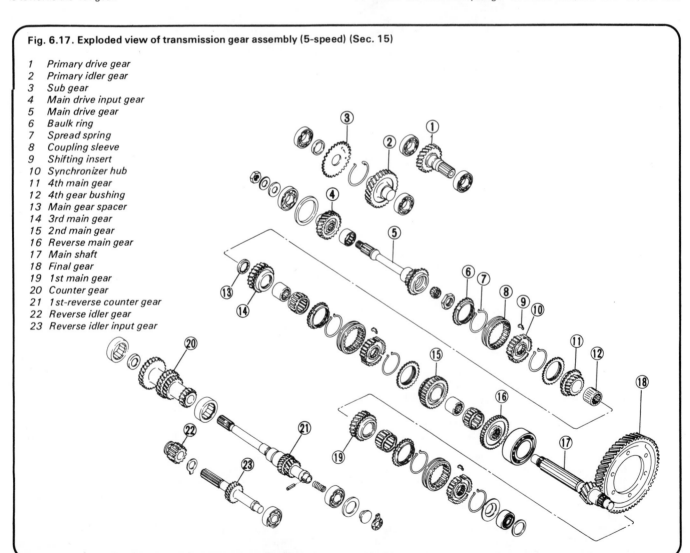

Fig. 6.17. Exploded view of transmission gear assembly (5-speed) (Sec. 15)

1   Primary drive gear
2   Primary idler gear
3   Sub gear
4   Main drive input gear
5   Main drive gear
6   Baulk ring
7   Spread spring
8   Coupling sleeve
9   Shifting insert
10   Synchronizer hub
11   4th main gear
12   4th gear bushing
13   Main gear spacer
14   3rd main gear
15   2nd main gear
16   Reverse main gear
17   Main shaft
18   Final gear
19   1st main gear
20   Counter gear
21   1st-reverse counter gear
22   Reverse idler gear
23   Reverse idler input gear

shafts then fit the 4th/5th fork shaft.
11 Fit the countershaft needle bearing and bearing retainer.
12 With a suitable selected shim fit the differential unit in the casing.
13 Fit the 1st gear needle bearing, 1st gear, baulk ring, synchronizer assembly, 1st shift fork, retainer washer, 1st/reverse counter gear with ball bearing, reverse idler input gear with ball bearing and washer, reverse idler gear and reverse shift fork at the same time and then fit the taper roller bearing using a suitable drift. Ensure that the claw on the reverse idler input gear washer is pointed towards the bottom cover and that the counter gear thrust washer is set as shown in Figs.

6.20 and 6.21.
14 Insert the interlock plunger between 2nd/3rd and 1st/reverse fork shafts and fit the 1st/reverse fork shaft.
15 Measure the 1st/reverse counter gear bearing height H, in Fig. 6.22 and select the required number of shims from the following table:

Available shim thickness

Height 'H' in (mm)	Required thickness in (mm)	Number of shims
3.472 to 3.480 (88.20 to 88.40)	0	0
3.465 to 3.471 (88.00 to 88.19)	0.008 (0.2)	1
3.457 to 3.464 (87.80 to 87.99)	0.016 (0.4)	2
3.449 to 3.456 (87.60 to 87.79)	0.024 (0.6)	3

16 Determine the mainshaft bearing shim thickness as follows:

  a) Fit the bearing outer race on the mainshaft bearing and measure dimension 'B' in Fig. 6.23.
  b) Measure depth of mainshaft bearing outer race housing of case cover, 'A' in Fig. 6.24.
  c) The required thickness of adjusting shim required can be determined by the formula, $T = A - B + 0.5$.
  T – Required thickness of mainshaft bearing adjusting shim (mm)
  A – Measured case cover depth (mm).
  B – Measured mainshaft bearing height (mm)

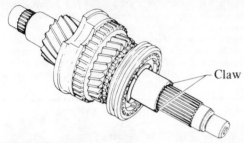

Fig. 6.18. Fitting the 3rd main gear bush (Sec. 16)

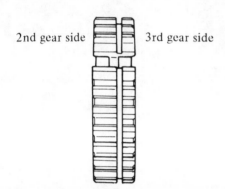

Fig. 6.19. Fitting direction of 2nd/3rd synchrohub (Sec. 16)

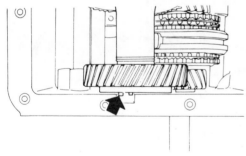

Fig. 6.21. Counter gear thrust washer fitted in position (Sec. 16)

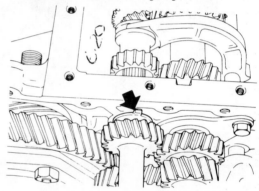

Fig. 6.20. Reverse idler input gear washer fitted in position (Sec. 16)

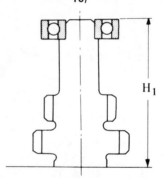

Fig. 6.22. Measure the 1st/reverse counter gear bearing height (Sec. 16)

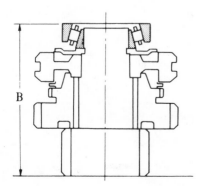

Fig. 6.23. Mainshaft bearing height (Sec. 16)

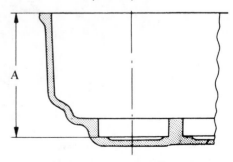

Fig. 6.24. Case cover depth (Sec. 16)

Select the required shim from the following.

Available shims in (mm)
Thickness
0.0012 (0.03)
0.0019 (0.05)
0.0028 (0.07)
0.0039 (0.1)
0.0118 (0.3)
0.0197 (0.5)
0.0276 (0.7)
0.0354 (0.9)

17 Fit the selected mainshaft bearing adjusting shim onto the case cover and press the mainshaft bearing outer race completely into the case cover.
18 Attach with grease the counter thrust bush to 1st/reverse counter gear, and the thrust washer and selected shims to the case cover.

19 With the fork shafts in neutral positions, fit the case cover on the transmission case. Do not forget to fit the 1st shift fork detent ball.
20 Fit the differential side flanges and primary gear.

17 Gearchange linkage – removal, inspection and refitting

1 Remove the bolts which secure the gear lever to its mounting bracket. Take out the split pin and remove the circlip which secures the control rod to the gear lever (photo).
2 Remove the bolts which secure the radius link assembly to the transmission case cover, then remove the circlip to free the radius link assembly from the subframe (photo).
3 Remove the bolts that secure the select lever to the tranmission case cover and detach the selector lever from the transmission case cover. Take out the pin that secures the shift rod to the lever and detach the shift rod from the lever. Withdraw the control linkage from the vehicle.

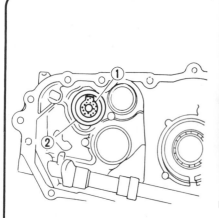

17.1   Removing the control rod from the gear lever

17.2   Remove the bolts securing radius link assembly to the transmission casing

Fig. 6.25. Attach the thrust washer (1) and selected shims (2) with grease (Sec. 16)

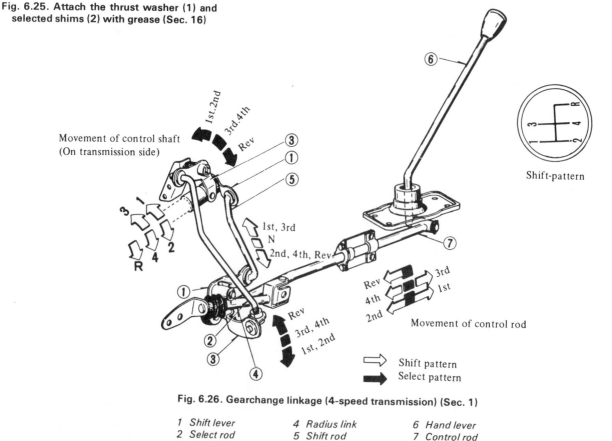

Fig. 6.26. Gearchange linkage (4-speed transmission) (Sec. 1)

1 Shift lever	4 Radius link	6 Hand lever
2 Select rod	5 Shift rod	7 Control rod
3 Select lever		

Shift pattern

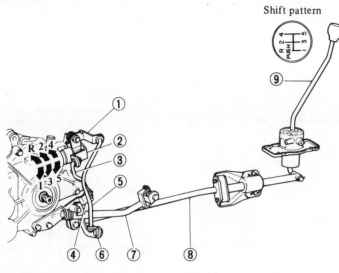

Fig. 6.27. Gearchange linkage (5-speed transmission) (Sec. 17)

1 *Select lever*
2 *Shift lever*
3 *Shift rod*
4 *Shift lever*
5 *Select rod*
6 *Select lever*
7 *Radius link*
8 *Control rod*
9 *Hand lever*

4   Each linkage is securely retained with various fasteners such as washers and circlips. Special care should be taken so that they may be reinstated in exactly the same location when reconnecting the linkage.

5   Inspect all the linkage components for general wear, corrosion or distortion. If general sloppiness is apparent in the linkage it is recommended that all the circlips, springs and clips are renewed as a matter of course.

6   Installation of the linkage is a reversal of the removal procedures, noting the following points:

7   O-rings are fitted between the shift lever and radius link assembly and between gear lever and control rod.

    The O-rings and radius link bosses should be lubricated with multi-purpose grease.

8   The shift lever and selector lever should also be greased.

18 Gear change linkage (4-speed transmission) – adjustment

1   Set the hand lever to the neutral position and loosen the adjusting nuts fully.

2   Under this condition, measure the initial clearance between the transmission case cover and protector, 'A' in Fig. 6.28, when the protector is pushed fully into the transmission case.

3   Now relocate the protector in order to increase the clearance by

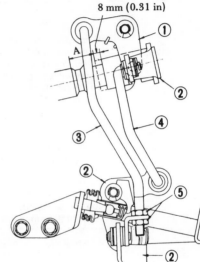

8 mm (0.31 in)

Fig. 6.28. Gearchange linkage adjustment (4-speed transmission) (Sec. 18)

1 *Select lever*
2 *Shift lever*
3 *Select rod*
4 *Shift rod*
5 *Adjusting nuts*

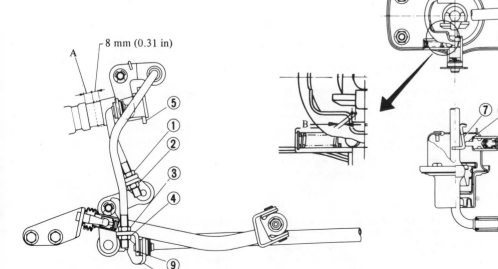

8 mm (0.31 in)

Fig. 6.29. Gearchange linkage adjustment (5-speed transmission) (Sec. 19)

1 *Nut*
2 *Nut*
3 *Nut*
4 *Nut*
5 *Shift lever*
6 *Select lever*
7 *Hand lever guide plate*
8 *Detent pin*
9 *Trunnion*

0.31 in (8 mm) over the initial clearance 'A', and then shift the hand lever into the 4th gear position.

4   Pull down on the selector lever and tighten the adjusting nuts.

19 Gear change linkage (5-speed transmission) – adjustment

1   Refer to Fig. 6.29 and loosen nuts (1), (2), (3) and (4).

Select adjustment

2   With the shift lever (5) moved fully towards the transmission case cover, move it back 0.31 in (8 mm), then move the shift lever (5) down so that 3rd gear is selected.

3   Push the select lever (6) fully down so that the hand lever guide plate (7) touches the detent pin (8). Turn the nut (3) in until it comes in contact with the trunnion (9), then screw it in a further 1 – 2 turns and lock nut (3) with nut (4).

Shift adjustment

4   Move the hand lever into neutral.

5   Adjust dimension 'B' of the hand lever assembly to between 0.039 and 0.079 in (1 and 2 mm) and then tighten nuts (1) and (2).

20 Fault diagnosis – Transmission

Symptom	Reason/s	Remedy
Gearbox		
Obstructive gearchange	*When difficulty in changing gear is encountered, it is necessary to determine whether the transmission or the remote control system is causing the trouble.*	
	If this condition is accompanied by a dragging clutch, trouble may be due to failure of clutch to disengage. Under such conditions, check to ensure that it couples or uncouples the engine and transmission properly. If upon inspection the clutch is in good condition, then check the cause of trouble to determine whether the transmission or the remote control system is causing trouble.	
	Control linkage out of adjustment or lack of lubrication to balljoint.	Re-adjust or lubricate.
	Failure of parts to reach their full measurement due to worn sliding contact surfaces or excessive free-play	Check and, if necessary, repair or renew worn parts.
	Improper contact pattern of baulk ring-to-gear cone or worn parts	Renew worn parts.
	Worn or deformed insert	Renew.
Jumping out of gear	*Jumping out of gear is often experienced when wear occurs to the interlock plunger, steel ball, locking spring, etc., or when the control linkage is out of adjustment.*	
	Interlock plunger worn	Renew
	Steel ball worn, or locking spring fatigued or broken	Renew faulty parts.
	Worn groove in shift rod	Renew.
	Gear tip worn or damaged	Renew gear.
	Bushes worn	Renew.
	Excessive end play	Renew faulty parts.
	Mainshaft mounting nut loose	Re-tighten
Excessive noise	*Noise in the transmission indicates a fault if it is heard when the engine is running at idling speed or when gears are shifted from one speed position to another, and if it ceases when the clutch is disengaged. To determine whether the transmission (included primary gear) or the differential is producing the noise, run the vehicle with top gear selected. Under this condition if noise ceases, it is produced in the transmission.*	
	Lack of lubricating oil or use of improper oil	Lubricate or use recommended lubricant.
	Bearing worn (humming at a high speed travel).	Renew.
	Bearing damaged (rattling noise at a low speed travel).	Renew.
	Worn splines	Renew worn shaft or gear.
	Gear contact surfaces damaged	Renew damaged gears.
	Oil leakage or insufficient oil due to damaged oil seal or gasket, or clogged breather.	Clean or renew.
Gearchange linkage		
Failure of gears to mesh or hard to mesh gears	Control linkage out of adjustment (or lack of lubricating oil to ball joint).	Re-adjust or lubricate.
	Excessive free-play to worn control linkage	Check and correct.
Jumping out of gear	Control linkage out of adjustment	Re-adjust.
	Excessive free-play – due to worn control linkage	Repair or renew faulty parts.

Symptom	Reason/s	Remedy
Gearlever drag or failure of gearlever to respond quickly	Control rod deformed or bent	Repair or renew.
	Lack of oil to sliding contacts or sliding resistance excessive owing to deformed parts	Lubricate, repair, or renew, as required.
Shifting noise	Worn bearing or excessive free-play in linkage	Repair or renew.
	Interference of lever, link, etc, with adjacent parts	Repair.

Final drive
Damage to final drive

Renew any damaged parts. Also check every possible part for condition.

	Improper backlash in final gear	Renew final gear.
	Excessive backlash in differential gear	Renew differential gear or thrust washer.
	Final gear mounting bolt loose	Re-tighten.
	Damage due to overloading	Renew damaged parts.
Abnormal noise when steering	Differential gear damaged	Renew.
	Thrust washer worn excessively or damaged	Renew.
	Pinion main shaft damaged	Renew.
	Side bearing seized or damaged	Renew.

Excessive gear noise

To clearly determine whether noise is produced in transmission gears (including primary gear), engine, wheel bearings, tyres, or body, check and locate cause of noise in the following manner:
a)   Run the vehicle at a creeping speed and then at a constant speed, accelerating engine as necessary.
b)   Jack-up front portion of vehicle, and run engine with top gear selected. After cause of trouble is located, use a systematic procedure to repair or replace defective parts.

	Improper backlash in final gear	Renew final gear.
	Final gear tooth tip damaged	Renew final gear.
	Side bearing seized, broken or damaged	Renew.
	Oil leakage (or lack of oil) due to defective oil seal or gasket.	Renew faulty parts.

Chapter 7 Driveshafts

Contents

Specifications

Driveshaft
Inner joint type . . . . Double offset joint
Outer joint type . . . . Birfield joint

Maximum swivel movement
Double offset joint . . . . 20°
Birfield joint . . . . 42°

Torque wrench settings

	lbf ft	kgf m
Wheel hub nut	87 – 116	12 – 16
Driveshaft attaching bolt	29 – 36	4 – 5

1 General description

1   Power is transmitted to the front wheels by two driveshafts which are carried by knuckle arms attached to the lower ends of the struts. Each driveshaft is supported on two ball bearings mounted back to back, and is splined to the wheel hub.

2   Constant velocity (CV) joints are incorporated at each end of the driveshafts. The joint at the wheel end of the shaft provides a forty-two degree swivel movement, while the double offset type of joint at the other end of the shaft allows for a movement of twenty degrees.

3   The outer universal joints are of the Birfield constant velocity type. The driveshaft fits inside the circular outer CV joint which is also the driven shaft. Drive is transmitted from the driveshaft to the driven shaft by six steel balls which are located in curved grooves machined in line with the axis of the shaft on the inside of the driven shaft and outside of the driveshaft. This allows the driven shaft to hinge freely on the driveshaft, but at the same time keeps them together. Enclosing the CV joint is a rubber boot.

2 Routine maintenance

1   At intervals of 6000 miles (10 000 km) inspect the rubber boots which protect the constant velocity joints. If they are torn, split or show signs of deterioration they should be renewed as soon as possible. When the boot splits the CV joint becomes contaminated by water, road dust and grit, which soon results in rapid failure of the bearings in the joint.

2   Wear in the joints is detected by a regular knocking when the front wheels are turned on full lock. In very severe cases it is only necessary to turn the wheels slightly for the noise to begin.

3 Driveshaft – removal

1   Remove the wheel trim from the wheel from which the driveshaft is to be removed.

2   Place the car in gear and apply the handbrake firmly. Extract the split pin from the hub nut, and undo and remove the nut and thrust washer.

3   Loosen the front roadwheel securing nuts and jack-up the car on the same side.

4   As it will be necessary to work underneath the car, supplement the jack with a stand or support blocks. This will minimise the danger should the jack collapse.

5   Remove the roadwheel.

6   Remove the bolts which secure the driveshaft to the final drive assembly, then use the subframe to support the detached driveshaft.

7   It will now be possible to partially free the end of the driveshaft from the centre of the hub. With a soft drift and hammer tap the end of the shaft until it is seen to move inwards slightly. Sometimes the shaft can be completely removed this way but great care must be taken or thesplines, bearings or oil seals will be damaged. If the resistance to the initial taps is significant it is better to obtain a special tool from your Datsun agent (ST35100000).

8   Place the special removal tool 'ST35100000' on the hub and secure it with the wheel nuts. The driveshaft can now be removed by screwing in the removal tool, but take care not to damage the oil seals.

9   Inspect the driveshaft for distortion, corrosion or cracks. Replace if necessary.

4 Constant velocity joint (inner) - dismantling

1   The double offset type of constant velocity joint used at the final drive end of the driveshaft can be dismantled if defective parts are to be renewed.

2   Place the driveshaft in a vice equipped with soft jaws. Expand and remove the band which secures the rubber boot, and remove the boot from the joint.

3   Use a screwdriver to prise off the retaining ring and withdraw the flanged outer ring of the joint (Fig.7.4) You will also need to remove the sealing plate from the other end of the joint.

4   Wipe grease from the ball cage and take out the ball bearings. Rotate the cage by approximately half a turn, and detach it from the

inner ring.
5   Take off the retaining circlip, using a pair of circlip pliers, and with-draw the inner ring of the joint by lightly tapping it with a soft-faced mallet.
6   Finally, withdraw the flanged outer ring and the rubber boot.

5   Constant velocity joint (inner) – inspection and reassembly

1   Thoroughly clean all the component parts of the joint by washing in paraffin.
2   Examine each ball in turn for cracks, flat spots, or signs of surface pitting.
3   The cage which fits between the inner and outer races must be examined for wear in the ball cage windows and for cracks which are especially likely to develop across the narrower portions between the outer rims and the holes for the balls.
4   Wear is most likely to be found in the ball tracks on the inner and outer races. If the tracks have widened the balls will no longer be a tight fit and, together with excessive wear in the ball cage windows, will lead to the characteristic 'knocking' on full lock described previously.
5   If wear is excessive then all the parts must be renewed as a

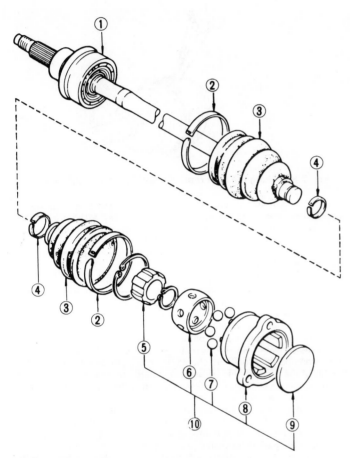

Fig. 7.1 Exploded view of driveshaft assembly

1 Outside joint assembly (Birfield joint)	7 Ball
2 Band	8 Outer ring
3 Dust cover	9 Plug
4 Band	10 Inside joint assembly (Double offset joint)
5 Inner ring	
6 Cage	

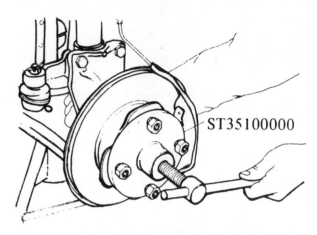

Fig. 7.2 Removing the driveshaft (Sec. 3)

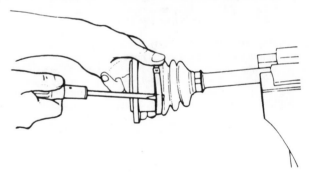

Fig. 7.3 Removing the boot band (Sec. 4)

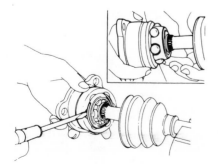

Fig. 7.4 Prising off the retaining ring (Sec. 4)

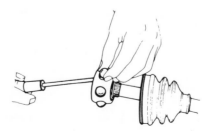

Fig. 7.5 Taking out the ball bearings (Sec. 4)

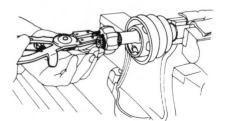

Fig. 7.6 Removing the inner ring retaining circlip with circlip pliers (Sec. 4)

Fig. 7.7 Tightening the boot retaining band (Sec. 7)

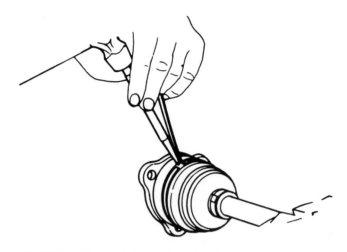

Fig. 7.8 Locking the boot retaining band with a punch (Sec. 7)

matched set.

6   Examine the rubber boot and renew if there is evidence of splits, wear or deformation. It is sound policy to renew it anyway since it could save another strip later on.

7   Reassembly is a reversal of the dismantling procedure.

6   Constant velocity joint (outer) – removal and refitting

1   If the Birfield joint assembly shows any sign of rust or excessive play the joint should be renewed.

2   Remove the driveshaft as described in Section 3.

3   The next task is to remove the joint from the driveshaft. First remove the boot by expanding the clips and then easing it back from the joint. Remove the joint by tapping the outer edge of the CV joint with a hide or plastic headed hammer. The CV joint is held to the shaft by an internal circular section circlip and tapping the joint in the manner described forces the circlip to contract into a groove so allowing the joint to slide off. Remove the boot.

4   At this stage it is just as well to fit a new boot, since it might well save a major operation later on. Slide the boot over the shaft and do not secure at this stage. Obtain a new CV joint and ensure that it is packed with the correct molybdenum disulphide compound grease.

5   Fit the CV joint onto the shaft the correct way round and with the joint pressing against the circlip. Contract the circlip right into its groove in the shaft with the aid of two screwdrivers, so the inner race of the CV joint will slide over. It may be necessary to tap the outside

end of the joint smartly with a soft faced hammer in order to close the circlip completely. Tap the joint until it is fully home with the inner race resting against the large retaining clip. The circular section circlip should now have expanded inside the joint.

6   Secure the rubber boot, and refit the driveshaft to the car, asdescribed in Section 7.

7   Driveshaft – reassembly and refitting

1   Assembly is a reversal of the dismantling procedures. Tie the band twice round the rubber boot before tightening it with screwdriver and pliers, as shown in Fig. 7.7. A punch should be used to lock the clip to the band and then the band should be secured by bending it over. The width of the band should be used as a guide to determine how much to bend over. Exercise great care in securing the band, not to scratch the boot. When renewing grease, take great care to prevent the ingress of dirt or other foreign matter into the joint.

2   When installing the driveshafts make sure that the lips of the oil seals are lubricated with multi-purpose grease and are not damaged on installation. The driveshaft can be tapped into position with a hammer until the threads are sufficiently exposed, but the flange of the shaft should be protected with a soft pad so that the seal plate does not suffer damage

3   When fitting the driveshaft attaching bolts ensure that the nuts are to the driveshaft side. Fit the correct bolts.

4   Tighten the wheel hub nut to 87-116 lbf ft (l2-16 kgf m) and the driveshaft attaching bolts to 29-36 lbf ft (4-5 kgf m).

Chapter 8 Steering

Contents

Specifications

Type	Rack-and-pinion
Steering gear ratio	18 : 1
Steering wheel turns (lock to lock)	3.2
Turning angle of front wheel:	
Inside	38° 00′
Outside	32° 30′
Minimum turning radius	15.7 ft (4.8m)
Steering wheel free play	0–1.4 in (0 – 35 mm)
Rack stroke	2.6 in (65 mm).
Lubrication interval	30 000 miles (50 000 km)
Retainer spring:	
Free length	0.720 in (18.3 mm)
Load x length	55.1 lb (25 kg) x 0.591 in (15 mm)
Tie-rod inner balljoint:	
Swing torque	1.1 – 5.4 lbf ft (0.15 – 0.75 kgf m)
Axial play	0 in (0 mm)
Tie-rod outer balljoint:	
Swing torque	0.36 – 1.1 lbf ft (0.05 – 0.15 kgf m)
Axial play	0 in (0 mm)
Pinion axial play	less than 0.0118 in (0.3 mm)
Pinion rotary torque	less than 17 lbf in (20 kgf cm)
Force to pull rack	33–66 lbs (15–30 kg)

Torque wrench settings

	lbf ft	kgf m
Steering wheel nut	14 – 18	1.9 – 2.5
Column clamp bolt	6.5 – 10	0.9 – 1.4
Upper joint shaft to column bolt	14 – 17	1.9 – 2.4
Lower joint to pinion bolt	14 – 17	1.9 – 2.4
Tie-rod balljoint nut	40 – 47	5.5 – 6.5
Tie-rod outer socket locknut	27 – 34	3.8 – 4.7
Tie-rod inner socket locknut	58 – 72	8 – 10
Gear housing clamp bolt	16 – 25	2.2 – 3.4
Retainer locknut	29 – 43	4 – 6

1 General description

The steering assembly is a direct acting rack-and-pinion type. The steering wheel, which is splined to the upper inner column, is a cone type which provides excellent safety characteristics.

There are two types of steering columns; collapsible and conventional. The steering column is connected to the steering gearbox pinion through two universal joints. The pinion teeth mesh with those machined in the rack so that rotation of the pinion moves the rack from one side of the housing to the other. Located at each end of the rack are tie-rods and balljoints which are attached to the steering arms on the steering knuckles.

One other point is that, unlike so many contemporary vehicles, it is possible to lubricate the balljoints at the ends of the tie-rods.

2 Steering wheel – removal and refitting

1   Disconnect the battery terminal
2   Remove the horn pad by unscrewing the bolts from the underside of the steering wheel bar (photo). On Hatchback models, take off the horn pad and remove the screws securing the contact plates, 'A' and

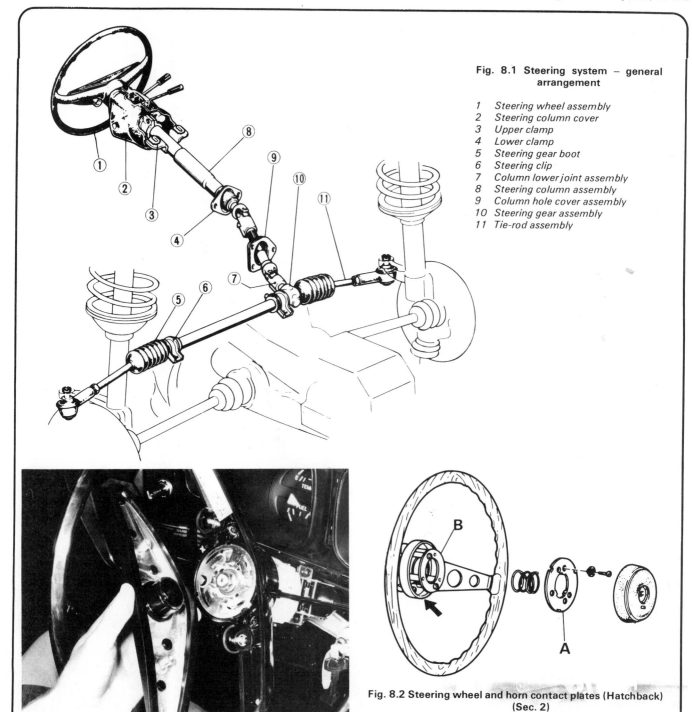

Fig. 8.1 Steering system – general arrangement

1   Steering wheel assembly
2   Steering column cover
3   Upper clamp
4   Lower clamp
5   Steering gear boot
6   Steering clip
7   Column lower joint assembly
8   Steering column assembly
9   Column hole cover assembly
10 Steering gear assembly
11 Tie-rod assembly

2.2   Removing the horn pad (F-II models)

Fig. 8.2 Steering wheel and horn contact plates (Hatchback) (Sec. 2)

'B' in Fig.8.2, then detach the contact plates. Remove the screws securing the contact plate base and detach the plate.
3   Remove the steering wheel nut and then remove the steering wheel by striking it with the heel of your hand. Do not use a hammer; if it is difficult to remove, a puller should be used, located in the threaded holes provided on the steering wheel.
4   Refitting is the reverse of removal procedure. Tighten the steering wheel nut to I4-18 lbf ft (2-2.5 kgf m).

3   Steering column assembly – removal

1   Remove the steering wheel as described in Section 2.
2   Remove the bolt securing the lower column universal joint to the pinion gear.
3   Remove the screws securing the steering column cover and take off the cover (photo).
4   Remove the two screws attaching the multi-switch assembly to the steering column and remove the switch.
5   Support the steering column at the top and remove the bolts securing the upper and lower steering column clamps.
6   Remove the screws securing the column hole cover assembly to the bulkhead.
7   Pull the steering column assembly into the interior of the car.

4   Steering column assembly – dismantling, inspection and reassembly

1   After removing the circlip at the top of the steering shaft, remove the washers and spring.
2   Remove the steering shaft from the casing.
3   Because the steering system is such a critical element in driving, inspect it with particular care. The collapsible type steering column

should not be disassembled; if, on inspection, any damage to the collapsible section is noticed, it is recommended that the complete assembly is renewed.
4   Check the column bearings for wear or damage; if necessary renew them and lubricate them with multi-purpose grease.
5   Inspect the column shaft and casing for evidence of distortion, corrosion or cracks.
6   Check the column shaft spring, and renew if damaged or weakened; the length should be 0.512 in (13mm) with 66 lb (30 kg) load.
7   Inspect the universal joints for excessive play or damage and renew as necessary.
8   Reassembly is the reverse of the dismantling procedure.

5   Steering column assembly – refitting

1   Refitting is the reverse of the removal procedure, but note the following points.
2   Set the road wheels in the straight ahead position.
3   Tighten the lower clamp first (photo), then the upper clamp bolts and the column hole cover screws in that order. Make sure that the seal of the column hole cover is not twisted or turned over and that the lip makes correct contact with the lower joint shaft.
4   Refit the steering wheel as described in Section 2.
5   After refitting check that the steering wheel turns smoothly and that the horn operates.

6   Steering tie-rod outer balljoint – removal and refitting

1   The removal of the balljoints (photo) is necessary if they are to be renewed, or if the rubber boots on the steering gear are being renewed.

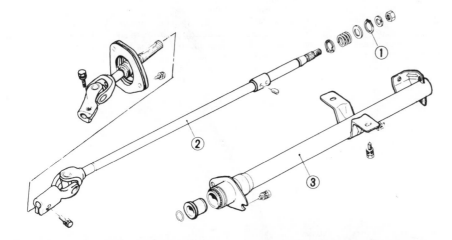

Fig. 8.3 Exploded view of steering column (Sec. 3)

1 Circlip
2 Steering shaft assembly
3 Jacket tube assembly

3.3   Removing the steering column cover

5.3   Steering column lower clamp and universal joint

6.1   Steering tie-rod outer balljoint attached to the steering arm

2   It is not necessary to jack-up the car but the increase in height above ground level may make it more convenient to do so.

3   Slacken the nut after removing the split pin; completely remove it to clear the threads, and replace it after oiling them until the head of the nut is level with the end of the stud. This will protect the threads in subsequent operations if the same joint is being replaced.

4   If a claw clamp is being used to 'break' the taper of the joint pin from the steering arm, the joint may be disconnected without further ado.

5   If no clamp claw is available and it is necessary to strike the pin out, it is essential to provide a really firm support under the steering arm first. A firm tap with a normal weight hammer is all that is then necessary to move the pin out of the steering arm. Another way is to strike one side of the arm whilst holding the head of another hammer against the opposite side. This tends to 'jump' the taper pin out.

6   If the nut turns the pin when trying to remove it, (despite the precaution taken in paragraph 3) jam the pin back into the arm with the jack to hold it whilst the nut is removed. If difficulty is experienced with a joint being renewed then cut it off.

7   Once the balljoint is clear, slacken the locknut on the rod but leave it at its original position. The joint may be removed and a new one fitted by screwing it up as far as the locknut. The pin should point upwards and then be fitted into the steering arm.

8   Replace the castellated locknut and secure with a split pin. See Specifications for the correct torque. Tighten the locknut on the tie-rod.

9   It is advisable to have the front wheel alignment checked as soon as possible.

7   Steering mechanism – inspection

1   The steering mechanism is uncomplicated and easy to check. As the statutory test for vehicles more than three years old pays particular attention to it, the owner can save himself a lot of trouble by regular examination, apart from, of course, keeping a check on his own safety.

2   Assuming that the suspension joints and bushes and front wheel bearings have been checked and found in order the steering check involves tracing the amount of lost motion between the rim of steering wheel and the roadwheels. If the rim of the steering wheel can be moved more than 2 inches (50mm) at its periphery with no sign of movement at either or both of the front wheels it may be assumed that

there is wear at some point. If there are signs of lost motion, jack-up the car at the front and support it under the front crossmember so that both wheels hang free.

3   Grip each wheel in turn and rock it in the direction it would move when steering. It will be possible to feel any play. Check first for any sign of lateral play on the balljoints which connect the tie-rods from the steering gear to the steering arms on the wheel hubs. This is the more common area for wear to occur and if any is apparent the balljoint(s) must be renewed. The joints are spring loaded up and down so they can move in this plane, but not without considerable pressure. If the socket moves easily then the joint needs renewal.

4   Having checked the balljoints, next grip the tie-rod and get someone to move the steering wheel. Do this with the bonnet open and if there is any play still apparent look first to see whether the universal joints in the steering column assembly are causing the trouble or if the rack-and-pinion-unit mounting bolts are loose. Renew the joint(s) or tighten the mounting bolts as necessary.

5   Finally, if play still exists it must be in the steering gear itself. This is more serious (and expensive). If either of the rubber boots at each end of the gear housing is damaged, resulting in loss of oil from the unit then various bearings and teeth on the rack and pinion may have been severely worn. In such cases renewal of the complete steering gear assembly may be necessary. Certainly adjustments will be required

8   Rack-and-pinion unit – removal and refitting

1   Jack-up the front of the car, chock the rear wheels and support the front end on axle stands or wooden blocks.

2   Remove the front wheels.

3   Remove the split pins and castellated nuts from the ends of each tie-rod balljoint. Separate the tie-rods from the steering arms as described in Section 6.

4   Remove the bolt securing the bottom universal joint assembly to the steering gear pinion (photo).

5   Remove the bolts that secure the steering gear clamps to the sub-frame (photo) and pull the steering gear assembly out to the side.

6   Before refitting the steering gear make sure that the wheels are in the straight-ahead position, also that the rack is in the middle of its travel. This can be done by ensuring that the distance between the

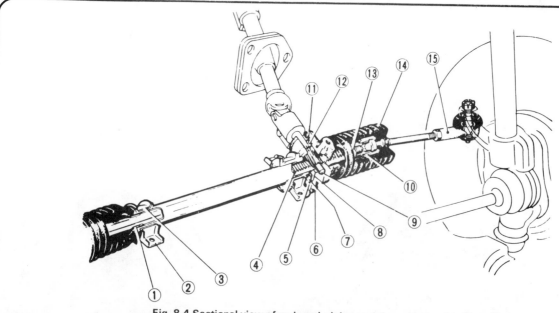

Fig. 8.4 Sectional view of rack-and-pinion and tie-rod assembly (Sec. 8)

1	Steering rack bushing	6	Adjusting nut	11	Oil seal
2	Steering clip	7	Retainer spring	12	Steering pinion bearing
3	Steering gear mount	8	Steering gear retainer	13	Locknut
4	Steering gear rack	9	Steering gear pinion	14	Steering gear boot
5	Retainer adjusting screw	10	Inner socket assembly	15	Tie-rod socket assembly

8.4   Remove the bolt securing the bottom universal joint to the pinion ...

8.5   ... and then the bolts attaching the steering gear clamps to the sub-frame

8.9   The black clamp is fitted at the gear housing

ends of the tie-rods and the steering gear housing on both sides is the same.

7   Position the steering gear in its location on the subframe and at the same time mate the splines on the pinion with the splines of the lower universal joint of the steering column.

8   Make sure that the subframe bracket is aligned with the mount on the side of the steering gear housing by turning and/or moving the mounting as necessary.

9   Fit and tighten the securing clamps. The black clamp is 0.126in (3.2mm) thick and is used on the gear housing (photo), while the white clamp is 0.079in(2mm) and is fitted on the rubber mounting.

9   Rack-and-pinion – dismantling

1   Clean the outside of the steering gear housing and the tie-rods with a grease solvent and wipe dry.

2   Clamp the rack-and-pinion assembly in a vice, taking care not to damage the housing.

3   Remove the boot clamps from the steering gear boots (Fig. 8.6).

4   Loosen the tie-rod locknuts and inner socket assemblies.

5   Unscrew and remove the tie-rods. Do not dismantle the inner socket assemblies.

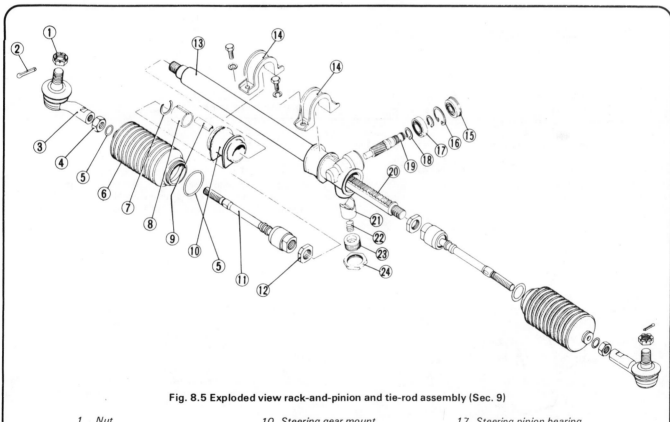

Fig. 8.5 Exploded view rack-and-pinion and tie-rod assembly (Sec. 9)

1 Nut	10 Steering gear mount	17 Steering pinion bearing
2 Split cotter pin	11 Inner socket assembly	18 Pinion bearing inner
3 Tie-rod socket assembly	12 Locknut	circlip
4 Nut	13 Steering gear housing	19 Steering gear pinion
5 Boot clamp	assembly	20 Steering rack gear
6 Steering gear boot	14 Steering clip	21 Steering gear retainer
7 Circlip	15 Oil seal	22 Retainer spring
8 Steering rack bushing	16 Pinion bearing outer	23 Retainer adjusting screw
9 Plate	circlip	24 Adjusting nut

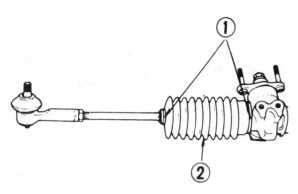

Fig. 8.6 Removing the steering gear boots (Sec. 9)

1 Boot clamp   2 Boot

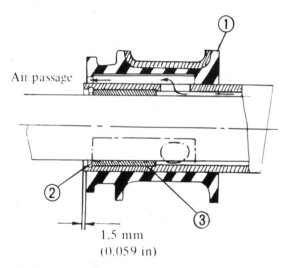

Fig. 8.7 Section through rubber mounting and bushing (Sec. 11)

1 Steering gear mount   3 Steering rack bushing
2 Circlip

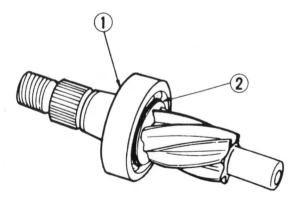

Fig. 8.8 Pinion bearing and circlip (Sec. 11)

6   Loosen the adjusting screw locknut and remove the retainer adjusting screw then take out the retainer spring and steering gear retainer.
7   Remove the oil seal.
8   Using circlip pliers, remove the circlip from the pinion housing and withdraw the pinion.

9   Pull the rack out of the gear housing.
10   Remove the circlip securing the pinion bearing and press the bearing off the pinion shaft.
11   Remove the circlip retaining the rack bushing in the steering gear housing and take out the rack bushing.

10 Rack-and-pinion assembly – inspection

1   Clean all parts in paraffin, thoroughly, and then either let dry naturally or, if available, use compressed air. Check each part for evidence of deterioration, (ie burrs, cracks, chipped rack or pinion). If damaged, the rack-and-pinion must be replaced as a matching pair.
2   Check the tie-rod inner and outer balljoints for excess axial play. Use an ordinary spring balance to check the torque necessary to move the balljoints axially. Limits are detailed in the Specifications.
3   Visually inspect the bearing for cracked, pitted or worn balls and races. Ensure that it runs freely. Renew if at all doubtful. The oil seal should be renewed as a matter of policy, since they are reasonably inexpensive.
4   Compare the spring dimensions with the Specifications and renew if necessary.
5   Renew the rack bushing if it is scored, cracked or excessively worn.

11 Rack-and-pinion and tie-rods – reassembly and adjustment

1   Using a suitable drift and hammer, drive the bushing into the rack and secure with a circlip.
2   Fit the rubber mounting on the end of the tube ensuring that the cut-out in the mounting is lined up with the hole in the tube. Ensure that the ventilation hole is free from grease. (Fig.8.7).
3   Press the bearing over the pinion and secure it with circlips, ensuring that the circlips are located in the correct grooves. Circlip sizes are selected from the table below. Item (2) in Fig.8.8 will always be (d) in the table, while item (1) must be chosen to give an axial play of less than 0.0039 in (0.1mm).

Circlip thickness in (mm)

a   0.041 to 0.043 (1.04 to 1.09)
b   0.043 to 0.045 (1.09 to 1.14)
c   0.045 to 0.047 (1.14 to 1.19)
d   0.047 to 0.049 (1.19 to 1.24)
e   0.049 to 0.051 (1.24 to 1.29)

4   Place the housing in a vice; then lightly grease all the mating surfaces and teeth. Insert the rack from the housing side, mesh the pinion with the rack and secure with a circlip selected from the following table.

Circlip thickness in (mm)

a   0.067 to 0.069 (1.70 to 1.75)
b   0.065 to 0.067 (1.65 to 1.70)
c   0.063 to 0.065 (1.60 to 1.65)
d   0.061 to 0.063 (1.55 to 1.60)

5   Insert the oil seal with the lip face towards the outside, over the pinion stem and onto the circlip. Pack the seal with grease. Check that the pinion assembly rotates smoothly.
6   Measure the axial play of the pinion; it should be less than 0.0118in (0.3mm).
7   Fit the gear retainer and retainer spring into the housing.
8   Screw in the adjusting screw until the retainer is tight and then back-off the screw approximately 20 to 25 degrees. Apply a coat of thread-locking compound round the adjusting screw and tighten the locknut to 29-43 lbf ft (4-6 kgf m).
9   When assembly is completed, check the torque required to keep the rack-and-pinion in motion;

   a) Using a spring balance check that the pinion rotary torque is less than 17 lbf in (20 kgf cm).
   b) Check that the force required to pull the rack is between 33 and 66 lb (15 and 30 kg).

Screw the adjusting screw in or out as necessary to obtain these figures. Check that the rack moves smoothly over its full travel

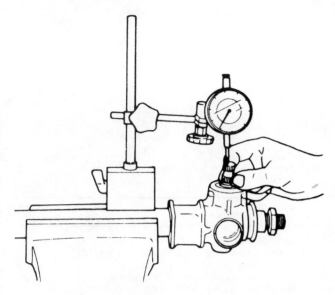

Fig. 8.9 Measuring the pinion axial play (Sec. 11)

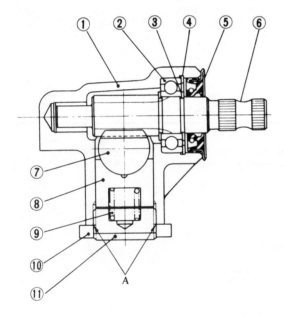

Fig. 8.10 Sectional view of steering gear unit (Sec. 11)

1	Steering gear housing	8	Steering gear retainer
2	Steering pinion bearing	9	Retainer spring
3	Circlip	10	Locknut
4	Pinion bearing outer circlip	11	Retainer adjusting screw
5	Oil seal		
6	Steering gear pinion	A	Sealant location
7	Steering rack gear		

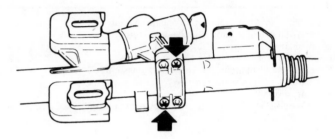

Fig. 8.11 Measuring force to pull the rack (Sec. 11)

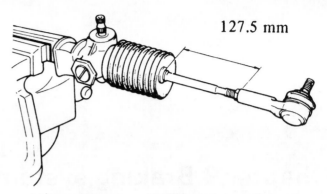

Fig. 8.12 Temporary tie-rod adjustment figure (Sec. 11)

127.5 mm

Fig. 8.13 Steering lock securing screws (Sec. 12)

distance.

10   Connect the outer sockets to the tie-rods. Adjust the exposed length of each tie-rod to 5.02 in (127.5mm) and tighten the locknuts temporarily.

11   Fit the rubber boots, first greasing the groove in the tie-rods where the boots are secured. This will facilitate rotation of the boots if they twist in subsequent adjustment of the tie-rods.

12   Connect the tie-rods to the inner sockets, after fitting the inner socket springs. Screw in the inner sockets, as far as they will go, then apply thread-locking compound to the threads of the locknuts and tighten them to the specified torque of 58-72 lbf ft (8-10 kgf m).

13 Mate the boot with the groove in the gear housing and ensure that the boot is not distorted when securing it.

14 Recheck that the exposed length of the tie-rods is 5.02in (127.5mm) and tighten the locknuts to a torque of 27-34 lbf ft (3.8-4.7 kgf m).

12 Steering lock – removal and refitting

1   As an anti-theft device, two self-shear type screws are used to secure the steering lock. The heads of the screws are sheared off after fitting so that the steering lock cannot easily be removed.

2   To remove the lock drill out the securing screws and remove the steering lock from the steering column casing.

3   To refit, align the steering lock-hole in the casing with the mating part of the steering lock and fit the securing screws. Tighten the screws until the heads are sheared off.

13 Fault diagnosis

Fault diagnosis of the steering system is included in the fault diagnosis for the suspension; refer to Chapter 11, Section 18.

Chapter 9 Braking system

Contents

Specifications

System type . . . . Four wheel, dual hydraulic circuit with servo assistance

Front brake
Type . . . . Single cylinder disc brake (Annette)
Cylinder inner diameter . . . . 1.78 in (48.1 mm)
Disc outer diameter . . . . 9.45 in (240 mm)
Minimum disc thickness . . . . 0.339 in (8.6 mm)
Pad dimensions
    Width . . . . 1.67 in (42.5 mm)
    Length . . . . 2.09 in (53.1 mm)
    Thickness . . . . 0.406 in (10.3 mm)
    Minimum thickness . . . . 0.063 in (1.6 mm)

Rear brake
Drum inner diameter . . . . 7.09 in (180 mm)
Out of round (maximum) . . . . 0.0012 in (0.03 mm)
Minimum diameter of drum . . . . 7.13 in (181 mm)
Lining dimensions:
    Width . . . . 1.181 in (30 mm)
    Thickness . . . . 0.157 in (4 mm)
    Length . . . . 6.81 in (173 mm)
    Minimum thickness . . . . 0.04 in (1.0 mm)
Wheel cylinder inner diameter . . . . 0.687 in (17.46 mm)

Master cylinder inner diameter . . . . 0.687 in (17.46 mm)

Pedal height:
    Left-hand drive . . . . 6.85 – 7.09 in (174 – 180 mm)
    Right hand drive . . . . 6.50 – 6.73 in (165 – 171 mm)

Torque wrench settings

	lbf ft	kgf m
Caliper attaching bolt	40 – 47	5.5 – 6.5
Disc attaching bolt	18 – 25	2.5 – 3.4
Master cylinder attaching nut	6 – 8	0.8 – 1.1
Brake pipe connections	11 – 13	1.5 – I.8
Brake hose connections	12 - 14	1.7 – 2.0
Vacuum line non-return valve	5 – 6	0.7 – 0.9

1 General description

The braking system is hydraulically operated on all four wheels with discs on the front and drum on the rear.

The hydraulic system is of the dual line type, whereby the front brakes and the rear brakes are operated by separate hydraulic circuits from the tandem type master cylinder, so that should one circuit fail braking action will still be effective on two wheels.

A Master-Vac servo booster, brake fluid leakage warning device and a pressure regulating valve are fitted in the system. The servo increases braking force and the pressure regulator ensures greater safety by preventing the rear wheels locking before the front wheels.

The handbrake lever is mounted between the front seats and operates on the rear wheels by a system of cables, equalizer and adjuster. When the handbrake is applied a warning light on the instrument panel illuminates.

The rear drum brakes are a leading-trailing type, expanded by a wheel cylinder to move outwards into contact with the rotating brake drum.

The front brake is a single cylinder type disc brake (Annette). It has two pistons on one side of the brake disc. With the aid of the yoke, the pads grip the disc equally from both sides. Brake adjustment is not necessary as pad clearance is automatically adjusted due to the elasticity of the piston seal.

2 Routine maintenance

1   Every 250 miles (400 km) or weekly, whichever occurs first, check the fluid level in both the master cylinder reservoirs. If necessary, top-up with fluid of the specified type which has been stored in an airtight container and has remained unshaken for the previous 24 hours.

2   Check that the reservoir cap breather holes are clear.
3   If topping-up is required frequently in one reservoir, inspect the hydraulic pipes of that particular circuit for leaks.
4   Every 6000 miles (10 000 km) or more frequently if pedal travel becomes excessive, adjust the rear brakes, as described in Section 3.
5   At similar mileage intervals, remove the rear brake drums, inspect the linings and renew them if they are worn to 0.04 in (1.0 mm) with the bonded type, or with riveted linings, down to the rivet heads. Where the linings are in good condition, brush out any dust from the rivet head recesses and the interior of the drums before refitting the drums.
6   Examine the thickness of the friction lining material of the front disc brake pads. If it is worn down to 0.06 in (1.6 mm) then all the disc, pads should be renewed as a set or both front wheels. No adjustment is required to disc brakes.
7   Every 24 000 miles (38 000 km), bleed the hydraulic system of old fluid and refill with fresh.
8   Every 48 000 miles (77 000 km) renew all flexible hoses and rubber seals within the hydraulic components.

3 Rear drum brakes – adjustment

1   Release the handbrake fully and depress the brake pedal several times to position the shoes.
2   Chock the front wheels and then raise the rear roadwheels.
3   Align the hole in the brake drum with the brake adjuster, after removing the rubber plug from the wheel hole (photo).
4   To adjust the brake shoes, turn the outer side of the toothed adjuster with a screwdriver until by turning the wheel, the brakes can be felt to bind. Now back-off the adjuster until the wheel is just free (photo).
5   Apply the brake pedal hard and re-check the adjustment.

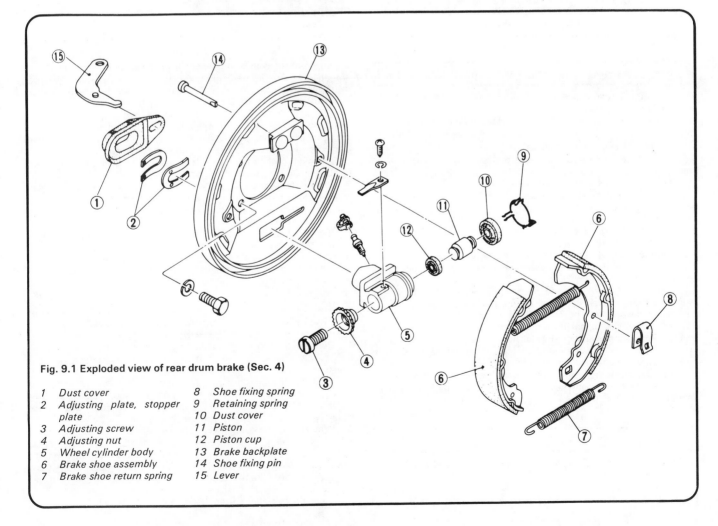

Fig. 9.1 Exploded view of rear drum brake (Sec. 4)

1 Dust cover	8 Shoe fixing spring
2 Adjusting plate, stopper plate	9 Retaining spring
	10 Dust cover
3 Adjusting screw	11 Piston
4 Adjusting nut	12 Piston cup
5 Wheel cylinder body	13 Brake backplate
6 Brake shoe assembly	14 Shoe fixing pin
7 Brake shoe return spring	15 Lever

3.3   Remove the rubber plug from the brake adjusting access hole

3.4   Adjusting the brakes with a screwdriver through the access hole in the wheel and drum

4.3   Rear brake with drum removed

4.7a   The upper return spring

4.7b   Shoe fixing spring and pin

4   Rear brake shoes – inspection, removal and refitting

1   Slacken the rear wheel nuts, jack-up the rear of the car and support it on axle stands.
2   Back-off the brake drum adjuster to aid brake drum removal.
3   Remove the roadwheel and brake drum/hub assembly. Refer to Chapter 11, Section 9 for details of this procedure (photo).
4   Clean any accumulated dust from the brake shoes and internal components.
5   The brake linings must be renewed if they are worn to less than 0.04 in (1.0 mm). If the shoes are being removed to give access to the wheel cylinders, then protect the linings to prevent any possibility of their becoming contaminated with grease or oil.
6   Before removing the shoes, note the location of the shoes and the position of the shoe return springs.
7   Using a pair of pliers, unhook the return springs from the elongated holes in the shoe webs, then remove the shoe fixing spring and pin (photos).
8   Remove the brake shoes and use rubber bands to retain the wheel cylinder pistons in their cylinders. On no account depress the brake pedal while the drum and brake shoes are removed.
9   Fit the new shoes, making sure they are the right way round and that the return springs are correctly located.
10   Check the condition of the drum. If the friction surface is scored, it must be skimmed on a lathe or renewed.
11   Refit the brake drum/hub assembly as described in Chapter 11, Section 9. Refit the roadwheel. Adjust the brakes as described in Section 3 and lower the car.

5   Front brake pads – renewal

1   Raise the front of the vehicle, support securely and remove the roadwheels.
2   Remove the spring clips from the retaining pins and then extract the retaining pins, coil springs and pad springs (photos)(Fig.9.4)

3   Using pliers, withdraw the pads from the caliper, together with the anti-squeal shims (if fitted) (photos).
4   With the pads removed, on no account depress the brake pedal.
5   Brush out any dust from within the caliper body.
6   Unscrew the caliper bleed nipple so that by using the fingers, held square to the face of the outer piston, the piston can be depressed into the cylinder far enough to accommodate the new, thicker, inner pad. Only depress the piston the minimum amount needed to provide a wide enough gap for the pad; if it is pushed in too far, the piston seal will be damaged by the piston groove.
7   Now depress the inner piston into its cylinder by pulling the yoke of the caliper until sufficient gap is made to enable the new thicker outer pad to be installed. Install the anti-squeal shims (where fitted) with the arrow pointing upwards.
8   Tighten the bleed nipple, fit the pad pins and clips and then depress the brake pedal several times to settle the new pads.
9   Refit the roadwheel and lower the vehicle to the ground.
10   Check the reservoir fluid level for the front hydraulic circuit.

6   Flexible brake hoses – inspection, removal and refitting

1   Periodically, inspect the condition of the flexible brake hoses. If they appear swollen, chafed or when bent double with the fingers tiny cracks are visible, then they must be renewed.
2   Always uncouple the rigid pipe from the flexible hose first, then release the end of the flexible hose from the support bracket. Now unscrew the flexible hose from the caliper or connector. If this method is followed, no kinking of the hose will occur.
3   When fitting the hose, always use a new copper sealing washer.
4   When fitting is complete, check that the flexible hose does not rub against the tyre or other adjacent components. Its attitude may be altered to overcome this by releasing its bracket support locknut and twisting the hose in the required direction by not more than one quarter turn.
5   Bleed the hydraulic system (Section 16).

5.2a   Remove the spring clips from the retaining pins ...

5.2b   ... and then withdraw the retaining pins

5.3a   Remove the disc pads

5.3b   A front disc pad and spring

Fig. 9.2 Depressing the outer piston to accept new pad (Sec. 5)

Fig. 9.3 Pulling the yoke to depress the inner piston (Sec. 5)

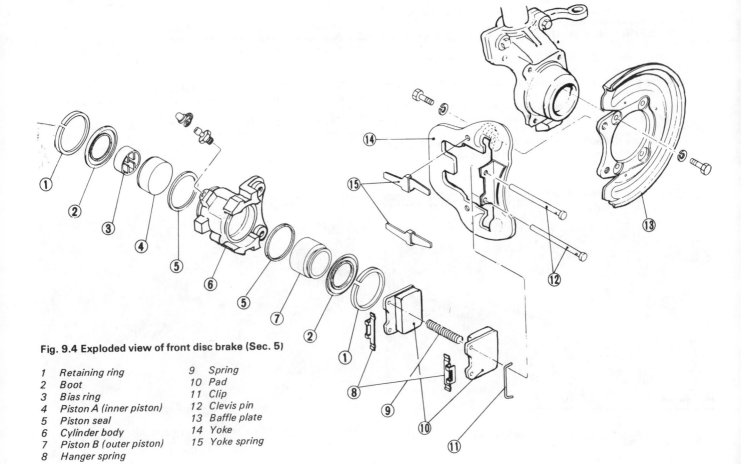

Fig. 9.4 Exploded view of front disc brake (Sec. 5)

1   Retaining ring
2   Boot
3   Bias ring
4   Piston A (inner piston)
5   Piston seal
6   Cylinder body
7   Piston B (outer piston)
8   Hanger spring
9   Spring
10 Pad
11 Clip
12 Clevis pin
13 Baffle plate
14 Yoke
15 Yoke spring

7　Rigid brake lines – inspection, removal and refitting

1　At regular intervals wipe the steel brake pipes clean and examine them for signs of rust or denting caused by flying stones.
2　Examine the fit of the pipes in their insulated securing clips and bend the tongues of the clips if necessary to ensure a positive fit.
3　Check that the pipes are not touching any adjacent component or rubbing against any part of the vehicle. Where this is observed, bend the pipe gently away to clear.
4　Any section of pipe which is rusty or chafed should be renewed. Brake pipes are available to the correct length and fitted with end unions from most Datsun dealers and can be made to pattern by many accessory suppliers. When refitting the new pipes use the old pipes as a guide to bending and do not make any bends sharper than is necessary.
5　The system will of course have to be bled when the circuit has been reconnected.

8　Wheel cylinder seals – renewal

1　If hydraulic fluid is leaking from one of the brake cylinders it will be necessary to dismantle the cylinder and replace the dust cover and piston sealing rubber. If brake fluid is found running down the side of the wheel, or it is noticed that a pool of liquid forms alongside one wheel and the level in the master cylinder has dropped, and the hoses are in good order proceed as follows, there being no need to remove the wheel cylinder from the brake backplate.
2　Remove the brake drum and shoes as described in Section 4, and remove the circlip and dust cover from the cylinder.
3　Take the piston complete with its seal out of the cylinder bore. Should the piston and seal prove difficult to remove, gentle pressure on the brake pedal will push it out of the bore. If this method is used place a quantity of rag under the brake backplate to catch the hydraulic fluid as it pours out of the cylinder.
4　Inspect the cylinder bore for score marks caused by impurities in the hydraulic fluid. If any are found the cylinder and piston will require renewal together as an exchange unit.
5　If the cylinder bore is sound, thoroughly clean it out with fresh hydraulic fluid.
6　The old rubber seal will probably be visibly worn or swollen. Detach it from the piston, smear a new rubber seal with hydraulic fluid and assemble it to the piston with the flat face of the seal next to the piston rear shoulder.
7　Reassembly is a direct reversal of the above procedure. If the rubber dust cap appears to be worn or damaged this should also be renewed.
8　Replenish the hydraulic fluid, replace the brake shoes and drum and bleed the braking system, as described in Section 16.

9　Wheel cylinder – removal and refitting

1　Remove the brake drums and shoes as described in Section 4 (photo).
2　Pull out the clevis pin and disconnect the handbrake cable from the operating lever (photo).
3　Unscrew the union and disconnect the brake pipe from the wheel cylinder. Plug the line to prevent loss of fluid and ingress of dirt.
4　Remove the dust cover from the wheel cylinder aperture and slide out the lockplates and adjustment shims. Note their sequence of fitting and number.
5　Refitting is a reversal of the removal sequence but smear the lockplates and shims with grease before fitting them.
6　After refitting, bleed the hydraulic system and check the sliding resistance of the cylinder with a spring balance; it should be 4.4 – 15.4 lb (2 – 7 kg).

10　Caliper unit – removal and refitting

1　Remove the disc pads as described in Section 5.
2　Disconnect the brake hose from the caliper. To do this, first disconnect the rigid pipe from the flexible hose at the support bracket union and then unscrew the flexible hose. Plug the open ends of the pipes.
3　Remove the bolts securing the caliper to the steering knuckle and lift the caliper assembly away from the disc.
4　Refitting is the reverse of the removal procedure. Tighten the caliper securing bolts to the specified torque, given in the Specifications at the beginning of this Chapter. Bleed the hydraulic system as described in Section 16.

11　Caliper unit – dismantling, servicing and reassembly

1　Drain the brake fluid from the caliper through the flexible hose connection.
2　Unscrew and remove the bleed nipple.
3　Depress each piston in turn as described in Section 5.
4　Secure the longer edge of the caliper yoke in a vice and tap the top of the yoke lightly with a hammer. This action will disconnect the caliper body from the yoke.
5　Remove the bias ring from the inner piston.
6　Remove the retaining rings and boots from the ends of both pistons.
7　Eject both pistons. This may be achieved by blocking the fluid inlet hole and applying air pressure at the bleed nipple hole.
8　Carefully extract the piston seals from their grooves in the cylinders.

9.1　Rear brake wheel cylinder

9.2　Handbrake clevis and operating lever

Fig. 9.5. Separating caliper body from yoke (Sec. 11)

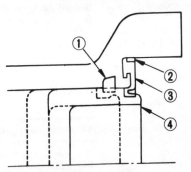

Fig. 9.6. Correct location in caliper cylinder groove (Sec. 11)

1 Piston seal   3 Boot
2 Retaining ring   4 Normal position

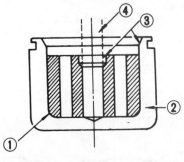

Fig. 9.7 Fitting bias ring in caliper inner piston (Sec. 11)

1 Round portion   3 Chamfer
2 Piston A   4 Yoke

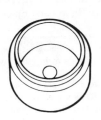

Piston A   Piston B

Fig. 9.8 Caliper piston identification (Sec. 11)

Piston A – inner piston   Piston B – outer piston

Yoke spring

Fig. 9.9 Yoke with yoke spring (Sec. 11)

Fig. 9.10 Assembling caliper body and yoke (Sec. 11)

9   Detach the spring from the yoke.
10 Clean all components in methylated spirit or clean hydraulic fluid. Inspect the cylinder walls for scoring, bright spots or corrosion. Where these are evident, renew the complete caliper assembly.
11 Obtain a repair kit which will contain all the necessary seals and new parts. Check that the rubber seals have not deteriorated or become deformed in storage.
12 Dip the new seals in hydraulic fluid and locate them in their grooves in the cylinder bores. Use only the fingers to manipulate them into position. Note the correct fitting of the seal chamfer.
13 Insert the bias ring into the inner piston so that the radiused corner of the ring is to the bottom. Make sure that the inner and outer pistons are correctly identified.
14 Dip each of the pistons in clean hydraulic fluid and insert them into their respective cylinders. Do not push the pistons too far into their cylinders or the seal will be damaged by the piston groove. Position the inner piston so that the yoke groove of the bias ring coincides with the yoke groove of the cylinder.
15 Install the boots and retaining rings.
16 Install the yoke spring.
17 Fit the bias spring to the yoke.
18 Apply a smear of brake grease to the yoke sliding surface of the cylinder body then reposition the bias ring so that the groove of the bias ring coincides with the yoke.
19 With the yoke spring located in the groove in the cylinder, connect the cylinder body and yoke by applying pressure with the thumbs.
20 Screw in the bleed nipple.

12 Master cylinder – removal and refitting

1   Disconnect both fluid pipes from the master cylinder body and push a cap over the open ends of the pipes to prevent dirt entering the system.
2   Unscrew and remove the two master cylinder flange securing nuts and withdraw the unit from the front of the brake vacuum servo unit (photo).

12.2   The master cylinder is attached to the brake servo unit

3   Refitting is the reverse of the removal procedure. After refitting, bleed the hydraulic system as described in Section 16.

13 Master cylinder – dismantling, servicing and reassembly

1   Clean all dirt from the external surfaces of the master cylinder body, taking care that none enters the fluid outlet holes.
2   Remove the reservoir caps and filters and tip out the brake fluid.
3   Extract the circlip from the end of the cylinder body.
4   Unscrew and remove the stop bolt and then extract the stop ring,

the primary piston assembly, the spring and the secondary piston assembly.

5   At this stage examine the surfaces of the pistons and cylinder bore. If there is evidence of scoring or 'bright' wear areas, the complete master cylinder must be renewed as an assembly.

6   Where the components are in good condition, discard all rubber seals and obtain a repair kit which will contain all the necessary items for renewal.

7   Do not detach the reservoirs from the master cylinder body.

Should this be necessary for any reason, new reservoirs must be fitted.

8   If the non-return valves require attention, secure the master cylinder body in the jaws of a vice and unscrew the plugs.

9   Clean all components in methylated spirit or clean hydraulic fluid.

10   Manipulate the new seals into position using the fingers only.

11   Dip the internal components in clean hydraulic fluid and insert them into the master cylinder body in the reverse sequence to dismantling.

14 Pressure regulating valve – checking operation

1   This device is installed on the engine rear bulkhead and regulates the pressure applied in the front and rear hydraulic circuits to prevent the rear wheels locking before the front ones.

2   Periodically, test the functioning of the valve by driving the vehicle on a quiet or private road at about 30 mph (50 km/h) and apply the brakes suddenly. Observe the tyre tracks which should show that the front wheels lock ahead of the rear ones.

3   Where this is not the case, renew the valve and bleed the system.

15 Pressure differential indicator switch – description and operation

1   With dual circuit hydraulic braking systems, a switch is fitted to the engine rear bulkhead to monitor any drop in pressure in either of the circuits (photo).

2   The switch is essentially a piston which is kept in balance when the pressure in the front and rear hydraulic circuits is equal. Should a leak occur in either circuit then the piston is displaced by the greater pressure existing in the non-leaking circuit and makes an electrical contact to illuminate a warning lamp on the vehicle facia.

3   In the event of the warning lamp coming on, check immediately to establish the source of fluid leakage. This may be in the rigid or flexible pipes or more likely, at the wheel operating cylinders, master cylinder or caliper units.

4   When the faulty component has been repaired or renewed, bleed the brakes as described in Section 16, of this Chapter, when thepressure differential switch piston will automatically return toits 'in balance' position.

5   In the event of a fault developing in the switch itself, renew it as an assembly.

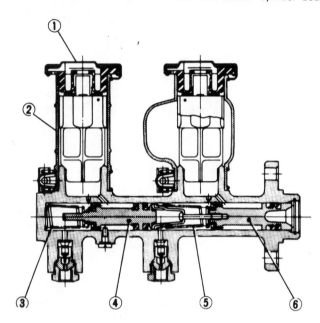

Fig. 9.11 Sectioned view of master cylinder (Sec. 13)

1 *Reservoir cap*
2 *Reservoir*
3 *Secondary piston return spring*
4 *Secondary piston*
5 *Primary piston return spring*
6 *Primary piston*

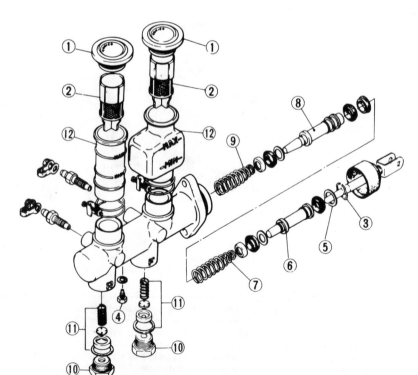

Fig. 9.12 Exploded view of master cylinder (Sec. 13)

1 *Reservoir cap*
2 *Filter*
3 *Stopper ring*
4 *Stopper screw*
5 *Stopper*
6 *Primary piston assembly*
7 *Primary piston return spring*
8 *Secondary piston assembly*
9 *Secondary piston return spring*
10 *Plug*
11 *Check valve*
12 *Reservoir*

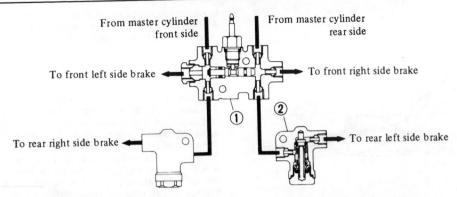

From master cylinder front side

From master cylinder rear side

To front left side brake

To front right side brake

To rear right side brake

To rear left side brake

①

②

Fig. 9.13 Location of pressure indicator switch and pressure regulating valve (Sec. 14)

1 Pressure indicator switch   *2 Pressure regulating valve*

15.1   The pressure differential switch and pressure regulating valve are mounted on the bulkhead

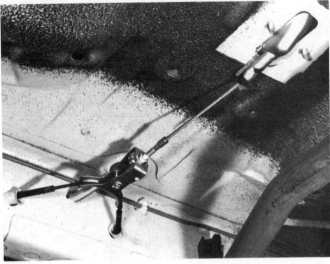

17.2   The handbrake adjuster

16 Hydraulic system – bleeding

1   Removal of air from the hydraulic system is essential to the correct operation of the brakes. Whenever either of the hydraulic circuits has been 'broken' or a component removed and refitted, the system must be bled.

2   If the master cylinder has been removed and replaced, initial bleeding should be carried out using the nipples on the master cylinder body.

3   An indication of air in the system is a 'spongy' pedal or when the pedal travel is reduced by repeated applications of the brakes. In the latter case, the trouble may be due to a worn or faulty master cylinder and this should be rectified immediately.

4   If there is any possibility of incorrect fluid having been put into the system, drain all the fluid out and flush through with methylated spirit. Renew all piston seals and cups since these will be affected and could possibly fail under pressure.

5   Gather together a clean glass jar, a length of tubing which fits tightly over the bleed nipples, and a tin of the correct brake fluid.

6   To bleed the system clean the areas around the bleed valves, and start on the front brakes first by removing the rubber cap over the bleed valve, and fitting a rubber tube in position.

7   Place the end of the tube in a clean glass jar containing sufficient fluid to keep the end of the tube submerged during the operation.

8   With an assistant to operate the pedal open the bleed valve with a spanner and quickly press down the brake pedal. After slowly releasing the pedal, pause for a moment to allow the fluid to recoup in the master cylinder and then depress again. This will force air from the system. Continue until no more air bubbles can be seen coming from

the tube. At intervals make certain that the reservoir is kept topped up, otherwise air will enter at this point again. Tighten the bleed valve when the pedal is fully depressed.

9   Continue the operations on the rear brakes.

10   Always discard fluid which has been bled from the system and top-up the system with new fluid which has been stored in an airtight container and has remained unshaken for the preceding 24 hours.

17 Handbrake – adjustment

1   The handbrake is adjusted automatically whenever the rear brake shoes are adjusted. However, due to cable stretch, additional adjustment may be required when the handbrake lever can be pulled more than six notches (clicks) to the full-on position (Figs. 9.14 and 9.15).

2   Carry out the adjustment by slackening the locknut on the equalizer (saloon) and on the counter lever (station wagon). Rotate the knurled adjusting nut sufficiently to bring the handbrake lever movement within that specified and tighten the locknut (photo).

3   Jack-up the rear roadwheels and check that the rear brake shoes do not bind when the handbrake is fully off.

18 Handbrake cables – renewal

1   *Front cable (Saloon):* Disconnect the return spring, then remove the locknut and adjustment nut (knurled) on the equalizer.

2   Remove the pin securing the clevis to the handbrake lever; the front cable should now be free to lift away (photo).

3   *Front cable (Station wagon):* Disconnect the return spring, then

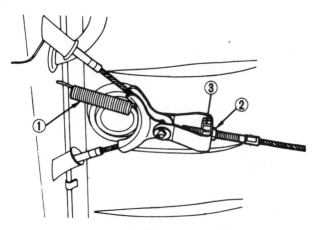

Fig. 9.14 Handbrake adjustment (saloon) (Sec. 17)

1 Spring   3 Adjuster
2 Locknut

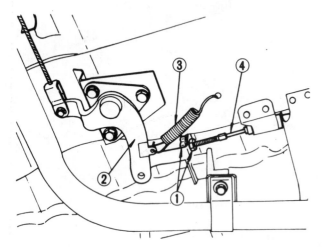

Fig. 9.15 Handbrake adjustment (station wagon) (Sec. 17)

1 Locknut and adjuster nut   3 Spring
2 Counter lever   4 Rear cable

18.2   Remove the split pin and withdraw the pin securing the clevis to the handbrake lever

loosen the locknut and adjusting nut on the counter lever.
4   Remove the clevis pin securing the front cable clevis to the counter lever, then the clevis pin securing the cable to the handbrake lever. Remove the cable.
5   *Rear cable (Saloon):* Remove the clevis pin securing the rear brake cable to the rear brake lever. Disconnect the cable clamp at the rear suspension arm.
6   Ease the rear cable out through the cable guide and equalizer.
7   *Rear cable (Station wagon):* Remove the clevis pin securing the rear brake cable to the rear brake lever. Disconnect the return spring, adjusting nut and locknut at the counter lever. Ease the front end of the rear cable out through the bracket and hole in the chassis.
8   Remove the brackets on the left rear spring and on the axle tube.
9   Remove the circlip from the sliding section of the bracket. Pull out the rear cable assembly, towards the left rear spring, through the guide bracket. Finally, disconnect the left-hand rear cable from the equalizer.
10   Check the cables for chafing or corrosion and the handbrake lever ratchet for wear. Renew as necessary.
11   Reassembly is a reversal of dismantling. Apply a small quantity of grease to the handbrake lever ratchet and to the threads of the adjusters to prevent corrosion. Use new split pins in the clevises which connect the cable end fittings to the wheel cylinder operating levers and apply a drop of oil to the clevis pins.
12   When installation is complete, adjust the handbrake as described in Section 17.

19 Handbrake warning switch – removal and refitting

1   The handbrake warning switch is mounted on a bracket on the handbrake operating lever mounting. It is actuated when the handbrake is applied, and a warning light on the instrument panel lights up when the ignition is switched on.
2   Apart from checking the electrical connections any fault will necessitate renewal of the switch.
3   To remove the switch, disconnect the lead wire at the connector, remove the switch bracket securing screw and separate the switch from the bracket.
4   Refitting is the reverse of the removal procedure.

20 Brake pedal and stop lamp switch – adjustment, removal and refitting

1   The pedal height, 'H' in Fig. 9.20 must be adjusted to the following dimension:

   Left-hand drive – 6.85 – 7.09 in (174 – 180 mm)
   Right-hand drive – 6.50 – 6.73 in (165 – 171 mm)

2   Adjust, if necessary, by slackening the pushrod locknut and adjusting the length of the pushrod. Tighten the locknut.
3   Adjust the stop lamp switch so that the pedal lightly touches the stopper rubber on the end of the stop lamp switch. Tighten the stop lamp switch locknut.
4   To remove the brake pedal remove the snap pin fitted at the end of the clevis pin. Pull out the clevis pin and separate the pushrod from the brake pedal. Remove the nut securing the fulcrum pin and pull out the fulcrum pin. The brake pedal can now be removed along with the return spring and clutch pedal (Fig. 9.21).
5   Refitting is the reverse of the removal sequence. Apply a coating of multi-purpose grease to the sliding parts and return spring (Fig. 9.22).

21 Master-Vac brake servo unit – removal and refitting

1   Remove the master cylinder as described in Section 12.
2   Disconnect the vacuum hose from the servo unit (Fig. 9.23).
3   Release the locknut on the pushrod and unscrew the pushrod from the clevis.
4   Remove the four servo unit securing nuts and withdraw the servo unit from the engine compartment bulkhead.
5   Refitting is the reverse of the removal procedure. Adjust the brake pedal position as described in Section 20 and bleed the hydraulic system as described in Section 16.
6   Whenever the fluid levels in the master cylinder reservoirs are

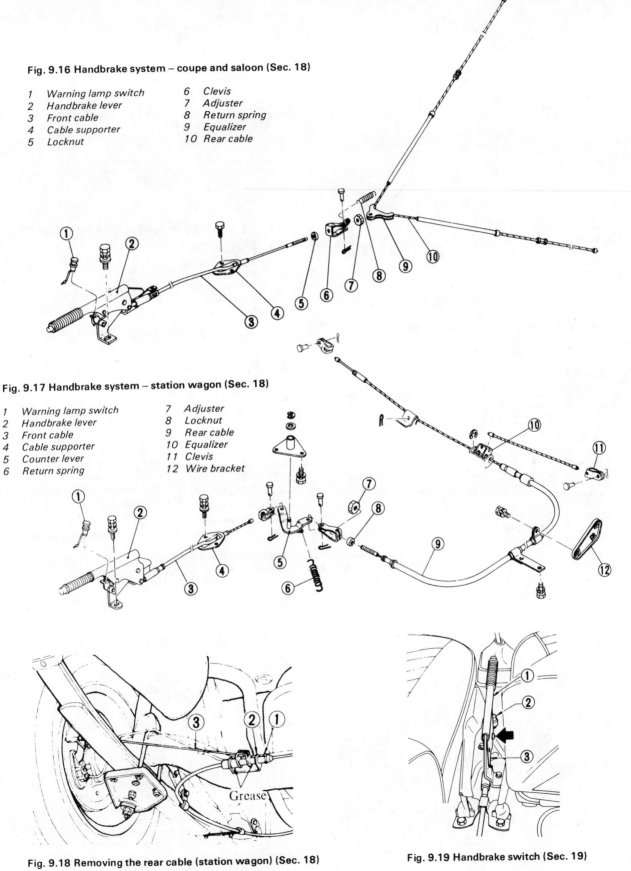

Fig. 9.16 Handbrake system – coupe and saloon (Sec. 18)

1 Warning lamp switch
2 Handbrake lever
3 Front cable
4 Cable supporter
5 Locknut
6 Clevis
7 Adjuster
8 Return spring
9 Equalizer
10 Rear cable

Fig. 9.17 Handbrake system – station wagon (Sec. 18)

1 Warning lamp switch
2 Handbrake lever
3 Front cable
4 Cable supporter
5 Counter lever
6 Return spring
7 Adjuster
8 Locknut
9 Rear cable
10 Equalizer
11 Clevis
12 Wire bracket

Fig. 9.18 Removing the rear cable (station wagon) (Sec. 18)

1 Washer
2 Bracket
3 Left-hand rear cable

Fig. 9.19 Handbrake switch (Sec. 19)

1 Handbrake lever
2 Handbrake switch
3 Bracket

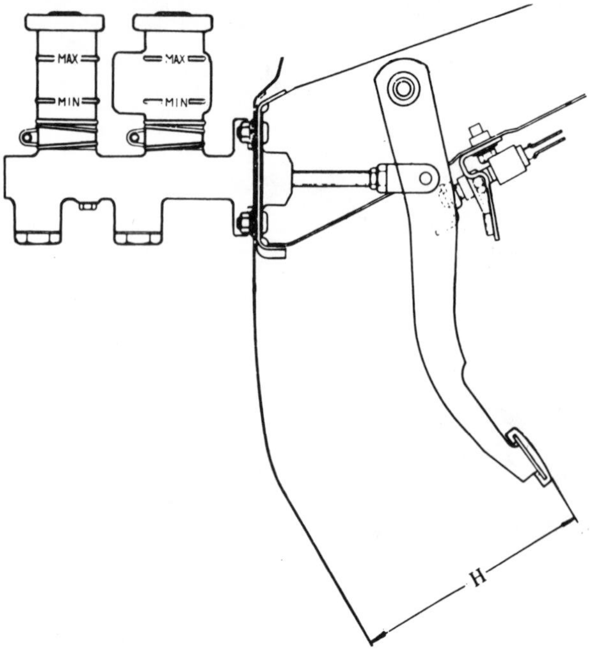

Fig. 9.20 Adjusting the brake pedal (Sec. 20)

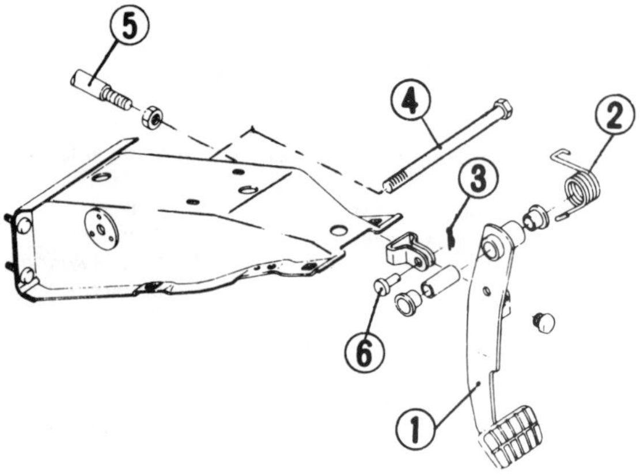

Fig. 9.21 Exploded view of brake pedal (Sec. 20)

1 Brake pedal
2 Return spring
3 Lockpin
4 Fulcrum pin
5 Pushrod
6 Clevis pin

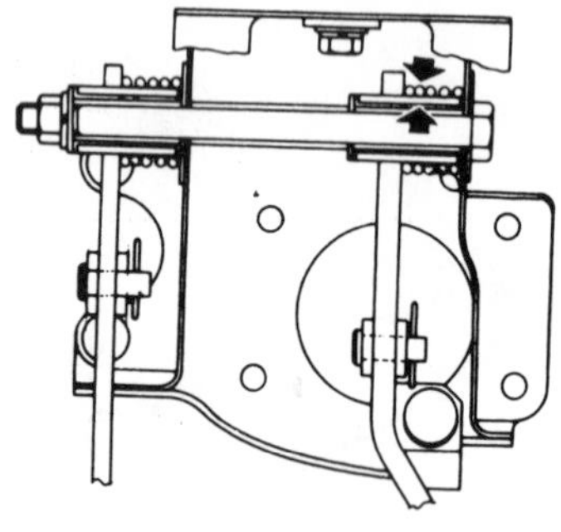

Fig. 9.22 Brake pedal assembly grease points (Sec. 20)

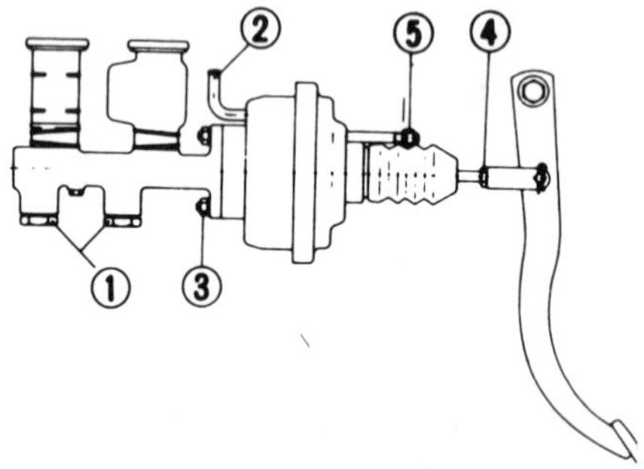

Fig. 9.23 Brake servo unit and master cylinder assembly (Sec. 21)

1 Master cylinder   4 Pushrod locknut
2 Vacuum connection 5 Filter silencer
3 Nut

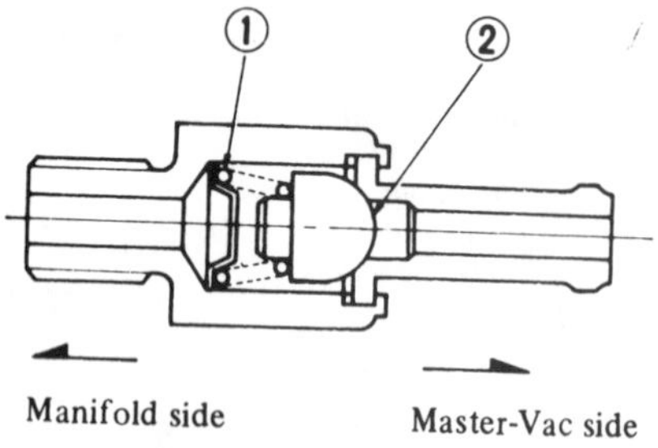

Fig. 9.24 Sectional view of non-return valve (Sec. 21)

Manifold side   Master-Vac side

1 Spring   2 Valve

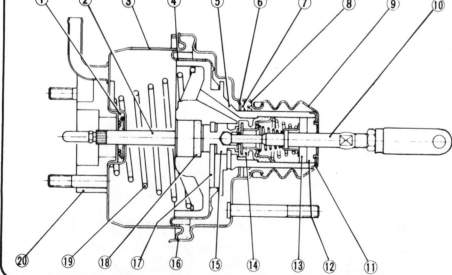

Fig. 9.25 Sectional view of vacuum servo unit (Sec. 22)

1 Plate and seal assembly
2 Pushrod
3 Front shell
4 Diaphragm
5 Diaphragm plate and valve body
6 Retainer
7 Bearing
8 Valve body seal
9 Valve body guard
10 Valve operating rod
11 Silencer retainer
12 Silencer filter
13 Silencer
14 Poppet assembly
15 Plunger assembly
16 Rear shell
17 Valve plunger stop key
18 Reaction disc
19 Diaphragm return spring
20 Flange

being checked, inspect the condition and security of the vacuum hose which runs from the inlet manifold to the servo unit.

7 Incorporated in this hose is a non-return valve which is the most likely component to cause faulty operation of the brake booster facility.

8 Should the valve require renewal, make sure that it is installed in the vacuum hose the correct way round as shown in Fig. 9.24.

22 Brake servo unit – overhaul

1 A brake vacuum servo unit will normally give trouble-free service over a very high mileage and when a fault does eventually develop, it is recommended that the unit is renewed complete on an exchange basis.

2 For those wishing to undertake the servicing however, the following operations should be carried out (Fig. 9.25).

3 Clean the external surfaces of dirt and grease.

4 Mark the relationship of the front and rear shells so that they can be refitted in their original positions.

5 Secure the unit vertically in a vice fitted with jaw protectors. Grip the edges of the front flange in the vice jaws (Fig. 9.26).

6 Remove the pushrod locknut and the flexible bellows.

7 A tool will now have to be made up to unlock the rear shell from the front shell. The tool must locate securely on the four mounting studs of the rear shell and a diagram of a suitable device is shown in Fig. 9.27. Do not improvise by placing a lever between two of the studs or irreparable damage will result.

8 Using the tool release the rear shell by turning it in an anticlockwise direction.

9 Remove the diaphragm plate and valve body, followed by the diaphragm spring and pushrod.

10 Prise off the retainer and extract the bearing and valve body seal.

11 Place the diaphragm plate assembly on a clean surface and detach the diaphragm from the groove in the plate.

12 Prise the air silencer retainer from the diaphragm plate.

13 Extract the silencer and filter.

14 Extract the valve plunger stop key and remove the plunger assembly (Fig. 9.32).

15 Remove the reaction disc (Fig. 9.33).

16 Now dismantle the front shell by unscrewing the two flange securing nuts and removing the flange and the plate and seal assembly.

17 Obtain a repair kit which will contain new seals and specified grease. Commence reassembly by applying some of the grease supplied to the valve body seal lip and then install it in the rear shell using a tubular drift. The seal should be installed in accordance with the dimensions shown in Fig. 9.34. Install the bearing and retainer.

18 Apply specified grease to the new plunger assembly at the points indicated and install it, using a new stop key (Fig. 9.35).

19 Fit a new silencer, silencer filter and silencer retainer.

20 Install a new diaphragm to the diaphragm plate/valve body assembly.

21 Lightly smear a new reaction disc with specified grease and install it in the diaphragm plate.

22 Install the plate and seal assembly to the front shell after smearing specified grease to the edge of the seal and the contact surface of the shell.

23 Apply a little specified grease to the shell contact surfaces of the diaphragm and then locate it correctly so that with the diaphragm spring in position, the rear shell can be assembled to the front shell by using the special tool and turning the shell in a clockwise direction to the limit of its travel in the retaining notches.

24 Adjust the projection of the pushrod, 'B' in Fig. 9.36, to 0.384 - 0.394 in (9.75 - 10.00 mm). To do this, grip the serrated portion of the pushrod and release the locknut. Tighten the locknut after adjustment.

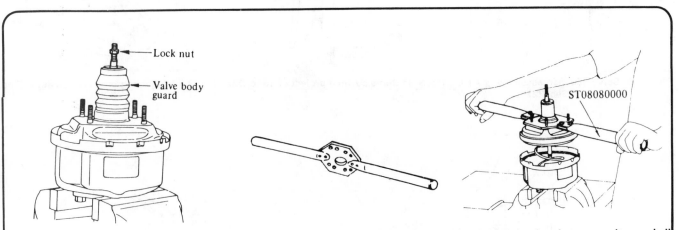

Fig. 9.26 Servo unit secured in a vice ready for dismantling (Sec. 22) Fig. 9.27 Tool for unlocking the rear shell (Sec. 22) Fig. 9.28 Releasing the servo unit rear shell (Sec. 22)

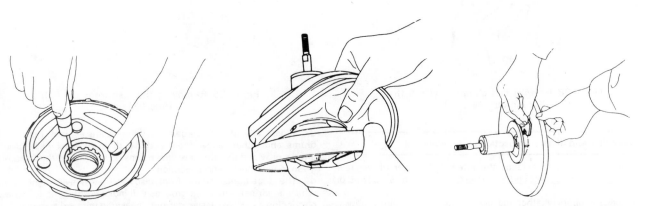

Fig. 9.29 Removing retainer from rear shell (Sec. 22) Fig. 9.30 Separating the diaphragm from the plate assembly (Sec. 22) Fig. 9.31 Removing the servo unit valve plunger stop key (Sec. 22)

Fig. 9.32 Removing the valve plunger assembly (Sec. 22)

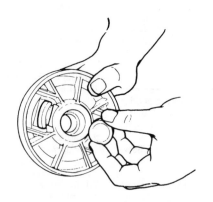

Fig. 9.33 Removing the reaction disc (Sec. 22)

Length "A"
6.7 to 7.0 mm
(0.264 to 0.276 in)

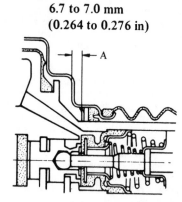

Fig. 9.34 Position of valve body seal (Sec. 22)

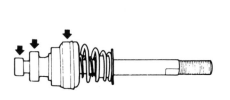

Fig. 9.35 Servo plunger assembly grease points (Sec. 22)

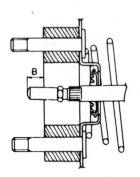

Fig. 9.36 Servo pushrod projection (Sec. 22)

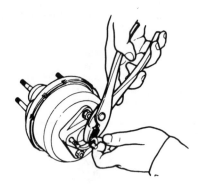

Fig. 9.37 Adjusting the servo pushrod (Sec. 22)

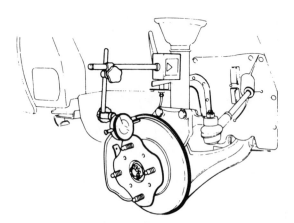

Fig. 9.38 Using a dial gauge to check the disc run-out (Sec. 23)

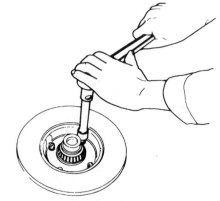

Fig. 9.39 Removing the disc from the hub (Sec. 23)

23 Brake disc and drum – inspection and renovation

1   After a considerable mileage the internal diameter of the rear drums may become out of round, worn beyond the permissible limit, or tapered.

2   Dependent upon whether the brake shoes have been renewed before the rivets have scored the internal surface of the drum, so the drums may require renewal or regrinding particularly if deep scoring is visible.

3   Where any of the foregoing conditions are evident, remove the drums and either renew them or have them professionally ground, always provided that the new dimensions do not exceed the tolerances given in the Specifications Section.

4   The appearance of the front discs will show even light scoring which is normal. Any deep grooves will indicate the need for renewal or grinding as will excessive run-out, measured with a dial gauge.

5   Always check the tolerances specified in the Specifications Section before having an original disc ground or refaced. A disc can be detached from the hub after unscrewing the securing bolts.

24 Fault diagnosis – Braking system

Symptom	Reason/s
Brake grab	Out of round drums. Excessive run-out of discs. Rust on drums or discs. Oil stained linings or pads.
Brake drag	Faulty master cylinder. Foot pedal return impeded. Reservoir breather blocked. Seized caliper or wheel cylinder piston. Incorrect adjustment of handbrake. Weak or broken shoe return springs. Crushed, blocked or swollen pipe lines.
Excessive pedal effort required	Linings or pads not yet bedded-in. Drum, disc or linings contaminated with oil or grease. Scored drums or discs. Faulty vacuum servo unit.
Brake pedal feels hard	Glazed surfaces of friction material. Rust on disc surfaces. Seized caliper or wheel cylinder piston.
Excessive pedal travel	Low reservoir fluid level. Disc run-out excessive, Worn front wheel bearings. Air in system. Worn pads or linings. Rear brakes require adjustment.
Pedal creep during sustained application	Fluid leak. Internal fault in master cylinder. Faulty servo unit non-return valve.
Pedal 'spongy'	Air in system. Perished flexible hose. Loose master cylinder mounting nuts. Cracked brake drum. Faulty master cylinder. Reservoir breather blocked. Linings not bedded-in.
Fall in reservoir fluid level	Normal due to pad or lining wear. Leak in hydraulic system.

Chapter 10 Electrical system

Contents

Specifications

Battery

Type	Lead/acid
Voltage	12V
Capacity at 12 hour rate	60 amp/hour
Polarity	Negative earth

Alternator

	A10 and A12 engine	A14 engine
Make	Hitachi	Hitachi
Type	LT135–13B	LT150–26
Nominal rating	12V/35A	12V/50A
Polarity	Negative earth	Negative earth
No-load minimum revolutions		Less than 1000 rpm
Output current A/rpm	28/2500	37.5/2500
	35/5000	50/5000
Brush:		
Length		More than 0.30 in (7.5 mm)
Spring pressure		9.0 – 12.2 oz (255 – 345 gm)
Slip ring diameter		More than 1.18 in (30 mm)

Voltage regulator

Type	TL1Z–57	TL1Z–85C
Regulating voltage		14.3 – 15.3 at 68°F (20°C)
Core gap		0.024 – 0.039 in (0.6 – 1.0mm)
Point gap	0.0118 – 0.0157 in (0.3 – 0.4 mm)	0.014 – 0.018 in (0.35 – 0.45 mm)

Charge relay

Release voltage		4.2 – 5.2V at 'N' terminal
Core gap		0.031 – 0.039 in (0.8 – 1.0 mm)
Point gap	0.016 – 0.023 in (0.4 – 0.6 mm)	0.012 – 0.016 in (0.3 – 0.4 mm)

Fuses
Type . . . .   Cartridge
Rating . . . .   3 x 10A, 4 x 15A, 1 x 20A
Fusible link:
    Colour and size . . . .   Green 0.008 in² (0.5 mm²)
                                       Red 0.0013 in² (0.85 mm²)

Starter motor
Make and type . . . .   Hitachi S114–161
System voltage 12V
No load:
    Current . . . .   Less than 60A
    Revolution . . . .   More than 7000 rpm
    Terminal voltage 12V
Commutator outer diameter . . . .   More than 1.22 in (31 mm)
Brush length . . . .   More than 0.47 in (12 mm)
Brush spring tension . . . .   3.1 – 4.0 lb (1.4 – 1.8 kg)
Gap between pinion and pinion stopper . . . .   0.012 – 0.059 in (0.3 – 1.5 mm)

Bulbs

	General areas (watts)	US and Canada (watts)
Headlamp (sealed beam)	50/40	50/40
Headlamp (semi-sealed)	45/40	—
Front turn signal lamp	21	23
Clearance lamp	5	8
Side marker lamp	5	8
Interior lamp	10	10
Rear turn signal lamp	21	23
Reverse lamp	21	23
Stop and tail lamp	21/5	23/8
Number plate lamp	10	7.5
Instrument panel lamp	3.4	3.4
Clock illumination lamp	3.4	3.4
Tachometer illumination lamp	3.4	3.4
Indicator lamp	3.4	3.4
Warning lamps	3.4	3.4

1 General description

The electrical system is of the 12 volt negative earth type and the major components comprise a 12 volt battery of which the negative terminal is earthed, an alternator which is driven from the crankshaft pulley and a starter motor.

The battery supplies a steady amount of current for the ignition, lighting, and other electrical circuits and provides a reserve of electricity when the current consumed by the electrical equipment exceeds that being produced by the alternator.

The alternator has its own regulator which ensures a high output if the battery is in a low state of charge or the demand from the electrical equipment is high, and a low output if the battery is fully charged and there is little demand for the electrical equipment.

When fitting electrical accessories to cars with a negative earth system it is important, if they contain silicone diodes or transistors, that they are connected correctly, otherwise serious damage may result to the components concerned. Items such as radios, tape players, electronic ignition systems, automatic headlight dipping etc., should all be checked for correct polarity.

It is important that the battery positive lead is always disconnected if the battery is to be boost charged. Also if body repairs are to be carried out using electric arc welding equipment, the alternator must be disconnected otherwise serious damage can be caused to the more delicate components. Whenever the battery has to be disconnected it must always be reconnected with the negative terminal earthed.

2 Battery – removal and refitting

1 The battery is mounted on a carrier at the front right-hand side of the engine compartment. It should be removed every six months for cleaning and testing.
2 Disconnect the negative and the positive leads from the battery terminals by slackening the clamp bolts and lifting off the clamps.
3 Remove the nuts securing the battery securing clamp and take off the clamp. Carefully lift the battery from its carrier and hold it vertically to ensure that none of the electrolyte is spilled.

4 Refitting is the reverse of the removal procedure. Smear the terminals and clamps with petroleum jelly to prevent corrosion. Never use a mineral base grease.

3 Battery – maintenance and inspection

1 Normal weekly battery maintenance consists of checking the electrolyte level of each cell to ensure that the separators are covered by ½ inch (12 mm) of electrolyte. Do not overfill. If the level has fallen top-up the battery using distilled water only. If a battery is overfilled or any electrolyte spilled, immediately wipe away the excess as electrolyte attacks and corrodes very rapidly any metal it comes into contact with.
2 As well as keeping the terminals clean and covered with petroleum jelly, the top of the battery, and especially the top of the cells, should be kept clean and dry. This helps to prevent corrosion and ensures that the battery does not become partially discharged by leakage through dampness and dirt.
3 Once every few months remove the battery and inspect the clamp nuts, clamps, tray and battery leads for corrosion (white fluffy deposits on the metal which are brittle to the touch). If any corrosion is found, clean off the deposits with ammonia and paint over the clean metal with an anti-rust/anti-acid paint.
4 At the same time inspect the battery case for cracks. If a crack is found, clean and plug it with one of the proprietary compounds marketed. If leakage through the crack has been excessive it will be necessary to refill the appropriate cell with fresh electrolyte as detailed later. Cracks are frequently caused to the top of a battery case by pouring in distilled water in the middle of winter *after* instead of *before* a run. This gives the water no chance to mix with the electrolyte and so the former freezes and splits the battery case.
5 If topping-up the battery becomes excessive and the case has been inspected for cracks that could cause leakage, but none are found, the battery is being overcharged and the alternator control unit will have to be checked and reset.
6 With the battery on the bench, every few months measure its specific gravity with a hydrometer to determine the state of the charge and condition of the electrolyte. There should be very little variation

between the different cells and, if variation in excess of 0.025 is present, it will be due to either:

a) *Loss of electrolyte from the battery caused by spillage or a leak resulting in a drop in the specific gravity of the electrolyte, when the deficiency was replaced with distilled water instead of fresh electrolyte.*

b) *An internal short circuit caused by a buckled plate or a similar malady pointing to the likelihood of total battery failure in the near future.*

7   The specific gravity of the electrolyte from fully charged conditions at the electrolyte temperature indicated is listed in Table A. The specific gravity of a fully discharged battery at different temperatures of the electrolyte is given in Table B.

8   Specific gravity is measured by drawing up into the body of a hydrometer sufficient electrolyte to allow the indicator to float freely. The level at which the indicator floats shows the specific gravity.

Table A

A Specific gravity - battery fully charged
1.268 at 100°F or 38°C electrolyte temperature
1.272 at 90°F or 32°C electrolyte temperature
1.276 at 80°F or 27°C electrolyte temperature
1.280 at 70°F or 21°C electrolyte temperature
1.284 at 60°F or 16°C electrolyte temperature
1.288 at 50°F or 10°C electrolyte temperature
1.292 at 40°F or 4°C electrolyte temperature
1.296 at 30°F or – 1.5°C electrolyte temperature

Table B

Specific gravity - battery fully discharged
1.098 at 100°F or 38°C electrolyte temperature
1.102 at 90°F or 32°C electrolyte temperature
1.106 at 80°F or 27°C electrolyte temperature
1.110 at 70°F or 21°C electrolyte temperature
1.114 at 60°F or 16°C electrolyte temperature
1.118 at 50°F or 10°C electrolyte temperature
1.122 at 40°F or 4°C electrolyte temperature
1.126 at 30°F or –1.5°C electrolyte temperature

4   Electrolyte – replenishment

1   If the battery is in a fully charged state and one of the cells maintains a specific gravity reading which is 0.025 or lower than the others, and a check of each cell has been made with a voltage meter to check for short circuits (a four to seven second test should give a steady reading of between 1.2 and 1.8 volts), then it is likely that electrolyte has been lost from the cell with the low reading at some time.

2   Top-up the cell with a solution of 1 part sulphuric acid to 2.5 parts of water. If the cell is already fully topped-up draw some electrolyte out of it with a pipette.

3   When mixing the sulphuric acid and water **never add water to sulphuric acid** - always pour the acid slowly onto the water in a glass container. **If water is added to sulphuric acid it will explode.**

4   Continue to top-up the cell with the freshly made electrolyte and to recharge the battery and check the hydrometer readings.

5   Battery – charging

1   In winter time when a heavy demand is placed on the battery, such as when starting from cold, and much electrical equipment is continually in use, it is a good idea to occasionally have the battery fully charged from an external source at a rate of 3.5 to 4 amps.

2   Continue to charge the battery at this rate until no further rise in specific gravity is noted over a four hour period.

3   Alternatively, a trickle charger, charging at the rate of 1.5 amps can be safely used overnight.

4   Special rapid 'boost' charges which are claimed to restore the power of the battery in 1 to 2 hours are most dangerous unless they are thermostatically controlled as they can cause serious damage to the battery plates through overheating.

5   While charging the battery note that the temperature of the electrolyte should never exceed 100°F (37.8°C).

6   Take extreme care when making circuit connections to any vehicle fitted with an alternator and observe the precautions given in Section 8.

6   Alternator – general description

The main advantage of the alternator over a dynamo lies in its ability to provide a high charge at low revolutions.

An important feature of the alternator system is its output control, this being based on thick film hybrid integrated circuit techniques.

The alternator is of the rotating field, ventilated design. It comprises principally, a laminated stator on which is wound a star connected 3 phase output, and an 8 pole rotor carrying the field windings. The front and rear ends of the rotor shaft run in ball races each of which is lubricated for life, and natural finish die cast end brackets incorporating the mounting lugs.

The rotor is belt driven from the engine through a pulley keyed to the rotor shaft and a pressed steel fan adjacent to the pulley draws cooling air through the alternator. This fan forms an integral part of the

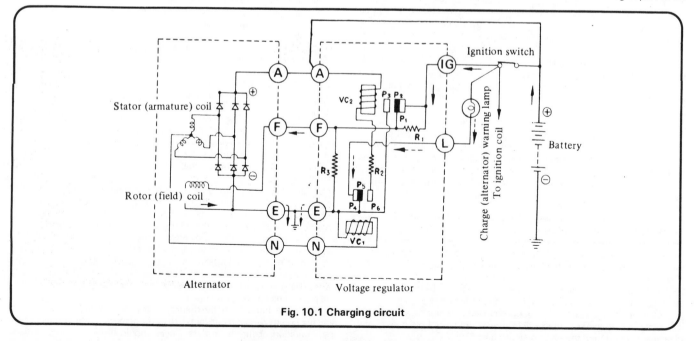

Fig. 10.1 Charging circuit

alternator specifications. It has been designed to provide adequate air flow with a minimum of noise and to withstand the high stress associated with maximum speed.

The brush gear of the field system is mounted in the slip ring end brackets. Two carbon brushes bear against a pair of concentric brass slip rings carried on a moulded disc attached to the end of the rotor. Also attached to the slip ring end bracket are six silicone diodes connected in a three phase bridge to rectify the generated alternating current for use in charging the battery and supplying power to the electrical system.

The alternator output is controlled by an electric voltage regulator unit and warning light control unit to indicate to the driver when there is a fault in the system.

7 Alternator – maintenance

1 The equipment has been designed for the minimum amount of maintenance in service; the only items subject to wear are the brushes and bearings.
2 Brushes should be examined after about 75 000 miles (120 000 km) and renewed if necessary. The bearings are pre-packed with grease for life and should not require further attention
3 Check the V-belt drive regularly for correct adjustment which should be 0.47-0.63 in (12-16 mm). Depress the finger and thumb between the alternator and water pump pulleys.

8 Alternator – precautions

Whenever the electrical system of the car is being attended to or an external means of starting the engine is used there are certain precautions that must be taken otherwise serious and expensive damage can result.
1 Always make sure that the negative terminal of the battery is earthed. If the terminal connections are accidentally reversed or if the battery has been reverse charged the alternator will burn out.
2 The output terminal of the alternator must never be earthed but should always be connected directly to the positive terminal of the battery.
3 Whenever the alternator is to be removed, or when disconnecting the terminals of the alternator circuit, always disconnect the battery first.
4 The alternator must never be operated without the battery to alternator cable connected.
5 If the battery is to be charged by external means always disconnect both battery cables before the external charger is connected. Never start the car with a battery charger connected.
6 Should it be necessary to use a booster charger or booster battery to start the engine always double check that the negative cables are connected to negative terminals and positive cables to positive terminals.
7 Before using electric-arc welding equipment to repair any part of the vehicle, disconnect the connector from the alternator and disconnect the positive battery terminal.

9 Alternator – removal and refitting

1 Disconnect both battery leads.
2 Make a note of the terminal connections at the rear of the alternator and disconnect the cables and terminal connector.
3 Undo and remove the alternator adjustment arm bolt, slacken the alternator mounting bolts and remove the V-drivebelt from the pulley (photo).
4 Remove the remaining two mounting bolts and carefully lift the alternator away from the car (photos).
5 Take care not to knock or drop the alternator; this can cause irreparable damage.
6 Refitting the alternator is the reverse sequence to removal. Adjust the V-drivebelt so that it has 0.47-0.63 in (12-16 mm) maximum deflection between the alternator and water pump pulleys (Fig. 9.2).

9.3 The alternator adjustment arm bolt

9.4a Removing the alternator

9.4b The alternator mounting bracket is bolted to the crankcase

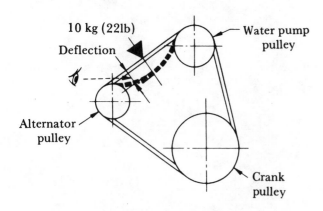

Fig. 10.2 Check drivebelt tension (Sec. 9)

10 Alternator – testing and servicing

1   It is not recommended that testing of an alternator should be undertaken at home owing to the testing equipment required and the possibility of damage occurring during testing. It is best left to automotive electrical specialists.

2   To dismantle the alternator in order to renew faulty components carry out the following operations.

3   Remove the pulley nut and withdraw the pulley using a suitable extractor. Lift off the fan and spacer.

4   Unscrew the brush holder cover screws and remove the cover.

5   Push the brush holder forward and remove it together with the brushes. Do not disconnect the 'N' terminal from the stator coil lead.

6   Unscrew and remove the tie bolts.

7   Separate the rotor/front cover assembly from the stator/rear cover by carefully tapping the front bracket with a soft-faced mallet.

8   Unscrew the three set screws from the bearing retainer and separate the rotor from the front cover.

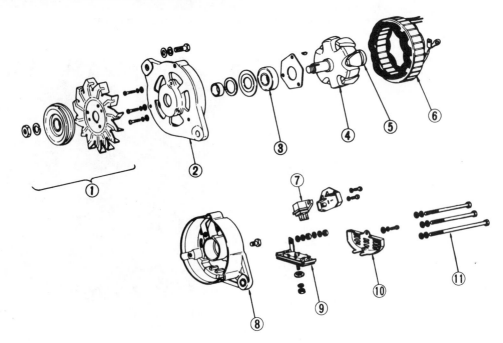

Fig. 10.3 Exploded view of alternator (Sec. 10)

1	Pulley assembly	7	Brush assembly
2	Front cover	8	Rear cover
3	Front bearing	9	Diode (set plate) assembly
4	Rotor	10	Diode cover
5	Rear bearing	11	Through bolts
6	Stator		

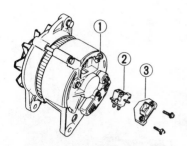

Fig. 10.4 Removing the brushes (Sec. 10)

1   'N' terminal   3   Brush holder cover
2   Brush holder

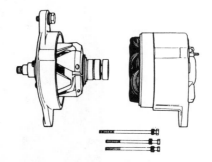

Fig. 10.5 Separating front cover with rotor from rear cover (Sec 10)

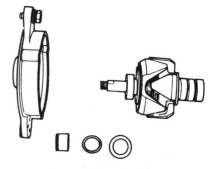

Fig. 10.6 Rotor separated from front cover showing spacer and washers (Sec. 10)

9   Remove the rear bearing from the rotor shaft using a two-legged extractor.,
10 Remove the securing screw and withdraw the diode cover.
11 Disconnect the three stator coil leads from the diode terminal by the careful use of soldering iron.
12 Unscrew the 'A' terminal nut and diode securing nut and withdraw the diode assembly.
13 If the brushes are worn beyond their specified limit (indicated by a line on some brushes), renew them, making sure that they move freely in the holder.
14 Reassembly is a reversal of dismantling but observe the following:-

(i)   When soldering each stator coil lead to the diode assembly, work as quickly as possible in order to localise the heat
(ii) When fitting the diode 'A' terminal, check that the components are installed in the correct sequence as illustrated.

15 Tighten the pulley retaining nut to the specified torque. In order to avoid distorting the pulley, locate an old drivebelt in the pulley groove and then grip the belt as close to the pulley as possible in the jaws of a vice. When the nut is tightened, the pulley will be prevented from turning.

11 Voltage regulator – general description

The regulator basically comprises a voltage regulator and a charge relay. The voltage regulator has two sets of contact points, lower and upper sets to control the alternator voltage. An armature plate placed between the two sets of contacts, moves upward, downward or vibrates. When closed the lower contacts complete the field circuit direct to earth, and the upper contacts when closed, complete the field circuit to earth through a field coil resistance, thereby producing the alternator output.

The charge relay is basically similar to that of the voltage

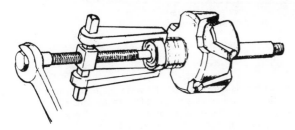

Fig. 10.7 Removing the rear bearing (Sec. 10)

Brush wear limiting line

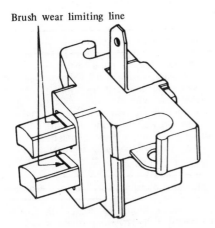

Fig. 10.8 Checking brush wear (Sec. 10)

regulator. When the upper contacts are closed the ignition warning light extinguishes. The construction of the voltage regulator is basically identical to the charge relay. If the regulator performance is suspect the services of a reputable auto electrician should be sought.

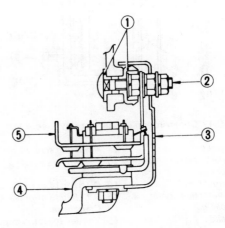

Fig. 10.9 Assembly of 'A' terminal and diodes (Sec. 10)

1 Insulating bush	4 Rear cover
2 'A' terminal bolt	5 Diode assembly
3 Diode cover	

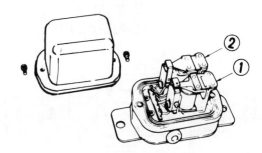

Fig. 10.10 Voltage regulator with cover removed (Sec. 11)

1 Charge relay	2 Voltage regulator

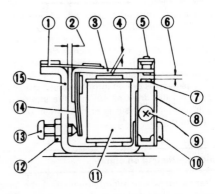

Fig. 10.11 Construction of voltage regulator (Sec. 11)

1 Connecting spring	9 0.118 in (3 mm) dia. screw
2 Yoke gap	10 0.157 in (4 mm) dia. screw
3 Armature	11 Coil
4 Core gap	12 Locknut
5 Low speed contact	13 Adjusting screw
6 Point gap	14 Adjusting screw
7 High speed contact	15 Yoke
8 Contact set	

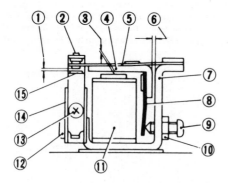

Fig. 10.12 Construction of charge relay (Sec. 11)

1	Point gap	9	Adjusting screw
2	Charge relay contact	10	Locknut
3	Core gap	11	Coil
4	Armature	12	0.157 in (4 mm) dia. screw
5	Connecting spring	13	0.118 in (3 mm) dia. screw
6	Yoke gap	14	Contact set
7	Yoke	15	Voltage regulator contact
8	Adjusting spring		

14.2   Disconnect the starter motor wiring

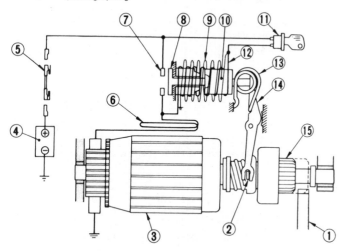

Fig. 10.13 Starting circuit (Sec. 12)

1	Ring gear	9	Shunt coil
2	Shift lever guide	10	Plunger
3	Armature	11	Ignition switch
4	Battery	12	Series coil
5	Fusible link	13	Torsion spring
6	Field coil	14	Shift lever
7	Stationary contact	15	Pinion
8	Movable contactor		

12 Starter motor – general description

The starter motor comprises a solenoid, a lever, starter drive gear and the motor. The solenoid is fitted to the top of the motor. The plunger inside the solenoid is connected to a centre pivoting lever the other end of which is in contact with the drive sleeve and drive gear.

When the ignition switch is operated, current from the battery flows through the series and shunt solenoid coils thereby magnetizing the solenoid. The plunger is drawn into the solenoid so that it operates the lever and moves the drive pinion into the starter ring gear. The solenoid switch contacts close after the drive pinion is partially engaged with the ring gear.

13 Starter motor – testing on engine

1   If the starter motor fails to operate then check the condition of the battery by turning on the headlights. If they glow brightly for several seconds and then gradually dim, the battery is in an undercharged condition.

2   If the headlights continue to glow brightly and it is obvious that the battery is in good condition, then check the tightness of the earth lead from the battery terminal to its connection on the body frame. Also check the positive battery lead connections. Check the tightness of the connections at the rear of the solenoid. If available check the wiring with a voltmeter or test light for breaks or short circuits.

3   If the wiring is in order check the starter motor for continuity using a voltmeter.

4   If the battery is fully charged, the wiring is in order and the motor electrical circuit continuous and it still fails to operate, then it will have to be removed from the engine for examination. Before this is done, however, make sure that the pinion has not jammed in mesh with the ring gear due either to a broken solenoid spring or dirty pinion gear splines. To release the pinion, engage a low gear and with the ignition switch off rock the car backwards and forwards which should release the pinion from mesh with the ring gear; if the pinion still remains jammed the starter motor must be removed.

14 Starter motor – removal and refitting

1   Disconnect the earth lead from the battery negative terminal.

2   Disconnect the black wire with the yellow stripe from the 'S' terminal on the solenoid and the black from the 'B' terminal also on the end cover of the solenoid (photo).

3   Unscrew and remove the two bolts securing the starter motor to the transmission casing. Pull the starter forward, tilt it slightly to clear the motor shaft support from the flywheel ring gear and withdraw it.

4   Refitting is the reverse of the removal procedure.

15 Starter motor – dismantling, servicing and reassembly

1   Servicing operations should be limited to renewal of brushes, renewal of the solenoid, the overhaul of the starter drive gear and cleaning the commutator.

2   The major components of the starter should normally last the life

of the unit and in the event of failure, a factory exchange replacement should be obtained.

3 Disconnect the solenoid 'M' terminal connecting plate.

4 Unscrew the two solenoid (magnetic switch) securing screws and remove the solenoid.

5 Remove the dust cover, E-ring and thrust washer(s).

6 Undo and remove the two long through-bolts and the rear cover.

7 Remove the brushes from their holders by moving each brush spring away from the brush with a wire hook, and then remove the brush holder.

8 Remove the yoke assembly, tapping it with a soft-faced mallet, if necessary, to free it. Take care not to damage the field coils of the yoke by catching them on the armature during removal.

9 Withdraw the armature with the shift fork/pinion assembly attached.

10 Push the pinion stopper to the clutch side and after removing the stopper clip, remove the stopper with the overrunning clutch assembly from the armature shaft.

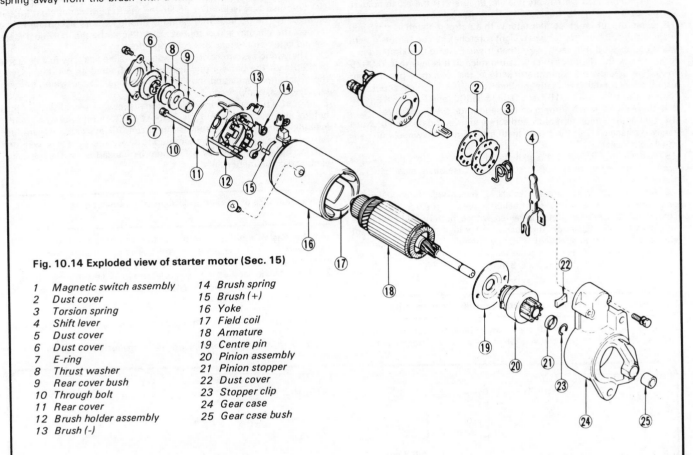

Fig. 10.14 Exploded view of starter motor (Sec. 15)

1 Magnetic switch assembly	14 Brush spring
2 Dust cover	15 Brush (+)
3 Torsion spring	16 Yoke
4 Shift lever	17 Field coil
5 Dust cover	18 Armature
6 Dust cover	19 Centre pin
7 E-ring	20 Pinion assembly
8 Thrust washer	21 Pinion stopper
9 Rear cover bush	22 Dust cover
10 Through bolt	23 Stopper clip
11 Rear cover	24 Gear case
12 Brush holder assembly	25 Gear case bush
13 Brush (-)	

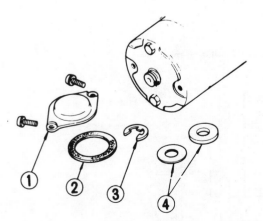

Fig. 10.15 Removing the dust cover and E-ring (Sec. 15)

1 Dust cover	3 E-ring
2 Packing	4 Thrust washer

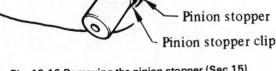

Fig. 10.16 Removing the pinion stopper (Sec.15)

11 Clean all the dismantled parts, but do not use a grease dissolving solvent for cleaning the overrunning clutch, armature assembly, solenoid and field coils as the grease packed in the clutch mechanism would be dissolved, and damge may be caused to the field coils and other insulation.

12 Check the condition of the brushes. If a brush is worn to a length of less than 0.472 in (12 mm) it must be renewed. Check that the brushes move freely in their holders. If they tend to stick, then clean them with a petrol moistened cloth and, if necessary, lightly polish the sides of the brushes with a very fine file. Ensure that the brush holders are not deformed in any way.

13 Clean the armature commutator with a petrol moistened cloth and inspect the commutator for wear. Light scratches can be removed with glass paper but if it is badly worn then it will have to be skimmed in a lathe. Check the depth of the insulating mica; if it is less than 0.0079 in (0.2 mm) below the commutator surface, the mica must be undercut using an old hacksaw blade ground to suit. The mica should be undercut to between 0.0197 and 0.0315 in (0.5 and 0.8 mm). Ensure that there are no sharp corners on the segments; see Fig.10.17.

14 Check the pinion assembly and screw sleeve; if damaged or worn renew as necessary. If the pinion teeth are worn the flywheel ring gear must be checked.

15 Reassembly is the reverse of the dismantling procedure. Apply grease to the rear cover bush and the gear case bush, also lightly oil the pinion.

16 After assembly actuate the solenoid, which will throw the drive gear forward into its normal flywheel engagement position. Do this by connecting the starter motor in series with a battery and switch as shown in Fig.10.18. Check the clearance 'l' with a feeler gauge; if not within the dimension specified adjust by changing or adding adjusting washers. Adjusting washers are available in two different thicknesses, 0.020 in (0.5 mm) and 0.032 in (0.8 mm).

16 Starter motor bushes – inspection, removal and refitting

1 With the starter motor stripped down check the condition of the bushes. They should be renewed when they are sufficiently worn to allow visible side movement of the armature shaft.

2 The old bushes are simply driven out with a suitable drift and new bushes inserted by the same method.

3 As the bushes are of the phospher bronze type it is essential that they are allowed to stand in SAE 30 engine oil for at least 24 hours.

17 Fuses and fusible link

1 The fuse box is located under the instrument panel close to the door pillar. The number and rating of the fuses vary according to the model. The circuits and components protected by the individual fuses are indicated on the fuse box cover (photos).

2 The wiring system contains a special fusible link. The fusible link is located near the battery positive terminal. Should an overload occur, the fusible link melts and thus prevents damage to the wiring harness and electrical equipment.

3 If a fuse blows or the fusible link melts, always establish the cause before fitting a new one. This is most likely to be caused by faulty insulation somewhere in the wiring circuit. Always carry a spare fuse for each rating and never be tempted to substitute a piece of wire or a nail for the correct fuse or a fire may be caused or, at the least, the electrical component ruined.

18 Flasher circuit (direction indicator) – fault tracing and rectification

1 The flasher unit is a small metal container located under the dashboard near to the fusebox. The unit is actuated by the direction indicator switch.

2 If the flasher unit fails to operate, or works very slowly or rapidly, check out the flasher indicator circuit as detailed below, before assuming that there is a fault in the unit:

a) *Examine the direction indicator bulbs both front and rear for broken filaments.*

b) *If the external flashers are working but either of the internal*

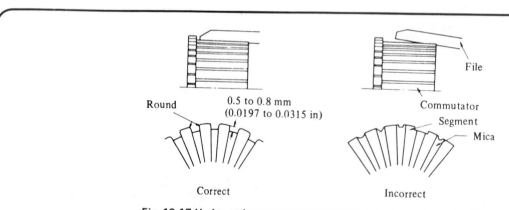

Fig. 10.17 Undercutting starter motor commutator insulating mica (Sec. 15]

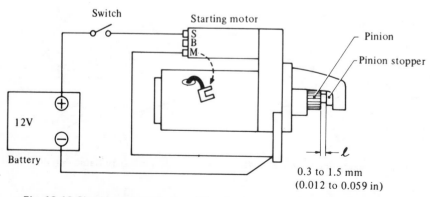

Fig. 10.18 Checking starter motor pinion face-to-stop clearance (Sec. 15)

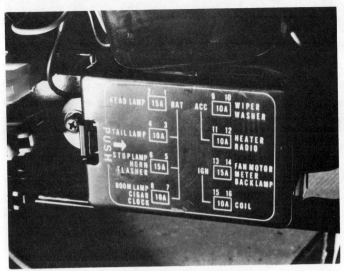

17.1a   Fuse box cover showing circuits protected

17.1b   Fuse box with cover removed

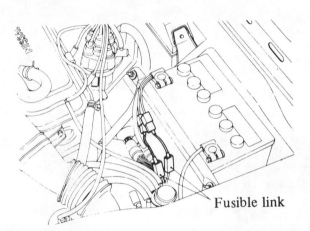

Fig. 10.19 Location of fusible link (Sec. 17)

flasher warning lights have ceased to function, check the filaments in the warning light bulbs and replace with a new bulb if necessary.

c) If a flasher bulb is sound but does not work check all the flasher circuit connections with the aid of the wiring diagram found at the end of this Chapter.

d) With the ignition switch on check that the current is reaching the flasher unit by connecting a voltmeter between the 'plus' terminal and earth. If it is found that current is reaching the unit connect the two flasher unit terminals together and operate the direction indicator switch. If one of the flasher warning lights comes on this proves that the flasher unit itself is at fault and must be replaced as it is not possible to dismantle and repair it.

19 Hazard warning lamp circuits – description

1   This system comprises a switch and independent flasher unit. When the switch is actuated, all the direction indicator flashers illuminate silmultaneously as a warning to other drivers that the vehicle is stationary owing to breakdown.

20 Headlamp flasher circuit – description

Irrespective of whether the headlamp switch is off or on, the headlamps may be flashed for signalling purposes by pulling the direction indicator switch forward.

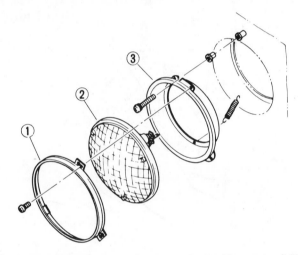

Fig. 10.20 Exploded view of headlamp (sealed beam type) (Sec. 21)

1 *Retaining ring*   3 *Mounting ring*
2 *Beam*

21 Headlamp sealed beam unit or bulb – renewal

1   Remove the three headlamp moulding screws and take off the moulding (photo).

Sealed beam headlamp units

2   Unscrew the headlamp retaining ring by rotating it in a counterclockwise direction after the three securing screws have been loosened (not removed). Do not confuse these screws with the adjusting screws which should not be disturbed (photos).

3   Withdraw the headlamp sealed beam unit forward, peel back the rubber cover at the rear and disconnect the connecting plug (photo).

4   Installation of the new lamp is a reversal of the removal operations but make sure that the work 'TOP' is correctly positioned.

Bulb type headlamps

5   Remove the ring by rotating it counterclockwise and then withdraw the lamp unit.

6   Disconnect the electrical plug and peel back the dust excluding boot. Remove the bulb holder by rotating it in a clockwise direction. Renew the bulb and then reassemble by reversing the removal process.

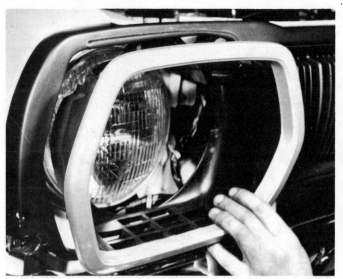

21.1   Removing the headlamp moulding

21.2a   Unscrew the retaining ring securing screws ...

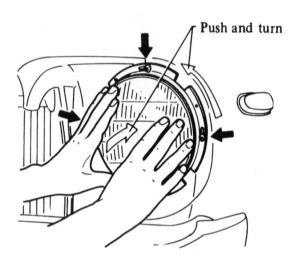

Fig. 10.21 Removing the headlamp retaining ring (Sec. 21)

21.2b   ... and remove the retaining ring

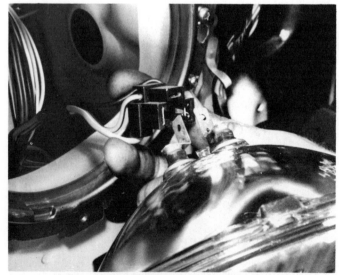

21.3   Disconnecting the headlamp connecting plug

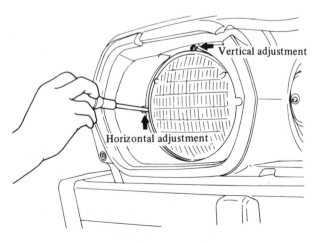

Fig. 10.22 Adjusting the headlamp beam (Sec. 22)

22 Headlamp – adjustment

1   Although it is recommended that the headlamp beams are adjusted by a service station having modern optical beam setting equipment, as a temporary measure they can be adjusted as follows.
2   Remove the headlamp moulding to expose the lateral and vertical adjustment screws.
3   Place the vehicle on a level surface with the tyres correctly inflated and check that the tops of the main beams do not rise above the level of the centres of the headlamps when projected onto a wall or screen.
4   In the dipped position, the beams should incline to the left or right (according to drive) to pick up the kerb for the maximum distance ahead compatible with there being no inclination to dazzle oncoming traffic. If necessary adjust by turning the adjustment screws.
5   Replace the headlamp moulding.

23 Front indicator and parking lamps – bulb renewal

1   Remove the two screws securing the lens and remove the lens (photo).
2   The bulb is of the normal bayonet type with offset pins to prevent incorrect refitting.

24 Rear lamp cluster – bulb renewal

1   Tail, stop and flasher bulbs are removed from the rear of the lamp cluster without the necessity of removing the lens or lamp unit.

Saloon

2   Remove the bulb holder by turning it in an counterclockwise direction and pulling it from the lamp housing. The bulb is of the normal bayonet type fitting (photo).
3   The complete lamp assembly can be removed from inside the boot, if required, by removing the six retaining flange nuts.

Coupe

4   Pull the knob in the rear panel trim and remove the cover (Fig. 10.24).
5   Turn the bulb holder counterclockwise and remove the holder with bulb from the lamp body. The bulb has a bayonet type fitting.
6   The complete lamp assembly can be removed from inside the boot by removing the rear panel trim and then removing the six flange nuts securing the lamp to the rear panel.

Station wagon

7   To replace the bulb, remove the lens cover and lens. Remove the bulb which has a bayonet type fitting (Fig. 10.25).
8   To remove the lamp the luggage compartment side trim must be removed, then the three flange nuts which secure the lamp body.

25 Side marker and number plate lamp – bulb renewal

The bulbs of these two units are accessible after removal of the lens securing screws and lens (photos) (Figs. 10.26, 10.27 and 10.28).

26 Interior lamp – bulb renewal

Remove the lamp lens by turning it counterclockwise. The bulb is of the festoon type and is pulled from the end contact supports (photo).

27 Lighting switch – removal and refitting

1   Disconnect the earth cable from the battery negative terminal.
2   Remove the steering column cover; refer to Chapter 8.
3   Disconnect the switch by uncoupling the connector on the wiring harness.
4   Remove the two securing screws and the switch (Fig. 10.29).
5   Refitting is the reverse of the removal procedure.

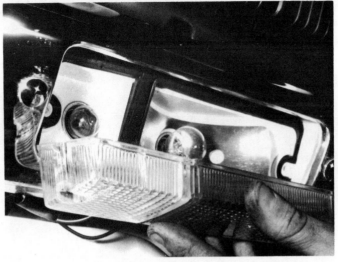

23.1   Removing the lens from the front indicator and parking lamp

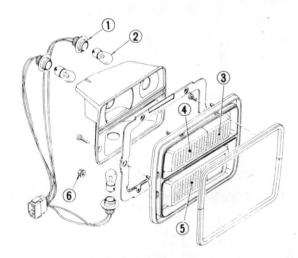

Fig. 10.23 Exploded view of rear lamp cluster – saloon (Sec. 24)

1 Socket	4 Turn
2 Bulb	5 Stop and tail
3 Reverse	6 Nut

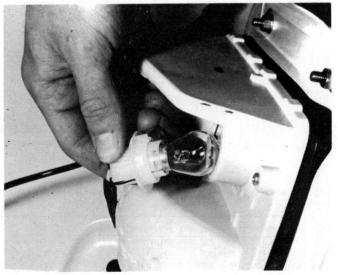

24.2   Renewing a rear lamp cluster bulb

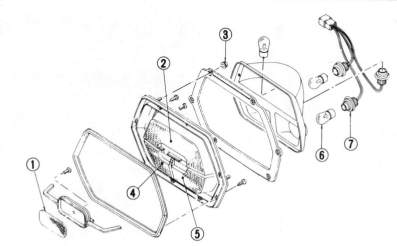

Fig. 10.24. Exploded view of rear lamp cluster – coupe (Sec. 24)

1 Reflector   5 Reverse
2 Stop and tail   6 Bulb
3 Nut   7 Socket
4 Turn

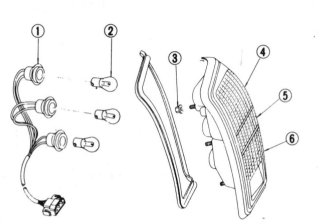

Fig. 10.25. Exploded view of rear cluster lamp – station wagon (Sec. 24)

1 Socket   4 Turn
2 Bulb   5 Reverse
3 Nut   6 Stop and tail

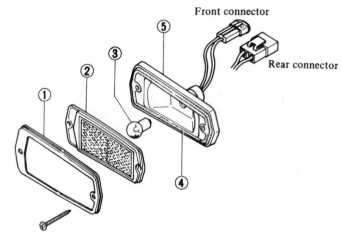

Front connector

Rear connector

Fig. 10.26 Exploded view of side marker lamp (Sec. 25)

1 Retainer   4 Rim
2 Lens   5 Lamp body
3 Bulb

25.1a   Removing the side marker lamp lens

25.1b   Undoing the number plate lamp securing screws ...

25.1c   ... and removing the lens

28 Direction indicator and headlamp flasher switch – removal and refitting

1   Disconnect the earth cable from the battery negative terminal.
2   Remove the horn ring, steering wheel and steering column cover as described in Chapter 8.
3   Disconnect the wiring harness connector.
4   Remove the two securing screws and then the switch assembly.
5   Refitting is the reverse of the removal procedure.

29 Courtesy light/warning buzzer switch – removal and refitting

1   The switch is a press fit in the door pillar.
2   To remove it, simply pull it from its location or carefully prise it out using a small screwdriver.
3   With the switch and leads withdrawn, disconnect the leads from the switch at the snap connectors, noting that of the three leads, two are for the warning buzzer and the third for the vehicle interior lamp.
4   The switch may cease to operate due to corrosion, causing a poor

Fig. 10.27. Exploded view of number plate lamp (Sec. 25)

1 Screw   4 Lens
2 Washer   5 Bulb
3 Lens cover

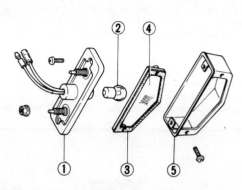

Fig. 10.28 Exploded view of licence plate lamp (US model) (Sec. 25)

1 Light body   4 Lens
2 Bulb   5 Cover
3 Rim

26.1   Interior lamp with lens removed

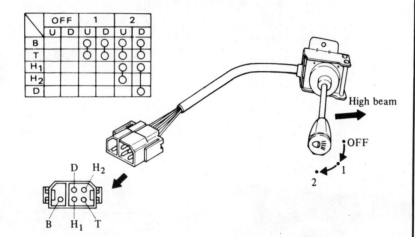

	OFF		1		2	
	U	D	U	D	U	D
B			◯	◯	◯	◯
T			◯	◯	◯	◯
H₁				◯	◯	
H₂					◯	◯
D						◯

Fig. 10.29 Lighting switch (Sec. 27)

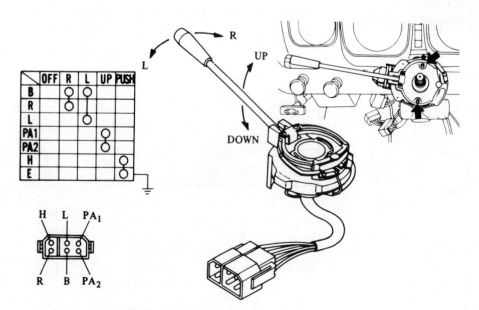

	OFF	R	L	UP	PUSH
B		◯	◯		
R	◯	◯			
L			◯		
PA1				◯	
PA2				◯	
H					◯
E					◯

Fig. 10.30 Direction indicator and headlamp flasher switch (Sec. 28)

earth or bad switch electrical contact, in which case it should be renewed complete.

5　Installation is the reverse of the removal sequence.

30　Ignition switch – removal and refitting

1　Disconnect the earth cable from the battery negative terminal.

2　Remove the steering column cover (refer to Chapter 8) and

disconnect the wiring harness connector.

3　Undo the small screw securing the switch body to the steering lock and remove the switch.

4　Refitting is the reverse of the removal procedure.

31　Horns – description and checking

1　The dual horns are mounted under the battery (photo), one is low

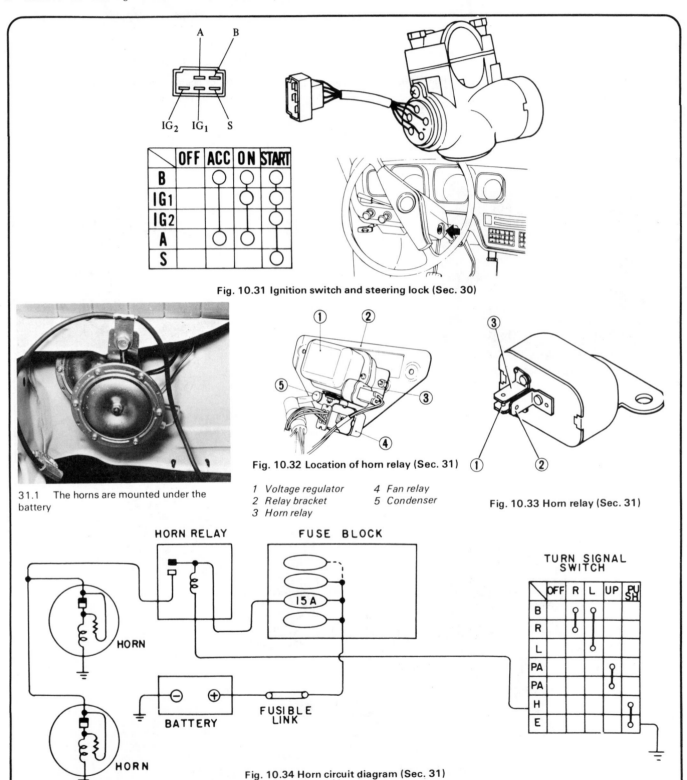

	OFF	ACC	ON	START
B		○	○	○
IG1			○	○
IG2				○
A		○	○	○
S				○

Fig. 10.31 Ignition switch and steering lock (Sec. 30)

31.1　The horns are mounted under the battery

Fig. 10.32 Location of horn relay (Sec. 31)

1　Voltage regulator　　4　Fan relay
2　Relay bracket　　　　5　Condenser
3　Horn relay

Fig. 10.33 Horn relay (Sec. 31)

HORN RELAY　　　FUSE BLOCK

15 A

HORN

HORN

BATTERY

FUSIBLE LINK

TURN SIGNAL SWITCH

	OFF	R	L	UP	PU SH
B		○	○		
R		○			
L			○		
PA				○	
PA				○	
H					○
E					○

Fig. 10.34 Horn circuit diagram (Sec. 31)

tone and the high tone. The horn relay is mounted on the battery carrier support.

2   Normal maintenance consists of checking the security of the connecting wiring to the horns and the relay.

3   If the horns fail to operate test the continuity of the circuit with a test lamp or ohmmeter. When testing the horn relay there must be continuity between terminals (1) and (3) when there is 12V between terminals (1) and (2); refer to Fig. 10.33. The horn fuse is of 15A rating. Renew a faulty horn or horn relay.

32 Instrument cluster – removal and refitting

1   Disconnect the earth cable from the battery negative terminal.

2   Remove the knobs and nuts as shown in Fig 10.35.

3   Remove the ashtray and then remove the instrument cover retaining screws.

4   Pull the cover forward, disconnect the cigarette lighter harness at the connector and remove the cover.

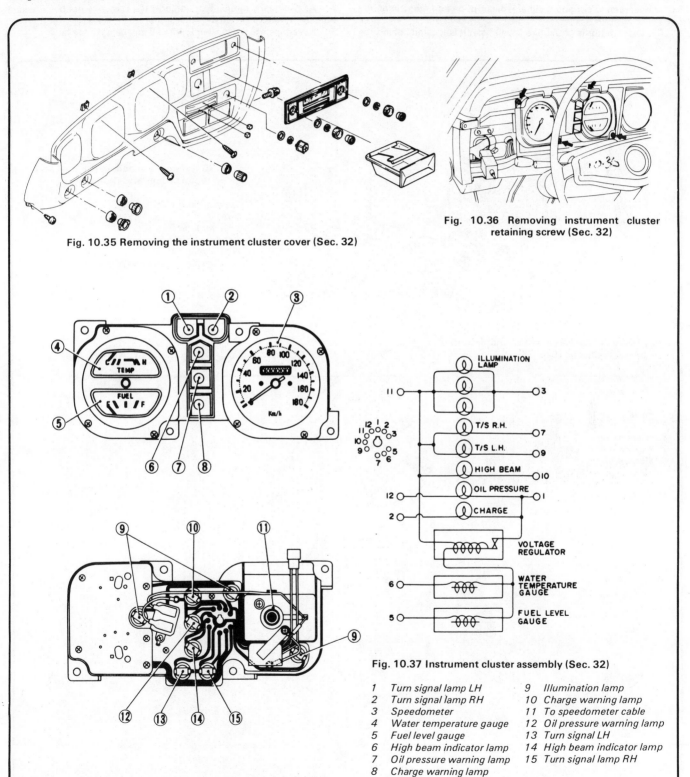

Fig. 10.35 Removing the instrument cluster cover (Sec. 32)

Fig. 10.36 Removing instrument cluster retaining screw (Sec. 32)

Fig. 10.37 Instrument cluster assembly (Sec. 32)

1   Turn signal lamp LH
2   Turn signal lamp RH
3   Speedometer
4   Water temperature gauge
5   Fuel level gauge
6   High beam indicator lamp
7   Oil pressure warning lamp
8   Charge warning lamp
9   Illumination lamp
10 Charge warning lamp
11 To speedometer cable
12 Oil pressure warning lamp
13 Turn signal LH
14 High beam indicator lamp
15 Turn signal lamp RH

5   Remove the instrument cluster retaining screws and disconnect the multi-pole connector plug.
6   Disconnect the speedometer cable and lift out the instrument cluster.
7   Speedometer, gauges and bulbs can now be removed from the instrument cluster panel (Fig. 10.38).
8   Refitting the instrument cluster is the reverse of the removal procedure.

33 Windscreen wiper and washer – description and maintenance

1   The wiper motor is of the two speed type. It is located behind the glove box and drives the wiper arms through linkage mechanism located behind the instrument panel.
2   The electrically operated windscreen washer unit (motor, tank and pump) is located to the left of the engine compartment.
3   A combined wiper/washer switch is fitted. The switch operates the wipers by a two position push-pull action and the washer by twisting the switch knob clockwise. The washer knob is spring loaded and it should not be held in the 'ON' position for more than 30 seconds at a time.
4   At two yearly intervals or earlier if the screen is not being wiped effectively, renew the wiper blades.
5   Never operate the washer without liquid being in the tank.

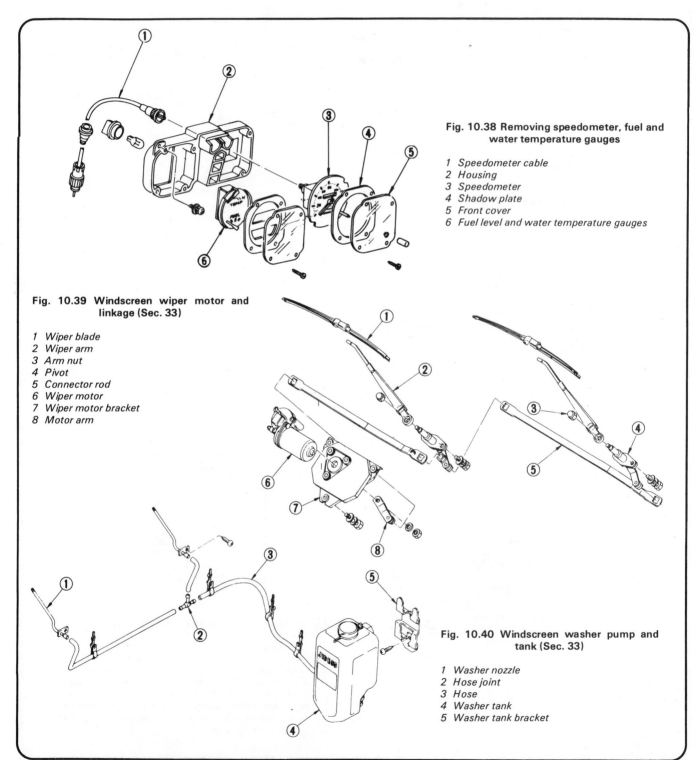

Fig. 10.38 Removing speedometer, fuel and water temperature gauges

1 *Speedometer cable*
2 *Housing*
3 *Speedometer*
4 *Shadow plate*
5 *Front cover*
6 *Fuel level and water temperature gauges*

Fig. 10.39 Windscreen wiper motor and linkage (Sec. 33)

1 *Wiper blade*
2 *Wiper arm*
3 *Arm nut*
4 *Pivot*
5 *Connector rod*
6 *Wiper motor*
7 *Wiper motor bracket*
8 *Motor arm*

Fig. 10.40 Windscreen washer pump and tank (Sec. 33)

1 *Washer nozzle*
2 *Hose joint*
3 *Hose*
4 *Washer tank*
5 *Washer tank bracket*

34.2a   Unscrew the wiper arm securing nut ...

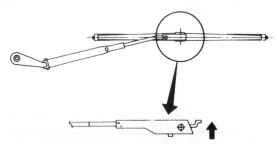

Fig. 10.41 Removing windscreen wiper blade (Sec. 34)

34 Windscreen wiper arm and blade – removal and refitting

1   Pull the wiper arm/blade assembly forward to raise it from the windscreen glass.
2   Unscrew and remove the arm to spindle securing nut and remove the arm/blade assembly from the spindle (photos).
3   To remove the wiper blade, depress the tab to release the dimple from its recess and pull the blade from the arm (photo).
4   Installation is a reversal of removal but with the wiper motor in the parked position, install the wiper arm/blade assemblies so that they are parallel with the bottom of the windscreen and tighten the arm to spindle nuts to the specified torque. Any fine adjustment can be made by releasing the nut and slightly moving the position of the arm on the spindle. Incorrect parking of the wiper arms may be caused by incorrect setting of the auto-stop device. Remove the cover and bend the relay plates as required.

34.2b   ... and remove the wiper arm from the spindle

35 Windscreen wiper – fault tracing

Should the windscreen wipers fail, or work very slowly then check the terminals for loose connections, and make sure the insulation of the external wiring is not broken or cracked. If this is in order then check the current the motor is taking by connecting a 1-20 volt ammeter in series in the circuit and turning on the wiper switch. Consumption should be less than 1.5 amps on low speed, and less than 2.0 amps on high.
    If no current is flowing check that the fuse has not blown. The correct rating is 10 amps. If it has, check the wiring of the motor and other electrical circuits serviced by this fuse for short circuits. If the fuse is in good condition check the wiper switch.
    Should the motor take a very low current ensure that the battery is fully charged. If the motor takes a high current then it is an indication that there is an internal fault or partially seized linkage.
    It is possible for the motor to be stripped and overhauled but the availability of spare parts could present a problem. Either take a faulty unit to the local automobile electricians or obtain a replacement unit.

36 Windscreen wiper motor and linkage – removal and refitting

1   Disconnect the earth cable from the battery negative terminal.
2   Remove the instrument cluster cover (see Section 32) and the glove box. Remove the wiper arms.
3   Remove the wiper motor attaching bolts and the ball joint connecting the motor shaft to the linkage (Fig. 10.44).
4   Remove the wiper motor from the cowl dash panel.
5   Remove the pivot attaching bolts and then the linkage assembly.
6   Refitting is the reverse of the removal sequence but when fitting the wiper arms ensure that they are positioned at the bottom when the motor is in the 'OFF' (parked) position before tightening the securing nut.

37 Windscreen washer tank and pump – removal and refitting

1   The washer pump is fitted under the washer tank and the assembly is located on a bracket on the left-hand side in the engine compartment.
2   Remove the washer tank from the bracket by pulling it upwards.
3   Remove the hoses from the washer pump and drain the fluid.

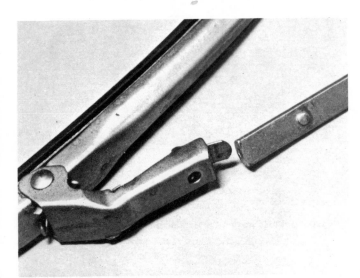

34.3   Wiper blade disconnected from wiper arm

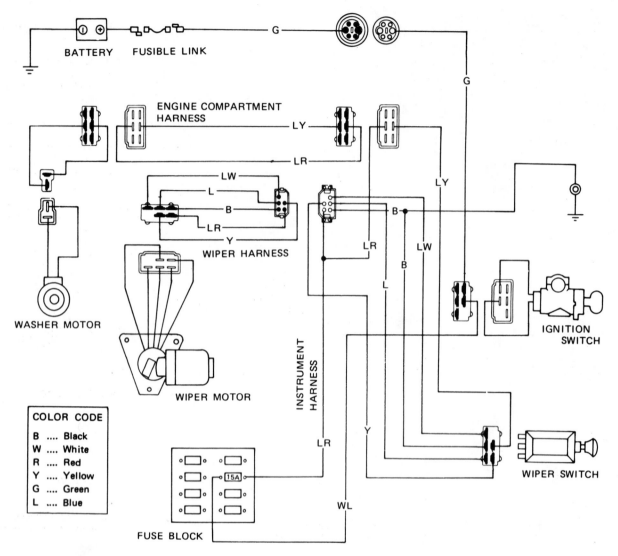

Fig. 10.42 Windscreen wiper and washer circuit diagram (Sec. 35)

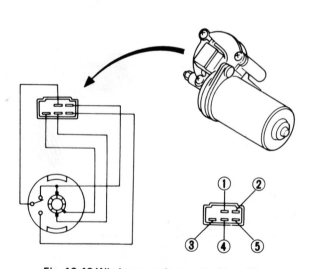

Fig. 10.43 Windscreen wiper motor (Sec. 36).

1 Yellow wire   4 Blue wire
2 Blue/red wire   5 Black wire
3 Blue/white wire

Fig. 10.44 Removing the windscreen wiper motor (Sec. 36)

4   Disconnect the electrical leads at the connector and lift the tank and pump assembly out.

5   Refitting is the reverse of the removal procedure.

38 Cigarette lighter – removal and refitting

1   Disconnect the earth cable from the battery.
2   Pull the lighter from the housing.
3   Remove the instrument cluster cover as described in Section 32.
4   Disconnect the wiring harness at the connector.
5   Turn the housing counterclockwise to remove it.
6   Refitting is the reverse of the removal procedure.

39 Heated rear window – general

1   The heater element is controlled by a switch and indicator lamp. On left-hand drive models the switch is fitted on the left side of the heater control unit and on right-hand drive models it is fitted on the instrument panel.
2   The system is wired in conjunction with the ignition switch to prevent the heater being left on when the car is parked.
3   A break in the heating element can be repaired by your Datsun dealer using conductive silver composition (Dupont 4817) without the expense of a new rear window being incurred.

40 Radio – removal, refitting and aerial trimmer adjustments

1   Remove the instrument cluster cover as described in Section 32.
2   Remove the radio bracket to instrument panel attaching screws and disconnect the speaker wires at the connector.

3   Disconnect the radio wires to the instrument harness at the connectors.
4   Disconnect the aerial feeder to radio receiver cable and lift the radio from the instrument panel.
5   Refitting is the reverse of the removal procedure.
6   To adjust the aerial trimmer, extend the aerial fully and tune to the weakest station between 1200 and 1600 KHz. Then, using a small screwdriver, turn the trimmer first to the left and then to the right until receiving sensitivity is at its best.

41 Clock – testing, removal and refitting

1   If the clock fails to work, check the blue cable to verify the presence of 12 volts, using a test lamp or voltmeter. If this is satisfactory, check the black cable for a good earth connection. If the clock is not illuminated suspect the red/white cable connection
2   If all the cables are satisfactory, and the power supplies and earth are present at the clock terminals, then the fault must lie in the clock.

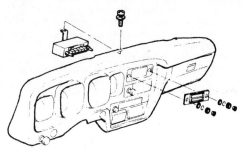

Fig. 10.45 Removing the radio (Sec. 40)

Fig. 10.46 Radio and aerial (Sec. 40)

1 Aerial	6 Fuse
2 Escutcheon	7 Harness for power inlet
3 Feeder cable	8 Illumination light connector
4 Radio receiver	9 Earth
5 Speaker harness	

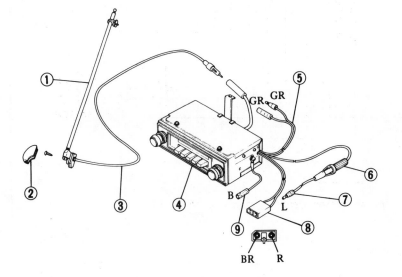

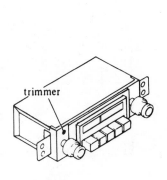

HITACHI

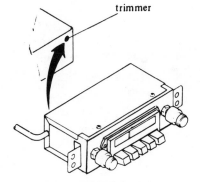

CLARION

Fig. 10.47 Location of aerial trimmer (Sec. 4C)

3   Remove the clock by releasing the two screws that secure it to the instrument panel. No further breakdown is possible and a replacement unit should be obtained.

Note: If the fuse that supplies the clock is faulty, several other circuits will also be defective, including the interior light, the cigarette lighter and the beam indicator.

42 Fuel and water temperature gauges – general description

1   The fuel gauge circuit comprises a tank sender unit located in the fuel tank (Chapter 3) and the fuel gauge. The sender unit has a float attached and this rides on the surface of the petrol in the tank. At the end of the float arm is a contact and rheostat which control current flowing to the fuel gauge.

2   The water temperature gauge circuit comprises a meter and thermal transmitter which is screwed into the side of the engine cylinder block. This is fitted with a thermistor element which converts any cooling system water temperature variation to a resistance. This therefore controls the current flowing to the meter.

3   The fuel gauge and water temperature gauge are provided with a bi-metal arm and heater coil. When the ignition is switched on, current flows so heating the coil. With this heat the bi-metal arm is distorted and therefore moves the pointer.

4   Because a slight tolerance may occur on the fuel or water temperature gauge due to a fluctuation in voltage a voltage regulator is used to supply a constant voltage resulting in more consistent readings. The output voltage to the meter circuits is 8 volts.

5   If it is found that both the fuel gauge and water temperature gauge operate inaccurately then the voltage regulator should be suspect.

43 Warning lights – general

Oil pressure warning light

A switch is fitted to the engine lubrication system so that with the ignition switched on, a warning lamp will light when the engine is either stationary or the oil pressure has fallen below 2.7-5.7 lb/in^2 (0.2-0.4 kg/cm^2). When the engine is running normally and the oil pressure passes the minimum pressure mark so the pressure switch opens the circuit and the light is extinguished.

Handbrake warning light

Whenever the handbrake is applied and the ignition switched on, the warning lamp will light. When the handbrake is released so the light is extinguished.

44 Theft protection system (where fitted)

1   The system comprises the ignition switch, the door pillar switch and a buzzer and is designed to prevent the driver leaving the vehicle while the ignition key is still in the lock.

2   Where a fault occurs in the system, first check the connecting wiring. The door pillar switch which also operates the interior courtesy

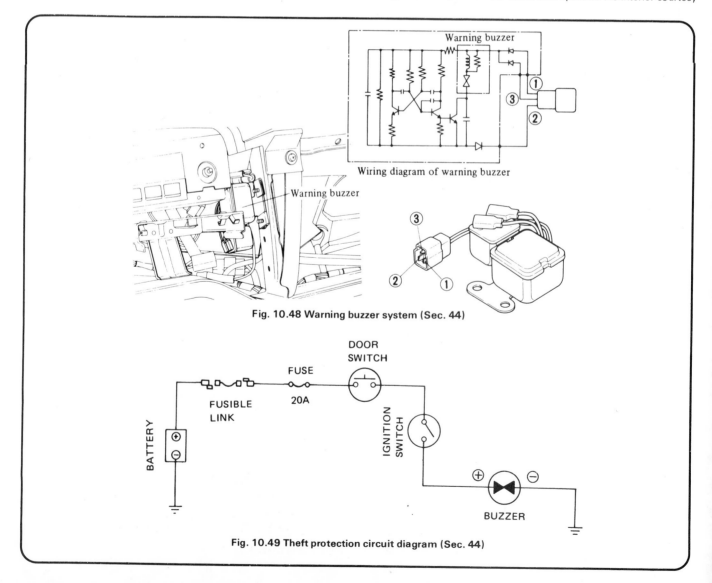

Fig. 10.48 Warning buzzer system (Sec. 44)

Fig. 10.49 Theft protection circuit diagram (Sec. 44)

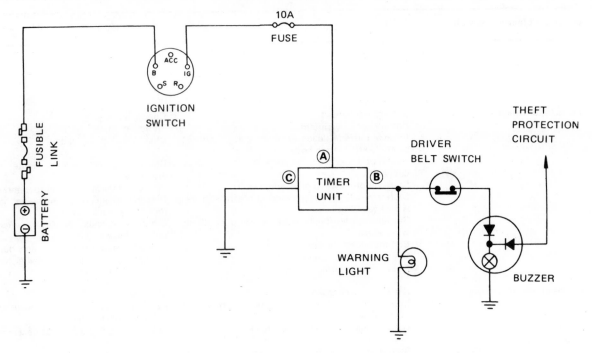

Fig. 10.50 Seat belt warning system circuit diagram.

lamp can be removed as described in Section 29.
3   The warning buzzer is located behind the instrument panel adjacent to the interlock relay.
4   Refer to Chapter 8 for details of the steering column lock.

45 Seat belt warning system – description and operation

1   This system is installed to meet regulations in North America and certain other territories. The engine can only be started when the following conditions have been complied with, otherwise a warning buzzer and lamp will be actuated;
   a) The seat belts are fastened after each of the front seats is occupied.
   b) The gearshift lever is in neutral.
2   The system consists of a belt switch, a warning buzzer, a warning light, a timer unit (not Canada) and the ignition switch. When the ignition switch is turned to the 'ON' position, the warning light comes on and remains on for 4 to 8 seconds. The warning buzzer sounds for 4 to 8 seconds intermittently if the driver's seat belt is not fastened properly.
3   For tuning and maintenance purposes, the engine can be started by reaching into the car, through the door window, to switch on the ignition without any weight on the front seats.
4   Do not leave objects on the front seats or the seat switch will be actuated and discharge the battery.

46 Seat belt switch – removal and refitting

1   Remove the seat belt fastener securing bolt.
2   Disconnect the belt switch lead at the connector and remove the seat belt fastener.
3   Refitting is the reverse sequence of removal.

47 Timer unit – removal and refitting

1   The timer is located behind the left lower dash panel.
2   Remove the panel shelf.
3   Remove two relay securing screws and disconnect the timer unit connector, then take out the timer unit.
4   Refitting the timer unit is the reverse of the removal sequence.

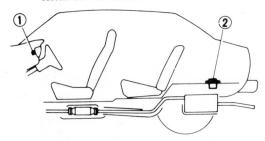

Hatchback and Sedan

Station Wagon

Fig. 10.51 Location of floor temperature sensing switch

   1 Warning light   2 Floor temperature sensing switch

48 Floor temperature warning system (California model) – description

The floor temperature warning system consists of a floor temperature sensing switch, fitted on the floor of the car, a floor temperature relay, a floor temperature warning light and wiring harness.
When the floor temperature rises to an abnormal level, the warning light comes on. The warning light also comes on during operation of the starter motor, and then goes out after the engine starts.

49 Fault diagnosis – Electrical system

Symptom	Reason/s	Remedy
Starter motor		
Starter motor fails to turn engine	Battery discharged	Charge battery.
	Battery defective internally	Fit new battery.
	Battery terminal leads loose or earth lead not securely attached to body	Check and tighten leads.
	Loose or broken connections in starter motor circuit	Check all connections and tighten any that are loose.
	Starter motor switch or solenoid faulty	Test and replace faulty components with new.
	Starter motor pinion jammed in mesh with flywheel gear ring	Disengage pinion by engaging gear and rocking car back and forth.
	Starter brushes badly worn, sticking or brush wires loose	Examine brushes, replace as necessary, tighten down brush wires.
	Commutator dirty, worn or burnt	Clean commutator, recut if badly burnt.
	Starter motor armature faulty	Overhaul starter motor, fit new armature.
	Field coils earthed	Overhaul starter motor.
Starter motor turns engine very slowly	Battery in discharged condition	Charge battery.
	Starter brushes badly worn, sticking, or brush wires loose	Examine brushes, replace as necessary, tighten down brush wires.
	Loose wires in starter motor circuit	Check wiring and tighten as necessary.
Starter motor operates without tuning engine	Starter motor pinion sticking on the screwed sleeve	Remove starter motor, clean starter motor drive.
	Pinion or flywheel gear teeth broken or worn	Fit new gear ring to flywheel, and new pinion to starter motor drive.
Starter motor noisy or excessively rough	Pinion or flywheel gear teeth broken or worn	Fit new gear teeth to flywheel, or new pinion to starter motor drive.
	Starter drive main spring broken	Dismantle and fit new main spring.
	Starter motor retaining bolts loose	Tighten starter motor securing bolts. Fit new spring washer if necessary.
Battery		
Battery will not hold charge for more than a few days	Battery defective internally	Remove and fit new battery.
	Electrolyte level too low or electrolyte too weak due to leakage	Top up electrolyte level to just above plates.
	Plate separators no longer fully effective	Remove and fit new battery.
	Battery plates severely sulphated	Remove and fit new battery.
	Alternator belt slipping	Check belt for wear, replace if necessary, and tighten.
	Battery terminal connections loose or corroded	Check terminals for tightness, and remove all corrosion.
	Alternator not charging properly	Take car to specialist.
	Short in lighting circuit causing continual battery drain	Trace and rectify.
	Regulator unit not working correctly	Take car to specialist.
Ignition light fails to go out, battery runs flat in a few days	Drive belt loose and slipping or broken	Check, replace and tighten as necessary.
	Alternator faulty	Take car to specialist.

Failure of individual electrical equipment to function correctly is dealt with alphabetically, item-by-item, under the headings listed below

Symptom	Reason/s	Remedy
Fuel gauge		
Fuel gauge gives no reading	Fuel tank empty!	Fill fuel tank.
	Electric cable between tank sender unit and gauge earthed or loose	Check cable for earthing and joints for tightness
	Fuel gauge case not earthed	Ensure case is well earthed
	Fuel gauge supply cable interrupted	Check and replace cable if necessary.
	Fuel gauge unit broken	Replace fuel gauge.
Fuel gauge registers full all the time	Electric cable between tank unit and gauge broken or disconnected	Check over cable and repair as necessary.
Horn		
Horn operates all the time	Horn push either earthed or stuck down	Disconnect battery earth. Check and rectify source of trouble.
	Horn cable to horn push earthed	Disconnect battery earth. Check and rectify source of trouble.

Symptom	Reason/s	Remedy
Horn fails to operate	Blown fuse Cable or cable connection loose, broken or disconnected Horn has an internal fault	Check and renew if broken. Ascertain cause. Check all connections for tightness and cables for breaks. Remove and overhaul horn.
Horn emits intermittent or unsatisfactory noise	Cable connections loose Horn incorrectly adjusted	Check and tighten all connections. Adjust horn until best tone obtained.
Lights Lights do not come on	If engine not running, battery discharged Light bulb filament burnt out or bulbs broken Wire connections loose, disconnected or broken Light switch shorting or otherwise faulty	Push-start the car, charge battery (not automatics). Test bulbs in live bulb holder. Check all connections for tightness and wire cable for breaks. Bypass light switch to ascertain if fault is in switch and fit new switch as appropriate.
Lights come on but fade out	If engine not running battery discharged	Push-start car and charge battery (not automatics).
Lights give very poor illumination	Lamp glasses dirty Lamps badly out of adjustment Incorrect bulb with too low wattage fitted Existing bulbs old and badly discoloured	Clean glasses. Adjust lamps correctly. Remove bulb and replace with correct grade. Renew bulb units.
Lights work erratically — flashing on and off, especially over bumps	Battery terminals or earth connections loose Lights not earthing properly Contacts in light switch faulty	Tighten battery terminals and earth connection. Examine and rectify. Bypass light switch to ascertain if fault is in switch and fit new switch as appropriate.
Wiper motor Wiper motor fails to work	Blown fuse Wire connections loose, disconnected or broken Brushes badly worn Seized motor shaft	Check and replace fuse if necessary. Check wiper wiring. Tighten loose connections. Renew wiper motor. Renew wiper motor.
Wiper motor works but blades remain stationary	Disconnected linkage or broken linkage	Reconnect linkage or renew broken linkage.
Wiper operating speed too slow	Brushes worn Linkage sticking Armature faulty	Renew wiper motor. Examine and rectify. Renew wiper motor.
Incorrect parking of wiper arms	Auto-stop device incorrectly set	Remove cover and bend the relay plate as necessary.

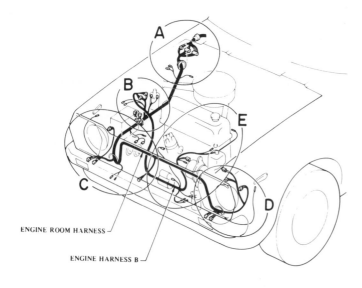

**Fig. 10.52 Engine compartment harness –
120A F-II (Europe)**

Detail 'A'

1   To engine bay harness
2   To instrument harness
3   To circuit breaker (Sweden)
4   To brake switch

Detail 'B'

1   To fusible link (Sweden)
2   To fusible link
3   To engine harness B
4   To engine bay harness
5   To condenser
6   To voltage regulator
7   To fan relay
8   To horn relay
9   To ignition coil
10   To lighting relay (Sweden)

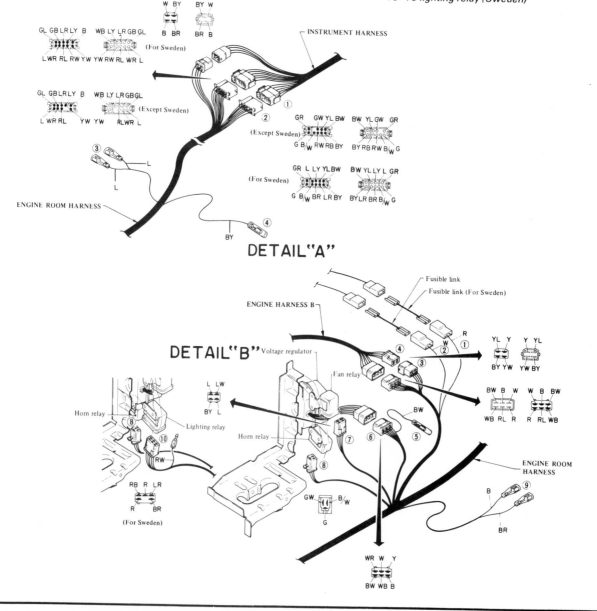

DETAIL "A"

DETAIL "B"

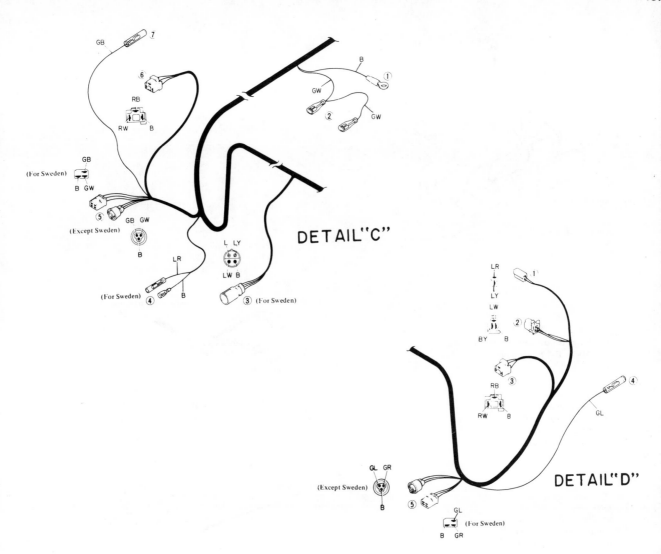

DETAIL"C"

DETAIL"D"

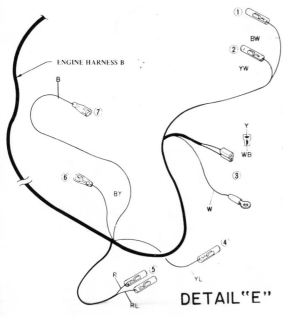

DETAIL"E"

Fig. 10.52 Engine compartment harness – 120A F-II (Europe) – continued

Detail 'C'

1   Earth
2   To horn
3   To headlamp wiper motor (Sweden)
4   To headlamp washer motor (Sweden)
5   To front combination lamp (RH)
6   To headlamp (RH)
7   To side turn signal lamp (RH)

3   To headlamp (LH)
4   To side turn signal lamp (LH)
5   To front combination lamp (LH)

Detail 'E'

1   To anti-dieseling solenoid valve
2   To thermal transmitter
3   To alternator
4   To oil pressure switch
5   To reverse lamp switch
6   To starter motor
7   To distributor

Detail 'D'

1   To washer motor
2   To fan motor

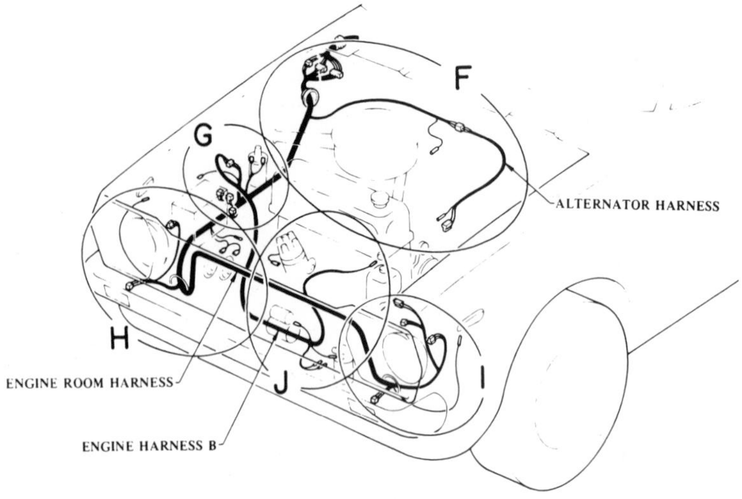

F

G

ALTERNATOR HARNESS

H

ENGINE ROOM HARNESS

J

I

ENGINE HARNESS B

Fig. 10.53 Engine compartment harness – 100A F-11 (Europe)

Detail 'F'

1   To engine bay harness
2   To instrument harness
3   To brake indicator switch
4   To alternator harness
5   To engine bay harness
6   To alternator

Detail 'H'

1   Earth
2   To horn
3   To headlamp (RH)
4   To side turn signal lamp (RH)
5   To front combination lamp (RH)

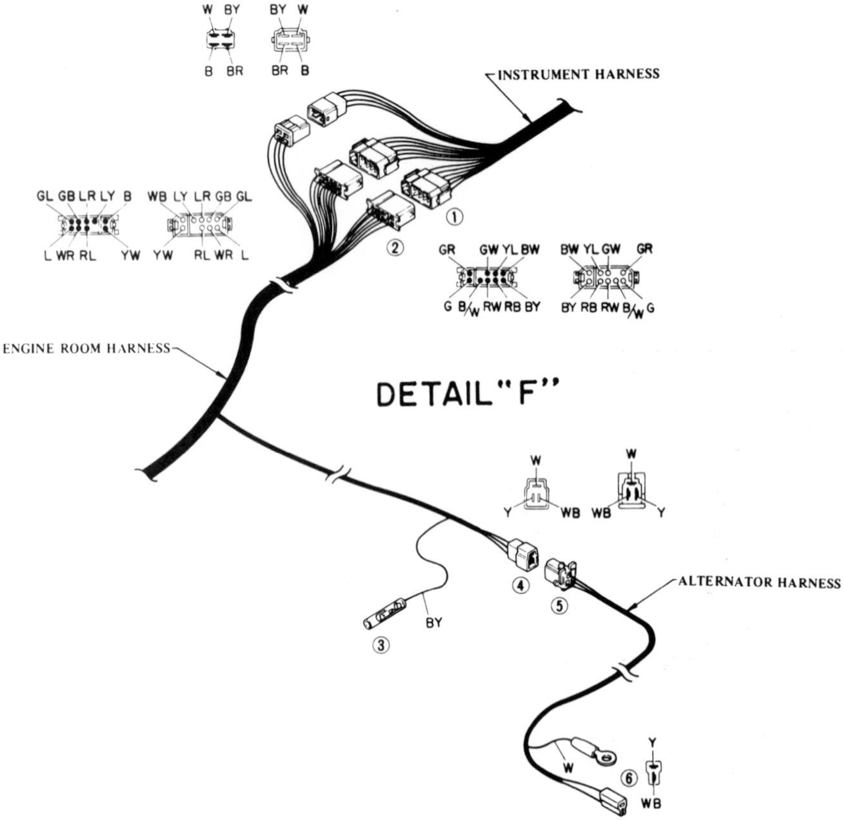

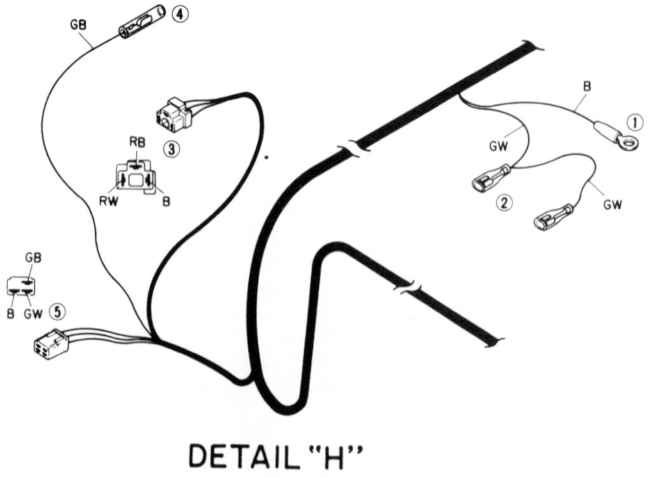

INSTRUMENT HARNESS

W BY   BY W

B BR   BR B

GL GB LR LY B   WB LY LR GB GL

L WR RL   YW   YW   RL WR L

① ②

GR   GW YL BW   BW YL GW   GR

G B/W RW RB BY   BY RB RW B/W G

ENGINE ROOM HARNESS

DETAIL "F"

W   W

Y   WB WB   Y

④   ⑤

ALTERNATOR HARNESS

③   BY

W   Y

⑥   WB

GB   ④

RB   ③

RW   B

B   ①

GW

② GW

GB

B GW ⑤

DETAIL "H"

Fig. 10.53 Engine compartment harness –
100A F-II (Europe) – continued

Detail 'G'

1   To fusible link
2   To engine bay harness
3   To engine harness B
4   To condenser
5   To voltage regulator
6   To fan relay
7   To horn relay
8   To ignition coil

Detail 'I'

1   To washer motor
2   To fan motor
3   To headlamp (LH)
4   To side turn signal lamp (LH)
5   To front combination lamp (LH)

Detail 'J'

1   To thermal transmitter
2   To distributor
3   To starter motor
4   To oil pressure switch
5   To reverse lamp switch

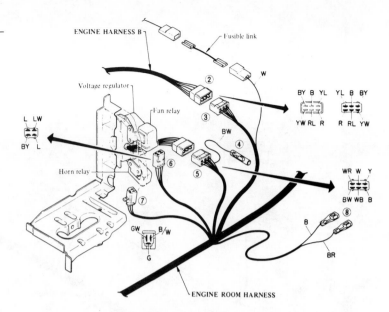

DETAIL "G"

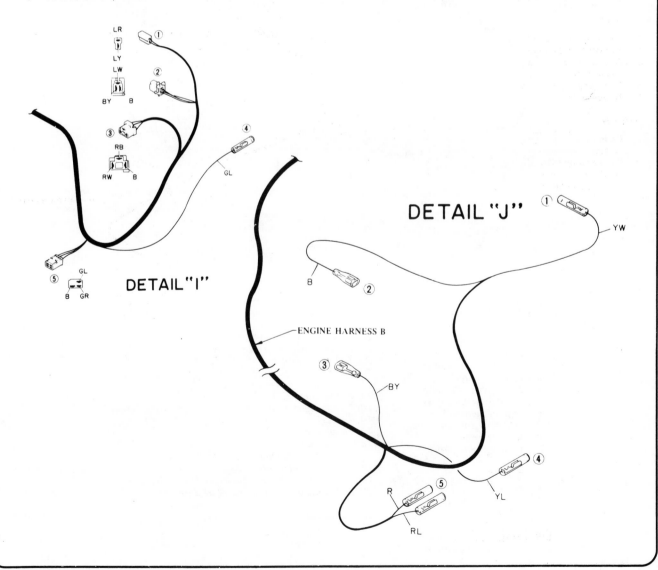

DETAIL "I"

DETAIL "J"

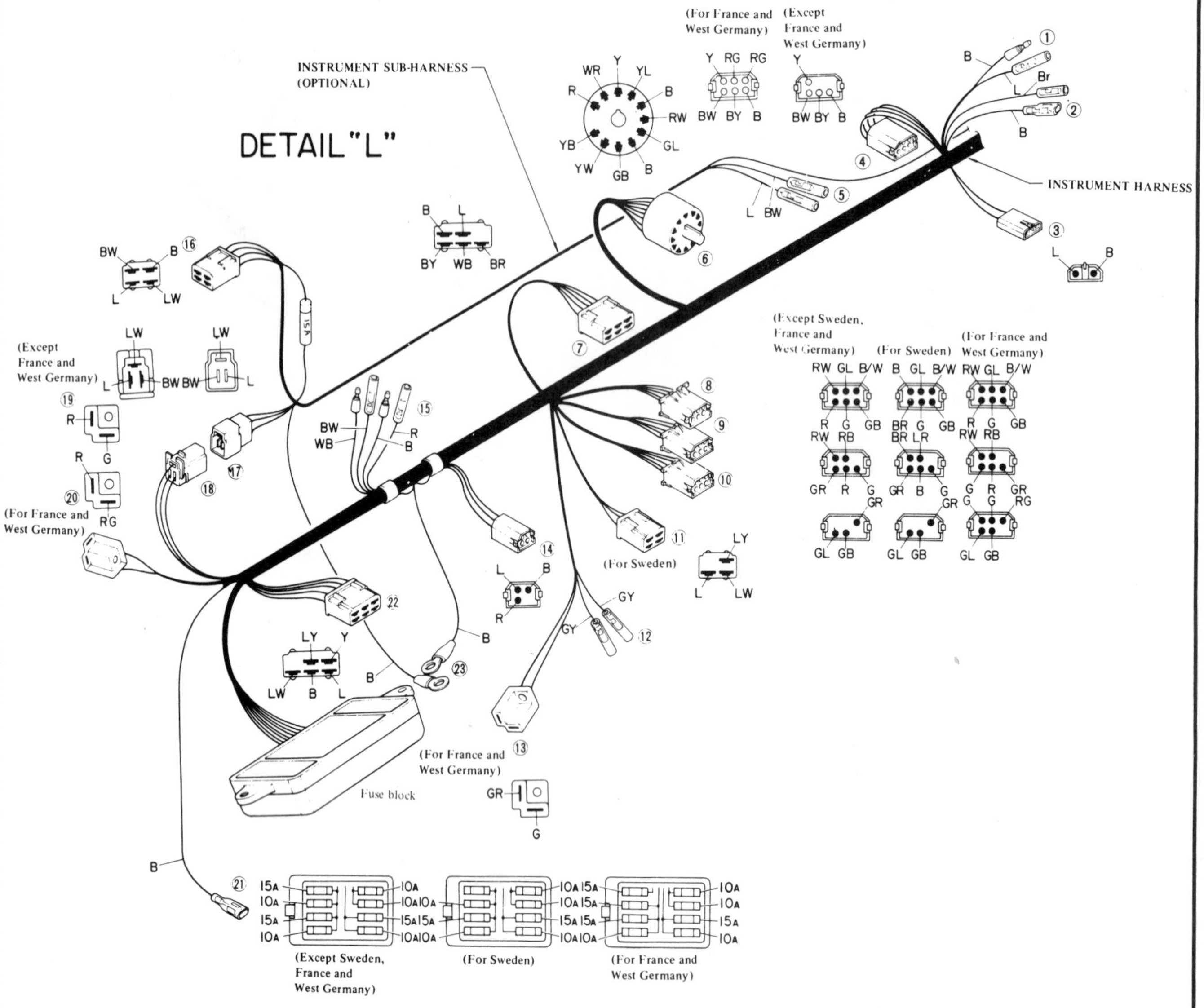

DETAIL "L"

INSTRUMENT SUB-HARNESS (OPTIONAL)

INSTRUMENT HARNESS

(For France and West Germany)

(Except France and West Germany)

(Except Sweden, France and West Germany)

(For Sweden)

(For France and West Germany)

(Except France and West Germany)

(For France and West Germany)

Fuse block

(For France and West Germany)

(Except Sweden, France and West Germany)

(For Sweden)

(For France and West Germany)

Fig. 10.54 Instrument harness – 100A and 120A F-II (Europe)

Detail 'K'

1   To wiper motor
2   To instrument harness
3   To wiper harness
4   To instrument harness
5   To room lamp harness
6   To body harness *
7   To instrument sub-harness
8   To body harness
9   To instrument harness

Detail 'L'

1   To radio
2   To cigarette lighter
3   To heater unit
4   To indicator lamp
5   To rear demister switch
6   To combination meter

7   To ignition switch
8   To turn signal lamp switch
9   To lighting switch
10 To hazard warning lamp switch
11 To headlamp wiper switch (Sweden)
12 To stop lamp switch
13 To turn signal flasher unit (France and West Germany)
14 To clock
15 To tachometer
16 To rear demister relay *
17 To instrument harness *
18 To instrument sub-harness
19 To flasher unit (Except France and West Germany)
20 To hazard unit (France and West Germany)
21 To door switch
22 To wiper switch
23 Earth

      * Optional

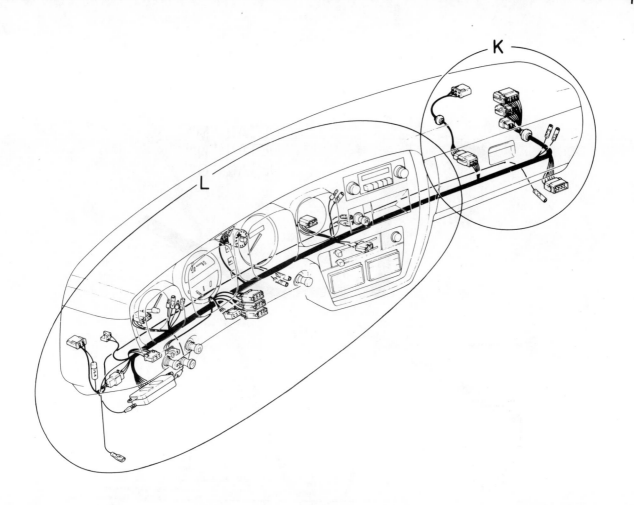

K

L

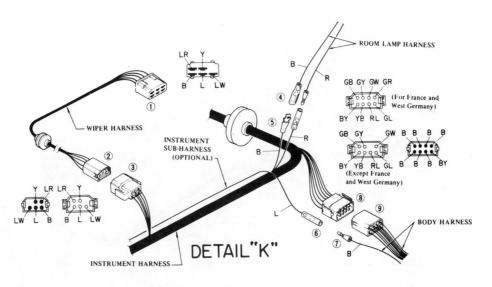

ROOM LAMP HARNESS

LR Y
B   L LW

B

R

GB GY GW GR

(For France and
West Germany)

BY YB RL GL

GB GY   GW   B B B B

BY YB RL GL

(Except France
and West Germany)

B B B BY

WIPER HARNESS

①

②

③

④

⑤

⑥

⑦

⑧

⑨

INSTRUMENT
SUB-HARNESS
(OPTIONAL)

R

L

B

B

BODY HARNESS

Y LR LR Y
LW L B   B L LW

R

DETAIL "K"

INSTRUMENT HARNESS

Fig. 10.54 Instrument harness – 100A and 120A F-II (Europe) – continued

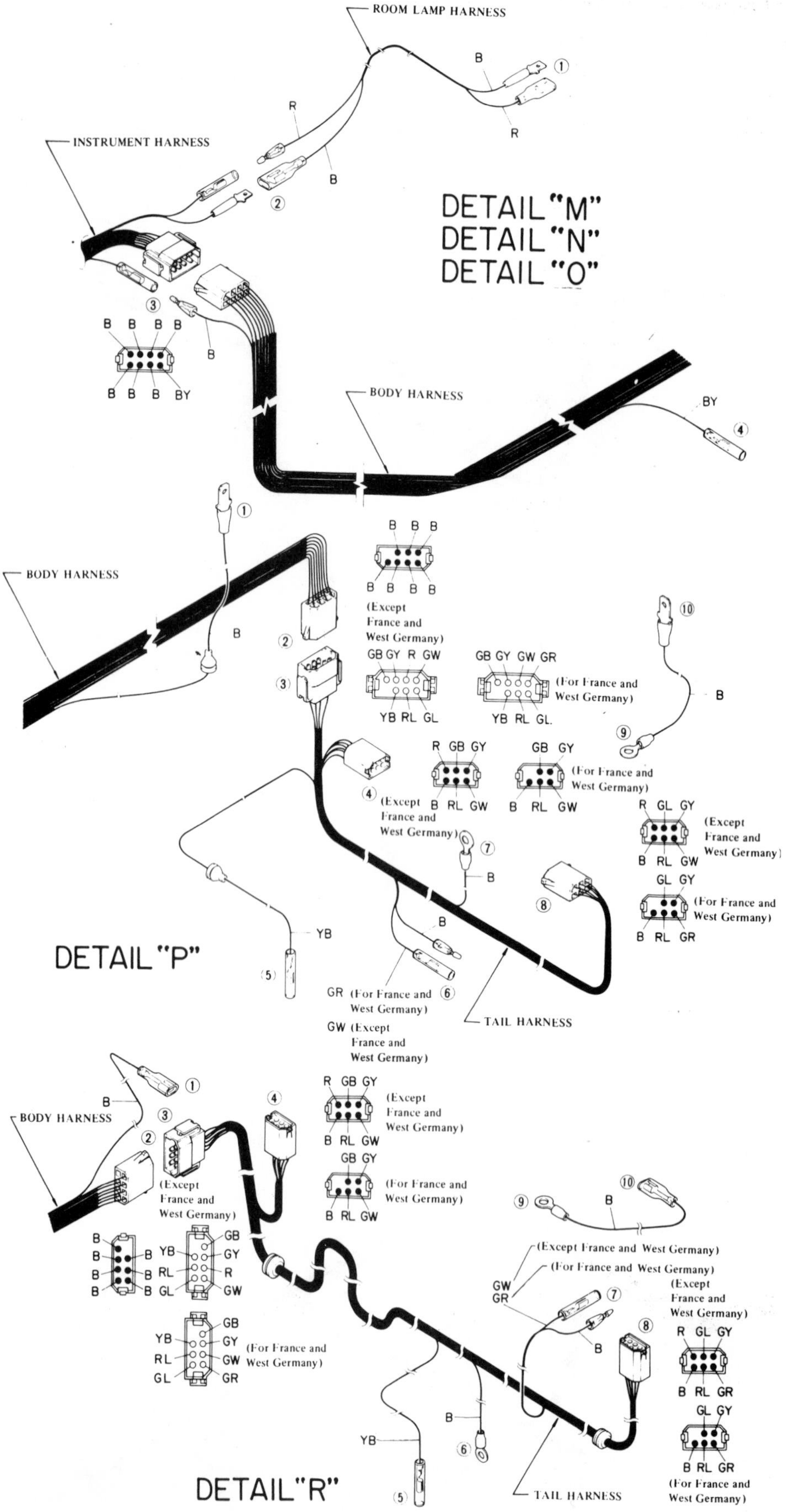

ROOM LAMP HARNESS

B

①

R

R

B

INSTRUMENT HARNESS

②

DETAIL "M"
DETAIL "N"
DETAIL "O"

③

B B B B

B B B BY

B

BODY HARNESS

BY

④

①

B B B

BODY HARNESS

B B B B

(Except France and West Germany)

B

②

GB GY R GW

GB GY GW GR

③

YB RL GL

YB RL GL

(For France and West Germany)

R GB GY

GB GY

B RL GW

B RL GW

(For France and West Germany)

④

(Except France and West Germany)

⑦

B

⑧

⑩

B

⑨

R GL GY

B RL GW

(Except France and West Germany)

GL GY

B RL GR

(For France and West Germany)

DETAIL "P"

⑤

YB

⑥

GR (For France and West Germany)

GW (Except France and West Germany)

B

TAIL HARNESS

①

B

BODY HARNESS

③

②

④

(Except France and West Germany)

R GB GY

B RL GW

(Except France and West Germany)

GB GY

B RL GW

(For France and West Germany)

⑩

B

⑨

(Except France and West Germany)

(For France and West Germany)

GW
GR

(Except France and West Germany)

⑦

⑧

B

B B GB YB
B B GY RL
B B R GW
B B GL

GB
YB GY
RL GW
GL GR

(For France and West Germany)

YB

⑥

B

⑤

R GL GY

B RL GR

GL GY

B RL GR

(For France and West Germany)

DETAIL "R"

TAIL HARNESS

Fig. 10.55 Body and tail harness 100A and 120A F-11 (Europe) (For Key see next page)

Fig. 10.55 Body and tail harness – 100A and 120A F-11 (Europe) - continued

Details 'M', 'N' and 'O'

1 To room lamp
2 To instrument harness
3 To instrument harness
4 To handbrake switch

Detail 'P'

1 To rear window demister *
2 To tail harness
3 To body harness
4 To rear combination lamp (RH)
5 To fuel tank unit
6 To number plate
7 Earth
8 To rear combination lamp (LH)
9 Earth *
10 To rear window demister *

Detail 'Q'

1 To rear window demister

2 To fuel tank unit
3 To tail harness
4 To body harness
5 To rear combination lamp (RH)
6 To license lamp
7 Earth
8 To rear combination lamp (LH)
9 Earth *
10 To rear window demister *

Detail 'R'

1 To rear window demister *
2 To tail harness
3 To body harness
4 To rear combination lamp (RH)
5 To fuel tank unit
6 Earth
7 To license lamp
8 To rear combination lamp (LH)
9 Earth *
10 To rear window demister

* *Optional*

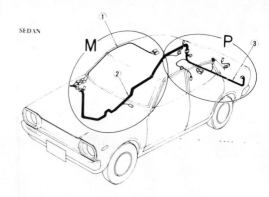

SEDAN

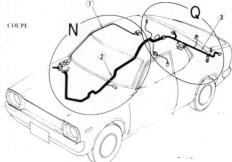

COUPE

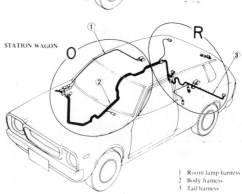

STATION WAGON

1 Room lamp harness
2 Body harness
3 Tail harness

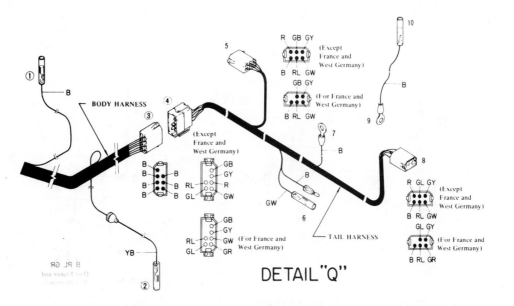

DETAIL "Q"

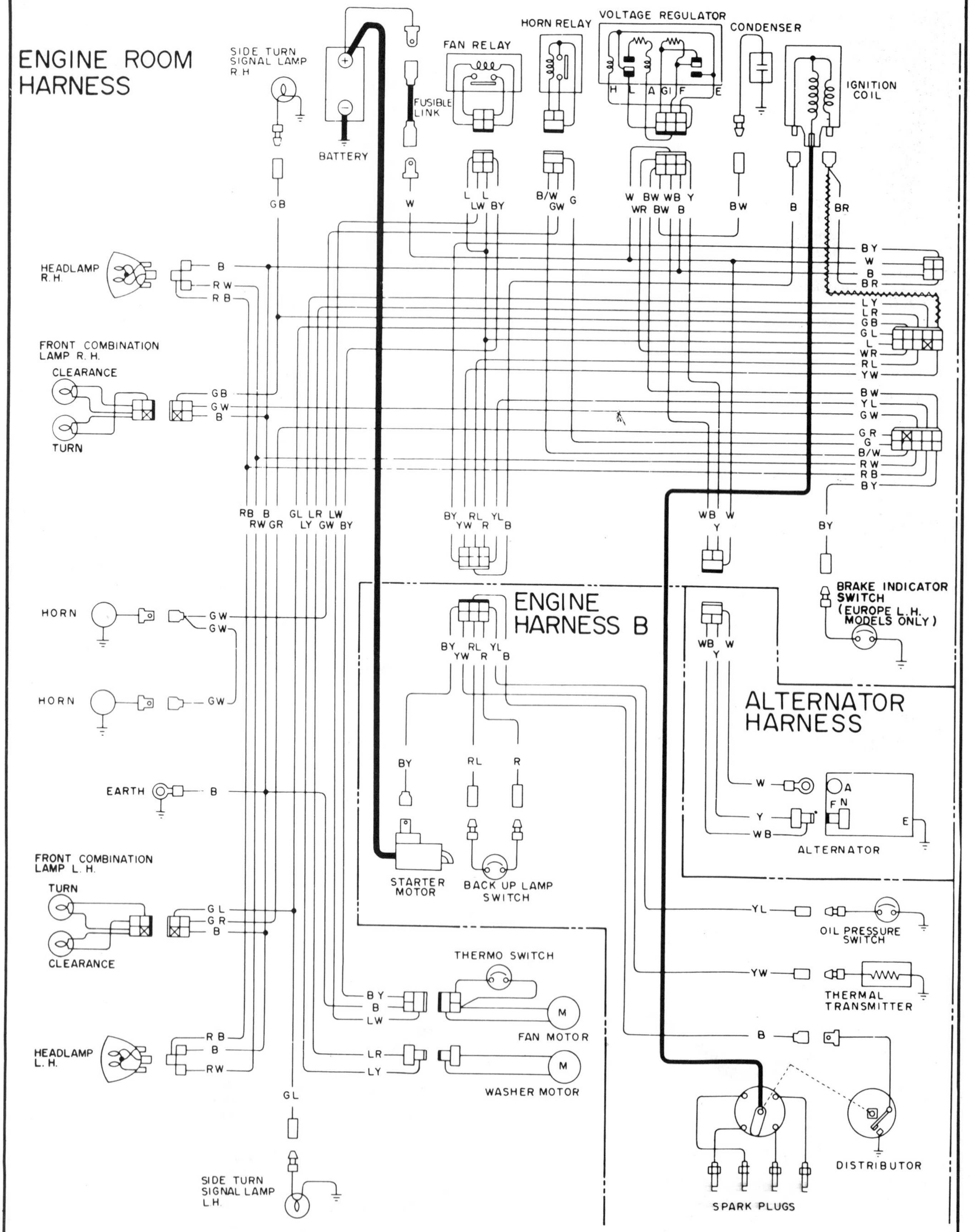

ENGINE ROOM HARNESS

SIDE TURN SIGNAL LAMP R.H.

GB

BATTERY

FUSIBLE LINK

W

FAN RELAY

HORN RELAY

VOLTAGE REGULATOR

H L A G I F E

CONDENSER

IGNITION COIL

L L LW BY

B/W GW G

W BW WB Y
WR BW B

BW

B

BR

HEADLAMP R.H.

B
R W
R B

BY
W
B
BR

LY
L
GB
G L
L
WR
R L
Y W

FRONT COMBINATION LAMP R.H.

CLEARANCE

GB
GW
B

TURN

BW
Y L
G W

G R
G
B/W
R W
R B
BY

RB B
RW GR
GL LR LW
LY GW BY

BY RL YL
YW R B

WB W
Y

BY

HORN

GW
GW

ENGINE HARNESS B

BY RL YL
YW R B

WB W
Y

BRAKE INDICATOR SWITCH
(EUROPE L.H. MODELS ONLY)

HORN

GW

ALTERNATOR HARNESS

EARTH

B

BY

RL

R

W

A

F N

E

Y

WB

ALTERNATOR

FRONT COMBINATION LAMP L.H.

TURN

GL
GR
B

STARTER MOTOR

BACK UP LAMP SWITCH

YL

OIL PRESSURE SWITCH

CLEARANCE

THERMO SWITCH

YW

THERMAL TRANSMITTER

B Y
B
LW

M

FAN MOTOR

B

HEADLAMP L.H.

R B
B
RW

LR
LY

M

WASHER MOTOR

GL

DISTRIBUTOR

SIDE TURN SIGNAL LAMP L.H.

SPARK PLUGS

Fig. 10.56 Engine compartment wiring diagram, 100A F-II

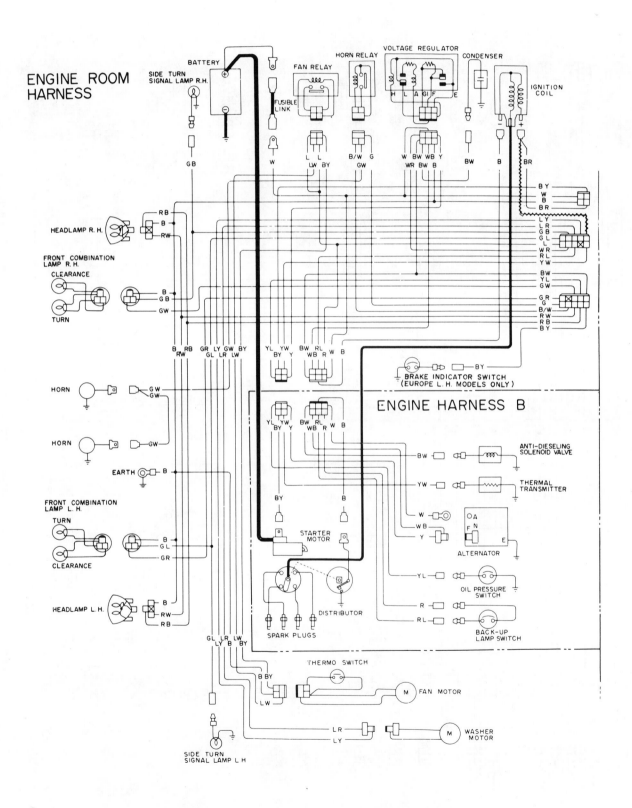

Fig. 10.57 Engine compartment wiring diagram, 120A F-II

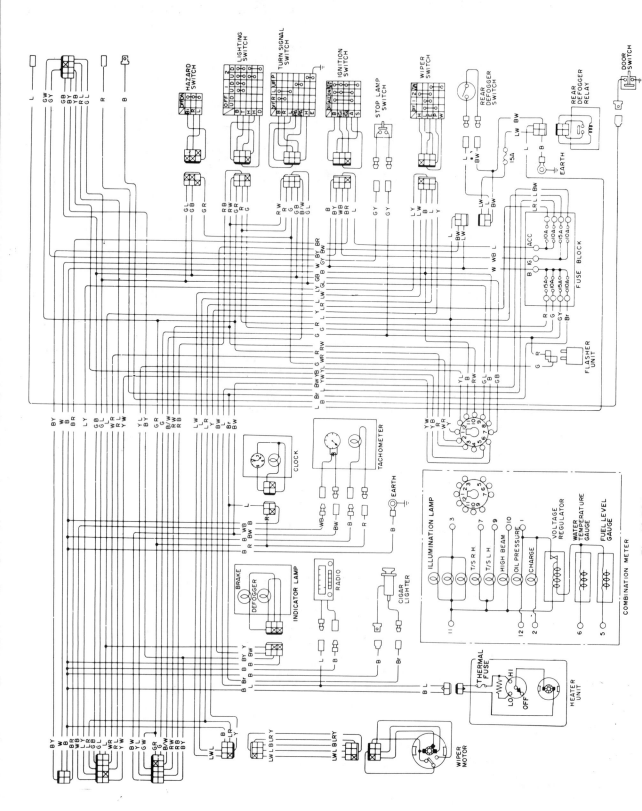

Fig. 10.58 Instrument harness wiring diagram, 100A F-II and 120A F-II

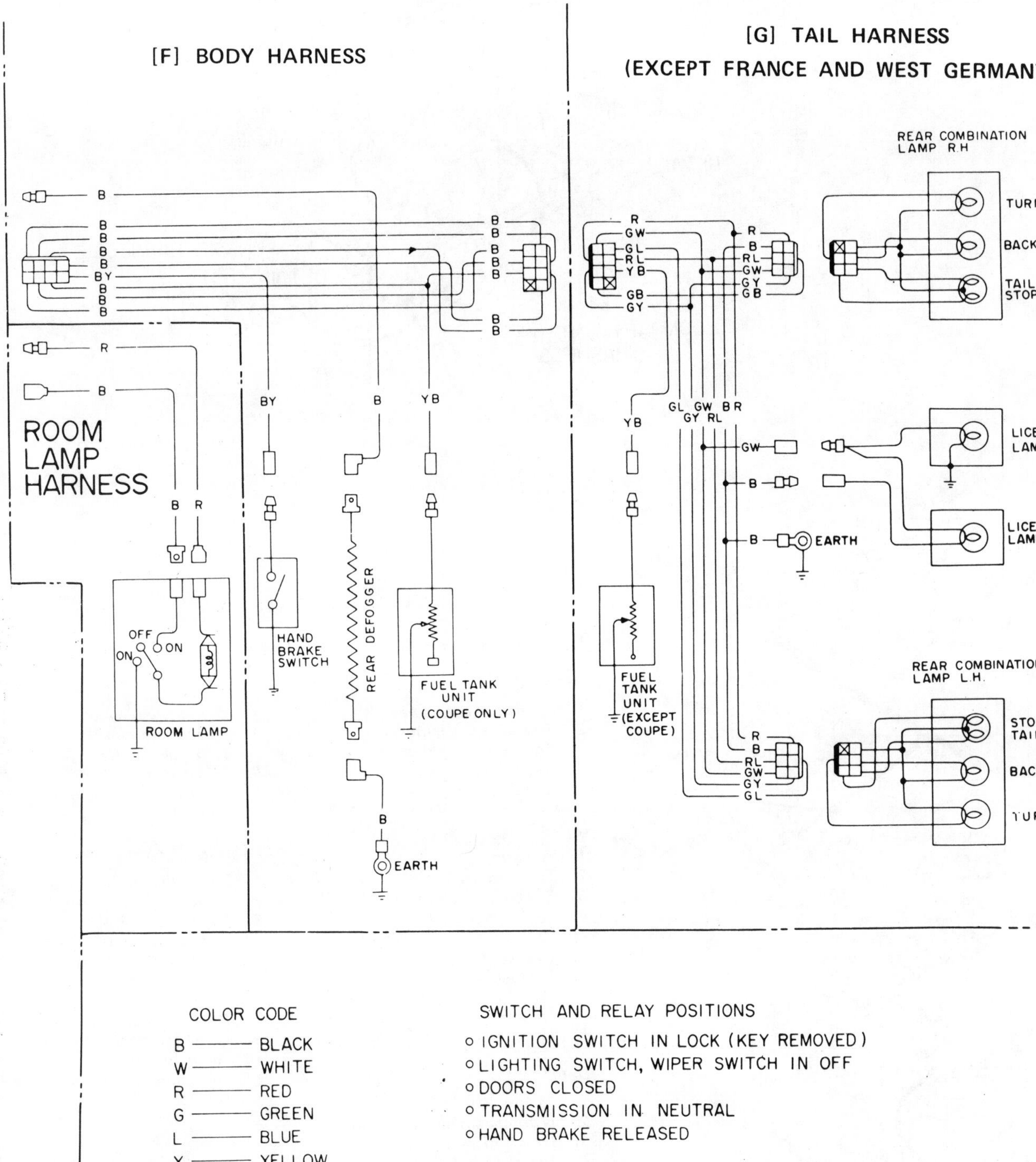

[F] BODY HARNESS

[G] TAIL HARNESS
(EXCEPT FRANCE AND WEST GERMANY)

REAR COMBINATION
LAMP R.H

TURN
BACK-UP
TAIL
STOP

LICENSE
LAMP R.H.

LICENSE
LAMP L.H.

EARTH

ROOM
LAMP
HARNESS

B R

OFF
ON ON

ROOM LAMP

HAND
BRAKE
SWITCH

REAR DEFOGGER

FUEL TANK
UNIT
(COUPE ONLY)

B EARTH

FUEL
TANK
UNIT
(EXCEPT
COUPE)

REAR COMBINATION
LAMP L.H.

STOP
TAIL
BACK-UP
TURN

COLOR CODE

B ——— BLACK
W ——— WHITE
R ——— RED
G ——— GREEN
L ——— BLUE
Y ——— YELLOW
Br —— BROWN

SWITCH AND RELAY POSITIONS

○ IGNITION SWITCH IN LOCK (KEY REMOVED)
○ LIGHTING SWITCH, WIPER SWITCH IN OFF
○ DOORS CLOSED
○ TRANSMISSION IN NEUTRAL
○ HAND BRAKE RELEASED

EXAMPLE

BW ——— BLACK WITH WHITE STRIPE
B/W ——— BLACK WIRE WITH WHITE TUBE

Fig. 10.59 Body harness and tail harness wiring diagram, 100A F-II and 120A F-II

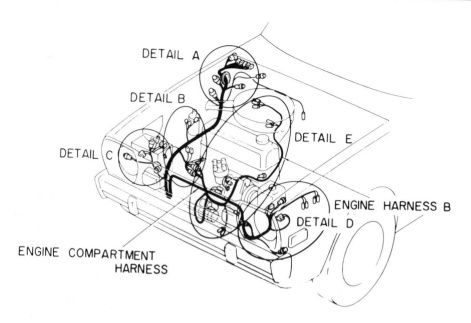

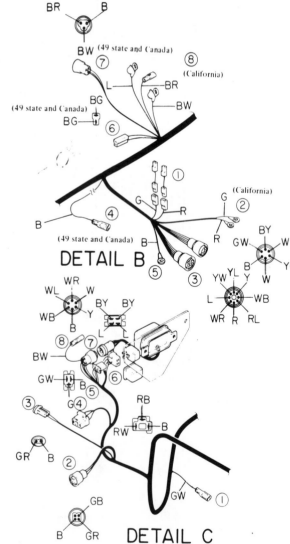

Fig. 10.60 Engine compartment harness – F10 (North America)

Detail 'A'

1 To instrument harness
2 To auxiliary electric fan
3 To brake indicator switch
4 Check connector
5 To auto-choke relay

3 To radiator fan motor
4 To washer motor
5 To headlight LH
6 To side marker light RH
7 To front combination light LH
8 To horn LH

Detail 'B'

1 To battery
2 To terminal block (California model)
3 To engine harness B
4 To distributor
   (Non-California model)
5 To earth point
6 To resistor
   (Non-California model)
7 To ignition coil
8 To ignition coil (California model)

Detail 'C'

1 To horn RH
2 To front combination light RH
3 To side marker light RH
4 To headlight RH
5 To horn relay
6 To fan relay
7 To voltage regulator
8 To condenser

Detail 'D'

1 To water temperature sensing
   switch (For auxiliary electric fan)
2 To water temperature sensing
   switch (For radiator fan)

Detail 'E'

1 To vacuum cut solenoid
2 To auto-choke heater
3 To fuel cut solenoid
4 To throttle opener solenoid
5 To thermal transmitter
6 To alternator
7 To oil pressure switch
8 To back-up switch
9 To starter motor
10 To top gear switch
11 To engine compartment
   harness

Colour code

B – Black
W – White
R – Red
G – Green
Y – Yellow
L – Blue
Lg – Light Green
BW – Black with white stripe
RL – Red with blue stripe
GB – Green with black stripe

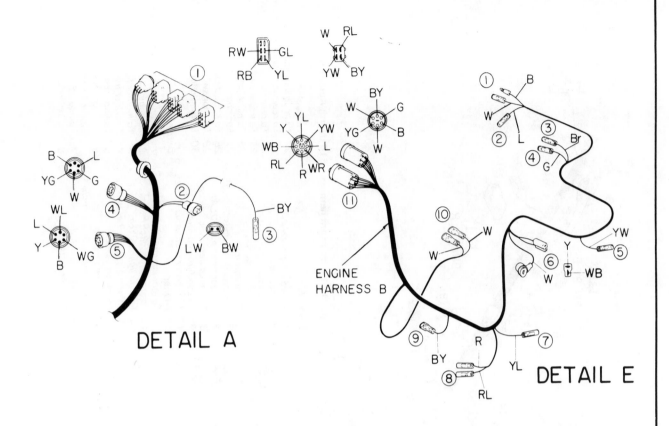

DETAIL A

ENGINE HARNESS B

DETAIL E

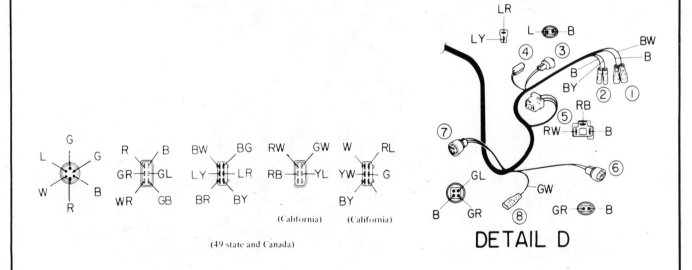

(California)   (California)

(49 state and Canada)

DETAIL D

Fig. 10.60 Engine compartment harness – F10 (North America) – continued

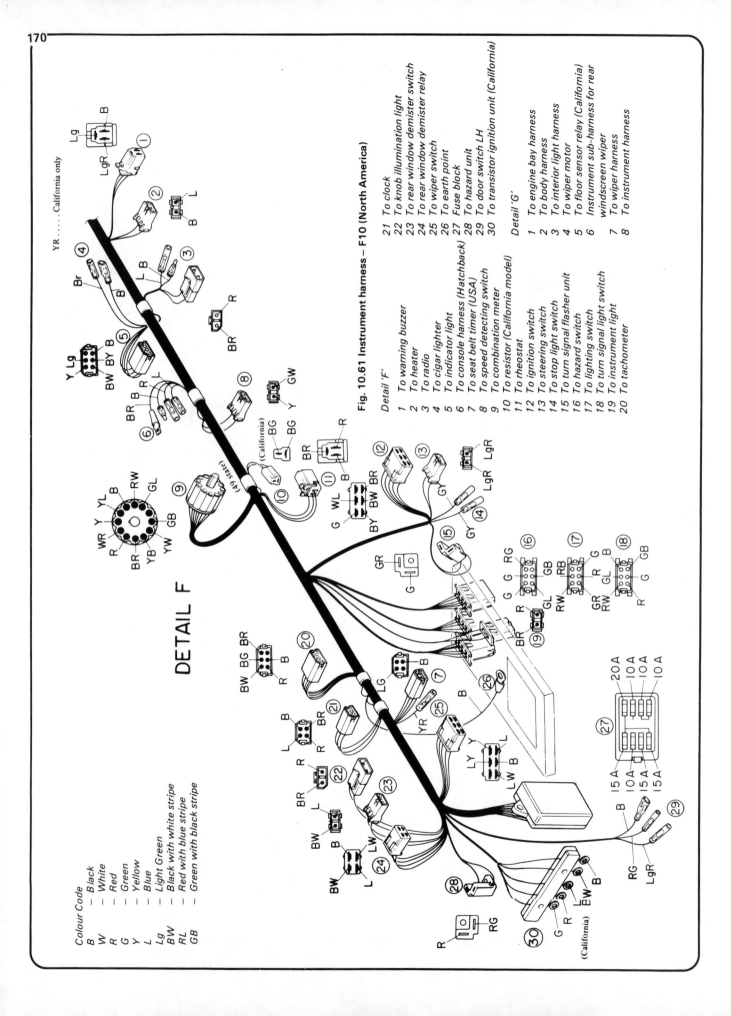

YR . . . . . California only

DETAIL F

Colour Code

B – Black
W – White
R – Red
G – Green
Y – Yellow
L – Blue
Lg – Light Green
BW – Black with white stripe
RL – Red with blue stripe
GB – Green with black stripe

Fig. 10.61 Instrument harness – F10 (North America)

Detail 'F'

1 To warning buzzer
2 To heater
3 To radio
4 To cigar lighter
5 To indicator light
6 To console harness (Hatchback)
7 To seat belt timer (USA)
8 To speed detecting switch
9 To combination meter
10 To resistor (California model)
11 To rheostat
12 To ignition switch
13 To steering switch
14 To stop light switch
15 To turn signal flasher unit
16 To hazard switch
17 To lighting switch
18 To turn signal light switch
19 To instrument light
20 To tachometer
21 To clock
22 To knob illumination light
23 To rear window demister switch
24 To rear window demister relay
25 To wiper switch
26 To earth point
27 Fuse block
28 To hazard unit
29 To door switch LH
30 To transistor ignition unit (California)

Detail 'G'

1 To engine bay harness
2 To body harness
3 To interior light harness
4 To wiper motor
5 To floor sensor relay (California)
6 Instrument sub-harness for rear
   windscreen wiper
7 To wiper harness
8 To instrument harness

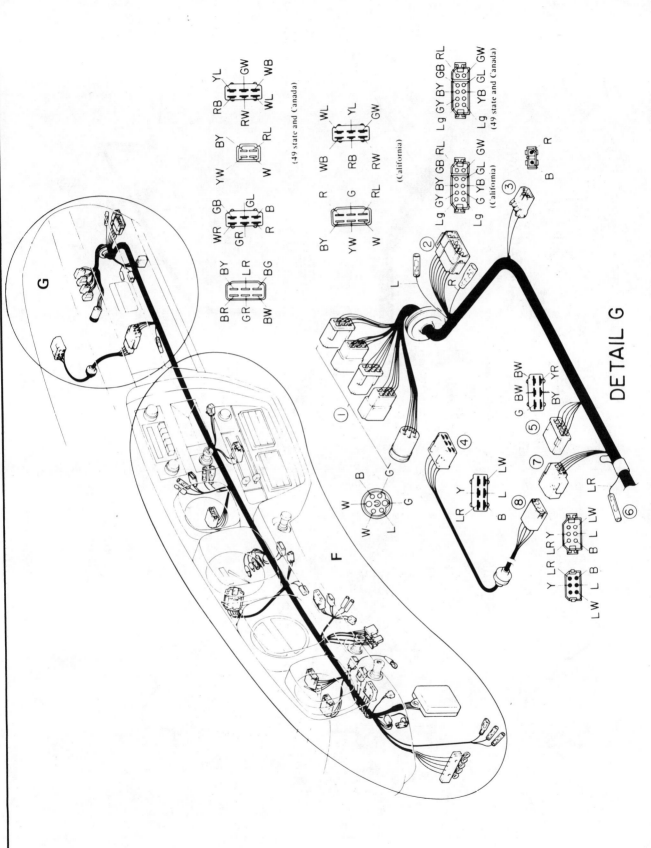

Fig. 10.61 Instrument harness – F10 (North America) – continued

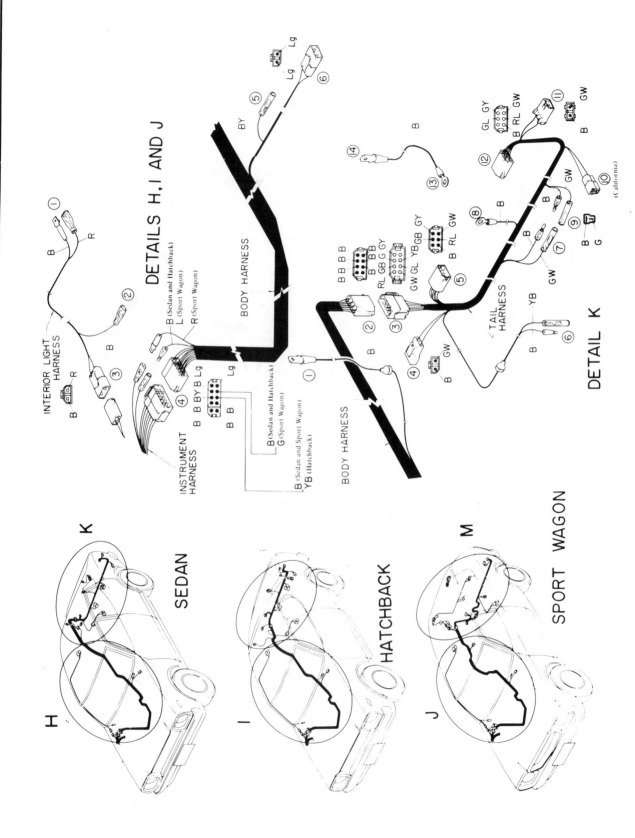

Fig. 10.62 Body and tail harness – F10 (North America) (For Key see next page)

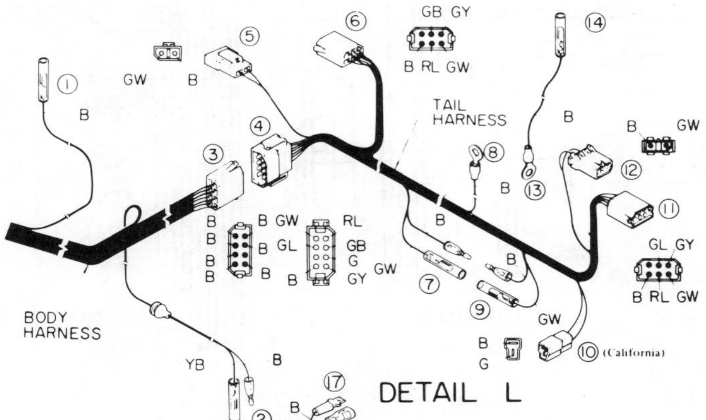

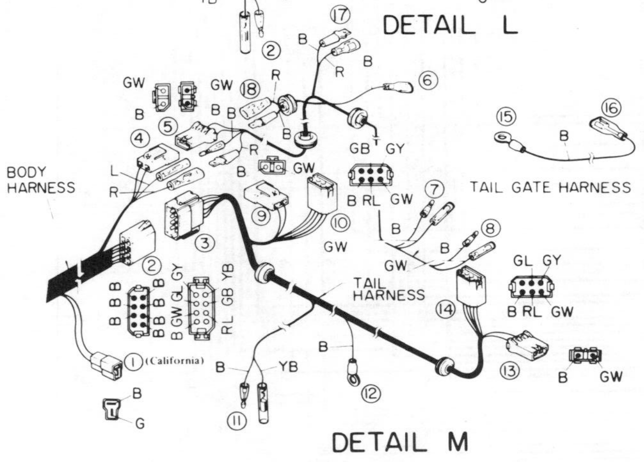

Fig. 10.62 Body and tail harness – F10 (North America) – continued

Details 'H', 'I' and 'J'

1   To interior light
2   To door switch RH
3   To instrument harness
4   To instrument harness
5   To handbrake switch
6   To driver seat belt switch

Detail 'K'

1   To rear window
2   To tail harness
3   To body harness
4   To rear side marker light RH
5   To rear combination light RH
6   To fuel tank
7   To number plate light RH
8   To earth point
9   To number plate light LH
10 To floor temperature sensing switch (California)
11 To rear side marker light LH
12 To rear combination light LH
13 To earth point
14 To rear window

Detail 'L'

1   To rear window demister
2   To fuel tank
3   To tail harness
4   To body harness
5   To rear side marker light RH
6   To rear combination light RH
7   To license plate light RH
8   To earth point
9   To license plate light LH
10 To floor temperature sensing switch (California)
11 To rear combination light LH

12 To rear side marker light LH
13 To earth point
14 To rear window demister

Detail 'M'

1   To floor temperature sensing switch (California)
2   To tail harness
3   To body harness
4   To tailgate harness
5   To body harness
6   To rear window demister
7   To license plate light RH
8   To license plate light LH
9   To rear side marker light RH
10 To rear combination light RH
11 To fuel tank
12 To earth point
13 To rear side marker light LH
14 To rear combination light LH
15 To earth point
16 To rear window demister
17 To back door switch
18 To luggage lamp

Colour code

B   – Black
W   – White
R   – Red
G   – Green
Y   – Yellow
L   – Blue
Lg – Light Green
BW – Black with white stripe
RL – Red with blue stripe
GB – Green with black stripe

DETAIL L

DETAIL M

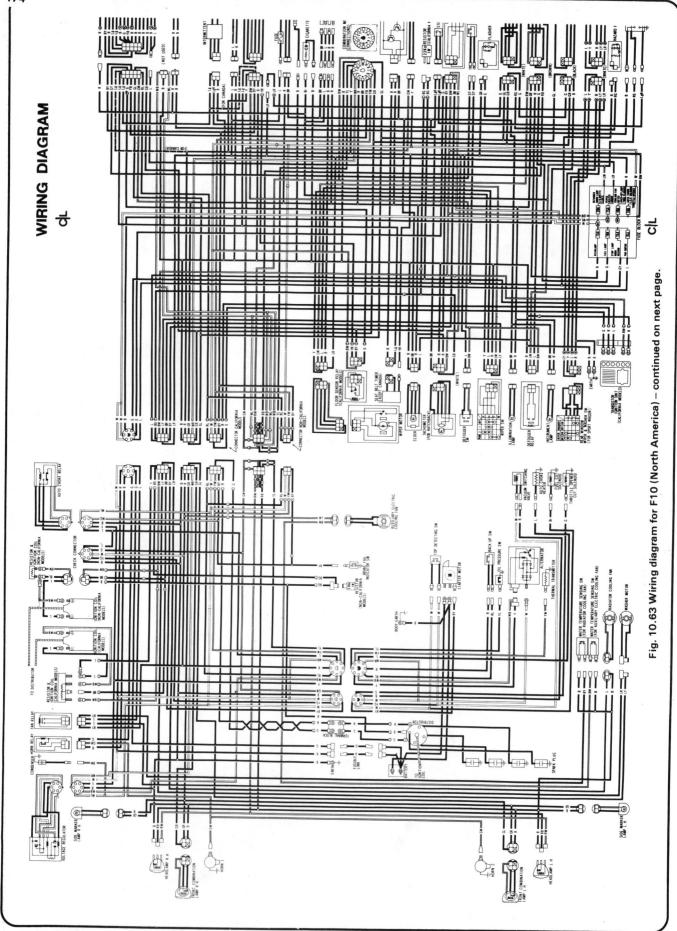

WIRING DIAGRAM

Fig. 10.63 Wiring diagram for F10 (North America) – continued on next page.

WIRING DIAGRAM

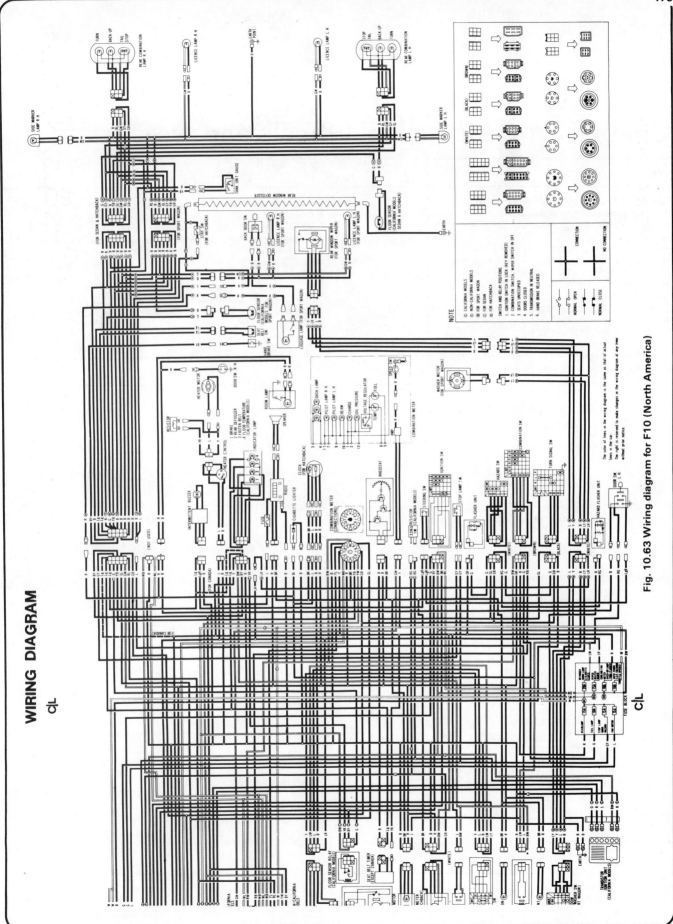

Fig. 10.63 Wiring diagram for F10 (North America)

Chapter 11 Suspension, wheels and tyres

Contents

Specifications

Front suspension

	A10	A12	A14
Wheel alignment			
Camber (non-adjustable)	0° 55′ – 2° 25′	0° 50′ – 2° 20′	0° 50′ – 2° 20′
Caster (non-adjustable)	0° 30′ – 2° 00′	0° 25′ – 1° 55′	0° 20′ – 1° 50′
Toe-in in (mm)	0.157 – 0.315 (4 – 8)	0.157 – 0.315 (4 – 8)	0.20 – 0.28 (5 – 7)
King pin inclination (non-adjustable)	9° 15′ – 10° 35′	9° 15′ – 10° 45′	9° 15′ – 10° 45′

Steering angle
Inner wheel . . . . 36° 30′ – 39° 30′
Outer wheel . . . . 31° – 34°

Coil spring (European models) — Right side / Left side
Wire diameter in (mm) . . . . 0.453 (11.5) / 0.441 (11.2)
Installed height/load in/lb (mm/kg) . . . . 8.39/619 (213/281) / 8.39/575 (213/261)

Coil spring (North American models) — Right side / Left side
Wire diameter in (mm) . . . . 0.472 (12) / 0.465 (11.8)
Installed height/load in/lb (mm/kg) . . . . 8.39/732 (213/332) / 8.39/686 (213/311)

Strut assembly
Damping force at piston speed of 0.98 ft (0.3 m)/sec:
 Expansion/compression lb (kg):
  Europe 163/97 (74/44)
  Except Europe 143/66 (65/30)

Balljoint stud swinging torque
Standard lbf in (kgf cm) 30 (35)
Minimum lbf in (kgf cm) 9 (10)

Wheel bearing rotating torque
Rotation starting force at wheel stud . . . . 3 – 11 lb (1.4 – 4.9 kg)

Rear suspension (Saloon and Coupe)

Type . . . . Trailing arm, independent suspension

Shock absorber
Type . . . . Gas filled, cylindrical, double action
Maximum stroke in (mm) 5.75 (146)

Coil spring — Europe / North America
Installed height/load in/lb (mm/kg) . . . . 5.98/802 (152/364) / 5.98/2 (152/382)

Wheel bearing rotating torque
Rotation starting force at wheel stud:
    New grease seal lb (kg) . . . .   1.0 – 2.4 (0.5 – 1.1)
    Used grease seal lb (kg) . . . .   1.5 (0.7) maximum

Rear suspension (Station wagon)

Type . . . .   Semi-elliptic leaf springs with double acting shock absorbers

Shock absorbers
Type . . . .   Gas-filled, cylindrical, double action
Maximum stroke in (mm) 7.01 (178)

Wheel bearing rotating torque . . . .   As for Saloon and Coupe

Torque wrench settings	**lbf ft**	**kgf m**
Front suspension		
Wheel hub nut	58 – 116	8.0 – 16.0
Balljoint stud nut	22 – 29	3.0 – 4.0
Strut to knuckle bolt	24 – 33	3.3 – 4.5
Strut mounting nut	11 – 17	1.5 – 2.4
Gland packing	43 – 47	6.0 – 6.5
Piston rod mounting nut	46 – 53	6.3 – 7.3
Transverse link attaching nut	42 – 56	5.8 – 7.8
Balljoint to transverse link bolt	40 – 47	5.5 – 6.5
Stabilizer connecting bolt nut	6 – 9	0.8 – 1.2
Stabilizer bracket bolt	6 – 9	0.8 – 1.2
Tie-rod ball stud nut	40 – 47	5.5 – 6.5
Tie-rod locknut	27 – 34	3.8 – 4.7
Rear suspension (Saloon and Coupe)		
Wheel bearing nut	18 – 22	2.5 – 3.0
Shock absorber lower bolt	11 – 17	1.5 – 2.4
Shock absorber upper locknut	12 – 16	1.6 – 2.2
Rear arm attaching bolt	42 – 51	5.8 – 7.0
Rear suspension (Station wagon)		
Shock absorber locknut (lower and upper side)	12 – 16	1.6 – 2.2
U-bolt attaching nut	25 – 29	3.4 – 4.0
Shackle attaching nut	12 – 14	1.6 – 2.0
Front pin nut	12 – 14	1.6 – 2.0
Front pin mounting bolt	7 – 10	0.9 – 1.4
Wheel nuts	58 – 65	8.0 – 9.0

1 General description

1   The front suspension on all models consists of independent struts with integral shock absorbers, and transverse links. The upper end of each strut is secured to the wing structure, while the lower end is retained by a knuckle fitting bolted to the rear of the wheel hub. Transverse links connect the lower end of each knuckle to the sub-frame via a balljoint and two rubber-bushed pivot points.

    The rear suspension on the saloon version is a conventional trailing arm independent suspension utilizing coil springs and gas-filled shock absorbers,

    The station wagon rear suspension is different in that it consists of a rigid axle tube transversely secured to semi-elliptic leaf springs. Shock absorbers are provided and are secured, at the lower end, to the spring seat, and at the top to the body structure.

2 Springs and shock absorbers – inspection

1   Have an assistant bounce the car up and down while you check any movement in the top and bottom mountings of the front and rear shock absorbers. On station wagon models check for movement in the rear road spring shackles and bushes and for broken or cracked spring leaves.

2   Shock absorbers may be checked by bouncing the car at each corner. Generally speaking the body will return to its normal position and stop after being depressed. If it rises and returns on a rebound the shock absorber should be suspect. Examine also the shock absorber mounting bushes for any sign of looseness and the cylinders themselves for traces of hydraulic fluid leaks. (Rear shock absorbers, however, are gas-filled). If there is any sign of leaks the unit must be renewed. Static tests of shock absorbers are not entirely conclusive and further indications of shock absorber failure are noticeable pitching; (bonnet going up and down when the car is braked and stopped sharply); excessive rolling on fast bends; and a definite feeling of insecurity on corners, particularly if the road surface is uneven. If you are in doubt it is a good idea to drive over a roughish road and have someone follow you to watch how the wheels behave. Excessive up and down 'patter' of any wheel is usually quite obvious, and denotes a defective shock absorber.

3 Front wheel hub, bearings and steering knuckle – removal, inspection and refitting

1   Jack-up the front of the car and support it on axle stands. Remove the roadwheels.

2   Disconnect the brake hose and plug the open end of the hose.

3   Pull out the cotter pin and remove the castellated hub nut and the washer.

4   Remove the brake caliper assembly as described in Chapter 9.

5   Attach a puller to the hub and secure it with the wheel nuts. Set the front knuckles to the straight-ahead position, so that the driveshaft constant velocity (CV) joint is not subjected to stress and remove the wheel hub.

6   Remove the driveshaft as described in Chapter 7. When removing the driveshaft be careful not to damage the knuckle seal.

7   Remove the wheel bearings and seals from the wheel hub and knuckle.

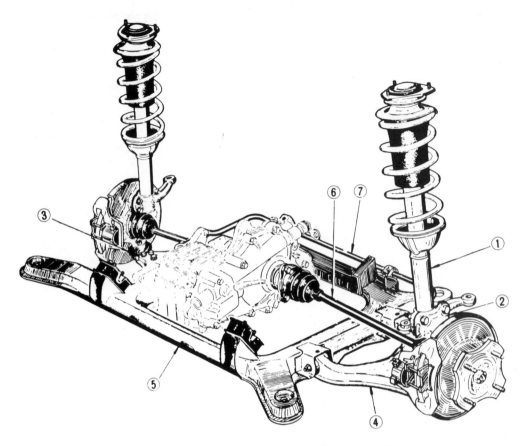

Fig. 11.1. Front suspension – general arrangement

1 Strut assembly
2 Knuckle
3 Balljoint
4 Transverse link

5 Subframe
6 Driveshaft
7 Stabilizer

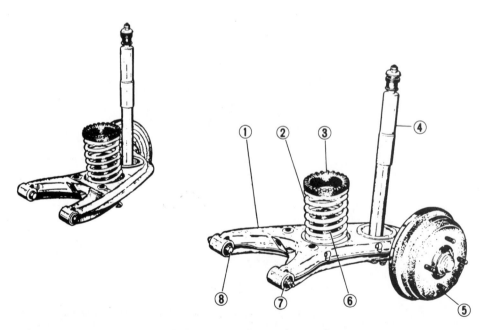

Fig. 11.2. Rear suspension – saloon and coupe

1 Rear arm
2 Coil spring
3 Rubber seat
4 Shock absorber

5 Drum
6 Bound bumper
7 Bushing
8 Rear arm bolt

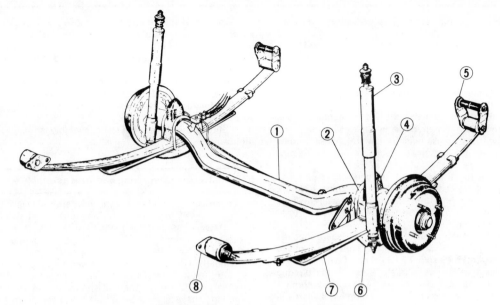

Fig. 11.3. Rear suspension – station wagon

1 Axle tube   5 Shackle
2 U-bolt   6 Spring seat
3 Shock absorber   7 Leaf spring
4 Bumper rubber   8 Front pin

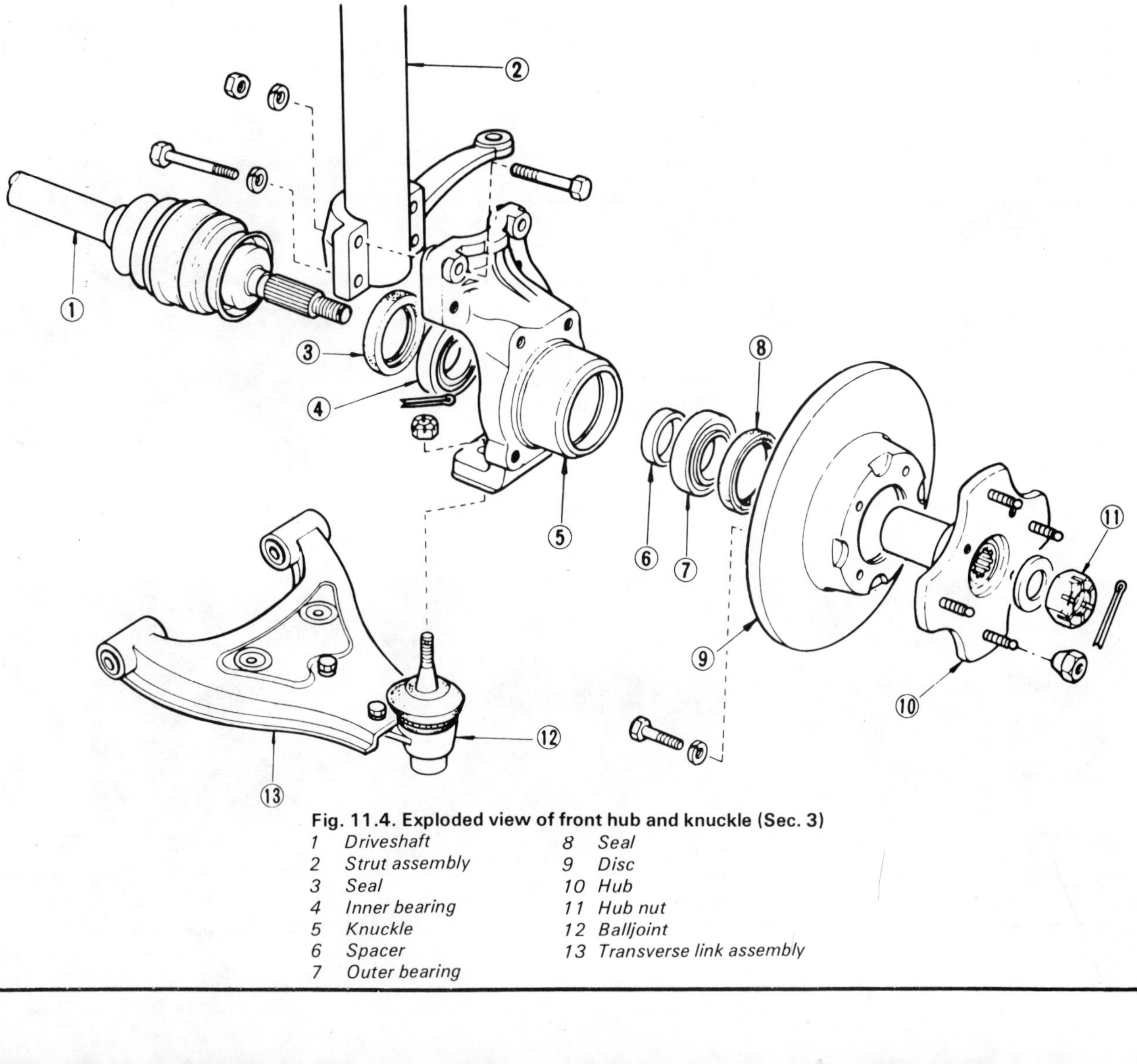

Fig. 11.4. Exploded view of front hub and knuckle (Sec. 3)

1 Driveshaft   8 Seal
2 Strut assembly   9 Disc
3 Seal   10 Hub
4 Inner bearing   11 Hub nut
5 Knuckle   12 Balljoint
6 Spacer   13 Transverse link assembly
7 Outer bearing

8   Undo the attaching bolts and remove the brake disc and back plate.

9   Separate the lower balljoint and tie-rod balljoint from the knuckle as described in Chapter 8.

10   Remove the bolts securing the knuckle to the strut and detach the knuckle.

11   Drive the wheel bearing outer race and grease seal out of the knuckle with a brass drift.

12   Clean all the parts thoroughly with paraffin and inspect for signs of overheating, scoring, corrosion or other damage. Check that the wheel bearings rotate freely without excess noise or any roughness. Renew all defective parts. Discard the old grease seals and always fit new ones after each dismantling.

13   If new bearings have to be fitted, special tools are required to determine the thickness of the spacer. As there are eighteen different thicknesses of spacer to select from, and six different special tools are needed, take the wheel hub to your Datsun dealer and get him to fit the new bearings and appropriate spacer.

14   Refitting is the reverse of the removal procedure. Ensure that the bearings are lubricated with multi-purpose grease. Tighten hub nut to 58 – 116 lbf ft (8 – 16 kgf m) then spin the wheel hub several times in both directions to check that it rotates freely. Measure the bearing preload with a spring balance, as shown in Fig. 11.6. It should be 3 – 11 lb (1.4 – 4.9 kg). If the preload is not correct a different spacer will have to be fitted; if preload is lower than specified, fit a thinner spacer, if greater fit a thicker spacer.

15   Bleed the brake system as described in Chapter 9.

4   Front suspension spring and strut assembly – removal and refitting

1   Chock the rear wheels, apply the handbrake, jack-up the front of the car and support on firmly based axle stands.

2   Remove the four bolts securing the strut to the knuckle and separate the two components (photo).

3   Detach the steering tie-rod, as described in Chapter 8 (photo).

4   Working in the engine bay, remove the cap over the top of the suspension strut and partially loosen the locknut securing the piston rod (photo).

5   Place a jack or suitable packing under the strut to support its weight during the next operation.

6   Working under the bonnet undo and remove the three nuts fastening the top of the strut to the inner wing panel.

7   Carefully lower the jack or remove the packing and lift away the suspension strut assembly (photo).

8   Refitting the suspension strut assembly is the reverse sequence to removal.

5   Front suspension spring and strut assembly – overhaul

It is recommended that, if the strut assembly is in need of overhaul or it is necessary for new coil springs to be fitted, this job be left to the local Datsun garage. The reason for this is that special tools are necessary to compress the spring, keep the spring in a compressed state and to dismantle the strut assembly.

The following instructions are given for those who wish to attempt the job. Before removing the strut assembly from the car it is necessary to fit clips to the coil spring to keep it in the compressed condition. These should be either borrowed from the local Datsun garage or made up using some high tensile steel rod at least 0.5 inch (12.70 mm) in diameter with the ends bent over. The length should accommodate as many coils as possible. Refer to Section 4, and follow the instructions given in paragraph 1. Then place a jack under the strut and compress the road springs by raising the jack. Fit the spring clips and tie firmly in place with strong wire or cord.

To overhaul the strut assembly proceed as follows:

1   Thoroughly clean the unit by working in paraffin and then wiping dry with a clean non-fluffy rag.

2   Fit the coil spring compressor to the suspension unit, make sure that it is correctly positioned and then compress the spring. This is not applicable if the spring clips are in position.

3   Carefully prise the circlip from the dust cover.

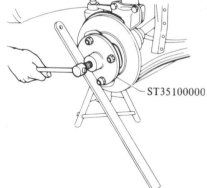

Fig. 11.5. Removing the front hub (Sec. 3)

ST35100000

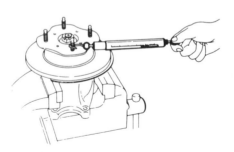

Fig. 11.6. Measuring wheel bearing pre-load (Sec. 3)

4.2   Strut to knuckle securing bolts

4.3   Detach the steering tie-rod from the knuckle

4.4   Remove the cap from the top of the suspension strut

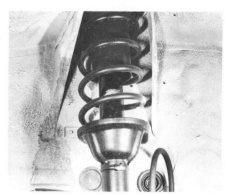

4.7   Front suspension coil spring

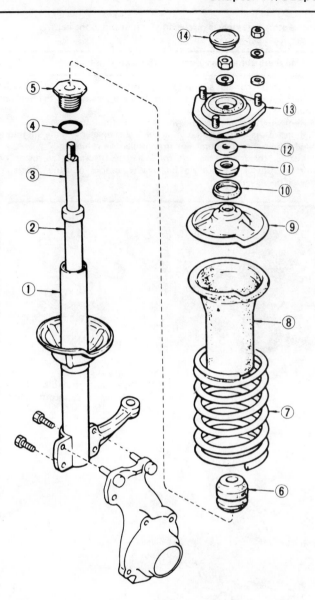

Fig. 11.7. Exploded view of front spring and strut assembly (Sec. 5)

1 Strut	8 Dust cover
2 Cylinder	9 Spring seat
3 Piston rod	10 Dust seal
4 O-ring	11 Seat
5 Gland packing	12 Plate
6 Bumper rubber	13 Mounting insulator
7 Coil spring	14 Cap

4   Undo and remove the self-locking nut. A new one will be necessary on reassembly.

5   Lift off the strut insulator, and the rest of the top mounting components. Note the order in which they are removed.

6   Remove the coil spring still in the compressed state.

7   Push the piston rod down until it reaches its fully retracted position.

8   It is now necessary for the gland packing to be removed. Ideally a special tool should be used but it may be improvised using a wrench.

9   Remove the O-ring from the top of the piston rod guide.

10 Lift out the piston rod together with the cylinder. **Important**: The piston and piston rod guide must never be removed from the cylinder as these are set relative to each other.

11 Tilt the inner cylinder and allow the hydraulic fluid to drain out into a container. Also drain out any fluid inside the outer casing. Fresh fluids will be required during reassembly.

12 Wash all parts in petrol and wipe dry. Make quite sure no dirt is allowed to contact any internal parts.

13 Always renew the gland packing, and O-ring when the strut has been dismantled.

14 Inspect the outer casing for signs of distortion, cracking or accident damage and obtain a new casing if any such condition is apparent.

15 Inspect the spindle for hair line cracks on the case or damaged threads. If evident the complete strut assembly should be renewed.

16 Inspect the rubber and metal joint for signs of damage or deterioration. Obtain new parts if evident.

17 If noise originated from the strut when driving over rough road surfaces the cause is probably due to the strut mounting bearing having worn. Obtain a new bearing assembly.

18 Before reassembly commences, make sure that every part is really clean and free from dust.

19 Fit the piston rod and cylinder into position in the outer casing.

20 Fill the assembly with the recommended grade of hydraulic fluid. For AMPCO (ATSUGI) units use 210 cc or KYB (KAYABA) units use 190 cc. Do not deviate from the quoted amounts otherwise the operating efficiency of the unit will be altered.

21 Place the rod guide on the top of the piston rod guide and refit the gland packing.

22 Lubricate the sealing lips with a little multi-purpose grease and tighten the gland packing to a torque wrench setting of 43 to 47 lbf ft (6.0 to 6.5 kgf m). This will have to be estimated if the special tool is not available. **Note.** When tightening the gland packing the piston rod must be extended approximately 4.724 in (120 mm) from the end of the outer casing to expel most of the air out of the strut.

23 It is now necessary to bleed the shock absorber system by holding the strut with the spindle end down and pulling the piston rod out completely.

24 Now invert the strut so that the spindle end is uppermost and push the piston rod inwards as far as it will go.

25 Repeat the procedure described in paragraph 23 several times, until an equal pressure is felt during both strokes.

26 Pull the piston rod out fully and fit the rebound rubber, to prevent the piston rod falling by its own weight.

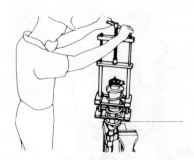

Fig. 11.8. Compressing the spring (Sec. 5)

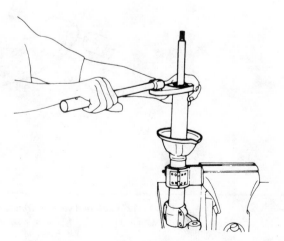

Fig. 11.9. Tightening the gland packing (Sec. 5)

27 Locate the spring on the lower spring seat with the end fitted into the recess and compress the spring with the special tool if spring clips are not fitted.

28 Refit the dust seals with the lip pointing downwards.

29 Lubricate the dust seals with a little multi-purpose grease. Fit the rest of the top mounting components as noted on removal and in accordance with Fig.11.10.

30 Refit the piston rod self-locking nut and tighten to a torque wrench setting of 43-47 lbf ft (6.00-6.5 kgf m).

31 With the spring correctly located release the spring compressor. If clips have been used leave in position until the strut has been reassembled to the car.

32 Raise the rebound rubber until it is seated under the upper spring seat.

33 The strut assembly is now ready for refitting to the car.

6 Transverse link – removal, overhaul and refitting

1   Jack up the car and support it on axle stands.

2   Remove the three bolts securing the transverse link to the balljoint (photo).

3   Remove the stabilizer attaching nut from the transverse link.

4   Remove the two bolts securing the transverse link to the subframe and withdraw the transverse link from under the vehicle.

5   Inspect the transverse link for evidence of cracks, corrosion or distortion. Check the bushes for ovality, cracks or other damage. Renew if necessary.

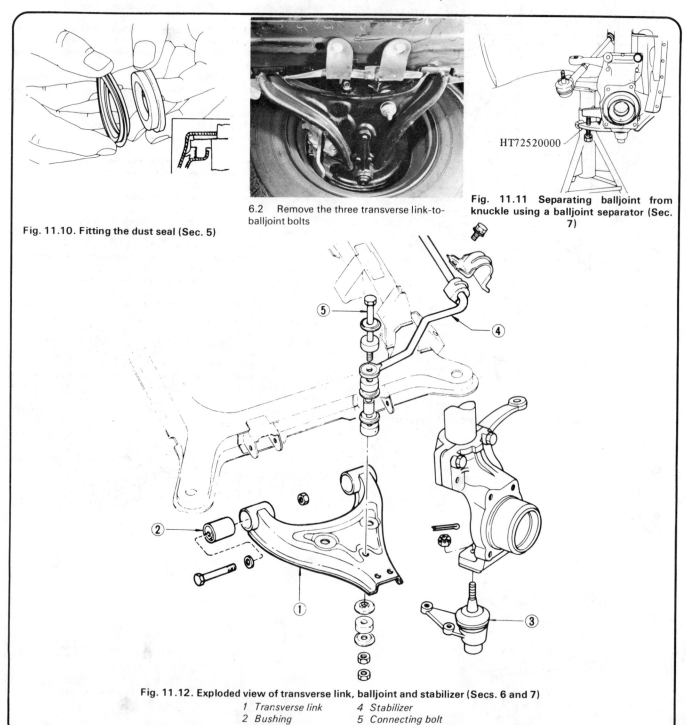

Fig. 11.10. Fitting the dust seal (Sec. 5)

6.2   Remove the three transverse link-to-balljoint bolts

HT72520000

Fig. 11.11 Separating balljoint from knuckle using a balljoint separator (Sec. 7)

Fig. 11.12. Exploded view of transverse link, balljoint and stabilizer (Secs. 6 and 7)

1 Transverse link   4 Stabilizer
2 Bushing   5 Connecting bolt
3 Balljoint

6   Renewal of the bushes calls for care as the transverse link must not be distorted during the course of removing and refitting the bushes. It is best to get the old ones out by cutting through them.
7   New bushes should be lubricated and drawn in using a long nut and bolt together with a tubular spacer (on the inside of the arm) and large washers to ensure the bushes are drawn in square. Do not attempt to drive the bushes in with a hammer. When installing the bushes should project equally either side of the link.
8   Refitting is the reverse of removal. Fit the mounting bolts from inside the link.
9   With the transverse link under standard load conditions, (i.e. the car weight off the jack), tighten the bolts so as not to deform the bushing excessively.

7   Transverse link balljoint – removal and refitting

1   Although the normal technique for removing this particular ball-joint involves removing the driveshaft beforehand, if great care is exercised it is possible to do it without this onerous task.
2   Remove the split pin and castellated locknut. Separate the joint from the knuckle. This can only be done with surety by using a claw clamp. However, it is possible to drive through but only if the knuckle is firmly supported. The joint will almost certainly be damaged in the process. Another method is to strike the side of the knuckle where the pin goes through whilst holding the head of another hammer on the opposite side, This has a squeezing out effect on the tapered pin. If any difficulty arises that looks as though it might cause damage to the driveshaft, then you must remove the driveshaft.
3   Remove the bolts securing the balljoint to the transverse link and detach the balljoint.
4   Inspect the balljoint for endplay and damage. Check the dust cover for cracks and deterioration. Should there be endplay or damage to the balljoint a new one must be fitted. Generally a new balljoint assembly is supplied complete with a dust cover. Replenish the grease, if the old balljoint is being refitted, by removing the dust cover and using a grease gun.
5   Make sure that the socket groove in which the dust cover clamps securely is free from oil or grease. Wipe clean if necessary.
6   After a new dust cover is installed, move the stud until the ball surface is coated with grease evenly. Make sure that the stud swing torque is correctly obtained. (See Specifications).
7   After the balljoint is installed on the vehicle, replace the plug with the grease nipple. Apply grease to the balljoint through this grease nipple until grease is forced out at the grease vent hole.

8   Front suspension stabilizer – removal and refitting

1   Jack-up the front of the car and support it on axle stands.
2   Remove the nuts securing the connecting bolt to the transverse link.
3   Remove the bolts securing the stabilizer bracket to the subframe, withdraw the connecting bolt and remove the stabilizer and rubber mountings.
4   Inspect the stabilizer for deformation and cracks. Check all the rubber parts for deterioration and cracks. Renew any defective parts.
5   Refitting the stabilizer is the reverse of the removal procedure. Tighten the connecting bolt nut and bracket attaching bolts to 6 – 9 lbf ft (0.8 – 1.2 kgf m).

9   Rear hub – removal and refitting

1   Chock the front wheels. Remove the rear wheel trim, slacken the wheelnuts, jack-up the rear of the car and support on firmly based stands. Remove the roadwheel.
2   Knock off the cap from the end of the hub, remove the split pin and unscrew and remove the castellated nut and thrust washer (photos).
3   Pull the hub assembly forward and extract the outer roller bearing then pull the unit from the stub axle.
4   To refit the hub, first clean out all traces of old grease and repack with fresh. To do this, carefully wipe clean the stub axle and seal track. Inspect the hub seal and axle threads for wear or damage. If there are any signs of leakage onto the brake backplate fit a new seal.
5   Wipe away as much old grease as possible from the hub and then insert new grease into the bearings. Do not overfill the hub cavity. Remove any surplus grease other than that shown in Fig.11.17.
6   Refit the hub assembly to the stub axle and secure it with the

Fig. 11.13. Removing the stabilizer connecting bolt nut (Sec. 8)

9.2a   Remove the hub cap, split pin, nut ...

9.2b   ... and thrust washer

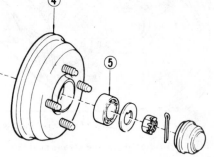

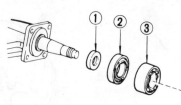

Fig. 11.14. Rear hub assembly (Sec. 9)

1 Bearing collar   4 Brake drum
2 Seal   5 Outer bearing
3 Inner bearing

washer and castellated hub nut.

7   Using a torque wrench, tighten the nut to 18 – 22 lbf ft (2.5 – 3.0 kgf m). Rotate the hub in both directions to settle the wheel bearings.

8   Loosen the hub nut until it can be turned by hand, then fit a socket on the nut and tighten it by hand, see Fig.11.15. Check that the hub rotates freely.

9   Align the castellated nut so that one of the slots lines up with the split pin hole in the stub axle and fit the split pin. If necessary, turn the hub nut clockwise, then fit a new split pin but do not bend it over at this stage.

10 If the adjustment is correct there should be no hub endfloat and, using a spring balance, the force required to rotate the hub should be 1.1 – 2.6 lb (0.5 – 1.2 kg) when a new grease seal is fitted and 1.5 lb (0.7 kg) maximum when the old seal is re-used. Attach the spring balance to a wheel stud as shown in Fig.11.16.

11 When adjustment is correct, bend over the ends of the split pin, fit the cap and roadwheel and lower the vehicle.

10 Rear hub – overhaul

1   Remove the rear hub as described in Section 9 paragraphs 1 to 3 inclusive.

2   Wash all internal grease from the hub using paraffin. If the bearings and seal are in good order, repack the interior of the hub and end cap with wheel bearing grease so that it occupies the area shown in Fig.11.17.

3   If the bearings are worn or damaged, prise out the grease seal from the inner and outer end of the hub and extract the inner roller race. Drift out the inner and outer bearing tracks using a thin rod.

4   Fit the new bearing tracks using a piece of tubing as a drift. If both hubs are being dismantled at the same time, ensure that the bearings

are kept as matched sets and do not mix up the races and tracks.

5   Press the new grease seal squarely into the inner end of the hub, with its lip towards the roller bearing.

6   Pack the hub with grease as described in paragraph 2.

7   Refitting is a reversal of removal, but adjust the bearing preload, as described in the preceding Section.

11 Rear axle tube (station wagon) – removal and refitting

1   Jack-up the rear of the car and support on firmly based axle stands. Also support the weight of the rear suspension by placing a jack under the tubular beam axle.

2   Remove the rear wheels if access to their inner face is not good.

3   Disconnect the brake pipe from the wheel cylinder.

4   Disconnect the handbrake cable by removing the split pin from the clevis pin.

5   Repeat operations 3 and 4 on the other wheel.

6   Remove the 3-way connector mounting bolts then ease off the connector and the brake pipe assembly from the axle tube.

7   Remove the handbrake equalizer bracket, then lift away the complete handbrake cable assembly.

8   Remove the shock absorber and U-bolts.

9   Undo and remove the bolts securing the rear end of the springs from the shackle. Detach the springs from the rear shackles.

10 Unbolt and remove the bolts holding the spring to the front pin.

11 Carefully lower the jack located under the tubular beam axle and wheel away the axle from the rear of the car.

12 Refitting is the reverse sequence to removal. It will be necessary to bleed the brake hydraulic system - details of this operation will be found in Chapter 9.

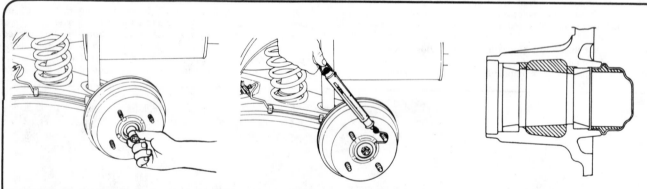

Fig. 11.15. Tightening the hub nut by hand (Sec. 9)   Fig. 11.16. Measuring the wheel bearing rotation force (Sec. 9)   Fig. 11.17. Pack shaded areas of hub with grease (Sec. 9)

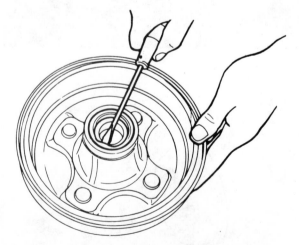

Fig. 11.18. Removing the grease seal (Sec. 10)

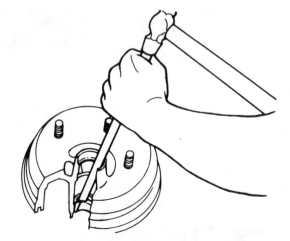

Fig. 11.19. Driving out the wheel bearing outer race (Sec. 10)

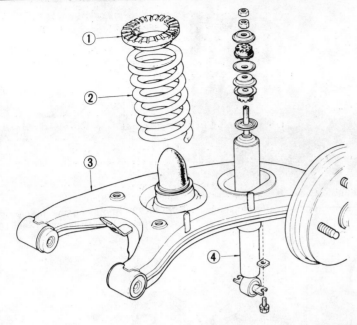

Fig. 11.20. Rear shock absorber and coil spring – saloon and coupe (Sec. 12)

1 *Rubber seat*   3 *Rear arm*
2 *Coil spring*   4 *Shock absorber*

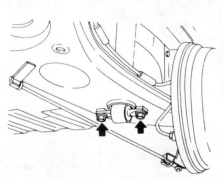

Fig. 11.21. Rear shock absorber lower attaching bolts (Sec. 12)

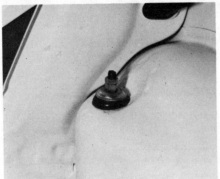

12.5a Rear shock absorber upper securing nuts ...

12.5b ... and the two lower mounting bolts

12 Rear shock absorber and coil spring (saloon and coupe) – removal, inspection and refitting

1 The rear shock absorbers will need renewal if their mounting bushes are worn or if indications are that the unit is no longer performing properly. Similarly, replace the coil springs if they are weak or fractured.

2 Jack-up the rear of the vehicle and support with axle stands.

3 Remove the rear wheel.

4 Support the lower end of the suspension arm by means of a jack.

5 Remove the two upper nuts that secure the shock absorber, then the two bolts from the shock absorber lower mounting. If only the coil spring is being replaced, remove the upper mounting bolts only (photos).

6 If the shock absorber only is being removed, it can be compressed and lifted out. Take care to collect the various washers and bushes that this will release from the top mounting. If the shock absorbers are definitely to be replaced, drill a hole on the lower portion of the tube to bleed high pressure gas out of it completely. This procedure makes it easy to remove the shock absorber.

7 Assuming both coil and shock absorber are to be removed, lower the jack under the suspension arm slowly to relieve the tension of the coil spring. Remove the spring, rubber seat and shock absorber (photo).

8 Inspect the shock absorber for signs of leakage, reduced damping properties or deformed shaft. Renew the thrust bushing if damage, cracks or deterioration is apparent.

9 Check the coil spring for cracks, corrosion and deformation. Check that the rubber seat is free from splits, distortion or excessive

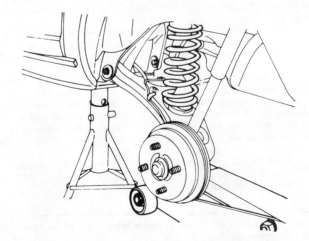

Fig. 11.22. Removing the coil spring (Sec. 12)

wear.

10 Refitting is the reverse of the removal procedure. When fitting the coil spring, first position the upper (flattened) end of the spring in place on its rubber seat, then attach the lower, open, end of the spring to the seating surface on the rear suspension arm. Gradually raise the jack to compress the spring.

12.7   Rear suspension coil spring

14.3   Rear suspension arm attaching bolts

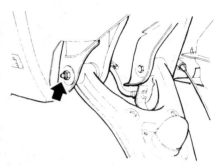

Fig. 11.23. Removing the rear suspension
arm – saloon and coupe (Sec. 14)

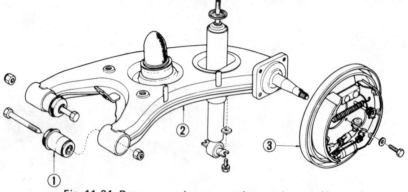

Fig. 11.24. Rear suspension arm – saloon and coupe (Sec. 14)

1   Bushing   3   Rear brake assembly
2   Rear arm

13 Rear suspension shock absorber (station wagon) – removal and refitting

1   Chock the front wheels, jack-up the rear of the car and support on firmly based stands. Remove the roadwheel.
2   Undo and remove the nuts that secure the upper end of the shock absorber to the body after removing the shock absorber cover.
3   Undo and remove the nut and washer that secure the shock absorber to the spring plate attachment. Detach the shock absorber and lift away from the car.
4   Inspect the shock absorber for signs of leaks, which, if evident, means the shock absorber must be discarded and a new one obtained. Since the shock absorbers are gas-filled, evidence of leakage is very difficult to detect.
5   Clean the exterior and wipe with a non-fluffy rag. Inspect the shaft for signs of corrosion or distortion and the body for damage.
6   Check the action by expanding and contracting to ascertain if equal resistance is felt on both strokes. If the resistance is very uneven the unit must be renewed. It may be found that resistance is greater on the upward stroke than on the downward stroke and this is permissible.
7   Check the rubber bushes and washers for deterioration and renew as necessary.
8   Refitting is the reverse sequence to removal.

14 Rear suspension arms (saloon and coupe) – removal, inspection and refitting

1   If the rubber mounting bushes on the arms are worn it will be necessary to remove the arms to renew them.
2   The initial operations to remove an arm are virtually identical with those given to remove a spring or shock absorber (Section 12): the only additions are that the brake pipe to brake hose joint must be disconnected, and the handbrake cable detached at the clevis pin on the wheel.

3   Having lowered the jack under the arm and removed the shock absorber and coil spring, next remove the two bolts that secure the arm to the body and detach the arm. (photo).
4   Inspect the arm for corrosion, distortion or cracks. Check the bushes for deterioration such as cracks or ovality; and check the rubber bump stop for damage.
5   If the arm is damaged it will have to be renewed.
6   Inspect the suspension arm bushes and if worn use a bolt, nut, washers and tubing to draw out the old bushes and fit new ones.
7   Refitting the rear suspension arm is the reverse sequence to removal. The following additional points should be noted:

   a)   Always use new self-locking washers
   b)   Finally tighten all suspension attachments when the car is resting on the ground
   c)   It will be necessary to bleed the brake hydraulic system, as described in Chapter 9.

15 Rear spring (station wagon) – removal and refitting

1   Chock the front wheels, jack-up the rear of the car and support on firmly based stands. Remove the roadwheel.
2   Place the jack under the centre of the rear axle and raise it until the strain is taken from the shock absorbers.
3   Undo and remove the nut and washer that secures the shock absorber to the spring plate attachments. Detach the shock absorber and compress it until it is clear of the axle housing.
4   Undo and remove the U-bolts nuts and lift away the mounting plate. If tight, tap with a hammer but take care not to damage the U-bolt threads.
5   Raise the jack until the weight of the axle has been taken from the spring.
6   Undo and remove the rear shackle nuts and washers.
7   Lift away the shackle plates noting the correct positioning of the shackle pins.
8   Rest the axle on wood blocks and lower the rear of the spring to

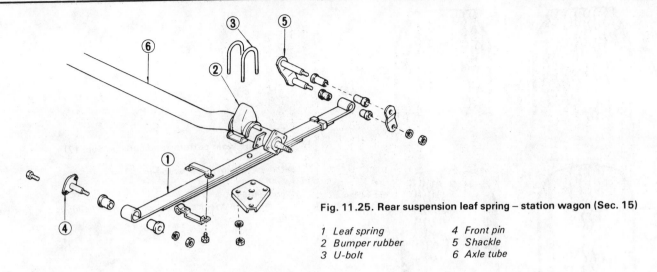

Fig. 11.25. Rear suspension leaf spring – station wagon (Sec. 15)

1 Leaf spring   4 Front pin
2 Bumper rubber   5 Shackle
3 U-bolt   6 Axle tube

the ground. Recover the two rubber bushes from the body spring shackle hanger.

9 Undo and remove the nut from the front pin bolt and tap out the bolt with a soft faced hammer.

10 The spring may now be removed from the car.

11 If any of the shackles or rubber bushes are worn they must be renewed together with the pins if they too show signs of wear.

12 The bushes fitted to the rear road spring eyes are of the bonded rubber type. They may be removed and new ones fitted with the spring in position on the axle by using a threaded bolt, distance piece of similar diameter to the outside diameter of the bush and a washer. Tightening the nut will draw the old bush from the spring eye or draw the new one into position.

13 Where the road spring has been removed from the car, then the bushes may be drifted out or in by using a piece of tubing of appropriate outside diameter. Do not attempt to use the inner shackle pin locating hole of the bush as a means of removing the bush or the bonding will be destroyed.

14 If a spring is broken or has lost its resilience then it should be replaced; in this event the other spring should be replaced at the same time.

15 Replacement is a straightforward reversal of the dismantling process. Do not fully tighten the attachments until the car has been lowered to the ground and the spring is in its normal position. If this is not done the rubber bushes will require frequent replacement.

16 Front wheel alignment – checking and adjustment

1 Accurate front wheel alignment is essential for good steering and tyre wear. Before considering the steering angle, check that the tyres are correctly inflated, that the front wheels are not buckled, the hub bearings are not worn or incorrectly adjusted and that the steering linkage is in good order, without slackness or wear at the joints.

2 Wheel alignment consists of four factors :

   Camber which is the angle at which the front wheels are set from the vertical when viewed from the front of the car. Positive camber is the amount (in degrees) that the wheels are tilted outwards at the top from the vertical.

   Castor is the right angle between the steering axis and a vertical line when viewed from each side of the car. Positive castor is when the steering axis is inclined rearward.

   Steering axis inclination is the angle, when viewed from the front of the car, between the vertical and an imaginary line drawn between the upper and lower suspension leg pivots.

   Toe-in is the amount by which the distance between the front inside edges of the roadwheels (measured at hub height) is less than the diametrically opposite distance measured between the rear inside edges of the front roadwheels.

3 All steering angles other than toe-in are set in production and are not adjustable. Front wheel tracking (toe-in) checks are best carried out with modern setting equipment but a reasonably accurate alterna-

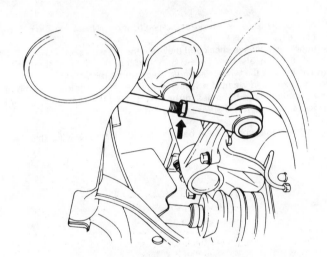

Fig. 11.26. Steering tie-rod locknut (Sec. 16)

tive and adjustment procedure may be carried out as follows:

4 Place the car on level ground with the wheels in the straight-ahead position.

5 Obtain or make a toe-in gauge. One may be easily made from tubing, cranked to clear the sump and bellhousing, having an adjustable nut and setscrew at one end.

6 With the gauge, measure the distance between the two inner rims of the front roadwheels, at hub height and at the rear of the wheels.

7 Pull or push the vehicle so that the roadwheel turns through half a turn (180°) and measure the distance between the two inner rims at hub height at the front of the wheel. This last measurement should be less than the first by the specified toe-in (see Specifications Section).

8 Where the toe-in is found to be incorrect, slacken the locknuts of each outer tie-rod and rotate each tie-rod an equal amount but in opposite directions, until the correct toe-in is obtained. Tighten the locknuts ensuring that the balljoints are held in the centre of their arc of travel during tightening.

17 Wheels and tyres

1 The roadwheels are of pressed steel type.

2 Periodically remove the wheels, clean dirt and mud from the inside and outside surfaces and examine for signs of rusting or rim damage and rectify as necessary.

3 Apply a smear of light grease to the wheel studs before screwing on the nuts and finally tighten them to specified torque.

4 The tyres fitted may be of crossply, bias belt or radical construc-

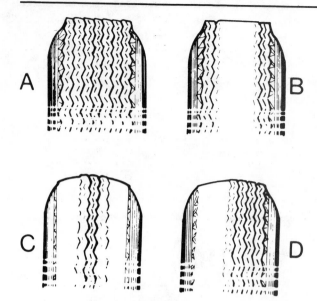

Fig. 11.27. Tyre wear patterns and causes (Sec. 17)

A 'Feathering' due to incorrect toe-in
B Over inflation
C Under inflation
D Wear due to incorrect camber, worn wheel bearings and fast cornering

tion according to territory and specification. Never mix tyres of different construction and always check and maintain the pressures regularly.

5 If the wheels have been balanced on the vehicle then it is important that the wheels are not moved round the vehicle in an effort to equalize tread wear. If a wheel is removed, then the relationship of the wheel studs to the holes in the wheel should be marked to ensure exact replacement, otherwise the balance of wheel, hub and tyre will be upset.

6 Where the wheels have been balanced off the vehicle, then they may be moved round to equalize wear. Include the spare wheel in any rotational pattern. If radial tyres are fitted, do not move the wheels from side to side but only interchange the front and rear wheels on the same side.

7 Balancing the wheels is an essential factor in good steering and road holding. When the tyres have been in use for about half their useful life the wheels should be rebalanced to compensate for the lost tread rubber due to wear.

8 Inspect the tyre walls and treads regularly for cuts and damage and, where evident, have them professionally repaired.

18 Fault diagnosis – Suspension and steering

Symptom	Reason/s	Remedy

Front suspension and steering

Vibration, shock and shimmying of steering wheel

Steering wheel oscillation is often experienced when there exists an excessive free-play in steering linkage, improper backlash in steering gear, or oscillation of front wheels.
Steering shock or kickback can be felt at the steering wheel when the front wheels encounter obstructions in road. This condition can be due to improper backlash in steering gear or other associated units.
Shimmy is rapid oscillation of front suspension system and related parts and is often experienced when vehicle picks up a certain speed.

	Reason/s	Remedy
	Incorrect tyre pressures	Adjust.
	Wheel out of balance or buckled	Correct or renew.
	Worn tyre or loose wheel	Renew or re-tighten.
	Worn suspension balljoint or lack of preload	Renew balljoint.
	Steering gear out of adjustment	Re-adjust.
	Improper wheel alignment	Re-adjust.
	Worn rubber bushing in transverse link	Renew.
	Excessive free-play in steering linkage	Check and correct.
	Excessive play or wear on front wheel bearing	Renew bearing, or adjust.
	Loose steering gearbox	Re-tighten.
	Loose or inoperative shock absorber (in strut assembly).	Re-tighten or renew.

Car pulls to one side

This condition becomes evident when vehicle is running on a level surface with your hands off steering wheel

	Reason/s	Remedy
	Incorrect tyre pressures, or loose wheelnuts	Correct. Tighten wheelnuts.
	Difference in right and left tyre treads, or tyre type	Renew tyres.
	Defective front wheel bearing	Renew.
	Fatigued front spring, or use of incorrect spring	Renew.
	Improper wheel alignment	Re-adjust.
	Brake drag (out of adjustment)	Re-adjust.
	Worn bushing in transverse link	Renew.
	Deformed steering linkage or suspension link	Renew.
	Defective radial tyre	Renew.

Vehicle wanders when steering wheel held stationary.

	Reason/s	Remedy
	Incorrect tyre pressures	Adjust.
	Improper wheel alignment	Re-adjust.
	Excessive free-play or wear on steering linkage or suspension linkage	Renew.
	Steering gear out of adjustment	Re-adjust.
	Wheel buckled or out of balance	Check and correct.
	Worn bushing in transverse link	Renew.

Steering stiff

Check and correct in the following manner:
Jack-up front portion of vehicle and support it on axle stands. Separate knuckle arm from tie-rod and manipulate steering wheel.
a) If steering wheel operation is now light, check and locate cause of trouble in steering linkage, suspension system, or front axle.
b) If steering wheel operation is now heavy, check and locate cause of trouble in steering gear or steering column.

	Reason/s	Remedy
	Incorrect tyre pressures	Adjust.
	Incorrect lubrication in steering gear housing or dirt in oil (b)	Lubricate, service or renew.
	Improper lubrication in steering linkage, dirt in grease, or abnormal wear on steering linkage (a)	Lubricate or renew.
	Seized, damaged suspension balljoint. Lack of lubrication to balljoint (a)	Renew.
	Worn or seized wheel bearing (a)	Renew or adjust.
	Steering gear out of adjustment (b)	Re-adjust.
	Deformed steering linkage(a)	Renew.
	Improper wheel alignment (a)	Re-adjust.
	Damaged thrust seal on upper end of strut (a)	Renew.
	Seized or damaged piston or piston rod of shock absorber (in strut) (a)	Renew.

Symptom	Reason/s	Remedy
Excessive play at steering wheel	Steering gear out of adjustment	Re-adjust.
	Worn steering linkage	Renew.
	Loose steering gearbox	Re-tighten.
	Defective wheel bearing	Renew.
	Worn bushing in transverse link	Renew.
Unusual noises	Incorrect tyre pressures	Adjust.
	Damaged or worn suspension balljoint or steering linkage, or lack of lubrication	Renew or lubricate.
	Loose steering gear linkage or suspension system	Re-tighten.
	Defective shock absorber (in strut)	Renew.
	Defective wheel bearing	Renew.
	Worn steering linkage or steering gear	Renew.
	Worn bushing in transverse link	Renew.
	Broken or fatigued coil spring	Renew.
	Loose mounting nut on strut mounting insulator	Re-tighten.
	Improper tightening of strut and gland packing	Re-tighten.
	Loose bolt on subframe	Re-tighten.
	Buckled wheel	Renew.
Tyre squeal	Incorrect tyre pressures	Adjust.
	Improper wheel alignment	Re-adjust.
	Deformed knuckle, spindle or suspension	Renew.
Abnormal or uneven tyre wear	Incorrect tyre pressures	Adjust.
	Improper wheel alignment	Re-adjust.
	Defective wheel bearing	Renew.
	Brakes out of adjustment	Re-adjust.

Rear suspension (Saloon and Coupe)

Symptom	Reason/s	Remedy
Unusual noises	Loose suspension linkages	Tighten.
	Tyres out of balance or incorrectly inflated	Adjust.
	Damaged rear arm bushing and shock absorber thrust bushing.	Renew.
	Defective shock absorber	Renew.
	Defective coil spring	Renew.
	Defective wheel bearing	Adjust or renew.
Unstable running	Loose wheelnuts	Tighten.
	Defective rear arm rubber bushing	Renew.
	Defective shock absorber	Renew.
	Defective coil spring	Renew.
	Faulty wheel bearings	Adjust or renew.
	Brakes out of adjustment (drag)	Adjust.
	Incorrect tyre pressures	Adjust.

Rear suspension (Station wagon)

Symptom	Reason/s	Remedy
	Defective leaf spring	Renew.
	Defective leaf spring bushing	Renew.
	Defective rear wheel bearing	Renew.
	Loose wheelnuts	Tighten.
	Loose or broken U-bolt	Tighten or renew.
	Loose shackle	Tighten.
	Defective shock absorber	Renew.
	Broken leaf spring	Renew.
	Worn or damaged leaf spring bushing	Renew.
	Faulty wheel bearing	Adjust or renew.
	Brakes out of adjustment (drag)	Adjust.
	Incorrect tyre pressures	Adjust.

Chapter 12 Bodywork and fittings

Contents

1 General description

The body shells are of rigid sheet metal construction with the outer roof and body panels welded together to form an integral structure. The shells also incorporate a subframe, contributing to engine and transmission accessibility. Because of very rigid box section load-carrying members, exceptional shell rigidity is obtained. Use of the subframe keeps noise and vibration from being carried to the bodyshell.

The front wings are of bolt-on detachable type for economy of replacement in the event of accident damage.

The bonnet is locked from the vehicle interior as are the passenger rear doors. The front doors are locked externally by key.

2 Maintenance – bodywork and underframe

1   The general condition of a car's bodywork is the one thing that significantly affects its value. Maintenance is easy but needs to be regular. Neglect, particularly after minor damage, can lead quickly to further deterioration and costly repair bills. It is important also to keep watch on those parts of the car not immediately visible, for instance the underframe, inside all the wheel arches and the lower part of the engine compartment.

2   The basic maintenance routine for the bodywork is washing - preferably with a lot of water, from a hose. This will remove all the loose solids which may have stuck to the car. It is important to flush these off in such a way as to prevent grit from scratching the finish.

The wheel arches and underframe need washing in the same way to remove any accumulated mud which will retain moisture and tend to encourage rust. Paradoxically enough, the best time to clean the underframe and wheel arches is in wet weather when the mud is thoroughly wet and soft. In very wet weather the underframe is usually cleaned of large accumulations automatically and this is a good time for inspection.

3   Periodically it is a good idea to have the whole of the underframe of the car steam cleaned, engine compartment included, so that a thorough inspection can be carried out to see what minor repairs and renovations are necessary. Steam cleaning is available at many garages and is necessary for removal of the accumulation of oily grime which sometimes is allowed to cake thick in certain areas near the engine, gearbox and back axle. If steam cleaning facilities are not available, there are one or two excellent grease solvents available which can be brush applied. The dirt can then be simply hosed off.

4   After washing paintwork, wipe off with a chamois leather to give an unspotted clear finish. A coat of clear protective wax polish will give added protection against chemical pollutants in the air. If the paintwork sheen has dulled or oxidised, use a cleaner/polisher combination to restore the brilliance of the shine. This is usually caused because regular washing has been neglected. Always check that the door and ventilator opening drain holes and pipes are completely clear so that water can be drained out. Bright work should be treated the same way as paintwork. Windscreens and windows can be kept clear of the smeary film which often appears if a little ammonia is added to the water. If they are scratched, a good rub with a proprietary metal polish will often clear them. Never use any form of wax or other body or chromium polish on glass.

3 Maintenance – upholstery and carpets

Mats and carpets should be brushed or vacuum cleaned regularly to keep them free of grit. If they are badly stained remove them from the car for scrubbing or sponging and make quite sure they are dry before refitting. Seats and interior trim panels can be kept clean by a wipe over with a damp cloth. If they do become stained (which can be more apparent on light coloured upholstery) use a little liquid detergent and a soft nail brush to scour the grime out of the grain of the material. Do not forget to keep the head lining clean in the same way as the upholstery. When using liquid cleaners inside the vehicle do not over-wet the surfaces being cleaned. Excessive damp could get into the seams and padded interior causing stains, offensive odours or even rot. If the inside of the car gets wet accidentally it is worthwhile taking some trouble to dry it out properly, particularly where carpets are involved. **Do not** leave oil or electric heaters inside the vehicle for this purpose.

4 Minor body damage – repairs

Refer to photo sequences on pages 198 and 199

Repair of minor scratches in the car's bodywork

If the scratch is very superficial, and does not penetrate to the metal of the bodywork, repair is very simple. Lightly rub the area of the scratch with a paintwork renovator, or a very fine cutting paste, to remove loose paint from the scratch and to clear the surrounding bodywork of wax polish. Rinse the area with clean water.

Apply touch-up paint to the scratch using a thin paint brush, continue to apply thin layers of paint until the surface of the paint in the scratch is level with the surrounding paintwork. Allow the new paint at least two weeks to harden; then blend it into the surrounding paintwork by rubbing the paintwork in the scratch area with a paintwork renovator, or a very fine cutting paste. Finally apply wax polish.

An alternative to painting over the scratch is to use Holts 'Scratch-Patch'. Use the same preparation for the affected area; then simply pick a patch of a suitable size to cover the scratch completely. Hold the patch against the scratch and burnish its backing paper; the patch will adhere to the paintwork, freeing itself from the backing paper at the same time. Polish the affected area to blend the patch into the surrounding paintwork. Where the scratch has penetrated right through to the metal of the bodywork, causing the metal to rust, a different repair technique is required. Remove any loose rust from the bottom of the scratch with a penknife, then apply rust inhibiting paint to prevent the formation of rust in the future. Using a rubber or nylon applicator fill the scratch with bodystopper paste. If required, this paste can be mixed with cellulose thinners to provide a very thin paste which is ideal for filling narrow scratches. Before the stopper-paste in the scratch hardens, wrap a piece of smooth cotton rag around the top of a finger. Dip the finger in cellulose thinners and then quickly sweep it across the surface of the stopper-paste in the scratch; this will ensure that the surface of the stopper-paste is slightly hollowed. The scratch can now be painted over as described earlier in this Section.

Repair of dents in the vehicle's bodywork

When deep denting of the car's bodywork has taken place, the first task is to pull the dent out, until the affected bodywork almost attains its original shape. There is little point in trying to restore the original shape completely, as the metal in the damaged area will have stretched on impact and cannot be reshaped fully to its original contour. It is better to bring the level of the dent up to a point which is about $\frac{1}{8}$ in (3 mm) below the level of the surrounding bodywork. In cases where the dent is very shallow anyway, it is not worth trying to pull it out at all.

If the underside of the dent is accessible, it can be hammered out gently from behind, using a mallet with a wooden or plastic head. Whilst doing this, hold a suitable block of wood firmly against impact from the hammer blows and thus prevent a large area of bodywork from being 'belled-out'.

Should the dent be in a section of the bodywork which has double skin or some other factor making it inaccessible from behind, a different technique is called for. Drill several small holes through the metal inside the dent area - particularly in the deeper sections. Then screw long self-tapping screws into the holes just sufficiently for them to gain a good purchase in the metal. Now the dent can be pulled out by pulling on the protruding heads of the screws with a pair of pliers.

The next stage of the repair is the removal of the paint from the damaged area, and from an inch or so of the surrounding 'sound' bodywork. This is accomplished most easily by using a wire brush or abrasive pad on a power drill, although it can be done just as effectively by hand using sheets of abrasive paper. To complete the preparation for filling, score the surface of the bare metal with a screwdriver or the tang of a file, or alternatively, drill small holes in the affected area. This will provide a really good 'key' for the filler paste.

To complete the repair see the Section on filling and respraying.

Repair of rust holes or gashes in the car's bodywork

Remove all paint from the affected area and from an inch or so of the surrounding 'sound' bodywork, using an abrasive pad or a wire brush on a power drill. If these are not available a few sheets of abrasive paper will do the job just as effectively. With the paint removed you will be able to gauge the severity of the corrosion and therefore decide whether to renew the whole panel (if this is possible) or to repair the affected area. New body panels are not as expensive as most people think and it is often quicker and more satisfactory to fit a new panel than to attempt to repair large areas of corrosion.

Remove all fittings from the affected area except those which will act as a guide to the original shape of the damaged bodywork (eg headlamp shells etc). Then, using tin snips or a hacksaw blade, remove all loose metal and any other metal badly affected by corrosion. Hammer the edges of the hole inwards in order to create a slight depression for the filler paste.

Wire brush the affected area to remove the powdery rust from the surface of the remaining metal. Paint the affected area with rust inhibiting paint; if the back of the rusted area is accessible treat this also.

Before filling can take place it will be necessary to block the hole in some way. This can be achieved by the use of one of the following materials: Zinc gauze, Aluminium tape or Polyurethane foam.

Zinc gauze is probably the best material to use for a large hole. Cut a piece to the approximate size and shape of the hole to be filled, then position it in the hole so that its edges are below the level of the surrounding bodywork. It can be retained in position by several blobs of filler paste around its periphery.

Aluminium tape should be used for small or very narrow holes. Pull a piece off the roll and trim it to the approximate size and shape required, then pull off the backing paper (if used) and stick the tape over the hole; it can be overlapped if the thickness of one piece is insufficient. Burnish down the edges of the tape with the handle of a screwdriver or similar, to ensure that the tape is securely attached to the metal underneath.

Polyurethane foam is best used where the hole is situated in a section of bodywork of complex shape, backed by a small box section (eg. where the sill panel meets the rear wheel arch - most cars). The usual mixing procedure for this foam is as follows: Put equal amounts of fluid from each of the two cans provided in the kit, into one container. Stir until the mixture begins to thicken, then quickly pour this mixture into the hole, and hold a piece of cardboard over the larger apertures. Almost immediately the polyurethane will begin to expand, gushing frantically out of any small holes left unblocked. When the foam hardens it can be cut back to just below the level of the surrounding bodywork with a hacksaw blade.

Having blocked off the hole, the affected area must now be filled and sprayed – see Section on bodywork filling and respraying.

Bodywork repairs – filling and respraying

Before using this Section, see the Sections on dent, deep scratch, rust hole and gash repairs.

Many types of bodyfiller are available, but generally speaking those proprietary kits which contain a tin of filler paste and a tube of resin hardener are best for this type of repair. A wide, flexible plastic or nylon applicator will be found invaluable for imparting a smooth and well contoured finish to the surface of the filler.

Mix up a little filler on a clean piece of card or board – use the hardener sparingly (follow the maker's instructions on the pack) otherwise the filler will set very rapidly.

Using the applicator, apply the filler paste to the prepared area; draw the applicator across the surface of the filler to achieve the correct contour and to level the filler surface. As soon as a contour that approximates the correct one is achieved, stop working the paste – if you carry on too long the paste will become sticky and begin to 'pick-up' on the applicator. Continue to add thin layers of filler paste at twenty-minute intervals until the level of the filler is just 'proud' of the surrounding bodywork.

Once the filler has hardened, excess can be removed using a Surform plane or Dreadnought file. From then on, progressively finer grades of abrasive paper should be used, starting with a 40 grade 'wet-and-dry' paper. Always wrap the abrasive paper around a flat rubber, cork, or wooden block – otherwise the surface of the filler will not be completely flat. During the smoothing of the filler surface the 'wet-and-dry' paper should be periodically rinsed in water – this will ensure that a very smooth finish is imparted to the filler at the final stage.

At this stage the 'dent' should be surrounded by a ring of bare metal, which in turn should be encircled by the finely 'feathered' edge of the good paintwork. Rinse the repair area with clean water, until all of the dust produced by the rubbing-down operation is gone.

Spray the whole repair area with a light coat of grey primer – this will show up any imperfections in the surface of the filler. Repair these imperfections with fresh filler paste or bodystopper, and once more smooth the surface with abrasive paper. If bodystopper is used, it can be mixed with cellulose thinners to form a really thin paste which is ideal for filling small holes. Repeat this spray and repair procedure until you are satisfied that the surface of the filler, and the feathered edge of the paintwork are perfect. Clean the repair area with clean water and allow to dry fully.

The repair area is now ready for final spraying. Paint spraying must be carried out in a warm, dry, windless and dust free atmosphere. This condition can be created artificially if you have access to a large indoor working area, but if you are forced to work in the open, you will have to pick your day very carefully. If you are working indoors, dousing the floor in the work area with water will 'lay' the dust which would otherwise be in the atmosphere. If the repair area is confined to one body panel, mask off the surrounding panels; this will help to minimise the effects of a slight mis-match in paint colours. Bodywork fittings (eg chrome strips, door handles etc) will also need to be masked off. Use genuine masking tape and several thicknesses of newspaper for the masking operation.

Before commencing to spray, agitate the aerosol can thoroughly, then spray a test area (an old tin, or similar) until the technique is mastered. Cover the repair area with a thick coat of primer; the thickness should be built up using several thin layers of paint rather than one thick one. Using 400 grade 'wet-and-dry' paper, rub down the surface of the primer until it is really smooth. While doing this, the work area should be thoroughly doused with water, and the wet-and-dry paper periodically rinsed in water. Allow to dry before spraying on more paint.

Spray on the top coat, again building up the thickness by using several thin layers of paint. Start spraying in the centre of the repair area and then using a circular motion, work outwards until the whole repair area and about 2 inches of the surrounding original paintwork is covered. Remove all masking material 10 to 15 minutes after spraying on the final coat of paint.

Allow the new paint at least 2 weeks to harden fully, then, using a paintwork renovator or a very fine cutting paste, blend the edges of the new paint into the existing paintwork. Finally, apply wax polish.

5 Major body repairs

Where serious damage has occurred or large areas need renewal due to neglect, it means certainly that completely new sections or panels will need welding in and this is best left to professionals. If the damage is due to impact it will also be necessary to completely check the alignment of the underframe structure. Owing to the principle of construction the strength and shape of the whole structure can be affected by damage to one part. In such instances the services of an official agent with specialist checking jigs are essential. If a frame is left misaligned it is first of all dangerous as the vehicle will not handle properly and secondly uneven stesses will be imposed on the steering, engine and transmission, causing abnormal wear or complete failure. Tyre wear may also be excessive.

6 Maintenance – hinges and locks

1   Oil the hinges of the bonnet, boot and doors with a drop or two of light oil periodically. A good time is after the car has been washed.
2   Oil the bonnet release catch pivot pin and the safety catch pivot pin periodically.
3   Do not over lubricate door latches and strikers. Normally a little oil on the rotary cam spindle alone is sufficient.

7 Doors – tracing rattles and their rectification

1   Check first that the door is not loose at the hinges, and that the latch is holding the door firmly in position. Check also that the door lines up with the aperture in the body.
2   If the hinges are loose or the door is out of alignment, it will be necessary to reset the hinge positions, as described in Section 13.
3   If the latch is holding the door properly, it should hold the door tightly when fully latched, and the door should line up with the body. If it is out of alignment, it needs adjustment as described in Section 13. If loose, some part of the lock mechanism must be worn out and requires renewal.
4   Other rattles from the door would be caused by wear or looseness in the window winder, the glass channels, and sill strips or the door buttons and interior latch release mecahnism. All these are dealt with in Sections 12 and 13.

8 Front wing – removal and refitting

1   Remove the front bumper body sill moulding, undo the radiator grille securing screws and take off the radiator grille.
2   Disconnect the side marker lamp
3   Unscrew the wing securing bolts from inside the engine compartment, the front edge of the wing and the front pillar (Fig.12.2).
4   Lift off the front wing; if necessary use a sharp knife to break the sealing.
5   Clean the mating joints on the body and fit the new wing in the reverse sequence to removal. Always fit a new seal.

9 Windscreen and rear window – removal and refitting

1   Where a windscreen is to be renewed owing to shattering, the facia air vents should be covered before attempting removal. Adhesive sheeting is useful to stick to the outside of the glass to enable large areas of crystallised glass to be removed.
2   Where the screen is to be removed intact then an assistant will be required. First release the rubber surround from the bodywork by running a blunt, small screwdriver around and under the rubber weatherstrip both inside and outside the car. This operation will break the adhesion of the sealer originally used. Take care not to damage the paintwork or cut the rubber surround with the screwdriver. Remove the windscreen wiper arms and interior mirror and place a protective cover on the bonnet (Fig.12.3).

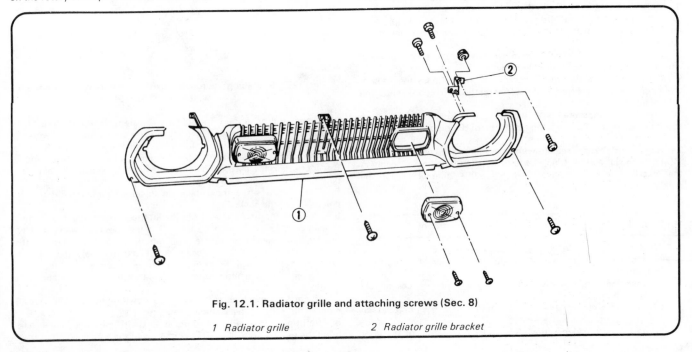

Fig. 12.1. Radiator grille and attaching screws (Sec. 8)

1 *Radiator grille*   2 *Radiator grille bracket*

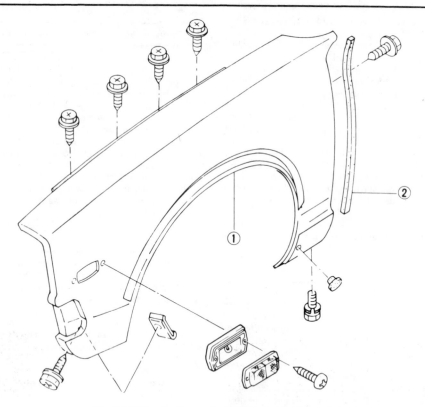

Fig. 12.2. Front wing and attaching bolts (Sec. 8)

1 Front wing   *2 Front wing seal*

3   Have your assistant push the inner lip of the rubber surround off the flange of the windscreen body aperture. Once the rubber surround starts to peel off the flange, the screen may be forced gently outwards by careful hand pressure. The second person should support and remove the screen complete with rubber surround and metal beading as it comes out.
4   Remove the beading from the rubber surround.
5   Before fitting a windscreen, ensure that the rubber surround is completely free from old sealant, glass fragments and has not hardened or cracked. Fit the rubber surround to the glass and apply a bead of suitable sealant between the glass outer edge and the rubber.
6   Refit the bright moulding to the rubber surround.
7   Cut a piece of strong cord greater in length than the periphery of the glass and insert it into the body flange locating channel of the rubber surround.
8   Apply a thin bead of sealant to the face of the rubber channel which will eventually mate with the body.
9   Offer the windscreen to the body aperture and pass the ends of the cord, previously fitted and located at bottom centre, into the vehicle interior.
10 Press the windscreen into place; at the same time have an assistant pulling the cords to engage the lip of the rubber channel over the body flange.
11 Remove any excess sealant with a paraffin soaked rag.
12 For removal and refitting of the heated rear window, disconnect the electrical lead and proceed in the same manner as for the windscreen.

10 Front door lock – removal, refitting and adjustment

1   Wind the window to the fully closed position and remove the retaining screw from the window regulator. Remove the regulator handle (photo).
2   Remove the single screw that secures the interior lock handle escutcheon (photo).
3   Unscrew and remove the door pull retaining screws and detach the door pull (photo).
4   Insert a broad-bladed screwdriver under one corner of the door

Fig. 12.3. Releasing the rubber surround before removing the windscreen (Sec. 9)

trim panel and prise the trim retaining clip from the door frame. Now insert the fingers between the trim and the door frame and working round the panel pull all the retaining clips out of engagement. Remove the trim panel sideways so that the interior lock handle passes through the aperture in the escutcheon plate. Remove the sealing panel taking care not to tear it excessively (photo).
5   Remove the screw that retains the lower sash and remove the run channel from the sash.
6   Remove the two screws from the interior lock handle and the two screws which secure the lock assembly to the door edge and withdraw the lock mechanism complete with remote control rod through the door aperture. The exterior door lock cylinder may be removed after releasing the retaining clip from within the door cavity and the exterior door release handle after removal of the securing screws and clips (photo).
7   If the lock mechanism is worn, do not attempt to dismantle or repair it but renew the assembly complete.
8   Refitting is a reversal of removal, but with the door fully locked, bring the remote control rod into contact with the locking knob.

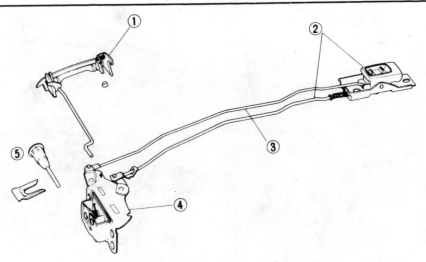

Fig. 12.4. Door lock and remote control (Sec. 10)

1 *Outside handle*   4 *Door lock*
2 *Remote control*   5 *Lock cylinder*
3 *Door lock rod*

10.1 Removing the window regulator handle securing screw

10.2 Removing the interior door handle escutcheon …

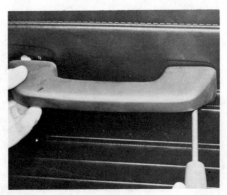

10.3 … and then the door pull

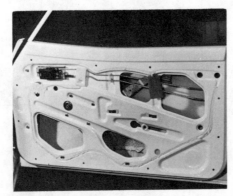

10.4 Door with trim panel removed

10.6 The interior door lock control is attached to the door panel with two screws

---

11 Rear door lock – removal, refitting and adjustment

1 The procedure for the removal of the front door lock described in the preceding Section will generally apply except that no exterior cylinder lock is fitted.

2 A door sash is not fitted on the rear door; therefore this instruction in the preceding Section can also be ignored.

3 Armrests are secured by two self-tapping screws located at their base.

4 Refitting is similar to that described for front door locks.

12 Door window and regulator – removal, refitting and adjustment

1 Remove the door interior trim and controls as described in Section 10.

2 Remove the outer weatherstrip, front lower sash and glass guide.

3 Temporarily fit the window regulator handle and lower the door glass until the regulator-to-glass holder connection appears in the aperture in the door panel.

4 Refer to Fig. 12.7 and remove screws (A) and (B).

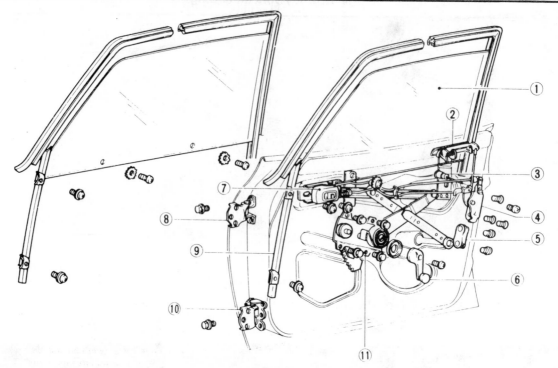

Fig. 12.5. Exploded view of front door (Sec. 12)

1	Front glass	5	Glass guide	9	Front lower sash
2	Outside handle	6	Regulator handle	10	Lower hinge
3	Key cylinder	7	Inside handle	11	Regulator
4	Door lock	8	Upper hinge		

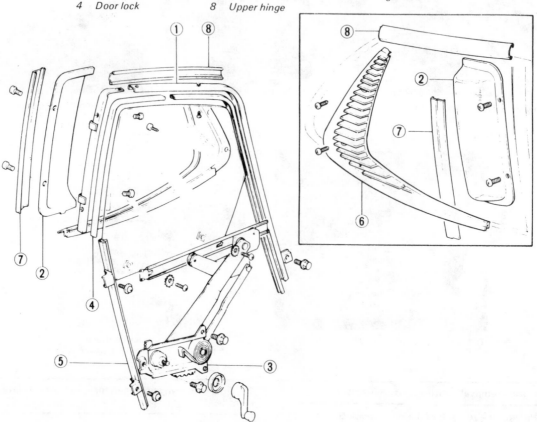

Fig. 12.6. Exploded view of rear side window (coupe) (Sec. 12)

1	Side window sash	5	Lower sash
2	Fillet	6	Drafter badge
3	Regulator	7	Centre pillar moulding
4	Weatherstrip	8	Side window moulding

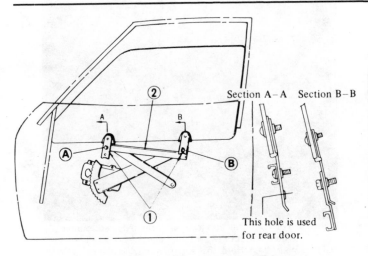

Section A–A   Section B–B

This hole is used for rear door.

Fig. 12.7. Door window adjustment (Sec. 12)

1 Glass holder   2 Guide channel

5   Carefully lower the glass, tilt it forward and then lift it out.
6   Remove the window winding regulator securing bolts and withdraw the regulator through the aperture in the door panel (photo).
7   Refitting is the reverse of the removal procedure.
8   To adjust, tighten screw (A) and temporarily tighten screw (B). Raise the window fully and then retighten screw (B). Front-to-rear adjustment of the window glass is by the front lower sash position.

13 Door – removal and refitting

1   Although the doors may be removed by unscrewing the hinge plates from their edges, it is recommended that the doors are removed complete with hinges by unbolting the hinges from the bodypillars.
2   Whichever method is used, first mark round the hinges for ease of refitting.
3   Remove the metal guard on the door step and peel off the side trim from inside the vehicle where it covers the access to the hinge bolts.
4   Remove the pin from the door stop then support the bottom of the door on jacks or blocks and unscrew and remove the hinge bolts from the door pillars and lift the doors away.
5   If the original doors and hinges are refitted, locate them in previously marked positions. If new hinges or doors are used, do not fully tighten the hinge bolts until the correct hanging of the door has been checked. Ensure that the gap all round the door is even and of consistent width, otherwise adjust the hinge plate position on either the door edge or pillar. Finally tighten the hinge bolts to 12 – 15 lbf ft (1.6 – 2.1 kgf m).
6   Check the closure of the door and adjust the pillar striker, if necessary, by loosening the three securing screws. Retighten the screws to 26 – 35 lbf ft (3.6 – 4.8 kgf m).

14 Tailgate torsion bar (station wagon) – removal and refitting

1   Remove the hinge cover.
2   Remove the upper rail welt and separate the headlining from the torsion bar housing area. Remove the headlining retainer.
3   With the tailgate fully open, put a steel pipe extension with a 90° bend over the bottom bar.
4   Lever the torsion bar in the direction of the arrow, as shown in Fig. 12.11, to free the bar from the hook.
5   Disconnect the bar at the opposite end and then remove it. The hinge base can be removed by backing–off the attaching bolts after the torsion bar has been removed.
6   Refitting is the reverse of the removal procedure. Coat the link-to-torsion bar faces with multi-purpose grease and the hinge base-to-torsion bar sliding faces with molybdenum disulphide grease.

15 Bonnet and boot lid – hinge and lock adjustment

1   The bonnet lid is hinged at the front and may be adjusted if necessary by loosening the retaining bolts and utilising the movement

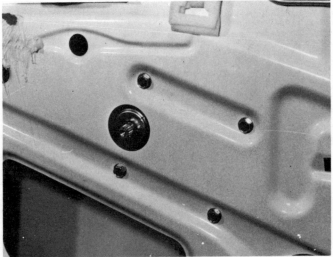

12.6   Window winding mechanism securing bolts

provided by the elongated hinge bolt holes. Vertical adjustment is by the body hinge holes and fore-and-aft by the bonnet hinge holes. An assistant will be required to remove the bonnet lid for major engine overhaul (photo).
2   The bonnet lock is controlled by a lever and cable located within the vehicle (photo).
3   Adjustment of the lock is correct when the bonnet lid striker engages centrally with the female section of the lock.
4   Vertical adjustment of both units is made by slackening the lock securing bolts and adjusting the position of the lock.
5   The boot lid is adjusted in the same manner as the bonnet; vertical adjustment by the nuts at the body, fore-and-aft adjustment by the bolts at the lid and right-left adjustment by both nuts and bolts.
6   The tailgate lock on station wagons is adjusted by elongated holes in the striker and by spacer and shims for vertical adjustment (Fig. 12.14).

16 Instrument panel – removal and refitting

1   The instrument cluster can be removed from the instrument panel as described in Chapter 10 or the panel assembly removed complete with the instrument cluster as described in this Section.
2   Disconnect the earth lead from the battery negative terminal.
3   Disconnect the speedometer cable from the speedometer.
4   Remove the parcel shelf. Disconnect the heater control cables at the heater.
5   Disconnect all the multi-pin wiring harness connectors. Tag them so that they can be easily identified at refitting.

This sequence of photographs deals with the repair of the dent and paintwork damage shown in this photo. The procedure will be similar for the repair of a hole. It should be noted that the procedures given here are simplified — more explicit instructions will be found in the text

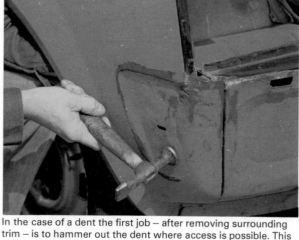

In the case of a dent the first job — after removing surrounding trim — is to hammer out the dent where access is possible. This will minimise filling. Here, the large dent having been hammered out, the damaged area is being made slightly concave

Now all paint must be removed from the damaged area, by rubbing with coarse abrasive paper. Alternatively, a wire brush or abrasive pad can be used in a power drill. Where the repair area meets good paintwork, the edge of the paintwork should be 'feathered', using a finer grade of abrasive paper

In the case of a hole caused by rusting, all damaged sheet-metal should be cut away before proceeding to this stage. Here, the damaged area is being treated with rust remover and inhibitor before being filled

Mix the body filler according to its manufacturer's instructions. In the case of corrosion damage, it will be necessary to block off any large holes before filling — this can be done with aluminium or plastic mesh, or aluminium tape. Make sure the area is absolutely clean before ...

... applying the filler. Filler should be applied with a flexible applicator, as shown, for best results; the wooden spatula being used for confined areas. Apply thin layers of filler at 20-minute intervals, until the surface of the filler is slightly proud of the surrounding bodywork

Initial shaping can be done with a Surform plane or Dreadnought file. Then, using progressively finer grades of wet-and-dry paper, wrapped around a sanding block, and copious amounts of clean water, rub down the filler until really smooth and flat. Again, feather the edges of adjoining paintwork

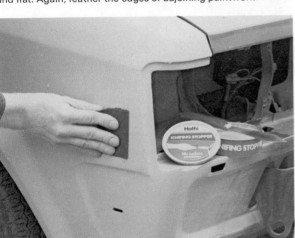

Again, using plenty of water, rub down the primer with a fine grade wet-and-dry paper (400 grade is probably best) until it is really smooth and well blended into the surrounding paintwork. Any remaining imperfections can now be filled by carefully applied knifing stopper paste

The top coat can now be applied. When working out of doors, pick a dry, warm and wind-free day. Ensure surrounding areas are protected from over-spray. Agitate the aerosol thoroughly, then spray the centre of the repair area, working outwards with a circular motion. Apply the paint as several thin coats

The whole repair area can now be sprayed or brush-painted with primer. If spraying, ensure adjoining areas are protected from over-spray. Note that at least one inch of the surrounding sound paintwork should be coated with primer. Primer has a 'thick' consistency, so will find small imperfections

When the stopper has hardened, rub down the repair area again before applying the final coat of primer. Before rubbing down this last coat of primer, ensure the repair area is blemish-free — use more stopper if necessary. To ensure that the surface of the primer is really smooth use some finishing compound

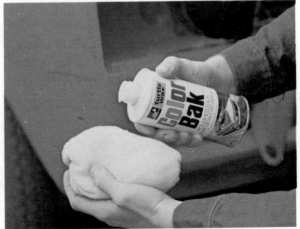

After a period of about two weeks, which the paint needs to harden fully, the surface of the repaired area can be 'cut' with a mild cutting compound prior to wax polishing. When carrying out bodywork repairs, remember that the quality of the finished job is proportional to the time and effort expended

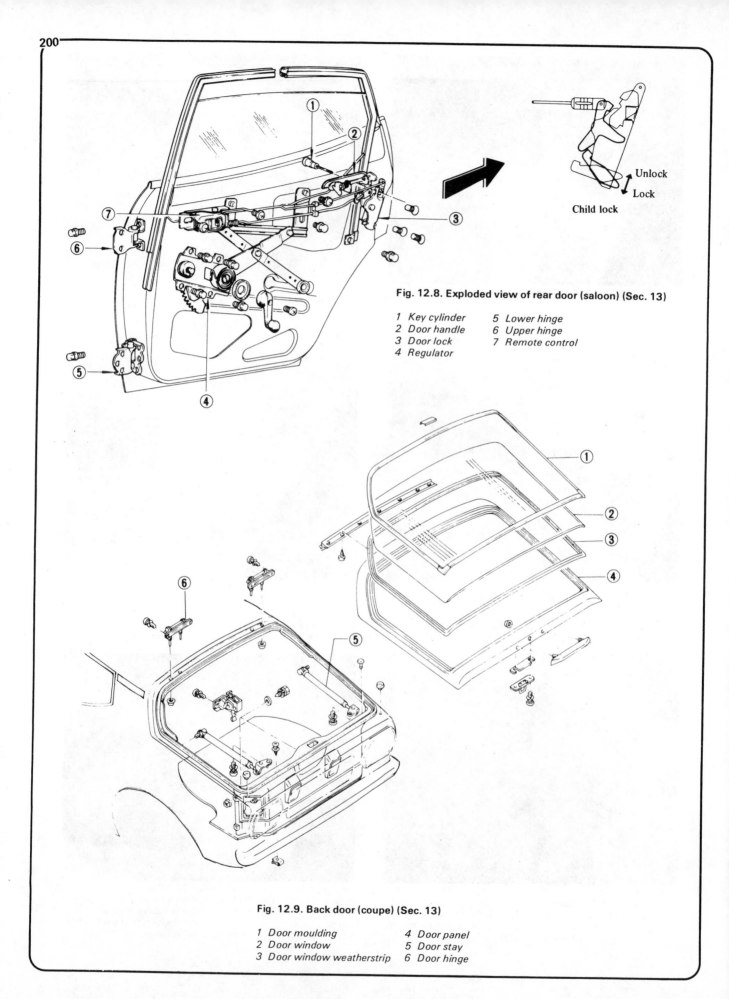

Fig. 12.8. Exploded view of rear door (saloon) (Sec. 13)

1 Key cylinder   5 Lower hinge
2 Door handle   6 Upper hinge
3 Door lock   7 Remote control
4 Regulator

Unlock
Lock
Child lock

Fig. 12.9. Back door (coupe) (Sec. 13)

1 Door moulding   4 Door panel
2 Door window   5 Door stay
3 Door window weatherstrip   6 Door hinge

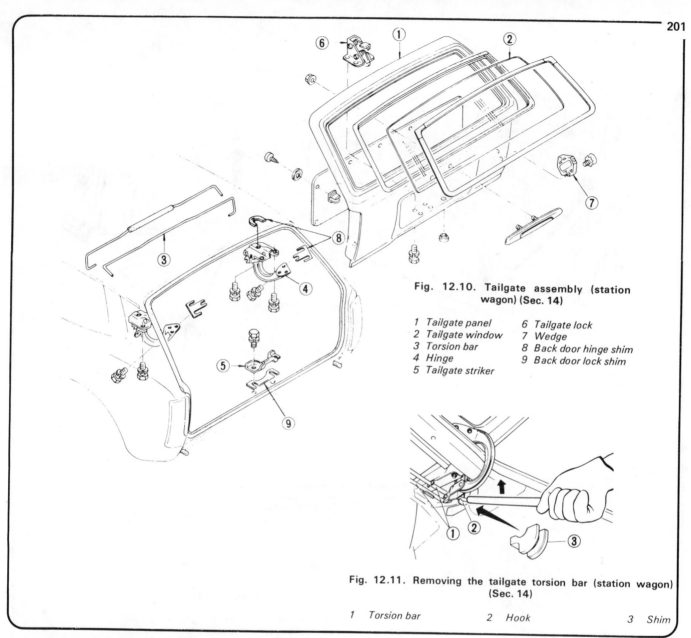

Fig. 12.10. Tailgate assembly (station wagon) (Sec. 14)

1 Tailgate panel
2 Tailgate window
3 Torsion bar
4 Hinge
5 Tailgate striker
6 Tailgate lock
7 Wedge
8 Back door hinge shim
9 Back door lock shim

Fig. 12.11. Removing the tailgate torsion bar (station wagon) (Sec. 14)

1 Torsion bar   2 Hook   3 Shim

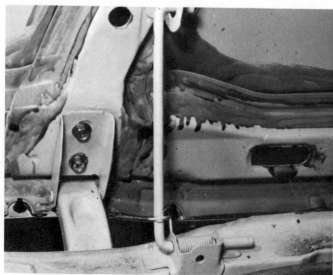

15.1   Bonnet hinge and stay

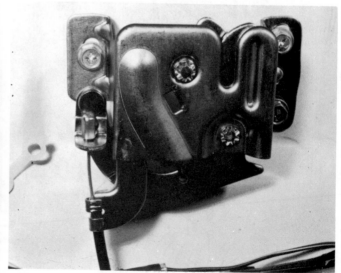

15.2   The bonnet lock and cable attachment.

Fig. 12.12. Bonnet and lock assembly (Sec. 15)

1 Hinge
2 Stay rod
3 Bonnet

4 Lock striker
5 Lock
6 Lock control knob

Fig. 12.13. Boot lid (Sec. 15)

1 Boot lid   4 Lock
2 Torsion bar   5 Lock striker
3 Hinge

Nylon nut

0.5 to 1 mm
(0.0197 to
0.0394 in)

Lock lever

Back door outer
panel

Striker

Fore-aft adjustment

Fig. 12.14. Tailgate lock adjustment (station wagon) (Sec. 15)

6   Remove the choke knob and nut.
7   Remove the steering column bracket attaching bolts.
8   Undo the instrument panel upper attaching screws, and remove the attaching bolts at each side of the panel.
9   Remove the bolts attaching the instrument panel to the pedal bracket and withdraw the instrument panel assembly carefully, ensuring that all the electrical connections and cable controls have been disconnected.
10 Refitting the instrument panel is the reverse of the removal procedure.

17 Front and rear bumpers – removal and refitting

1   The bumpers on the 100A F-II and 120A F-II models are simply attached by brackets and end bolts.
2   On the F10 models for North American the bumpers are secured to shock absorbers with bolts. After removing the bumper bar the shock absorbers can be removed by unbolting them from the bodyframe.
3   Removal of the front and rear bumper assemblies is similar except that with the shield fitted at the rear, the securing bolts are accessible from within the luggage boot.
4   The shock absorber units are gas-filled and must not be drilled or any attempt made to dismantle them. If they are faulty, renew them as complete units.
5   Refitting is the reverse of removal but the bumpers must be adjusted for height, as shown in Fig. 12.20, before fully tightening the securing nuts.

18 Seat belts

1   The front seat belt assembly is of a threepoint type consisting of a shoulder belt and outer and inner lap belts. The shoulder and outer lap belts are a combined unit and cannot be separated from each other. The rear seat belt is of a two-point type.
2   The belts which are made from synthetic fibre should be cleaned in a warm detergent solution only.
3   Periodically inspect the belts for wear or chafing and renew if necessary. The belts should also be renewed when they have been subjected to accident impact shock of severe proportions.
4   When fitting new belts, ensure that the fixing point attachment bolt assembly is correctly made.

19 Heater and ventilation system – general description

1   Two types of heater are used – one for right-hand drive models and one for left-hand drive models. The heater is controlled by the temperature control lever, air outlet lever and fan switch.
2   On right-hand drive models, the heater is equipped with three doors; the intake, the face and the floor. On left-hand drive models an air mix door is adopted in addition to the above doors.
3   On right-hand drive models, the temperature control lever regulates the hot water flow passing through the control valve. On left-hand drive models, the control lever controls the air mix door in addition to regulating the hot water flow.
4   The air outlet lever controls the intake door, face door and floor door positions.
5   The heater assembly comprises a matrix heated by coolant from the engine cooling system and a booster fan controlled by a two-position switch.
6   During normal forward motion of the car, air is forced through the air intake and passes through the heater matrix, absorbing heat and carrying it to the car interior. When the car is stationary or travelling at low speed then the booster fan may be switched on to increase the airflow.

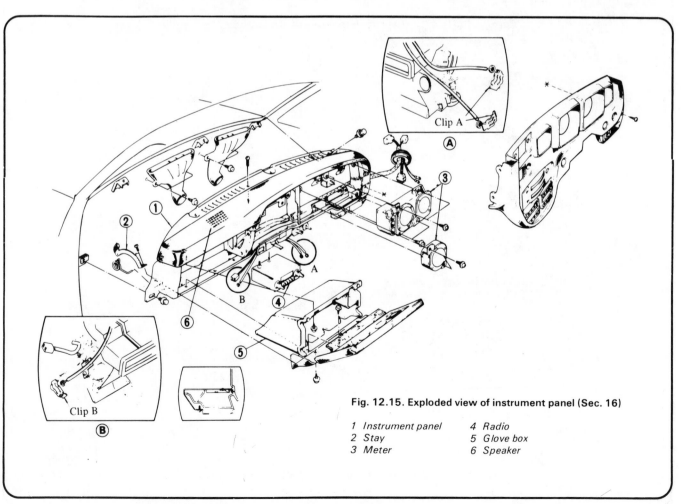

Fig. 12.15. Exploded view of instrument panel (Sec. 16)

1 Instrument panel   4 Radio
2 Stay   5 Glove box
3 Meter   6 Speaker

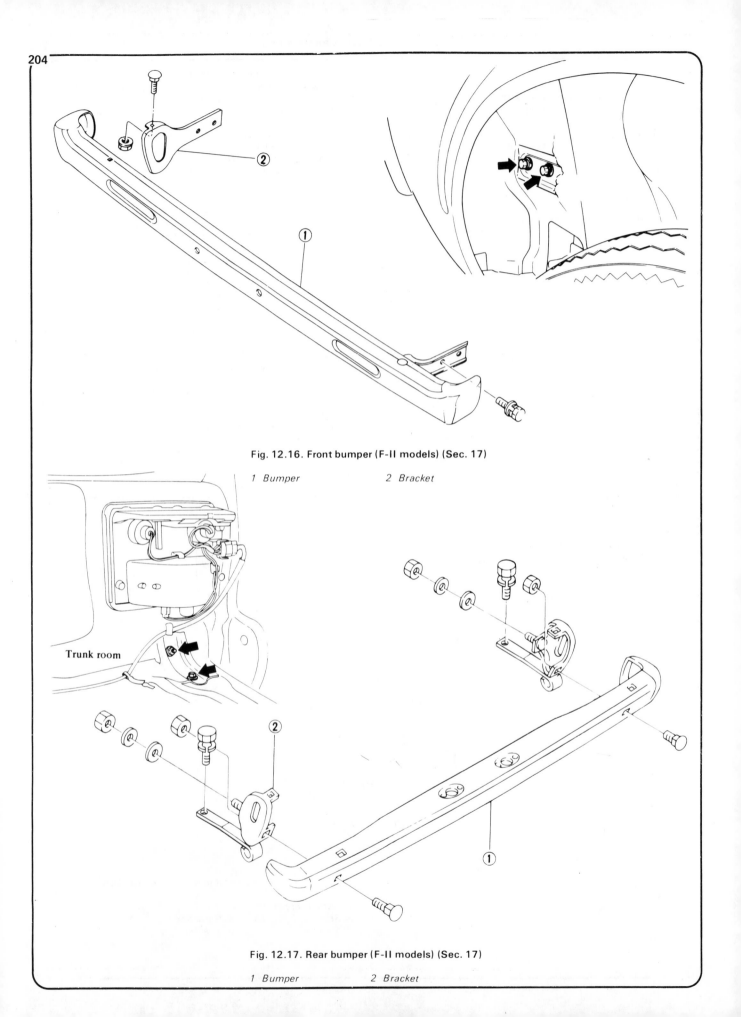

Fig. 12.16. Front bumper (F-II models) (Sec. 17)

1 Bumper   2 Bracket

Trunk room

Fig. 12.17. Rear bumper (F-II models) (Sec. 17)

1 Bumper   2 Bracket

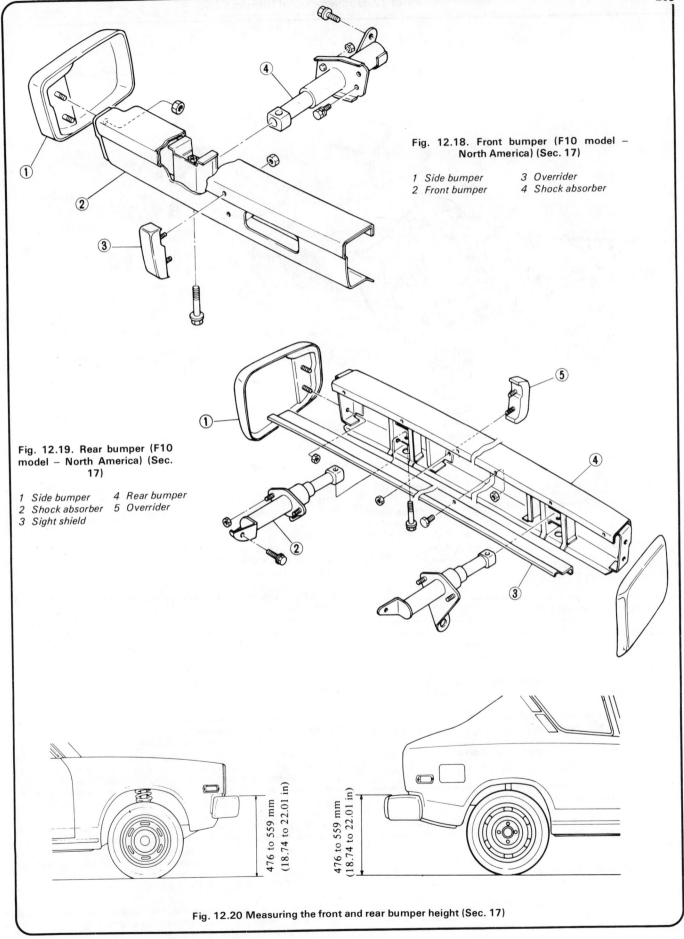

Fig. 12.18. Front bumper (F10 model – North America) (Sec. 17)

1 Side bumper   3 Overrider
2 Front bumper   4 Shock absorber

Fig. 12.19. Rear bumper (F10 model – North America) (Sec. 17)

1 Side bumper   4 Rear bumper
2 Shock absorber   5 Overrider
3 Sight shield

476 to 559 mm (18.74 to 22.01 in)

476 to 559 mm (18.74 to 22.01 in)

Fig. 12.20 Measuring the front and rear bumper height (Sec. 17)

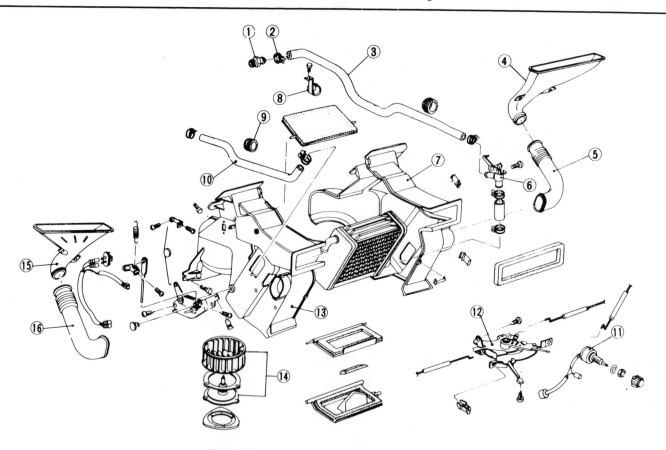

Fig. 12.21. Exploded view of heater assembly

1	Connector	9	Grommet
2	Clip	10	Heater hose (outlet)
3	Heater hose (inlet)	11	Heater switch
4	Defroster nozzle (RH)	12	Heater control
5	Defroster duct (RH)	13	Heater case (LH)
6	Valve	14	Fan and fan motor
7	Heater case (RH)	15	Defroster nozzle (LH)
8	Clamp	16	Defroster duct (LH)

20 Heater unit – removal and refitting

1   Disconnect the earth lead from the battery negative terminal.
2   Drain the engine cooling system as described in Chapter 2.
3   Remove the hose clamps a- disconnect the inlet and outlet coolant hoses.
4   Remove the defroster hoses from each side of the heater unit.
5   Remove the control cable retaining clamps for the control valve, floor door and intake door.
6   Disconnect the electrical connector.
7   Remove the four heater uni)   retaining screws and lift out the heater unit.
8   Refitting the heater unit is the reverse of the removal procedure.

21 Heater unit – inspection and servicing

1   The heater unit is simple and provided the electrical switches and wiring are securely connected, any fault must lie in the matrix or the booster motor.
2   If the heater fails to warm up, check the setting of the control levers and the control valve and ensure that the latter is passing coolant by pulling off the heater connecting hose for a moment with the engine running.
3   Reverse flush the heater matrix with a cold water hose (the heater need not be removed from vehicle); if the unit is clogged do not use chemical cleaners but renew it.

4   If the heater matrix is leaking, do not attempt to repair it yourself but renew the unit.
5   Failure of the booster motor may be due to faulty brushes or even a fuse blown, and these should be checked; otherwise remove the heater unit from the vehicle, dismantle the motor and refit a new one.
6   It should be remembered that the efficiency of the heater is largely dependent upon the engine cooling system and failure of the heater may be due to a defective thermostat or water pump or to air trapped in the heater pipes or matrix.

22 Body leaks – rectification

1   The nuisance of water entering the interior of the car or the luggage boot can usually be overcome by proper attention to the windscreen seal and the rubber sealing of doors. A suitable sealant may be squeezed between the glass of the screen and the rubber surround and between the rubber and the body. The windscreen may be left in position during the operation and should the bright moulding become detached, it can be refitted with the use of a small screwdriver. Tubes of suitable sealer are easily obtainable, and where a pressure gun is not available, then the small tubes available from most shops can have the nozzles pressed into a flattened spout to facilitate entry behind the rubber screen seal. Paraffin or white spirit, generously applied, will clean off any surplus sealant and impart a smooth finish to the seal.
2   Inspection of rubber grommets used in floor holes and to seal cables and controls entering from the engine compartment, should be regularly carried out and renewal implemented where necessary.

Metric conversion tables

Inches	Decimals	Millimetres
1/64	0.015625	0.3969
1/32	0.03125	0.7937
3/64	0.046875	1.1906
1/16	0.0625	1.5875
5/64	0.078125	1.9844
3/32	0.09375	2.3812
7/64	0.109375	2.7781
1/8	0.125	3.1750
9/64	0.140625	3.5719
5/32	0.15625	3.9687
11/64	0.171875	4.3656
3/16	0.1875	4.7625
13/64	0.203125	5.1594
7/32	0.21875	5.5562
15/64	0.234375	5.9531
1/4	0.25	6.3500
17/64	0.265625	6.7469
9/32	0.28125	7.1437
19/64	0.296875	7.5406
5/16	0.3125	7.9375
21/64	0.328125	8.3344
11/32	0.34375	8.7312
23/64	0.359375	9.1281
3/8	0.375	9.5250
25/64	0.390625	9.9219
13/32	0.40625	10.3187
27/64	0.421875	10.7156
7/16	0.4375	11.1125
29/64	0.453125	11.5094
15/32	0.46875	11.9062
31/64	0.484375	12.3031
1/2	0.5	12.7000
33/64	0.515625	13.0969
17/32	0.53125	13.4937
35/64	0.546875	13.8906
9/16	0.5625	14.2875
37/64	0.578125	14.6844
19/32	0.59375	15.0812
39/64	0.609375	15.4781
5/8	0.625	15.8750
41/64	0.640625	16.2719
21/32	0.65625	16.6687
43/64	0.671875	17.0656
11/16	0.6875	17.4625
45/64	0.703125	17.8594
23/32	0.71875	18.2562
47/64	0.734375	18.6531
3/4	0.75	19.0500
49/64	0.765625	19.4469
25/32	0.78125	19.8437
51/64	0.796875	20.2406
13/16	0.8125	20.6375
53/64	0.828125	21.0344
27/32	0.84375	21.4312
55/64	0.859375	21.8281
7/8	0.875	22.2250
57/64	0.890625	22.6219
29/32	0.90625	23.0187
59/64	0.921875	23.4156
15/16	0.9375	23.8125
61/64	0.953125	24.2094
31/32	0.96875	24.6062
63/64	0.984375	25.0031

Millimetres to Inches

mm	Inches
0.01	0.00039
0.02	0.00079
0.03	0.00118
0.04	0.00157
0.05	0.00197
0.06	0.00236
0.07	0.00276
0.08	0.00315
0.09	0.00354
0.1	0.00394
0.2	0.00787
0.3	0.01181
0.4	0.01575
0.5	0.01969
0.6	0.02362
0.7	0.02756
0.8	0.03150
0.9	0.03543
1	0.03937
2	0.07874
3	0.11811
4	0.15748
5	0.19685
6	0.23622
7	0.27559
8	0.31496
9	0.35433
10	0.39370
11	0.43307
12	0.47244
13	0.51181
14	0.55118
15	0.59055
16	0.62992
17	0.66929
18	0.70866
19	0.74803
20	0.78740
21	0.82677
22	0.86614
23	0.90551
24	0.94488
25	0.98425
26	1.02362
27	1.06299
28	1.10236
29	1.14173
30	1.18110
31	1.22047
32	1.25984
33	1.29921
34	1.33858
35	1.37795
36	1.41732
37	1.4567
38	1.4961
39	1.5354
40	1.5748
41	1.6142
42	1.6535
43	1.6929
44	1.7323
45	1.7717

Inches to Millimetres

Inches	mm
0.001	0.0254
0.002	0.0508
0.003	0.0762
0.004	0.1016
0.005	0.1270
0.006	0.1524
0.007	0.1778
0.008	0.2032
0.009	0.2286
0.01	0.254
0.02	0.508
0.03	0.762
0.04	1.016
0.05	1.270
0.06	1.524
0.07	1.778
0.08	2.032
0.09	2.286
0.1	2.54
0.2	5.08
0.3	7.62
0.4	10.16
0.5	12.70
0.6	15.24
0.7	17.78
0.8	20.32
0.9	22.86
1	25.4
2	50.8
3	76.2
4	101.6
5	127.0
6	152.4
7	177.8
8	203.2
9	228.6
10	254.0
11	279.4
12	304.8
13	330.2
14	355.6
15	381.0
16	406.4
17	431.8
18	457.2
19	482.6
20	508.0
21	533.4
22	558.8
23	584.2
24	609.6
25	635.0
26	660.4
27	685.8
28	711.2
29	736.6
30	762.0
31	787.4
32	812.8
33	838.2
34	863.6
35	889.0
36	914.4

1 Imperial gallon = 8 Imp pints = 1.16 US gallons = 277.42 cu in = 4.5459 litres

1 US gallon = 4 US quarts = 0.862 Imp gallon = 231 cu in = 3.785 litres

1 Litre = 0.2199 Imp gallon = 0.2642 US gallon = 61.0253 cu in = 1000 cc

Miles to Kilometres		Kilometres to Miles	
1	1.61	1	0.62
2	3.22	2	1.24
3	4.83	3	1.86
4	6.44	4	2.49
5	8.05	5	3.11
6	9.66	6	3.73
7	11.27	7	4.35
8	12.88	8	4.97
9	14.48	9	5.59
10	16.09	10	6.21
20	32.19	20	12.43
30	48.28	30	18.64
40	64.37	40	24.85
50	80.47	50	31.07
60	96.56	60	37.28
70	112.65	70	43.50
80	128.75	80	49.71
90	144.84	90	55.92
100	160.93	100	62.14

lb f ft to Kg f m		Kg f m to lb f ft		lb f/in^2: Kg f/cm^2		Kg f/cm^2: lb f/in^2	
1	0.138	1	7.233	1	0.07	1	14.22
2	0.276	2	14.466	2	0.14	2	28.50
3	0.414	3	21.699	3	0.21	3	42.67
4	0.553	4	28.932	4	0.28	4	56.89
5	0.691	5	36.165	5	0.35	5	71.12
6	0.829	6	43.398	6	0.42	6	85.34
7	0.967	7	50.631	7	0.49	7	99.56
8	1.106	8	57.864	8	0.56	8	113.79
9	1.244	9	65.097	9	0.63	9	128.00
10	1.382	10	72.330	10	0.70	10	142.23
20	2.765	20	144.660	20	1.41	20	284.47
30	4.147	30	216.990	30	2.11	30	426.70

Index

Printed by
Haynes Publishing Group
Sparkford Yeovil Somerset
England